Introduction to Homeland Security

INTRODUCTION TO
Homeland Security

EDITED BY

Keith Gregory Logan
Kutztown University

James D. Ramsay
Embry-Riddle Aeronautical University

Routledge
Taylor & Francis Group
New York London

First published 2012 by Westview Press

Published 2019 by Routledge
52 Vanderbilt Avenue, New York, NY 10017
2 Park Square, Milton Park, Abingdon, Oxon OX14 4RN

First issued in hardback 2019

Routledge is an imprint of the Taylor & Francis Group, an informa business

Every effort has been made to secure required permissions for all text, images,
maps, and other art reprinted in this volume.

Library of Congress Cataloging-in-Publication Data
Introduction to homeland security / edited by Keith Gregory Logan,
James D. Ramsay.

    p. cm.
   Includes bibliographical references and index.
   ISBN 978-0-8133-4598-7 (pbk. : alk. paper) —
ISBN 978-0-8133-4599-4 (ebook)
    1. Terrorism—United States—Prevention. 2. Terrorism—Prevention—
Government policy—United States. 3. National security—United
States—Management. 4. Emergency management—United States.
I. Ramsay, James D. II. Logan, Keith Gregory.
   HV6432.I59 2012
   363.325'160973—dc23

                             2011038041

ISBN 13: 978-0-367-31634-1 (hbk)
ISBN 13: 978-0-8133-4598-7 (pbk)

Chapter 14 was adapted from a May 2010 article that appeared in the
Homeland Security Affairs Journal

To my beautiful wife, Patricia,
the only woman I have ever loved.
—Keith

To my lovely wife, Trish, and my children, Margo and David,
for their unqualified love and support, which make
everything I do possible.
—Jim

Contents

Introduction

KEITH GREGORY LOGAN

September 11, 2001 (9/11) changed how the United States would view its security and its approach to counterterrorism (CT). No longer could terrorism, particularly Islamic extremist–based terrorism, be viewed as a problem that existed only in other countries. Although we have always recognized that it was a factor in how Americans were viewed and treated around the globe, it was never as significant an issue as on 9/11. As we have heard, the words uttered to President George Bush by Andrew Card, his chief of staff, "America is under attack," were shocking, and he was at a loss to immediately know how to respond, but that did not last very long.[1] What followed was an extensive reorganization of federal agencies and more than a decade of war. The events of 9/11 were totally unprecedented, even in comparison with December 7, 1941. But in each case, the sleeping tiger was awakened, and the world would never be the same.

At the time, everyone asked: What happened? How did this happen? What can be done to ensure that it will never happen again?[2] Nine days later, President Bush took the first major step to strengthen domestic national security and announced that Pennsylvania governor Tom Ridge would lead the new Office of Homeland Security (OHS), to "oversee and coordinate a comprehensive national strategy to safeguard our country against terrorism and respond to any attacks that may come."[3] President Bush and others recognized that our intelligence and law enforcement systems were not working as well as they should have been to prevent the attack. Technology could carry post–Cold War intelligence efforts just so far; changes were needed. The president commissioned the new OHS director to coordinate the "counterterrorism functions" that were scattered across several organizations, including the Central Intelligence Agency (CIA), Federal Bureau of Investigation (FBI), National Guard, state and local police, and numerous other agencies and departments. OHS director Ridge went on to become the first secretary of the Department of Homeland Security (DHS), shepherding the largest federal government reorganization since the passage of the National Security Act of 1947 that created the Department of Defense (DOD) and the CIA.

NOTES

1. http://www.msnbc.msn.com/id/32782623/ns/us_news-9_11_eight_years_later/t/he-told-bush-america-under-attack/.
2. Unfortunately, very similar questions were asked in the wake of Hurricane Katrina.
3. http://pittsburgh.about.com/library/weekly/aa100801a.htm.

Acronyms

ACP   area contingency plan
ADS   Active Denial System
AFIS   Automated Fingerprint Identification Systems
AG   attorney general
AOR   area of operations
ASME-ITI   American Society of Mechanical Engineers Innovative Technologies Institute
ATSA   Aviation and Transportation Security Act
AUMF   Authorization for Use of Military Force
BAC   Basic Access Control
BEOC   Business Emergency Operations Centers
Cal EMA   California Emergency Management Agency
CAT   United Nations Convention Against Torture and Other Cruel, Inhuman or Degrading Treatment or Punishment
CBIRF   Chemical and Biological Incident Response Force
CBP   Customs and Border Protection
CBRNE   chemical, biological, radiological, nuclear, or high-yield explosive
CCMRF   CBRN Consequence Management Response Force
CDC   Centers for Disease Control
CERFP   CBRN Enhanced Response Force Package
CFR   Code of Federal Regulations
CHDS   Center for Homeland Defense and Security
CI   critical infrastructure
CIA   Central Intelligence Agency
CI/KR   Critical Infrastructure/Key Resource
CIP   critical infrastructure and its protection
CIP/R   critical infrastructure protection and resilience
CNCI   Comprehensive National Cybersecurity Initiative

COI community of interest
CONPLAN contingency plan
COOP continuity of operations
COP community of practice
CRINT criminal intelligence
CT counterterrorism
C² command and control
C²CRE Command and Control CBRN Response Elements
DCI director of central intelligence
DCRF Defense CBRN Response Force
DEA Drug Enforcement Administration
DHS Department of Homeland Security
DHSES Division of Homeland Security and Emergency Service
DHS IP Department of Homeland Security Infrastructure Protection
DIA Defense Intelligence Agency
DMA2K Disaster Mitigation Act of 2000
DNI director of national intelligence
DOD Department of Defense
DPC Disaster Preparedness Commission
DSCA defense support of civil authorities
EAS Emergency Alert System
EM emergency management
EMAC Emergency Management Assistance Compact
EMPC Emergency Management Planning Commission
EO executive order
ES environmental security
ESF Emergency Support Function
FAR false acceptance rate
FBI Federal Bureau of Investigation
FEMA Federal Emergency Management Agency
FISA Foreign Intelligence Surveillance Act
FLETC Federal Law Enforcement Training Center
FMD foot-and-mouth disease
FPS Federal Protective Service
FRR false rejections rate
GAO Government Accountability Office
GEOINT geospatial intelligence
GHG greenhouse gas
HD homeland defense
HEAP Human Effects Advisory Panel
HHS Department of Health and Human Services

HRF	Homeland Response Forces
HS	homeland security
HSIN	Homeland Security Information Network
HSPD	Homeland Security Presidential Directive
HUMINT	human intelligence
IA	information assurance
I&A	Office of Intelligence and Analysis
IAFIS	Integrated AFIS
IAIP	Office of Information Analysis and Infrastructure Protection
IC	Intelligence Community
ICE	Immigration and Customs Enforcement
ICS	Incident Command System
IHL	international humanitarian law
IMINT	imagery intelligence
INS	Immigration and Naturalization Service
IP	infrastructure protection
IPCC	Intergovernmental Panel on Climate Change
IR	infrared radiation
IRTPA	Intelligence Reform and Terrorist Prevention Act of 2004
ISR	intelligence, surveillance, and reconnaissance
JDL	Jewish Defense League
JTF	Joint Task Force
JTTF	Joint Terrorism Task Force
LEINT	law enforcement intelligence
LRAD	Long Range Acoustic Device
LRE	launch-and-recovery element
MASINT	measurement and signatures intelligence
MCA	Military Commissions Act
MCE	mission-control element
MIP	Military Intelligence Program
M19CO	May 19th Communist Organization
MTI	moving-target indicator
NAS	National Airspace System
NCTC	National Counterterrorism Center
NGO	nongovernmental organization
NIC	National Intelligence Council
NIE	National Intelligence Estimate
NIMS	National Incident Management System
NIP	National Intelligence Program
NIPP	National Infrastructure Protection Plan
NMI	neuromuscular incapacitation

NORTHCOM	US Northern Command
NPG	National Preparedness Guidelines
NPS	Naval Postgraduate School
NRF	National Response Framework
NSB	National Security Branch
NSC	National Security Council
NSS	National Security Strategy
NVOAD	National Voluntary Organizations Active in Disaster
NYPD	New York Police Department
ODNI	Office of the Director of National Intelligence
ODP	Office for Domestic Preparedness
OEP	Office of Emergency Preparedness
OGC	Office of the General Counsel
OHS	Office of Homeland Security
OIA	Office of Intelligence and Analysis
OIG	Office of the Inspector General
OIP	Office of Infrastructure Protection
OKOHS	Oklahoma Office of Homeland Security
OMB	Office of Management and Budget
OS	Office of the Secretary
OSINT	open-source intelligence
PCA	Posse Comitatus Act
PD	presidential directive
PDD	presidential decision directive
PEMA	Pennsylvania Emergency Management Agency
PI	pulse induction
ppm	parts per million
PPP	private-sector and public-sector partnerships
PSO	Private Sector Office
PS-Prep	Private Sector Preparedness Accreditation and Certification Program
RAMCAP	Risk Analysis and Management for Critical Asset Protection
RCCC	Regional Consortium Coordinating Council
RFID	radio-frequency identification
RPV	remotely piloted vehicle
RTLS	real-time locating system
SCADA	supervisory control and data acquisition
SIGINT	signals intelligence
SIM	Subscriber Identity Module
SLTTGCC	State, Local, Tribal, and Territorial Government Coordinating Council

SOP standard operating procedure
SSP Sector-Specific Plan
SWOT strengths, weaknesses, opportunities, and threats
TFER Task Force for Emergency Readiness
TSA Transportation Security Administration
UAS Unmanned Aerial System
UCMJ Uniform Code of Military Justice
UGCS Universal Ground Control Station
UNFCCC UN Framework Convention on Climate Change
USA PATRIOT Uniting and Strengthening America by Providing Appropriate Tools Required to Intercept and Obstruct Terrorism Act
USBP US Border Patrol
USC United States Code
USCG US Coast Guard
USSS US Secret Service
VOAD Voluntary Organizations Active in Disaster
WHO World Health Organization
WMD weapons of mass destruction
XREP eXtended Range Electronic Projectile
ZOG Zionist Occupation Government

The Organization and Administration of Homeland Security

In Part I, the authors examine the basic structure of what has come to now be known as "homeland security" (HS). The concept of protecting our nation is not new, but the term is one that grew out of the devastating attacks on the American homeland, in New York, Washington, DC, and Pennsylvania. As we know, the United States is primarily a nation of immigrants, with a small percentage of our population being true "Native" Americans. But for all of us, naturally born American citizens or naturalized citizens, it is indeed our homeland. In a post-9/11 environment, there have been significant steps taken by all Americans to secure our homeland. The chapters that follow explore just a few of those steps.

Chapter 1: A First Look at the Department of Homeland Security

This chapter is an introduction to the Department of Homeland Security. But this is clearly just a first look. The author will present a very basic explanation of the DHS's mission and the organizations within the DHS that are charged with our security. We examine homeland security from the "top down," examining the responsibilities of the federal government and what it does. But many of the other authors will describe different structures, some starting at the bottom with local governments and others that rest with the private enterprise or even the military (state and federal).

Chapter 2: Homeland Security Law and Policy

In the United States, we would like to believe that homeland security is a straightforward mission. However, when it is carried out within a free society, with a complex legal structure designed with checks and balances on government power and protections for individual liberties, it is anything but straightforward. It is vital that those with homeland security or emergency management responsibilities (or both) have an understanding of the governmental and legal parameters in which homeland security policy and emergency operations function. This author presents the reader with an overview of areas of law and policy that impact homeland security in the United States, exploring the meaning of law and policy, sources of legal authority, basics of constitutional law, US agencies and government structures that address homeland security, and examples of major federal statutes, executive orders (EOs), and presidential directives (PDs) impacting homeland security. She also provides brief descriptions of several relevant areas of law, including public health law, laws impacting the detainment of terrorism suspects, and mutual aid agreements.

Chapter 3: Public- and Private-Sector Partnerships in Homeland Security

All too often, the assumption is made that homeland security is a strictly government function. That is not true, however. This chapter begins with a review of several key structural documents, particularly the pertinent Homeland Security Presidential Directives (HSPDs) that relate to the incorporation of the private sector within preparedness, prevention and mitigation, response, and recovery dimensions of emergency management. The author then addresses the role of the private sector as Critical Infrastructure Key Resource (CI/KR) owners and operators to include a review of the governance council structure currently in place within the Department of Homeland Security Infrastructure Protection (DHS IP) Directorate. This direction reflects the manner in which the DHS both interprets and implements the appropriate HSPDs, as well as the private-sector responsibilities as directed by the Federal Emergency Management Agency (FEMA) and US Northern Command (NORTHCOM). The chapter concludes with a description of several public-sector and private-sector models being considered by various jurisdictions as well as the salience and effectiveness of these models. Two key models examined by this author are the "top-down" model, which suggests private-sector partnerships need to be constructed and managed by the public sector, and the "bottom-up" model, based on community of practice and community of interest "grass-roots" initiatives.

CHAPTER 1

A First Look at the Department of Homeland Security

KEITH GREGORY LOGAN

They that can give up essential liberty to obtain a little temporary
safety deserve neither liberty nor safety.
—Benjamin Franklin, *Historical Review of Pennsylvania* (1759)

September 11

September 11, 2001, like many other days of tragedy and infamy, burned into the psyche of every American the mark of terrorism. We will never forget where we were and what we were doing when our homeland came under attack. The consequences of that day have challenged the freedom of all Americans. The loss of lives, the loss of property, and the loss of our security have changed us forever. We all asked how our intelligence and defense agencies failed to protect us. One response was to reorganize the government to ensure that this would not happen again.

Department of Homeland Security

On November 25, 2002, President Bush signed the Homeland Security Act of 2002 (Public Law [PL] 107-296; 116 Stat. 2135), creating the DHS, effective

January 24, 2003. The new department was intended to improve government operations and communications, by moving all the essential elements for domestic national security and intelligence under one manager. There have been numerous reorganizations at the DHS since 2003[1] to improve communications and operations (see Figures 1.1 and 1.2).[2]

The intent was to include within the DHS all of the federal organizations that had a primary responsibility for homeland security and the sharing of domestic intelligence in order to facilitate communication, policies, strategies, tactics, and control among them. Several agencies were moved under the aegis of the new department, including the US Secret Service (USSS), US Coast Guard (USCG), Federal Emergency Management Agency (FEMA), Transportation Security Administration (TSA), Federal Protective Service (FPS), and Federal Law Enforcement Training Center (FLETC).[3] Other organizations or functions were moved, in part, from their parent agencies to the DHS and assigned to various DHS directorates.[4] The new DHS Science and Technology Directorate included the CBRN (Chemical-Biological-Radiological-Nuclear) Countermeasures Programs, Environmental Measurements Laboratory, National BW Defense Analysis Center, and Plum Island Animal Disease Center.[5] The Nuclear Incident Response Team, Domestic Emergency Support Teams, National Domestic Preparedness Office, and Office for Domestic Preparedness (ODP) were included within FEMA's new structure.[6] The functions of the US Customs Service and the US Immigration and Naturalization Service (INS) were transferred into US Customs and Border Protection (CBP) and US Immigration and Customs Enforcement (ICE), both within the DHS.[7] The following other entities were also moved to the DHS: part of the Animal and Plant Inspection Service, Federal Computer Incident Response Center, National Communications System, National Infrastructure Protection Center, and Energy Security and Assurance Program.[8]

Key DHS Elements

The present DHS organization reflects refinements that have evolved since its initial creation in 2003.[9] The USSS, FEMA, USCG, and TSA remain within the DHS and are very similar to their initial organization. Other DHS components have refined their structure, function, and responsibilities. For example, when the FPS was transferred from the General Services Administration to the DHS, it was included as a part of ICE until 2009, and it is now part of the National Protection and Programs Directorate. There have been

Department of Homeland Security

Original Organization Chart, March 2003

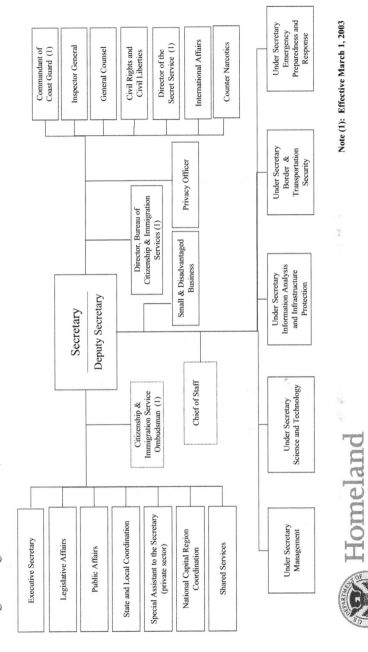

Secretary

Deputy Secretary

Executive Secretary

Legislative Affairs

Public Affairs

State and Local Coordination

Special Assistant to the Secretary (private sector)

National Capital Region Coordination

Shared Services

Citizenship & Immigration Service Ombudsman (1)

Chief of Staff

Director, Bureau of Citizenship & Immigration Services (1)

Small & Disadvantaged Business

Privacy Officer

Commandant of Coast Guard (1)

Inspector General

General Counsel

Civil Rights and Civil Liberties

Director of the Secret Service (1)

International Affairs

Counter Narcotics

Under Secretary Management

Under Secretary Science and Technology

Under Secretary Information Analysis and Infrastructure Protection

Under Secretary Border & Transportation Security

Under Secretary Emergency Preparedness and Response

Note (1): Effective March 1, 2003

For current information please visit www.dhs.gov/xabout

FIGURE 1.1 Department of Homeland Security, original organizational chart, March 2003

8

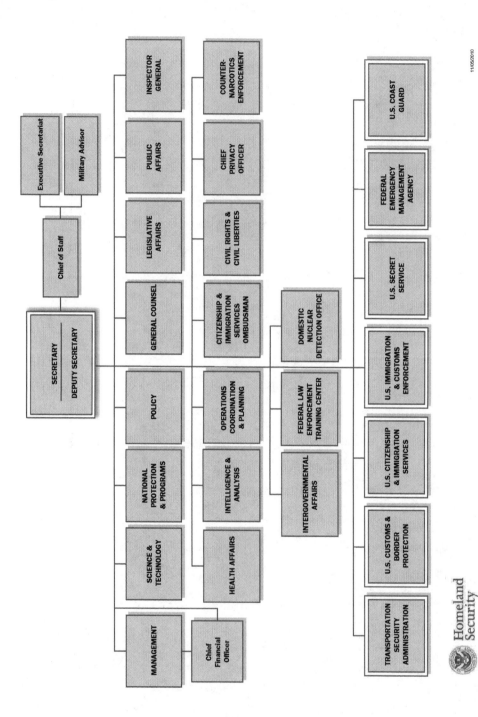

FIGURE 1.2 Department of Homeland Security, 2010

other refinements within the DHS organization as well. Although not all-inclusive, the list below provides a brief look at three distinct segments within the department: the Office of the Secretary (OS), key components and agencies, and advisory panels and committees.

The Office of the Secretary

The secretary and his or her staff are responsible for the management and strategic direction of the DHS. In particular, the secretary leverages resources among federal, state, and local governments to ensure that there is an integrated focus on protecting the American people and the homeland.[10] Reporting directly to the secretary are the following five functional and administrative areas:

1. Office of the General Counsel (OGC): The OGC is an OS staff office, responsible for providing legal advice and coordinating the activities of approximately seventeen hundred attorneys throughout the DHS and its components. The OGC works closely with the Department of Justice (DOJ) to ensure uniformity among the administration's legal actions.

2. Office of the Inspector General (OIG): By conducting audits, inspections, and investigations, the OIG is responsible for combating any fraud, waste, and mismanagement that may exist within the DHS or any of its programs, including contracts, grants, and so on. The OIG is considered an independent element of the DHS and makes only recommendations to the secretary for improving the department. The OIG is also responsible for reporting its findings to the US Congress. As with the DHS secretary, the inspector general is appointed by the president of the United States.

3. FLETC: FLETC is where most federal law enforcement officers receive the training necessary to fulfill their agencies' law enforcement or homeland security missions. The training center of FLETC is based in Glynco, Georgia. FLETC also has a western campus and several satellite centers for specialized training. Special agents, police officers, and security officers receive in-service and refresher training at FLETC's base or one of its campuses. The two exceptions, the Federal Bureau of Investigation and the Drug Enforcement Administration (DEA), train in Quantico, Virginia, at the FBI's National Academy facilities. Many agencies such as the US Border Patrol (USBP) and Secret Service also have their own specialized training schools for agency-specific courses

after officers complete their basic training at FLETC. FLETC is also involved in training foreign law enforcement personnel. Since 9/11 FLETC has expanded its homeland security training, along with its basic law enforcement training. In addition, FLETC has broadened into new subject areas, such as counterterrorism, security, intelligence, and law enforcement management. The increased FLETC curriculum is a positive reflection of the growth of homeland security as a discipline.

4. Directorate for Science and Technology: This directorate is the primary research and development segment of the DHS. It provides federal, state, and local agencies with improved technology capabilities that are essential to homeland security.

5. Office of Intelligence and Analysis (OIA): The OIA serves a critical mission that addresses weaknesses in communications and analyses that enabled the events of 9/11. The OIA represents the DHS in the Intelligence Community (IC), as one of the sixteen intelligence agencies under the guidance of the director of national intelligence (DNI). The USCG Intelligence program, another key DHS component, is also part of the IC because of its responsibilities for maritime security and safety. The OIA analyzes information from various sources to assess the threat to homeland security. It is also responsible for communicating the appropriate information to other members of the IC as well as to federal, state, local, and tribal counterparts directly and through Fusion Centers.[11]

Key DHS Components and Agencies

There are seven independent agencies that are clearly integral to the DHS, each with law enforcement authority. The inclusion of these components played a key role in the creation of the DHS and the centralization of homeland security.

1. US CBP: This is the primary organization that is responsible for border security. The CBP is the largest and most complex DHS organization and has the first-line responsibility of keeping terrorists and their weapons away from the homeland. The CBP has its roots in the USBP, INS, and US Customs Service (USCS). The USCS's origins date back to the Tariff Act of 1789, when the USCS was the primary source of revenue for our new nation.

2. US Citizenship and Immigration Services: This DHS component is responsible for overseeing lawful immigration to the United States.

(The responsibility for issuing passports and visas remains with the US Department of State.)

3. US Immigration and Customs Enforcement: ICE is responsible for homeland security law enforcement, encompassing both criminal and civil federal laws relating to border control, customs, trade, and immigration. Its agents are involved in an extensive array of criminal and national security investigations and are assigned to posts in forty-eight foreign countries.

4. US Secret Service: The USSS is responsible for protecting the president, vice president, and other leaders. It also safeguards the nation's financial infrastructure, with responsibility for conducting criminal investigations regarding the counterfeiting of US currency, credit card fraud, and other crimes.

5. US Coast Guard: The USCG's origin in 1790 predates that of the Department of the Navy; its initial purpose involved revenue enforcement. The USCG now has the primary responsibility for maritime and port security, including navigable domestic waterways, and enforcing US laws at sea. As a key player in fighting transnational crime, it works with the DEA, ICE, and CBP to prevent drug and human smuggling across US borders and waterways. Although not part of the Department of Defense, it is considered one of the nation's five military services. As noted above, it is a member of the IC.

6. TSA: This DHS component is renowned for ensuring the transportation safety of people and commerce. It is the most visible DHS element for the air-traveling public, as it represents the first line of security at the airport. When providing air marshals for flight security, the TSA represents the least-visible aspect of transportation security.[12]

7. FEMA: Whether confronted by natural or man-made disasters, FEMA is the first-responder federal agency.[13] FEMA is most visible during times of crisis, and it must be prepared to respond to any and every challenge, at any time. It is responsible for ensuring that first responders and emergency workers are qualified pursuant to the National Incident Management System (NIMS), so that workers from one area of the country operate under the same command and control (C^2) rules as workers from another area who arrive at the scene of a disaster to lend assistance. It has been the subject of criticism for its handling of the nation's response to Hurricane Katrina, and it has received high marks after other disasters. Some question whether it was more effective as an

independent agency before its affiliation with the DHS, whereas others favor its inclusion in the DHS as part of a unified homeland security response. It works to ensure that as a nation, we are able to "prepare for, protect against, respond to, recover from, and mitigate all hazards."[14]

Advisory Panels and Committees

There are a series of advisory groups that are part of the DHS. They include the Homeland Security Advisory Council, National Infrastructure Advisory Council, Homeland Security Science and Technology Advisory Committee, Critical Infrastructure Partnership Advisory Council, Interagency Coordinating Council on Emergency Preparedness and Individuals with Disabilities, Task Force on New Americans, and DHS Labor-Management Forum.

State and Local Homeland Security and Emergency Management (EM) Organizations

There are more than eighty-seven thousand federal, state, local, and tribal organizations that are responsible in some manner for homeland security and emergency management.[15] As was learned on 9/11, these organizations do not always follow the same procedures or connect all the dots. Key to being able to prevent and respond to terrorism and natural disasters is the ability to communicate effectively. Ensuring a clear and continuing line of communication is a primary responsibility of the DHS, working with the state, local, and tribal homeland security offices. One aspect of communication is the nationwide Emergency Alert System (EAS), an early warning system that was established to enable the president to address the American public during emergencies. The EAS was also designed for use by the National Oceanic and Atmospheric Administration's National Weather Service, state governors, and state and local authorities for emergency alerts. Under the law, each state is a sovereign, and it is a challenge for the DHS to ensure cooperation and communication, but the EAS is a move in the right direction.[16]

Each state has established its own homeland security or emergency management structure(s). It is important to note that both security and emergency response work from the bottom (such as a local township) up, as well as from the top (federal government) down, depending on the nature of the emergency. In Pennsylvania, for example, the Pennsylvania Emergency Management Agency (PEMA) takes the lead in homeland security, with the PEMA director also serving as the homeland security adviser to the governor and the

PEMA deputy as the director for homeland security.[17] PEMA is responsible for coordinating local and county governments in the areas of civil defense, disaster mitigation, and preparedness, planning, and response to and recovery from man-made or natural disasters.[18] Local governments also have emergency management structures. For example, Upper Uwchlan Township (Chester County), Pennsylvania, has an Emergency Management Planning Commission (EMPC), composed of volunteers who provide community assistance in coordinating disaster response. Like the police and fire departments, EMPC personnel receive training and participate in drills to be better prepared to respond to different disasters. The training includes what actions should be taken regarding evacuation; biological, chemical, or radiological hazards; explosions; dam breaches; and the like. The EMPC has a series of protocols to reflect how it handles certain disasters and when it is appropriate to look beyond its first responders to the county and state for assistance.

It is the responsibility of each township to provide the first responders to any disaster or emergency within its jurisdiction. If an incident expands beyond the township's ability to handle it, the local government will work with adjoining townships and then bring in the county's emergency management units for assistance. If the problem extends to multiple jurisdictions and grows beyond local or county abilities, the local leaders will look to the state and possibly to the federal government for assistance. At the local level, a township's (or city's) police and fire departments would likely be the first responders.

Even at the local level, it is important to look at communications, media relations, special equipment, and other resources, not the least of which is where the financial means necessary to pay for additional contractual services will derive. All the issues that confront these local township supervisors tend to be faced by other managers and elected officials, all the way up to the federal level. As reflected in several of the subsequent chapters, grants from the federal (DHS) and the state organizations (such as PEMA) assist in funding "top-down" training and the ability of each level of government to respond in a uniform manner. It is important that responders from one location are able to assist in another without additional training. This should include command, control, communications, policies, procedures, and more. It is also important to note that the type of resources needed at the federal level or in a large metropolitan city may be entirely different from that required in a small, rural town. The devastation from river flooding in the Dakotas may be just as "deadly" as a hurricane in the Gulf or a bomb in a city, but the preparation and response needs are entirely different.

Like the citizens of Pennsylvania and New York, Oklahomans have also experienced the devastation of terrorist acts on home soil. Unlike the organizations found in either the federal government or Pennsylvania, Oklahoma has two separate agencies, one for homeland security and another for emergency management. The Oklahoma legislature passed the Oklahoma Homeland Security Act (House Bill 2280) and established the Oklahoma Office of Homeland Security (OKOHS), the state agency responsible for countering terrorism. The responsibilities of OKOHS include the following: developing and implementing a comprehensive statewide homeland security strategy, planning and implementing a statewide response system, administering the homeland security advisory system, and implementing national homeland security plans. Oklahoma also has the Oklahoma Emergency Management Agency that handles most emergency management issues. Oklahoma's major threats involve natural disasters, such as the damage caused by tornadoes, which prompted the state to start the safe-room project, designed to provide shelter for those under the threat of a tornado. The implementation of this project starts at the community level; municipalities and townships raise a portion of the money needed, and the state provides the remaining funds to finish the project. Oklahoma has become more proactive in its emergency management initiations, attempting to prevent problems experienced in the past and mitigate the loss and damage from future natural disasters.[19]

New York State has a homeland security and emergency management structure that is different from those in both Pennsylvania and Oklahoma. New York has a Division of Homeland Security and Emergency Service (DHSES) that includes several offices with specific responsibilities for different aspects of homeland security and emergency management. Included within the DHSES are the Office of Counter Terrorism, Office of Cyber Security, Office of Interoperable and Emergency Communications, Office of Fire Prevention and Control, and Office of Emergency Management.

During World War II and the Cold War, US cities had developed civil defense programs through the Office of Civil Defense. In 1978 New York shifted its emphasis from civil defense to an "all-hazards" program approach, creating the Disaster Preparedness Commission (DPC). New York's DPC is composed of the commissioners, directors, and chairpersons of the thirty-three state agencies and one volunteer organization, the American Red Cross. The DPC's responsibilities include the preparation of state disaster plans, directing state disaster operations and coordinating those with local government operations, and coordinating federal, state, and private recovery efforts.[20]

The California model is similar to Pennsylvania's, including homeland security as part of its emergency management agency, reporting to the governor's office. The California Emergency Management Agency (Cal EMA) is vested with the duties, powers, purposes, responsibilities, and jurisdictions previously held within the governor's Offices of Homeland Security and Emergency Services. Cal EMA is responsible for designing and implementing homeland security initiatives, coordinating and supporting the emergency activities of all of California's state agencies that have an operational role in state emergencies, promoting and sustaining effective criminal justice programs, and ensuring California's readiness to respond to and quickly recover from the effects of all emergencies.[21]

Although it is relatively easy to examine an emergency management structure within a state, it is less obvious how the homeland security aspect is structured. Some states view homeland security as separate and distinct from emergency management; it is viewed as a law enforcement responsibility and assigned to a state police agency. As noted above, within the federal government, the DHS has responsibility for FEMA, and it is part of the IC (through both the OIA and the USCG), but the primary responsibility for domestic intelligence, antiterrorism, and counterterrorism law enforcement does not rest with either the DHS or FEMA. The FBI, operating under the direction of the attorney general (AG), is the domestic law enforcement agency responsible for domestic intelligence and counterterrorism and is also part of the IC. The FBI's National Security Branch, Intelligence Directorate, is primarily responsible for the coordination of domestic intelligence efforts that protect America. The FBI must identify security threats and transnational networks that have the intent and capability to harm America; these networks include terrorist organizations, foreign intelligence services, those groups that seek to proliferate weapons of mass destruction (WMD), and criminal enterprises.[22] The other members of the IC include the Central Intelligence Agency, Defense Intelligence Agency (DIA), National Geospatial-Intelligence Agency, National Reconnaissance Office, DEA, Department of State (Bureau of Intelligence and Research), Department of the Treasury (Office of Intelligence and Analysis), Department of Energy (Office of Intelligence and Counterintelligence), National Security Agency, and the four military service intelligence components. These IC members are responsible for the collection of national security intelligence gathering and counterterrorism activities outside the United States. However, several of the IC members are also involved with the gathering of law enforcement intelligence.

Fusion Centers

The DHS's OIA is responsible for collecting, analyzing, and sharing intelligence information, both within the IC[23] and among the appropriate state, local, and tribal agencies.[24] It is important to remember that the OIA does not have an active role in the collection of intelligence on a level that is comparable with the FBI; its collection is relative to the work that it does through the IC and Fusion Centers.[25] In order to collect and share information in a timely manner, the DHS has funded and participated in Fusion Centers throughout the United States. These centers serve as primary focal points for the receipt, analysis, gathering, and sharing of threat-related information. Fusion Centers empower frontline law enforcement, fire service, emergency management, public safety, public health, critical infrastructure and key resource protection, and private-sector security personnel to lawfully gather and share threat-related information. Although the centers are primarily supported by federal funding, they are the responsibility of the states and local entities for staffing and operations. The centers are effective at analyzing and sharing information to assist law enforcement and homeland security partners in preventing, protecting against, and responding to crime and terrorism.[26] The Department of Defense provides select state and major urban-area Fusion Center personnel with access to its Secret Internet Protocol Router Network to improve information sharing regarding terrorism-related classified information. These centers also work closely with the FBI's Joint Terrorism Task Forces (JTTFs), based in 106 cities; 71 JTTFs have been created since 9/11, involving 4,400 members and 650 federal, state, and local agencies.

Pursuant to the National Strategy for Information Sharing, the DHS is charged with improving information sharing as well as America's ability to gather, analyze, disseminate, and utilize information to prevent terrorist attacks. Fusion Centers provide actionable intelligence for dissemination, but do not usually participate in the related investigations.[27] Additional Fusion Center responsibilities include, but are not limited to:

1. fostering a culture that recognizes the importance of fusing all crimes with national security implications and all hazards information that may involve identifying criminal activity and other information that might be a precursor to a terrorist plot;
2. supporting critical counterterrorism, homeland security, and activities related to homeland defense (HD);

3. developing critical infrastructure protection plans to ensure security and resilience of infrastructure operations;

4. prioritizing emergency management, response, and recovery planning based on likely threat scenarios and high-risk targets;

5. ensuring that all locally generated terrorism-related information including suspicious activity and incident reports is communicated to the federal, state, and local governments through the appropriate mechanisms and systems.[28]

A First Look

The information in this chapter is provided to present a brief first look at the DHS. It is not intended to address whether it is successful or well organized, effectively managed or just the opposite. It is simply meant to present the reader with the basic structure of the department and the twenty-two federal agencies that were brought under the direction of one person in order to make America a safer place to live and work. It also provides a first look at state homeland security and emergency management structures. Each of the chapters that follow will address a different aspect of homeland security and emergency management. Each of the authors will provide the reader with another look at their respective subjects. When you have finished reading each of the chapters, and the events of the news each day, you will have a better understanding of the strength of our homeland security efforts to ensure that we continue to enjoy our freedom, our liberty, and security—our life in America.

NOTES

1. http://www.dhs.gov/xlibrary/assets/dhs-org-chart-2003.pdf.

2. *Final Report of the National Commission on Terrorist Attacks upon the United States* (July 22, 2004), 221–222.

3. The USSS was transferred from the Department of the Treasury to the DHS. The USCG was transferred from the Department of Transportation (DOT) to the DHS. FEMA and the TSA were independent agencies. The FPS was part of the General Services Administration. FLETC was transferred from the Department of the Treasury.

4. The Strategic National Stockpile and National Disaster Medical System was initially transferred from the Department of Health and Human Services (HHS) to the DHS, but is was returned to the HHS in July 2004.

5. The CBRN (Chemical-Biological-Radiological-Nuclear) Countermeasures Programs were transferred from the Department of Energy (DOE). The Environmental Measurements Laboratory was transferred from the Department of Energy. The National BW Defense

Analysis Center was transferred from the Department of Defense. The Plum Island Animal Disease Center was transferred from the Department of Agriculture.

6. The Nuclear Incident Response Team transferred from the Department of Energy. The Domestic Emergency Support Teams transferred from the Department of Justice. The National Domestic Preparedness Office transferred from the FBI. The Office for Domestic Preparedness transferred from the Department of Justice.

7. The US Customs Service transferred from the Department of the Treasury. The Immigration and Naturalization Service transferred from the Department of Justice.

8. The Animal and Plant Inspection Service transferred from the Department of Agriculture. The Federal Computer Incident Response Center transferred from the General Services Administration. The National Communications System transferred from the Department of Defense. The National Infrastructure Protection Center transferred from the FBI. The Energy Security and Assurance Program transferred from the Department of Energy.

9. http://www.dhs.gov/xlibrary/assets/dhs-orgchart.pdf.

10. http://www.dhs.gov/xabout/structure/#2.

11. Keith Gregory Logan, ed., *Homeland Security and Intelligence* (Santa Barbara, CA: Praeger Security International, 2010), 39, 41, 79.

12. http://www.tsa.gov/who_we_are/org/editorial_multi_image_with_table_0102.shtm.

13. http://www.fema.gov/.

14. http://www.dhs.gov/xabout/structure/#2.

15. See also PPD-8, National Preparedness, http://www.dhs.gov/xabout/laws/gc_1215 444247124.shtm; and http://www.dhs.gov/xlibrary/assets/NIPP_Plan.pdf.

16. FEMA and the Federal Communications Commission will conduct their first test of the EAS in late 2011. http://www.hstoday.us/single-article/first-ever-national-emergency -alert-test-set-for-november/3d09b530392bb786c1404f3f21c773a4.html.

17. Pennsylvania merged its Office of Homeland Security, an independent office that reported directly to the governor, into PEMA.

18. http://www.portal.state.pa.us/portal/server.pt/community/pema_home/4463.

19. http://www.ok.gov/homeland/documents/HB%202280%20(2004).pdf.

20. http://www.dhses.ny.gov/oem/.

21. http://www.oes.ca.gov/WebPage/oeswebsite.nsf/PDF/Cal%20EMA%20Consoli dation%20Plan/$file/CalEMAConsolidationPlan_FINAL.pdf.

22. http://www.fbi.gov/about-us/nsb/mission.

23. *United States Intelligence Community Information Sharing Strategy* (February 22, 2008), 17.

24. http://www.dhs.gov/xlibrary/assets/ia-fy2011-fy2018-strategic-plan.pdf.

25. DHS, *Fusion Center Guidelines*, 2005, it.ojp.gov/documents/fusion_center_guidelines _law_enforcement.pdf.

26. http://www.dhs.gov/files/programs/gc_1296484657738.shtm.

27. DHS, *Information Sharing Strategy*, 2008, http://www.dhs.gov/xlibrary/assets /dhs_information_sharing_strategy.pdf.

28. The White House, National Security Council, *National Strategy for Information Sharing, Appendix 1: Establishing a National Integrated Network of State and Major Urban Area Fusion Centers*, http://georgewbush-whitehouse.archives.gov/nsc/infosharing/sectionIX.html.

Homeland Security Law and Policy

EMILY BENTLEY

Introduction to Homeland Security Law and Policy

Homeland security and emergency management are part of a key function of government: protection of its citizens. Both policy and operational documents in homeland security and emergency management often refer to "protection of lives and property" or similar language, reflecting this foundation. In the United States, homeland security activities are conducted within a free society and complex government structures designed with checks and balances on government power and protections for individual liberties. It is vital that those who have homeland security or emergency management responsibilities have an understanding of the government and legal parameters in which homeland security policy and emergency operations function. This chapter provides an overview of areas of law and policy that impact homeland security in the United States. The chapter explores the meaning of law and policy, sources of legal authority, basics of constitutional law, US agencies and government structures that address homeland security, major federal statutes impacting homeland security, and relevant areas of law, such as hazardous materials law and laws impacting detention of terrorism suspects.

Laws are rules established by government that require compliance or adherence. They are mandatory rather than optional—"shall" rather than "should." James Madison stated the obvious in the Federalist No. 51 in 1788, noting, "If men were angels, no government would be necessary." Laws in the United States cover a wide range of topics, programs, and issues, from establishing a branch or agency of government to setting penalties for crimes and giving authority to isolate individuals ill with an infectious disease to protect the health of others. The term *law* refers to established governmental authority or requirements and can be found in several sources: constitutions (federal and state), statutes and ordinances, regulations, executive orders (EOs), and court decisions.

In general, laws determine the responsibility and authority to conduct a host of homeland security–related activities, from planning and preparedness to evacuation and surveillance. Policy is a defined course or method of action selected from among alternatives and in light of given conditions to guide and determine present and future decisions.[1] Policy refers collectively to laws, goals, programs, and other documents and actions that guide decision making and activities in a particular area, such as homeland security policy or flood mitigation policy. The first key step in creating policy is identifying the problem or issue to be addressed. Agreeing on the need for and the purpose of policy making can be a long-term process, such as developing an approach for mitigating and dealing with the effects of climate change, or quick developing, such as Congress's move to make airport security screening a government responsibility after the terrorist attacks of September 11, 2001. There are several recognized steps in formulating policy:

- *Problem recognition* involves identifying and agreeing on the issue. What is to be solved or addressed with the policy? Lack of agreement on the definition of the problem will result in challenges in other steps of policy making. The problem can also be confused or cluttered with collateral results caused by the problem. Make sure the stated issue is the problem and not a result of the problem. Problem identification may involve gathering data or other information that helps define the problem. Problem recognition should result in stated or implied objectives for the policy, against which policy impacts can later be measured.
- *Agenda setting* means bringing the issue to the attention of those who can do something about it. Information gathered in the previous step can be used to illustrate the problem with decision makers and the public.

- *Policy formulation* requires researching and exploring possible approaches to address the problem. If time is available, engaging diverse perspectives in brainstorming options can be beneficial. Results of this step should include a clear articulation of policy options, with benefits, risks, and practical considerations for each.
- *Policy adoption* requires settling on a policy option or a combination of options. This step is an action taken by the office or organization with the authority to adopt or approve the policy and task its implementation. It is ideal for those who make the decision on policy adoption to have input from those who will be charged with implementing the policy.
- *Budgeting* addresses how the policy will be funded, including within what agencies, over what time period, and with what benchmarks or expectations.
- *Implementation* of the policy involves putting the policy into action. In government, one or more agencies are generally tasked with specific roles in the implementation of a policy. Challenges can occur when roles and responsibilities regarding implementation—who or what is responsible for an action or an area of activity—are not clear.
- *Evaluation* measures the success of the policy in addressing the problem or issue. Objectives, timelines, and data from previous steps in the process are used to gauge to what degree the policy is having the intended effects—as well as unintended consequences. Evaluation should occur regularly and should result in adjustments to policy or implementation.

There is a wide range of policies put into place by each level of government, with the federal government sometimes taking the lead in establishing policy while other times incorporating policy tested or suggested by those in state government. For an example of policy that is not necessarily enacted as a law or regulation, see the Comprehensive National Cybersecurity Initiative:

President Obama has identified cybersecurity as one of the most serious economic and national security challenges we face as a nation, but one that we as a government or as a country are not adequately prepared to counter. Shortly after taking office, the President therefore ordered a thorough review of federal efforts to defend the U.S. information and communications infrastructure and the development of a comprehensive approach to securing America's digital infrastructure.

In May 2009, the President accepted the recommendations of the resulting Cyberspace Policy Review, including the selection of an Executive Branch Cybersecurity Coordinator who will have regular access to the President. The Executive Branch was also directed to work closely with all key players in U.S. cybersecurity, including state and local governments and the private sector, to ensure an organized and unified response to future cyber incidents; strengthen public/private partnerships to find technology solutions that ensure U.S. security and prosperity; invest in the cutting-edge research and development necessary for the innovation and discovery to meet the digital challenges of our time; and begin a campaign to promote cybersecurity awareness and digital literacy from our boardrooms to our classrooms and begin to build the digital workforce of the 21st century. Finally, the President directed that these activities be conducted in a way that is consistent with ensuring the privacy rights and civil liberties guaranteed in the Constitution and cherished by all Americans.

The activities under way to implement the recommendations of the Cyberspace Policy Review build on the Comprehensive National Cybersecurity Initiative (CNCI) launched by President George W. Bush in National Security Presidential Directive 54/Homeland Security Presidential Directive 23 (NSPD-54/HSPD-23) in January 2008. President Obama determined that the CNCI and its associated activities should evolve to become key elements of a broader, updated national U.S. cybersecurity strategy.[2]

The document then outlines a number of goals and objectives to improve cybersecurity.

It also is important to understand that policy and legal changes often follow a significant disaster. This is referred to as a "policy window."[3] This opportunity to expedite a shift in policy is the result of both the desire to improve capabilities to deal with disasters and the impacts of political reality. Elected officials experience pressure to take action to address damage and human suffering and to improve government response. This can be a positive in that we need to learn lessons from mistakes of the past so that we can prevent disasters when possible and improve outcomes from disasters when they occur. However, reacting to the specifics of a particular disaster or hazard can also create imbalances in policy focus and resource allocation.

Consider the reorganization of US federal government agencies after the terrorist attacks of September 11, 2001, combining twenty-two federal agencies and 175,000 employees in the new US Department of Homeland Security (DHS). In the years immediately following the creation of the DHS, some expressed concern that an accompanying shift in focus to terrorism prevention, post-9/11, negatively impacted comprehensive disaster preparedness and response activities at the federal level, as well as state and local priorities and funding.[4] This policy challenge of balancing corrective action based on lessons of recent incidents with the need to continue ongoing fundamental prevention and preparedness activities is evident in the development and evolution of homeland security; it continues to impact homeland security and emergency management law, policy, and practice.

Sources of Law

Law takes several forms. The US Constitution is the ultimate law of the land by which actions by the branches of government are established and limited. Statutes are laws passed by a legislative body and signed by the president. Regulations are rules adopted by executive branch agencies, such as the federal Environmental Protection Agency (EPA), the Internal Revenue Service, or the Transportation Security Administration (TSA, which is part of the DHS), to implement or carry out statutes passed by Congress. This is the same manner by which state agencies carry out responsibilities in statutes passed by their state legislature or assembly. Regulations are adopted following a formal administrative procedure that requires proposal of the regulation with time for public review and comment. Regulatory and administrative procedure is developed more fully in a special area of law called "administrative law."

Executive orders are written directives issued by the executive, meaning the president at the federal level or the governor at the state or territorial level, based on the powers granted to that office in the respective constitution. EOs cannot expand the power of the executive branch at the expense of the other branches, and because an EO can be rescinded or modified by the next person to hold that executive office, EOs are less durable than statutory law.

Court decisions collectively form what is known as case law, which amounts to judicial branch application of constitutional principles or language to statutes or actions of the two other branches or of lower levels of government. Case law from court decisions may assist with understanding how policies can be implemented in ways that are legally or constitutionally permissible; courts sometimes find laws or actions unconstitutional, which means they cannot continue as currently written or implemented.

Defining Homeland Security

Homeland security and emergency management activities cannot be separated from the policies of governments. Even something as seemingly simple as the definition of terrorism can be a matter of considerable policy debate, as illustrated by the multiple terrorism definitions used by federal agencies, the US Code, and state governments. Laws usually define terms to clarify the application of the powers and responsibilities addressed. Although there is no universally accepted definition of terrorism among various federal and state laws, Title 28 of the Code of Federal Regulations (CFR), the compendium of regulations promulgated by federal agencies, defines terrorism as "the unlawful use of force or violence against persons or property to intimidate or coerce a government, the civilian population, or any segment thereof, in furtherance of political or social objectives."[5] Implied in this definition and stated in most others is the element of "fear." It is fear that is the terrorist's key weapon when striking at noncombatant civilian populations. It was fear used during the French Revolution's Reign of Terror in the 1790s that gave birth to the use of the word *terrorism* in the twenty-first century.

Although the United States was familiar with terrorism long before September 11, 2001, the term *homeland security* was not commonly used until the aftermath of the 2001 terrorist attacks on New York and Washington, DC. With the creation of the White House Office of Homeland Security (OHS) in the fall of 2001 and then Congress's creation of the US Department of Homeland Security, the federal government adopted a previously little-used and now broadly accepted term: *homeland security.*

National security refers to protection of a nation's citizens and its interests. So how does homeland security differ? The term *homeland defense* had been used in military and national security materials. *Homeland security* was used around the turn of the twenty-first century in US military materials to address a combination of the prevention of external threats, the protection of critical assets, and the support for domestic response. The term was used in a US Army Homeland Security Initiative in June 2001, encompassing:

Active and passive measures taken to protect the population, area, and infrastructure of the United States, its possessions, and territories by:

- Deterring, defending against, and mitigating the effects of threats, disasters, and attacks;

- Supporting civil authorities in crisis and consequence management; and
- Helping to ensure the availability, integrity, survivability, and adequacy of critical national assets.[6]

The term *homeland security* was adopted by the Bush administration when it created the OHS in the White House after 9/11 to focus on improving terrorism prevention and response policy. Despite the assumed clarity of mission in preventing future terrorism attacks, the lack of definition of what is meant by *homeland security* and how it related to existing civilian agencies and their missions resulted in challenges for the new department, for agencies that were combined in it, and for state government counterparts. The federal government agencies that morphed into the new DHS had a range of responsibilities, separate and distinct from their "homeland security" missions, yet they were combined because of the post-9/11 focus on preventing terrorism.

Constitutional Law and Principles

The US Constitution is the basis for all law in the United States and establishes the three branches of government: legislative (Congress), executive (president and the executive departments and agencies), and judicial (Supreme Court and lower courts). Each branch has specific areas of authority and responsibility, as well as the authority to restrain or "check" one or both of the other branches. Although Congress passes laws, it also sets policy through its spending power. Congress determines the amount of money that federal agencies have in their budgets for various programs—called appropriations. The president establishes policy through his or her direction and supervision of executive branch agencies, which includes most of the federal government. The judicial branch, with the Supreme Court as the final arbiter, has the authority to determine the constitutionality of actions by the other branches as well as by state governments. The Constitution also establishes the relationship between state governments and the federal government.

In response to disasters, local and state governments and organizations prepare for and respond to local hazards, and they can be supported by the federal government when local and state capabilities are overwhelmed. State and local governments have a tiered system, providing on-the-ground capabilities for disaster prevention, preparedness, mitigation, response, and recovery and the federal government providing a dual and supplementary response capability.

Federalism refers to the concept of shared government between the central federal government and the state governments.[7] Each has responsibilities and authorities independent of the other, derived from the citizens and the US Constitution. Concurrent powers, or shared powers, include the power to levy taxes to raise money to fund government activities; both federal and state governments can levy taxes. Some powers are exclusive, such as the powers to establish a monetary system or enter into treaties with other countries; only the federal government has these powers. As James Madison, writing as Publius, said in Federalist Paper No. 45 in 1788 as part of his campaign to generate support for the proposed US Constitution:

> The powers delegated by the proposed Constitution to the federal government are few and defined. Those which are to remain in the State governments are numerous and indefinite. The former will be exercised principally on external objects, as war, peace, negotiation, and foreign commerce; with which last the power of taxation will, for the most part, be connected. The powers reserved to the several States will extend to all the objects which, in the ordinary course of affairs, concern the lives, liberties, and properties of the people, and the internal order, improvement, and prosperity of the State. The operations of the federal government will be most extensive and important in times of war and danger; those of the State governments, in times of peace and security.

The federal system adds to the complexity of a decentralized homeland security and emergency management system in the United States in that multiple agencies with diverse responsibilities, legal authority, and capabilities are involved and must be coordinated at each level of government: federal, state, and local. For example, both federal and state agencies (representing a sovereign power) have legal authority and responsibilities for law enforcement, including crime prevention. These powers are established in state and federal statutes for state and federal governments and by state laws and local ordinances for local law enforcement. Local law enforcement handles day-to-day incidents and crimes within its political jurisdiction; however, if an incident occurs that may involve terrorism, the Federal Bureau of Investigation (FBI) exercises its primary jurisdiction because of the national security implications of terrorism incidents.[8]

In addition to establishing the structure of government, the US Constitution includes the Bill of Rights, which guarantees civil liberties of individuals.

Passage of the Bill of Rights was vital to ratification of the US Constitution because of concerns that too much power was being vested in the federal government. Individual freedoms, such as freedom of speech, religion, and association, are recognized in the First Amendment; protection against unreasonable search and seizure is guaranteed in the Fourth Amendment. These rights and protections must be observed by the federal and state governments. Conflicts sometimes arise between actions to protect public safety and welfare and constitutionally protected individual liberties. Constitutional protections in the Fourth, Fifth, and Sixth Amendments restrict the conduct of criminal investigations and prosecution of suspects (e.g., probable cause, due process of law, and speedy and public trial, respectively).

Emergency situations may require extraordinary actions to protect life or ensure our national security. The powers of the president and other officials as well as federal and state agencies are initially established in their respective constitutions, with questions of the extent of authority at times reviewed and determined by the judicial branch. Emergency powers may also be further spelled out—and sometimes restricted—in statute, such as the National Emergencies Act. Under the powers delegated by statute, the president may seize property, organize and control the means of production, seize commodities, assign military forces abroad, institute martial law, seize and control all transportation and communication, regulate the operation of private enterprise, restrict travel, and, in a variety of ways, control the lives of US citizens. However, Congress may modify, rescind, or render dormant emergency authority delegated in statute.[9]

Government Agencies and Structures

The history of homeland security and emergency management law and policy follows the course of natural and human-caused disasters in the history of the United States. What we consider emergency management originated in case-by-case efforts to respond to disasters, such as the fire recovery assistance to a New Hampshire town provided for by the Congressional Act of 1803. With increasing urbanization and industrialization, local efforts also began to focus collectively on what we would now consider mitigation, prevention, and preparedness by forming fire brigades and taking steps to suppress the spread of infectious disease through improved sanitation. The 1930s saw increased federal activity in areas of major flood control projects, disaster recovery loans, and transportation-related infrastructure repairs after disasters.[10]

Many current programs and activities in homeland security and emergency management emerged during the Cold War era after World War II. In 1947 President Harry Truman signed into law the National Security Act,[11] which created the Department of Defense (DOD), the Central Intelligence Agency (CIA), and the National Security Council (NSC), the latter of which advises the president on matters of national security. Cold War tensions with the Soviet Union focused attention on the potential for nuclear attack, resulting in the Civil Defense Act of 1950 and public education campaigns about sheltering from nuclear fallout. The Civil Defense Act also resulted in the designation of local civil defense responsibilities and offices in local government throughout the nation. With the passage of time, recurring large natural disasters, including major hurricanes in the Southeast and earthquakes in Alaska and California in the 1960s and 1970s, required large-scale responses and recovery efforts. Federal response support at that time was spread among many federal agencies, including the Federal Disaster Assistance Administration in the Department of Housing and Urban Development.[12] Congress responded to the recognition of the significant damage caused by natural disasters by passing the National Flood Insurance Act[13] and the Disaster Relief Act, which created the presidential disaster declaration process that continues today under the Robert T. Stafford Disaster Relief and Emergency Act.[14] The term *civil defense* was slowly replaced by *emergency management* at the local and state levels to reflect an all-hazards approach to dealing with man-made and natural disasters.

In response to state governors' requests to simplify the process for gaining federal support in a disaster, particularly in states experienced in dealing with severe hurricanes and other problems such as the Three Mile Island nuclear disaster, President Jimmy Carter consolidated many federal disaster preparedness and response activities in a new federal agency he created by EO 2127 in 1978.[15] The Federal Emergency Management Agency (FEMA) combined multiple programs and agencies, including the civil preparedness responsibilities that had been housed in the DOD.

During the 1990s, federal officials, including some in Congress, expressed increasing concern about the likelihood of a terrorist strike against the United States. The 1993 bombing of the World Trade Center in New York City and the Oklahoma City bombing in 1995 raised awareness of the potential vulnerability to acts of terrorism. The Phase I report of the US Commission on National Security/21st Century, also called the Hart-Rudman Report for two of the commission's key members, noted the changing international landscape and predicted terrorist attacks on US soil: "States, terrorists, and other disaffected groups will acquire weapons of mass destruction and mass disruption, and some will use them. Americans will likely die on American soil, possibly in large numbers."[16]

In the fall of 2001, Senator Joseph Lieberman (D-CT) proposed combining a number of federal agencies into a new Department of National Homeland Security as a means of confronting challenges that led to US vulnerability in the September 11 attacks.[17] In 2002 President George W. Bush adopted this approach, proposing creation of a new Department of Homeland Security through the Homeland Security Act of 2002. The primary mission of the DHS is to prevent terrorist attacks within the United States, reduce the vulnerability of the United States to terrorism, and minimize the damage, and assist in the recovery, from terrorist attacks that do occur within the United States, as established in Public Law (PL) 107-296.

It must be noted that seventeen agencies and bureaus within the federal government make up the US Intelligence Community (IC) and have key roles in national and homeland security. Most of those agencies are not part of the DHS. There are also other departments, such as the US Department of Energy (DOE), US Department of Transportation (DOT), Drug Enforcement Administration (DEA), FBI, and EPA, for example, that are responsible for the security and safety of facilities and activities such as nuclear power, prohibition of illegal drug manufacturing, counterterrorism investigations, and transportation, storage, and maintenance of hazardous materials.

After the creation of the DHS at the federal level, states began creating offices or departments of homeland security. Some are independent agencies, while others are part of governors' offices; most are part of another state agency, such as emergency management or public safety.[18] At the local level, homeland security functions are usually addressed by police and sheriff's offices and emergency management. At each level of government, multiple agencies and organizations are involved in prevention, mitigation, preparedness, response, and recovery activities. Even with the creation of the DHS, no one agency has the capability to address or manage all of the activities required to deal with intentional or accidental disasters. The US EPA, for example, bears responsibility for the implementation and enforcement of federal laws related to reporting of hazardous materials and hazardous material releases. This is important for both responding to accidental releases as well as protecting locations—fixed sites—and shipments that involve substances that could be used to cause intentional harm. This is also relevant at the state and local levels, where the coordination of existing capabilities of diverse agencies to deal with natural and human-caused hazards forms the key mission of emergency management agencies. In most emergencies, including instances of terrorism, local first responders and officials deal with the initial incident before federal agency personnel are involved.

An example of the complexity of the overlapping missions of federal agencies lies in the Intelligence Community, the collective term for agencies and departments with intelligence collection and analysis roles. The IC in the United States includes sixteen federal agencies, bureaus, and offices, including the CIA, Coast Guard, DOE, DHS, Department of State, Department of the Treasury, DEA, FBI, National Geospatial-Intelligence Agency, National Reconnaissance Office, National Security Agency, intelligence offices in branches of the armed services, in addition to the Defense Intelligence Agency.[19] In 2004 Congress passed the Intelligence Reform and Terrorist Prevention Act of 2004 (IRTPA), which created the Office of the Director of National Intelligence (ODNI) to provide leadership and coordination among various federal intelligence activities; the ODNI is the seventeenth member of the IC. IRTPA was the culmination of long discussions regarding reforming the IC, but it became a priority in response to findings of the National Commission on Terrorist Attacks upon the United States (the 9/11 Commission) that intelligence agencies had failed to connect the dots on intelligence that might have discovered and thwarted the 9/11 terrorist attacks.[20]

Major Statutes and Other Forms of Law

Because of the nature of disasters—that they begin and end locally and that most emergencies are handled primarily at the local level—it is worth noting that powers are granted to local officials and responders in municipal and county ordinances based on authority granted by the respective state's constitution and statutes. For example, legal authority to require isolation or quarantine in a public health emergency or to call for evacuation of an area is typically set out in the state constitution or state statutory law. (The federal Centers for Disease Control and Prevention has authority as well, should state officials not act in a timely manner.) Below are examples of key federal laws related to homeland security; there are many others. Students who pursue studies in homeland security or emergency management will likely take at least one course that explores the details of these and other key legal authorities.

Aviation and Transportation Security Act (ATSA) of 2001

The ATSA created the TSA, bringing passenger airport screening under the responsibilities of the federal government.[21] Before passage of the act in November 2001, airport security screening had been the collective responsibility of the airlines. The act also establishes other duties of the TSA. The TSA was originally part of the US Department of Transportation and was moved to the new DHS after it was formed the next year.

Disaster Mitigation Act of 2000

The Disaster Mitigation Act of 2000 (DMA2K) amended the Robert T. Stafford Disaster Relief and Emergency Act to update requirements for state and local governments to create and maintain hazard mitigation plans and to create a mechanism for promoting long-term policies designed to reduce the impact of hazards.[22] Whereas hazard mitigation had generally been approached previously from a natural hazards perspective, DMA2K incorporated an all-hazards approach, calling for states to address both natural and human-caused hazards in mitigation planning.

Foreign Intelligence Surveillance Act

The Foreign Intelligence Surveillance Act (FISA) of 1978 (as amended) provides legal authority for gathering information and intelligence on "agents of foreign powers," meaning individuals that are not citizens of the United States.[23] The act deals with four areas of intelligence gathering: electronic searches, personal searches, trap and trace devices, and searches of personal and business records. The US attorney general (AG) can authorize searches without a court order in accordance with the provisions in FISA. The act establishes a FISA court, which reviews searches authorized by the attorney general under the act. The AG reports to congressional committees on how many times the government has conducted searches that fall under FISA as well as intelligence gained. The Uniting and Strengthening America by Providing Appropriate Tools Required to Intercept and Obstruct Terrorism (USA PATRIOT) Act modified portions of FISA.

Implementing Recommendations of the 9/11 Commission Act

The section "Implementing Recommendations" of the 9/11 Commission Act of 2007[24] addresses several of the issues raised in the 9/11 Commission report. It includes provisions for the State Homeland Security Grant Program and the Emergency Management Performance Grant Program. It includes provisions designed to improve information sharing among agencies and levels of government, including support of information Fusion Centers, and codifies use of the Incident Command System.

Intelligence Reform and Terrorism Prevention Act

The Intelligence Reform and Terrorism Prevention Act of 2004 reorganized the US IC and created the ODNI to improve coordination among intelligence agencies.[25] It also established the National Counterterrorism Center to serve as a multiagency center to better integrate intelligence related to terrorism that could impact US interests.

Homeland Security Act of 2002

After the terrorist attacks of September 11, 2001, elected officials and policy makers urgently discussed how to improve antiterrorism capabilities and activities of the US government. Senator Lieberman proposed legislation creating a new federal department to consolidate functions and agencies with responsibilities for preventing terrorism on US soil. After initially opposing the legislation and preferring a homeland security office as part of the White House staff, President Bush adopted the concept and advocated for reorganization of federal government agencies to create a new department to address homeland security. The Homeland Security Act of 2002 (PL 107-296) created the DHS with a mission of preventing terrorism against the United States. As noted above, the act combined twenty-two federal agencies (or parts thereof) under the supervision of one cabinet secretary.

National Security Act

The National Security Act of 1947,[26] passed in the wake of World War II, instituted a major reorganization of the US defense and intelligence agencies. It created the DOD, the CIA (in place of the Office of Strategic Services), and the NSC.

Oil Pollution Act (OPA)

The Oil Pollution Act of 1990, which was passed after the *Exxon Valdez* incident in 1989, provides requirements for contingency planning both by government and by industry.[27] Under OPA, the federal government directs public and private response efforts for certain types of spill events. Area committees that include federal, state, and local government officials develop detailed, location-specific area contingency plans, and owners or operators of vessels and certain facilities that pose a serious threat to the environment must prepare their own facility response plans. The act provides for penalties for noncompliance but also allows states to enact laws governing oil-spill prevention and response. OPA uses the concept of a "responsible party" for purposes of liability for costs of damages from an oil spill.

Posse Comitatus Act

The Posse Comitatus Act restricts the use of military forces for civilian law enforcement, with exceptions (for a more detailed explanation, see Chapter 6, "Defense Support of Civil Authorities"). The Posse Comitatus Act, passed by Congress in 1878, restricts the use of the military, except as otherwise authorized by the Constitution or by federal law. This prohibition has been applied to the US Army, Air Force, Navy, and Marine Corps as a matter of US Department of Defense policy. Exceptions to the Posse Comitatus Act are found in the Insurrection Act, which authorizes the president to direct the armed forces to enforce laws to suppress insurrections and domestic violence.[28]

Robert T. Stafford Disaster Relief and Emergency Act

The Robert T. Stafford Disaster Relief and Emergency Act established the process for federal disaster response assistance to state governments.[29] It amended the Disaster Relief Act of 1974 and sets the definitions for *emergency, major disaster,* and other terms used in determining disaster federal assistance. FEMA creates regulations, found in the Code of Federal Regulations, and policies for implementing the Stafford Act and its disaster assistance provisions.

USA PATRIOT Act

The USA PATRIOT Act was passed by Congress quickly in the aftermath of the September 2001 terrorist attacks, enacting intelligence-gathering tools that had been sought by the US Department of Justice. The act expanded the meaning of *terrorist organization* under federal law and expanded the surveillance powers of the federal government. It also includes provisions to interrupt terrorist financing through financial- and banking-system reporting requirements.[30] Because of concerns about invasion of privacy and the expansion of surveillance powers under the USA PATRIOT Act, the act has seen multiple revisions. Some modifications have been related to "sunset provisions," which preestablish from the original legislation a time at which specific sections expire unless they are reauthorized by Congress.

Public Health Security and Bioterrorism Preparedness and Response Act

The Public Health Security and Bioterrorism Preparedness and Response Act of 2002[31] was created to improve coordinated preparedness and response for a biological incident after the September 2001 terrorist attacks and the fall 2001 anthrax attacks, which killed five people and created significant public concern and uncertainty, as well as decontamination costs. The act is intended to improve the ability to prevent, prepare for, and respond to bioterrorism and public health emergencies and protection of the food supply. It tasks the US Department of Health and Human Services with creating a national biological preparedness plan.

National Emergencies Act

The National Emergencies Act[32] establishes procedures for presidential declaration and termination of a national emergency. Declaration of a national emergency is required for the exercise of certain special or extraordinary powers by the president.

Executive Orders and Presidential Directives

EOs and presidential directives (PDs) are examples of documents issued by the president in furtherance of his or her executive authority. EOs and directives establish an administration's policy in a particular area, often articulating goals or objectives for federal agencies in a specific policy area, such as critical infrastructure protection or incident management. EOs and PDs (also known as presidential decision directives, or PDDs) have the force of law to the extent they are consistent with the executive authority granted in the Constitution, including checks by the other branches of government. An EO is checked, for example, by the authority to appropriate funds—the budgeting authority or "power of the purse"—held by the legislative branch. Congress has specified that while a president can establish an executive agency by executive order or directive, the executive branch cannot use appropriated funds to support the agency for longer than one year unless Congress appropriates money specifically for it or authorizes expenditures for or by the agency. The president also has the ability to not carry forward a legislative program passed by Congress, but cannot use the appropriated funds in another program area.

PDs have been known by different labels in various presidential administrations, including presidential decision directive, national security action memorandum, national security decision memorandum, national security directive, national security decision directive, national security presidential directive, and homeland security presidential directive. All are the same level of presidential policy directive, issued under the executive authority of the president. They can be repealed or amended by a subsequent administration. Former president William J. Clinton, for example, issued a number of PDDs related to homeland security and emergency management:

- PDD 39 (1995) addressed responsibilities for crisis management (FBI) and consequence management (FEMA) in response to a disaster, particularly an act of terrorism;
- PDD 62 (1998) established a more systematic approach to fighting terrorism;
- PDD 63 (1998) enabled critical infrastructure protection (replaced by Executive Order 13231, October 2001, in the Bush administration);
- PDD 67 (1998) authorized continuity of government and continuity of operations planning for the federal government.

Former president George W. Bush used homeland security presidential directives to set objectives for federal agencies on a number of terrorism prevention and disaster response issues. For example, HSPD-5 directed the secretary of homeland security to develop and administer a National Incident Management System (NIMS). NIMS (under FEMA) formalizes expectations for disaster response, including resource management and use of a national incident management system called the Incident Command System to provide a common management framework for disaster operations. HSPD-7 called for initiatives to protect critical infrastructure. HSPD-8, which tasked the DHS with creating a national preparedness system, was modified to PDD-8 and updated by President Barack Obama in 2011.[33]

Examples of EOs include:

- EO 10450, April 27, 1953: established personnel security requirements for service in the US government;
- EO 12333, December 4, 1981: established the goals, directions, duties, and responsibilities of the Intelligence Community;

- EO 13224, September 23, 2001: defined terrorism and blocked certain property and prohibited transactions potentially related to terrorism;
- EO 13228, October 8, 2001: created the White House Office of Homeland Security and the Homeland Security Council, providing for coordination of federal terrorism prevention activities;
- EO 13470, July 30, 2008: amended EO 12333, amended by EO 13284, amended by 13355, and in compliance with PL 108-458,[34] regarding US intelligence activities and the role of the ODNI;
- Arizona EO 2010-14: Arizona governor's executive order establishing state policy on climate change.[35]

Specific Areas of Law

There are multiple diverse areas of homeland security law and policy that are specific to industries or aspects of society. Examples include administrative law, aviation law, criminal law, immigration policy and law, and maritime law (laws dealing with shipping vessels and legal jurisdiction in navigable waterways). Administrative law (as noted above) deals with procedures for government agencies to create regulations and with agency practices in implementing law and policy. We now turn to other specific areas of law that impact homeland security.

Hazardous Materials Law and Regulations

Multiple laws and regulations govern identification, storage, use, and transportation of hazardous materials. This also means multiple agencies are involved in regulating hazardous materials. The EPA creates and enforces regulations related to fixed-site hazardous materials and waste; the DOT creates and enforces regulations specific to the transportation of hazardous materials.[36] The US Coast Guard has a shared responsibility for hazardous materials safety and response regulation enforcement on and immediately adjacent to navigable waterways. State environmental protection departments and departments of natural resources also enforce federal environmental and hazardous material regulations.

International Law

Laws dealing with the interactions among nations are referred to as international law. Most people are familiar with the laws of their own communities, states, or nation, so to think in terms of how legal principles are addressed across national boundaries may initially be a challenge. Formal legal agreements among nations take the form of treaties, often called conventions if multiple nations are signatories to the agreement. While various agencies of the federal government may be involved in researching and developing treaties with other nations, the president has the power to enter into a treaty on behalf of the United States with the consent of two-thirds of the US Senate.[37] International treaties are written to address issues of common concern across national borders.

Situations that involve war—"armed conflict"—between nations, as well as humanitarian assistance in response to armed conflict, fall under an area of law known as international humanitarian law. International treaties, such as the Geneva Conventions, also govern detention and treatment of prisoners of war. According to the International Committee of the Red Cross, a key custodian of international humanitarian law materials and information:

> The basic premise underlying international humanitarian law (IHL), that even in an armed conflict only the weakening of the military potential of the enemy is acceptable, implies that IHL has to define who may be considered part of that potential and, therefore, may be attacked, participate directly in hostilities, but may not be punished for such participation under ordinary municipal law. Under the principle of distinction, all involved in armed conflict must distinguish between the persons thus defined, the combatants, on the one hand, and civilians, on the other hand. Combatants must, therefore, distinguish themselves (i.e., allow their enemies to identify them) from all other persons, the civilians, who may not be attacked nor directly participate in hostilities.[38]

In the post-9/11 world, international humanitarian law, military law, and US criminal law intersect in how the US government handles detention of suspected terrorist associates. The US policy of holding individuals—initially more than five hundred—at the US Naval Station at Guantánamo Bay, Cuba, created significant debate in the legal and military policy communities. As noted in a 2009 US government memorandum reviewing issues related to detainees:

> In the current conflict with al Qaeda, the Taliban, and affiliated forces, the unlawful activities of our adversaries can in many cases be fairly characterized both as violations of the law of war and as terrorism offenses under our federal criminal code. This reflects the nature of the conflict in which we

are engaged, in which the enemy is a non-state actor and criminal enterprise bent on attacking innocent civilians on a massive scale. The President has concluded that, just as the defeat of al Qaeda will require employment of all instruments of national power—military, intelligence, law enforcement, and diplomatic—so too must we have the ability to hold our enemies accountable for their crimes in more than one forum, namely both federal courts and military commissions.[39]

Full exploration of the legal issues associated with detainees at Guantánamo could fill a textbook. For the purposes of this chapter, the reader should note several key issues that have arisen with US policy and treatment of detainees: the rights of detainees to know the charges and evidence against them, rights to counsel and speedy trial, and application of US constitutional and statutory law and international law regarding procedures for trying the detainees or releasing them to other countries. These issues resulted in a series of US Supreme Court cases that each led to revisions in policy. The foundation for the debate lies in constitutional guarantees of individual rights and freedoms, including protection against being held without charge. An individual detained under US law has the privilege of habeas corpus[40] and can file a petition calling for the government to justify why the person is being detained.[41] Yet the system created by the United States for prisoners held at Guantánamo, first by Bush administration policy and then under the Detainee Treatment Act of 2005 passed by Congress, did not provide basic rights, including notification of charges, access to evidence against them, access to legal counsel, or a speedy trial. Individuals held at Guantánamo were primarily non-US citizens and were implicated as terrorists, terrorist associates, or those who might have information on terrorist groups. The US government under President George W. Bush considered the detainees "unlawful enemy combatants" who could be held indefinitely without trial.

The administration's justification was partially based in Congress's Authorization for Use of Military Force (AUMF) passed soon after September 11, 2001, which authorized the president "to use all necessary and appropriate force against those nations, organizations, or persons he determines planned, authorized, committed, or aided the terrorist attacks that occurred on September 11, 2001, or harbored such organizations or persons, in order to prevent any future acts of international terrorism against the United States by such nations, organizations or persons."[42] In *Hamdi v. Rumsfeld,* the Supreme Court held that as part of the AUMF, the president was authorized to detain persons captured while fighting US forces in Afghanistan for the duration of the conflict.[43] With this authority, the Department of Defense established Combatant Status Review Tribunals to determine whether Guantánamo detainees were "enemy combatants" who could be detained for the duration of what the administration called the "War on Terror" and prosecuted in military commissions for any war crimes committed.[44]

However, in *Rasul v. Bush,* the US Supreme Court was asked to review the tribunal process and said that "a state of war is not a blank check for the president" and held that individuals held as "enemy combatants" have the right to challenge their detention before a judge or neutral decision maker. The court ruled that the federal habeas statute[45] extended habeas corpus jurisdiction to individuals held in Guantánamo, rejecting the concept that the detainees had no right to habeas corpus because they were not US citizens and were held on foreign soil.[46] In *Hamdan v. Rumsfeld,* the US Supreme Court held that civilian courts could hear pending petitions for habeas corpus from Guantánamo detainees.[47] The court ruled that the Geneva Conventions—international agreements governing the conduct of armed conflict and treatment of civilians and prisoners—were applicable to Guantánamo detainees because of language in the Uniform Code of Military Justice (UCMJ) that states that "compliance with the law of war is the condition upon which the authority set forth in Article 21 is granted."

After the *Hamdan* decision, Congress passed the Military Commissions Act (MCA),[48] authorizing the president to convene military commissions without complying with the UCMJ language and eliminating detainees' access to federal courts for habeas review. As noted in a Congressional Research Service report summarizing Guantánamo detainee cases, "The complete elimination of habeas corpus review by Congress (via the MCA) compelled the courts to address directly an issue they had avoided reaching in earlier cases: Does the constitutional *writ of habeas corpus* extend to noncitizens held at Guantanamo?"[49] In the *Boumediene* and *Al Odah* consolidated case, the court found that aliens designated as enemy combatants at Guantánamo must be afforded the privilege of habeas corpus and that the MCA did not provide an adequate substitute for habeas corpus reviews.[50] The direct impact of the *Boumediene* case was that detainees could petition a federal district court for habeas corpus review of their detention.

The United States is a signatory to—meaning it agreed to and signed—a number of international agreements relevant to issues associated with Guantánamo detainees. Hamdan was captured in Afghanistan, for example, where the United States was at war, and the US Supreme Court said Hamdan met the criteria for treatment as a prisoner of war under Common Article 3 of the Geneva Conventions of 1949. Congress, in the MCA, tried to preclude the application of the Geneva Conventions to habeas or other civil proceedings.[51] The MCA also gave the president the authority to interpret the meaning and application of the Geneva Conventions, language the full meaning of which has not been tested.

The United Nations Convention Against Torture and Other Cruel, Inhuman, or Degrading Treatment or Punishment (CAT), to which the United States is a signatory, also is relevant in the issue of releasing detainees for resettlement in other countries. In some cases, detainees may be released to countries rather than tried by the United States. In addition to requiring signatories to take measures to prevent torture, the CAT states that signatory countries will not "expel, return ('refouler') or extradite a person to another State where there are substantial grounds for believing that he would be in danger of being subjected to torture."[52]

Although the US presidential administration changed in 2009, the issues of Guantánamo detainees continue. When President Barack Obama took office, he said he would close Guantánamo and begin the process of trying or releasing detainees. The Obama administration instituted a new standard to guide government authority to detain terrorist suspects, no longer using the phrase *enemy combatant* to refer to persons who may be detained. The new standard permits the detention of members of the Taliban, al-Qaeda, and associated forces and persons who provide "substantial support" to such groups regardless of where the individual was captured.[53] The Obama administration placed a moratorium on military tribunals for Guantánamo detainees as it reviewed procedures and sought to try detainees in civilian courts. However, in 2011, after opposition from Congress and some local and state officials regarding plans to bring detainees into the United States to be tried in federal courts, President Obama announced resumption of military trials for detainees under modified procedures. Some detainees could still be tried in civilian courts.[54]

A broader set of international agreements also is relevant in discussing criminal investigations, surveillance and intelligence gathering, business and finance, law of the sea, and human rights. For example, criminal investigations that may concern terrorist activity may involve laws of multiple nations and international agreements regarding evidence and extradition. Cyber crime and cyber terrorism, for example, require application of multiple nations' laws as well as international agreements since those who initiate a cyber attack can be in one or more countries external to that in which the most significant impact occurs, and impacts often cross national borders.

Public Health Law and Policy

Public health law encompasses authorities and powers for preserving public health—the health of the broader community as opposed to medical treatment of one individual. Public health law includes authority for isolation and quarantine, vaccination, and other protective measures. For example, while citizens typically have the right to choose the medical treatments they receive, the Supreme Court in *Jacobson v. Commonwealth of Massachusetts* held that a state's responsibility and authority in protecting public health can present a stronger interest than that of an individual who refuses to be vaccinated for smallpox. The state can limit individual rights by reasonable regulations to protect public health. (The state allows exceptions to the vaccination requirement when a doctor indicates that vaccination is not appropriate for the individual.)[55] Public health law also includes federal and state laws and regulations related to the reporting of disease, control of and testing for biological agents, and protection of food and water supplies. Much of the health care system in the United States is privately owned and operated, so interaction of public health authorities with private-sector health care organizations also is important.

Liability and Immunity

The act of responding to an emergency often involves the application of law, including the legal authorities to take specific actions or the potential legal liability for injury or death in the emergency incident. Liability is legal responsibility for a negative consequence. Those who respond as part of a government or other agency may be carrying out a legally designated responsibility or authority. When each of us acts toward others, we bear responsibility to act reasonably to avoid harming them. This is sometimes referred to as a duty of care. When the responding person is someone trained in the relevant profession (e.g., an emergency medical technician or firefighter), the duty may involve a standard of care for that professional role—the manner and level of training and expertise in exercising the duty. For those who respond in emergencies, offering response in an incident that already is dangerous could result in a situation in which he or she is considered responsible for a negative outcome (e.g., injury, death, property damage). Generally, those acting in a response role as part of a government entity enjoy governmental immunity for actions they take in their response role, as long as their actions are consistent with the standard of care for someone with the training and experience expected of their role. Governmental immunity, sometimes called sovereign immunity, also can be applicable as a defense to liability in the exercise of other government functions. Immunity, however, is not absolute, in that the person or entity may still be held liable for violations of law or may be held liable for damages if he or she was negligent in carrying out his or her duties. Immunity provisions are established in state and federal statutes.

Mutual Aid and Interstate Compacts

In emergencies and disasters, a local jurisdiction may need more resources and personnel than are available. Local and state governments enter into arrangements to provide assistance to each other in emergencies, called "mutual aid agreements." A mutual aid agreement is a pact between agencies or jurisdictions that they will assist one another on request, by furnishing personnel, equipment, or expertise in a specified manner during an emergency or disaster. The need for mutual aid agreements is related to the responsibilities of individual governments, such as a municipality, county, state, territory, or tribal nation. A government official or agency manager, such as a sheriff for one county, generally does not have the legal authority or responsibility for law enforcement in another county. However, through mutual aid agreements, supplemental response personnel, equipment, and supplies can cross jurisdictional boundaries to assist with emergency response and recovery. Because capabilities and political leadership change over time, mutual aid agreements should be in writing and updated regularly.

Mutual aid may be "intrastate" to address local-to-local mutual assistance across county or municipal boundaries within a state. Many states have intrastate mutual aid agreements for fire-suppression assistance. Mutual aid also may be "interstate," meaning between or among more than one state (think of the interstate highway system as it crosses multiple states).

Beginning in the early 1990s, states began developing what would become a nationwide mutual aid agreement. The Emergency Management Assistance Compact (EMAC) is an interstate agreement (similar to a contract among states) to provide assistance in emergencies and disasters. EMAC began as an agreement among southern states to assist each other in hurricane response and was later approved by Congress[56] and adopted by all states.[57] EMAC provides a mechanism to request and select mutual aid assistance from other states through a web-based tool and addresses consistently and in advance issues of liability and reimbursement for response costs.[58]

Mutual aid is a vital component of the nation's emergency response capability, providing additional support to impacted areas. Because it involves response and recovery personnel and resources that work across jurisdictional lines (where operational plans and procedures may be different from those in the home jurisdiction), mutual aid heightens the importance of common planning, incident management, and resource management processes and procedures throughout the nation.[59]

* * *

The study of law and policy is an integral part of the study of homeland security. Whether to appropriately implement surveillance or to understand the requirements to impose a quarantine in a biological emergency, a foundation of knowledge regarding legal powers, authorities, and constraints forms the basis of effective and efficient homeland security and disaster response.

NOTES

1. *Merriam-Webster OnLine,* s.v. "policy," accessed March 1, 2011, www.merriam-webster.com/dictionary/policy.

2. Barack Obama, "The Comprehensive National Cybersecurity Initiative," accessed April 2, 2011, http://www.whitehouse.gov/sites/default/files/cybersecurity.pdf.

3. John F. Kingdon, *Agendas, Alternatives, and Public Policies,* 2nd ed. (New York: Longman, 1995), 166.

4. Donald F. Kettl, *System Under Stress: Homeland Security and American Politics,* 2nd ed. (Washington, DC: CQ Press, 2007).

5. 28 CFR 0.85.

6. Greg Andreozzi, Center for Army Analysis, "Homeland Security Initiative," June 2001.

7. James Madison, Federalist Paper No. 45.

8. 28 USC §533, based on the US attorney general's designation of terrorism investigation authority to the FBI. PDD 39 (1995), US Policy on Counterterrorism.

9. Harold Relyea, Congressional Research Service, *CRS Report for Congress: National Emergency Powers,* updated 2007.

10. Ibid.

11. National Security Act of 1947, 50 USCA §402, as amended.

12. Federal Emergency Management Agency, "FEMA History."

13. 42 USC §4001 et seq. (2002).

14. Federal Emergency Management Agency, "FEMA History."

15. 43 FR 41943, 92 Stat. 3788 (1978); Executive Order 2127 of March 31, 1978, "Federal Emergency Management Agency," 3 CFR, 1979 Comp., p. 376; Executive Order 12148 of July 20, 1979, as amended, 3 CFR, 1979 Comp., p. 412 (implementation).

16. US Commission on National Security/21st Century, Phase I report, *New World Coming: American Security in the 21st Century*, September 15, 1999.

17. SB 1534 introduced October 2001; *Statements on Introduced Bills and Resolutions, 107th Congress, US Senate* (Washington, DC: Government Printing Office, October 11, 2001), 10647, available at http://www.thomas.gov.

18. National Governors Association Center for Best Practices, *Overview of State Homeland Security Governance Structures* (n.d.).

19. Office of the Director of National Intelligence, *National Intelligence: A Consumer's Guide* (2009).

20. Keith Gregory Logan, ed., *Homeland Security and Intelligence* (Santa Barbara, CA: Praeger, 2010), 229–230.

21. 49 USC §114 (2001).

22. Disaster Mitigation Act of 2000, Public Law 106-390 (2000), amending 42 USC 5121 et seq.

23. Foreign Intelligence Surveillance Act of 1978, 50 USC 36 §1802.

24. Public Law 110-53, August 3, 2007.

25. Public Law 108-458, December 17, 2004.

26. 50 USC §401 et seq., as amended.

27. 33 USC §2701 et seq.

28. 10 USC §§331–335 (2002).

29. 42 USC §5121 et seq., as amended.

30. Title III, International Money Laundering Abatement and Anti-Terrorism Financing Act of 2001.

31. 42 USC §201 et seq. (2002).

32. 50 USC §§1601–1651 (1988).

33. PPD-8, National Preparedness, accessed July 1, 2011, http://www.dhs.gov/xabout /laws/gc_1215444247124.shtm.

34. Intelligence Reform and Prevention Act of 2004.

35. EO 2010-14, Governor's Policy on Climate Change, superseding EO 2010-06, accessed April 2, 2011, http://azgovernor.gov/dms/upload/EO_2010-14.pdf.

36. 49 USC §5101 et seq.

37. US Constitution, Article 2, Section 2.

38. International Committee of the Red Cross, "How Does Law Protect in War?" (2006).

39. Detention Policy Task Force, "Memorandum for the Attorney General and Secretary of Defense," July 20, 2009, 1.

40. For the history of habeas corpus, see 39 Am. Jur. 2d *Habeas Corpus* §1 (1999).

41. US Constitution, Article 1, Section 9.

42. PL 107-40, 115 Stat. 224 (2001).

43. *Hamdi v. Rumsfeld*, 542 US 507 (2004).

44. Jennifer K. Elsea and Michael Johnson Garcia, Congressional Research Service, *Enemy Combatant Detainees: Habeas Corpus Challenges in Federal Court* (2010), 4.

45. 28 USC §2241.

46. *Rasul v. Bush*, 542 US 466, 124 S.Ct. 2686 (2004).

47. *Hamdan v. Rumsfeld*, 548 US 557 (2006).

48. PL 109-366 (2006).

49. Elsea and Garcia, Congressional Research Service, *Enemy Combatant Detainees*, 2.

50. 553 US 723 (2008).

51. 28 USC §2241n (2006).

52. UN Convention Against Torture and Other Cruel, Inhuman, or Degrading Treatment or Punishment, pt. 1, art. 3(1) (1975).

53. US Department of Justice, "Respondents' Memorandum Regarding the Government's Detention Authority Relative to Detainees Held at Guantanamo Bay," accessed April 20, 2011, http://www.justice.gov/opa/documents/memo-re-det-auth.pdf.

54. "Fact Sheet: New Actions on Guantánamo and Detainee Policy," accessed April 20, 2011, http://www.whitehouse.gov.

55. *Jacobson v. Massachusetts*, 197 US 11 (1905); Wendy E. Parmet, Richard A. Goodman, and Amy Farber, "Individual Rights Versus the Public's Health: 100 Years after *Jacobson v. Massachusetts*," *New England Journal of Medicine* 352 (February 17, 2005): 652–654.

56. Public Law 104-321, October 19, 1996, 110 Stat. 3877. Interstate compacts are similar to contracts except they are among states rather than among people or corporations. Interstate compacts do not have to be approved by Congress as long as the compact is not "directed to the formation of any combination tending to the increase of political power in the States, which may encroach upon or interfere with the just supremacy of the United States." *US Steel Corp. v. Multistate Tax Commission*, 434 US 452, 468 (1978).

57. Emergency Management Assistance Compact, "EMAC and Mutual Aid History," accessed February 1, 2011, http://www.emacweb.org/?321.

58. See also http://www.emacweb.org.

59. See also http://www.fema.gov/emergency/nims/.

Public- and Private-Sector Partnerships in Homeland Security

MICHAEL CHUMER

In 2002 President George Bush proposed the establishment of a Department of Homeland Security, to prevent terrorist attacks, reduce vulnerabilities to terrorism, and minimize damage and the time to recover from terrorist events and all other hazards. On November 25, 2002, the Homeland Security Act of 2002, Public Law 107-296, formally established the DHS. The new department not only had a profound effect on the organization of the federal government, but also began to shape the role of the private sector as well. Specifically, Section 508 of the act prescribes the use of private-sector networks during an all-hazard response: "To the maximum extent practicable, the Secretary shall use national private sector networks and infrastructure for emergency response to chemical, biological, radiological, nuclear, or explosive disasters, and other major disasters."

In parallel to the formation of the DHS, the Department of Defense planned for and developed a new combatant command called the US

Northern Command that became fully operational in October 2002. Part of the mission space of this combat command was defense support of civil authorities (DSCA). As will be explained later in this chapter, DSCA suggests a relationship with the private sector that was recognized and is addressed through the Interagency Coordination Directorate of NORTHCOM. Within the space created by two newly formed entities, the DHS and NORTHCOM, organizational structures and processes were established to formulate partnerships with the private sector both in homeland security and in homeland defense.

In this chapter the term *mission space* refers to the area of responsibility or field created by an organization's operation. The DHS's homeland security mission space is expanding, as the DHS defines and redefines what it is and where it is going. NORTHCOM is expanding in a similar manner. Both organizations are very young, and even though the DHS is an organizational collection of many more mature organizations and agencies (twenty-two), the entire collective is taking on an identity that shifts from year to year. With both the DHS and NORTHCOM, the private sector is viewed as a critical component, but is addressed differently.

There are four parts to analyzing the private sector and homeland security. The first part addresses a government approach to private-sector engagement and partnering. A series of structural documents shapes the role of the private sector from the view of the public sector. The second part addresses two major models of private-sector engagement that have emerged with the creation of the DHS and NORTHCOM. Both models are different. One is the "top-down model" that places emphasis upon the role that the structural documents play in private-sector behavior. The second is the "bottom-up model" that is based upon a "community of interest (COI) and community of practice (COP) model," suggesting a different type of behavior. Both need to be understood in order to fully grasp the role of the private sector within homeland security. The third part describes the nature of private-sector and public-sector partnerships (PPP) and further articulates several partnerships that are taking place at different jurisdictional levels (state, FEMA, the DHS, and NORTHCOM). These PPPs are beginning to center themselves on the concept of Business Emergency Operations Centers (BEOC), working with their public-sector counterparts. The fourth and last part addresses certain issues confronting the private sector in the mission space that has and is still being defined by HS and HD.

Structuring the Private Sector in Homeland Security

Structuring the private sector will focus upon the series of initiatives taken by government to incorporate the private sector within the four major dimensions of emergency management:

- *Preparedness*—Upon the establishment of the DHS, preparedness focused upon man-made disasters such as terrorism, but quickly grew to embrace natural disasters such as hurricanes, tornadoes, earthquakes, flooding, and a host of similar threats under an "all-hazards" approach to security. An integral component of this dimension is the exercises that are developed to establish the processes and procedures that would be used during an actual response.
- *Prevention and Mitigation*—This dimension places value on the gathering and dissemination of "actionable" information, such as intelligence, alerts, and notifications about a threat in order to prevent the threat from occurring or to mitigate its effects. The establishment of state Fusion Centers[1] and their approach to the fusing of sensitive law enforcement information coupled with information that carries a certain level of classification form the basis of activities within this EM dimension.
- *Response*—This dimension suggests everything from a single individual response to an event to a joint response that requires coordination and collaboration across agencies and sectors (private sector and public sector). It is during the response dimension where command and control thinking directly applies. The process model of C^2 suggests that increasing the speed of the process loop directly affects the overall ability of an actor (individual, collective, organization) to take appropriate action to reduce the effects of an emergency, especially in the reduction of casualties (Chumer and Turoff 2006).
- *Recovery*—This component suggests that both individual and joint efforts begun during response would continue in order to return to a state of normalcy. Some of the elements of this debate focus upon the nature of "normal," suggesting that a "new normal" direction may result as part of recovery scenarios.

A series of Homeland Security Presidential Directives[2] were developed to identify the needs and requirements of the United States in protecting the homeland from terrorist threats. The threat environment grew in a short period of time to include natural disasters. Two HSPDs (HSPD-5 and HSPD-7) in particular are highlighted here because they specifically identify a role for the private sector in HS. HSPD-5 identified a role for the private sector during a response to a catastrophic event, and HSPD-7 identified the role of the private sector in identifying and protecting critical infrastructure (CI). This infrastructure protection role grew as the DHS organized around the guiding principles contained within HSPD-7.

The Structuring Process

HSPDs and PDDs

Prior to the establishment of the DHS, HSPDs were issued and continue to be issued both as new directives and as modifications; these were followed by presidential decision directives. Of specific interest and relevance to the private sector are HSPD-5, Management of Domestic Incidents; HSPD-7, Critical Infrastructure Identification, Prioritization, and Protection; and PDD-8, National Preparedness.

HSPD-5 describes the importance of a joint effort between the public and private sectors during a response to an incident categorized as catastrophic or extreme. These incidents suggest large numbers of casualties, a high level of uncertainty and ambiguity during the initial response to the incident, and severe damage to infrastructure. Rising to this level are incidents such as:

- Katrina (a major hurricane affecting Louisiana, Mississippi, and neighboring states)
- the Gulf oil spill by British Petroleum in 2010
- 9/11
- the Australian floods in 2011
- the Christchurch earthquakes in 2011
- the Japan tsunami and earthquakes in 2011

HSPD-7 describes the importance of infrastructure to the United States and has resulted in an organizational function (infrastructure protection, or IP) created within the DHS. IP in turn focuses on infrastructure protection and infrastructure resilience through a series of coordinating councils. The roles of the private sector as both critical and noncritical infrastructure owners and operators were incorporated differently within the coordinating council structure. In addition, a coordinating council was established solely for public-sector integration and planning in the infrastructure mission space.

PDD-8 revised HSPD-8 and is aimed at strengthening the security and resilience of the United States "through systematic preparation for the threats that pose the greatest risk to the vulnerability of the Nation, including acts of terrorism, cyber attacks, pandemics, and catastrophic natural disasters" (PDD-8 2011).

DHS Office of Infrastructure Protection (OIP)

The DHS OIP "is a component within the National Programs and Protection Directorate. OIP leads the coordinated national program to reduce risks to the nation's critical infrastructure posed by acts of terrorism, and to strengthen national preparedness, timely response, and rapid recovery in the event of an attack, natural disaster, or other emergency" (DHS OIP 2011).

The OIP focuses upon both infrastructure protection and infrastructure resilience. As noted above, in carrying out this mission, it has created a governance structure that incorporates the private sector through a series of coordinating councils. These coordinating councils will be described in the sections that follow. There are three basic coordinating councils:

- **Sector Coordinating Councils (SCCs)** focus upon the unique infrastructure issues within each of the eighteen critical infrastructure sectors. These councils include some integration between formal sector structures in terms of planning and preparedness issues that may generalize between each sector. These coordinating councils are composed of private-sector and public-sector members, often at the agency level.
- **State, Local, Tribal, and Territorial Government Coordinating Councils (SLTTGCCs)** are composed of public-sector jurisdictions at various levels.
- **Regional Consortium Coordinating Councils (RCCCs)** are composed of private-sector entities that are not critical infrastructure owners and operators.

Sector Coordinating Council

The sector-partnership model incorporates the Sector Coordinating Councils and invites and encourages critical infrastructure owners and operators to create or identify Sector Coordinating Councils as the principal entities for coordinating with the government on a wide range of critical infrastructure protection activities and issues. Listed in alphabetical order are the current eighteen Critical Infrastructure/Key Resource sectors:

1. agriculture and food
2. banking and finance
3. chemical manufacturing
4. commercial facilities
5. commercial nuclear reactors, materials, and waste
6. critical manufacturing
7. dams
8. defense industrial base
9. drinking water and water treatment systems
10. emergency services
11. energy
12. government facilities
13. information technology
14. national monuments and icons
15. postal and shipping services
16. public health and health care
17. telecommunications
18. transportation systems

Each sector is headed by a Sector Coordinating Council that is involved in preparedness, protection, and resilience initiatives that may be unique to a specific sector. For example, the transportation sector, which addresses road, air, rail, and water transportation issues, is very large, requiring much coordination and planning. The energy sector is large as well, focusing on many dimensions, but an integral part is the electrical grid. Sector coordination is addressed by each individual sector through unique public-sector and private-sector integrating planning processes.

State, Local, Tribal, and Territorial Government Coordinating Council

The State, Local, Tribal, and Territorial Government Coordinating Council is a planning forum that ensures state, local, and tribal homeland security partners are fully integrated as public-sector participants in critical infrastructure protection and resilience efforts. The SLTTGCC also provides cross-jurisdiction coordination on state and local government–level critical infrastructure protection, strategies, and programs.

Regional Consortium Coordinating Council

Because of the specific challenges and interdependencies facing individual regions and the broad range of public- and private-sector security partners, regional efforts are often complex and diverse. The RCCC brings together representatives from regional partnerships, groupings, and governance bodies to enable critical infrastructure protection coordination among partners within and across geographical areas and in some instances across sectors.

DHS Private Sector Office

The DHS Private Sector Office (PSO) is also involved with integrating the private sector into the DHS, but does not focus upon the private sector strictly as CI/KR owners and operators, as does the DHS OIP. The DHS PSO focuses upon the needs of businesses and their ability to continue to do business when incidents of national significance occur. In this role and orientation, the DHS PSO and OIP coordinate to a large degree on all aspects of integrating the private sector within the major dimensions of emergency management. The following is a description of the roles and responsibilities of the DHS Private Sector Office:

The Private Sector Office:

- Advises the Secretary on the impact of the Department's policies, regulations, processes, and actions on the private sector.
- Creates and fosters strategic communications with the private sector to enhance the primary mission of the Department to protect the American homeland.
- Interfaces with other relevant Federal agencies with homeland security missions to assess the impact of these agencies on the private sector.
- Creates and manages private sector advisory councils composed of representatives of industries and associations designated by the Secretary to: (a) Advise the Secretary on private sector products, applications, and solutions as they relate to homeland security challenges; and (b) Advise the Secretary on homeland security policies, regulations, processes and actions that affect the participating industries and associations.
- Works with Federal laboratories, federally funded research and development centers, other federally funded organizations, academia, and the private sector to develop innovative approaches to address homeland security challenges to produce and deploy the best available technologies for homeland security missions.

- Promotes existing public-private partnerships and development of new public-private partnerships to provide for collaboration and mutual support to address homeland security challenges.
- Assists in the development and promotion of private sector best practices to secure critical infrastructure.
- Coordinates industry efforts regarding Department functions to identify private sector resources that could be effective in supplementing government efforts to prevent or respond to a terrorist attack.
- Consults with the various DHS elements and Department of Commerce on matters of concern to private sector including travel and tourism industries. (DHS PSO 2011)

FEMA's Private Sector Division

In addition to the DHS OIP and PSO, FEMA as part of its overall external affairs established a private-sector office in order to effect liaison, outreach, coordination, and planning with the private sector. As part of its outreach to the private sector, FEMA created and staffed private-sector liaisons within each FEMA region. These liaisons are currently reaching out to the private sector within each region in order to understand the different partnerships that have evolved as a result of both top-down (state-level) and bottom-up initiatives that are present to some degree within the regions. According to its website:

> FEMA established a Private Sector Division within the Office of External Affairs in October 2007. The division's overarching goals include improving information sharing and coordination between FEMA and the private sector during disaster planning, response and recovery efforts. The FEMA Private Sector Division cultivates public-private collaboration and networking in support of the various roles the private sector plays in emergency management, including: impacted organization, response resource, partner in preparedness, and component of the economy. The division also fosters internal collaboration and communication among FEMA programs that have an interest in private sector engagement. (FEMA 2011a)

NORTHCOM

In order to address issues of private-sector engagement, a private-sector nongovernmental organization (NGO) office was formed under the Interagency Coordination Directorate of NORTHCOM. This office provides outreach to private organizations, consortiums, associations, and NGOs. US NORTHCOM during a response scenario finds itself in an anticipatory role. They are not directly in the incident-command decision-making loop, but need to rely upon sources of information that can assist them in developing the situational awareness necessary in order to provide either direct support to citizens or support to civil authorities when called upon or when directed to do so. Building partnerships with the private sector permits a level of information sharing to occur that assists them in that role.

States and Regions

Each state approaches partnering with the private sector differently. Many of the states develop partnerships directly with CI/KR owners and operators. This is done in order to ensure that the critical infrastructure necessary to basic government and private-sector functioning is both protected and made resilient in order to withstand threat scenarios that may be unique to that state. In the fourth section, the growing role of Business Emergency Operations Centers is described. States are beginning to create these BEOCs as part of their response-preparedness efforts as well as Fusion Center information-sharing activities.

Summary

In this section we saw that there is an emerging role for the private sector that started with the HSPDs. This role was further shaped by the DHS in two ways: by creating both the DHS OIP and the DHS PSO. We also saw that there were initiatives in FEMA and US NORTHCOM designed to integrate the private sector within the four major dimensions of emergency management. Last, the states and in some instances regions, such as FEMA regions, are identifying different models that will allow private-sector integration to occur at the state and regional levels. What was not mentioned but is important is that there have been some initiatives undertaken by counties and municipalities to integrate with the private sector at those jurisdictional levels as well.

Private-Sector Models

This part will address the two basic directions and resulting models that emerge when investigating the private sector and its integration within HS. Part 1 addressed the formal structuring that occurred from the Office of the President. This structuring resulted in the creation of the DHS and NORTHCOM. Within both organizations the integration of the private sector resulted through a series of directives and standard operating procedures (SOPs) that in turn created a series of coordinating councils and committees through which private-sector involvement and private-sector roles were articulated. This direction is referred to as the "top-down model."

In contrast to the top-down model, there is activity occurring in the private sector that is self-directed in nature, emerging from both common interest and common practice. This activity is referred to in the sections that follow as the "bottom-up model." Both models will be described in the two sections that follow.

Top-Down Models

The first part addressed the initiatives taken by the federal government and state governments in defining the role and function of the private sector. However, as that section suggested, the private-sector role in HS is structured primarily upon the perceived needs of the public sector. This structuring that has its roots within government is referred to in this chapter as the top-down model of private-sector engagement and partnerships. This model is characterized by the following dimensions:

- the need for high-level formal directives as basic structuring artifacts (SOPs, frameworks, plans)
- a controlled governance structure or role based upon a set of processes and procedures
- a clear and oftentimes regulated communication structure
- a hierarchical decision-making model

Examples of this are as follows:

- DHS Office of Infrastructure Protection, its coordinating council framework, and eighteen critical infrastructure sectors
- FEMA and its private-sector initiatives
- state governments using infrastructure advisory committees
- National Incident Management System[3]
- National Infrastructure Protection Plan (NIPP)[4]
- National Response Framework (NRF)[5]

There are certainly many more examples of top-down structures, but they all, in a very formal way, suggest certain behaviors by the private sector during each dimension of emergency management.

The top-down model directs private-sector behavior within the four dimensions of emergency management as follows:

Preparedness—In the top-down model this dimension of emergency management is focused upon training, education, and planning at its core. An integral part of training is the role played by exercises such as tabletop exercises, command post exercises, communication exercises, and full-blown exercises. In the top-down model the exercises are predominantly developed and run by the public sector, with private-sector involvement oftentimes limited to CI/KR owners and operators. There is a suggested process for exercise development known as the Homeland Security Exercise Evaluation Program. This program was developed and formed primarily through top-down initiatives and suggests a certain controlled behavior when developing and evaluating exercises.

Another example is FEMA's Private Sector Preparedness Accreditation and Certification Program (PS-Prep). According to FEMA, "PS-Prep is a partnership between DHS and the private sector that will enable private entities—including businesses, non-profit organizations and universities—to receive emergency preparedness certification from a system DHS created in coordination with the private sector" (PS-Prep 2009). Both initiatives are examples of a top-down process within preparedness.[6]

Prevention and Mitigation—The top-down model formalizes the need to share information about an impending threat, whether that threat is manmade, such as a potential terrorist attack, or about a natural disaster that may be in the making. From the terrorist attack and law enforcement perspective, there are Fusion Centers created in just about each state; several states have more than one. Fusion Centers are "focal points within the state and local environment for the receipt, analysis, gathering, and sharing of threat-related information between the federal government and state, local, tribal, territorial (SLTT) and private sector partners." They are in states and major urban areas throughout the country and situated to empower law enforcement, public safety, fire service, emergency response, public health, CI/KR protection, and private-sector security personnel, thus enabling local officials to better protect their communities. Fusion Centers provide interdisciplinary expertise and situational awareness to inform decision making at all levels of government. A key component of Fusion Centers is the ability to develop procedures that permit information to flow from private-sector sources. In developing these private-sector information sources and subsequent data collection and analysis, most Fusion Centers embark upon a top-down process, resulting in structuring private-sector behavior as part of the overall process.[7]

Response—The top-down model is driven by NIMS and the NRF that structure, from the top down, behavior that should take place during a response to a catastrophic or extreme incident. Both documents suggest procedures and processes that should be followed in response to a catastrophic incident as well as suggested roles for responders at different levels. Both NIMS and the NRF suggest the role that should be played during a response by the private sector. These documents and the behaviors they suggest are examples of top-down structuration. (See also PDD-8 2011.)

Recovery—There is emerging "structural" guidance in this area in the NRF, which is limited. The NRF emphasizes that after the immediate response imperatives are addressed, the focus should shift to assisting individuals, households, CI, and businesses in meeting basic needs and returning to self-sufficiency. This phase requires significant contributions from all sectors of society.

Bottom-Up Models

Initiatives based upon the community of interest and community of practice model have emerged in the HS mission space since 2007. This initiative is becoming more and more widespread in the United States and includes groups of private-sector businesses with a common interest in business survivability in the face of a catastrophic or extreme event. In the top-down model the structuring of private-sector behavior was rooted in protecting infrastructure and creating more resilient infrastructure. This direction was set not by individual organizations but by government at the highest level. The bottom-up model movement is based upon supply- and value-chain survivability through information-sharing models that are driven by the needs of like-minded organizations.

According to the Techguide, the COI "is an organizational construct for working collaboratively to establish clusters of data interoperability that cross formal boundaries. COIs are important because they make explicit and widely visible (publish names, advertisements of what they doing, who's involved etc.) vital information sharing task groups that would not otherwise be even recognized as organizations" (2004). According to DOD Directive 8320.2, the COI is "a collaborative group of users that must exchange information in pursuit of its shared goals, interests, missions, or business processes and therefore must have shared vocabulary for the information exchanges" (2004). The key to both COI descriptions is that "shared goals" and "shared visions" hold the collective together.

The community of practice model takes this one step further. According to Wegner, "Communities of practice are formed by people who engage in a process of collective learning in a shared domain of human endeavor: a tribe learning to survive, a band of artists seeking new forms of expression, a group of engineers working on similar problems, a clique of pupils defining their identity in the school, a network of surgeons exploring novel techniques, a gathering of first-time managers helping each other cope" (2006).

The COP model moves from a common interest as being the coordinating principle to shared and collective learning being the predominant coordinating principle. The bottom-up model aligns itself with both COI and COP. In the HS space we find organizations that are self-organizing around a common interest and a common set of practices. Several entities have been formed under this model, such as the following business organizations:

- The Business Emergency Operations Center Alliance
- Southeast Emergency Response Network
- Safeguard Iowa
- Colorado Emergency Preparedness Partnership
- State BEOCs (Louisiana, Arkansas, Missouri, New Jersey, Kentucky)

Likewise, the following NGOs, among others, have formed:

- National Institute for Urban Search and Rescue
- Worldcares Center
- Halo Corporation
- Red Cross
- Catholic Charities
- Salvation Army

Summary

In this section the top-down and bottom-up models representing the involvement of the private sector within HS were described. It is important to note the different model orientations. The top-down model aligns itself with a vision and resulting set of goals developed at the top of the governance structure, in this case the Office of the President of the United States. This model was then contrasted with organizations as communities of practice and communities of interest. A vision and set of goals were established from a series of bottom-up collaborations that were largely informal. The research in this area is continuing and designed to understand the effectiveness and potential linkages of the two models within HS and EM.

Private-Sector and Public-Sector Partnerships

This part focuses on specific partnership initiatives. FEMA through its Private Sector Office has reached out to both top-down and bottom-up models in an attempt to capture some specific initiatives, while the DHS has stressed the importance and need for partnership frameworks (see FEMA 2011a). The major difference between the FEMA and DHS approaches is that FEMA realizes that a one-size-fits-all framework may not be the best way to understand partnerships and then build outreach to embrace the different partnership structures and frameworks. The DHS approach uses *framework* in the singular, suggesting that possibly a general framework may be the best way forward in shaping the private sector within HS.

According to the DHS CI Sector Partnerships, the protection of the nation's CI/KR requires an effective partnership framework that fosters integrated, collaborative engagement and interaction among both public- and private-sector partnerships.[8] These partnerships provide a framework to do the following:

1. exchange ideas, approaches, and best practices
2. facilitate security planning and resource allocation
3. establish effective coordinating structures among partners
4. enhance coordination with the international community
5. build public awareness

Though this partnership declaration focuses upon CI/KR, it is equally as important to HS issues that include response, recovery, and the growing concerns surrounding resilience. In addition, we will see that FEMA has recognized many PPPs that it describes as a "team approach to emergency management" (FEMA 2010).

FEMA Recognized Partnerships

According to FEMA, "States and big cities are actively entering into public-private partnerships to improve their capabilities in emergency management. In addition to participating in partnerships directly, public and private sector organizations can help bolster the nation's preparedness in other ways" (2011b). Since 2007 FEMA through its Private Sector Office has reached out to various PPPs in an attempt to develop an understanding about what they are and what their focus is. This is being done at the national level as well at the level of each FEMA region. Many of the PPPs align themselves with the top-down model, and many are a result of bottom-up initiatives. The following is a list of several of the partnerships:[9]

National
- Business Emergency Operations Alliance
- Citizen Corps
- Infragard
- Ready Campaign

Regional
- All Hazards Consortium
- DFW First
- KCP&L
- NorthEast Disaster Recovery Information X-Change
- Pacific NorthWest Economic Region
- South Central PA Region Task Force
- SouthEast Emergency Response Network
- Southeast Wisconsin Homeland Partnership
- Southern West Virginia Preparedness Partnership

State
- Alaska
- Arizona
- California
- California Direct Relief USA
- Colorado
- Illinois
- Iowa
- Louisiana
- Missouri
- New Jersey
- Utah
- Washington

Tribal Nation
- Indian Health Program—Emergency Preparedness
- Programa de Salud Indígena: Preparación para Emergencias

Big-City
- Arlington, Virginia
- Chicago, Illinois
- ChicagoFirst, Illinois
- Dallas, Texas
- New York, New York
- Providence, Rhode Island
- San Diego, California

County
- Fairfax County, Virginia
- Harris County, Texas
- Miami-Dade, Florida
- Santa Rosa County, Florida
- Victoria County, Texas
- Washoe County, Nevada

Event Specific
- Building Science Private Sector
- Consumer Electronic Association's "Public Alert Technology Alliance"
- Florida Emergency Management—Florida Outdoor Advertising Association Billboard Partnership
- Science Applications International Corporation

The Expanding Role of Business Emergency Operations Centers

The Business Emergency Operations Center concept grew in popularity during the summer and fall of 2007. A key source to its development was a requirement surfacing from certain private-sector organizations that needed to be able to anticipate organizational behavior (theirs and others') and provide for employee safety and security in a location affected by an incident of national significance. The mandate from these organizations was that during the first ninety-six hours, as an incident rises in severity, communication that can lead to better anticipation and subsequently better decision making about business continuity and employee safety and security was needed. The thinking was that the development of a business-oriented communication nexus that would permit better business anticipation and decision making would be required. A model of what a BEOC would consist of in terms of capabilities was developed in New Jersey and tested during four national-level exercises. Training opportunities are also available through FEMA.[10]

In addition to testing and experimenting with capabilities, the BEOC concept grew in terms of becoming a basis for private-sector and public-sector partnerships. The original vision of a BEOC becoming a communication nexus for private-sector anticipatory processes was coupled with the need by the public sector for response support. Response support suggests reaching out to the private sector for assistance during a response to a catastrophic event that requires both mutual assistance and resource support. A response shouldered strictly by the public sector is perceived as not being as effective as a joint response, where the private sector partners with the public sector in a mission space where both sectors have much as stake.

Currently, BEOCs are being developed in several states in order to interface with state offices of emergency management. Some examples are as follows:

BEOC Alliance—This is a consortium of BEOCs, associations, nongovernmental organizations, the military (NORAD and NORTHCOM), and the public sector (FEMA).

NJ Business Force BEOC—This is a partnership between business organizations headquartered in New Jersey and New York, academia (New Jersey Institute of Technology, Monmouth University, New Jersey City University), ARDEC (Picatinny Arsenal), and the New Jersey Office of Emergency Management.[11]

State of Arkansas BEOC—This is a partnership between Northwest Arkansas Community College, many private-sector organizations in Arkansas, and the State of Arkansas.

State of Louisiana BEOC—The Louisiana Business Emergency Operations Center is a joint partnership between Louisiana Economic Development, the Governor's Office of Homeland Security and Emergency Preparedness, the National Incident Management Systems and Advanced Technologies Institute at the University of Louisiana at Lafayette, and the Stephenson Disaster Management Institute at Louisiana State University. This indicates a partnership among the public sector, private sector, and academia within Louisiana.

What is emerging is that each BEOC engages communication-wise with the public sector and the private sector. The public-sector communication is one-to-one, suggesting a direct path between a BEOC and the public-sector partner. However, each BEOC communicates with multiple private-sector organizations. At this stage the Louisiana BEOC reaches out to approximately 40 private-sector organizations. The New Jersey and Arkansas BEOCs reach back and communicate with a similar amount of private-sector organizations, approximately 35 to 45 organizations each. The BEOC Alliance reaches 85 organizations. From these four BEOCs, between 195 and 215 business organizations will be communicated with over various communication media to include but not be limited to e-mail, Listservs, portals (secure or unsecure), peer-to-peer virtual private network technologies, and potentially other forms of social media.

In Arlington County, Virginia, for example, the Public/Private Partnership program consists of nonprofits, businesses, and public organizations working together as stakeholders in responding to any emergency. They have established three task forces in which volunteers work together to enhance the overall level of preparedness, response, and recovery: exercise and training, information and resource sharing, and emergency planning. Arlington County's goals are to:

- Strengthen private-sector involvement and communication;
- Improve private-sector knowledge of government plans and procedures, and visa-versa;
- Eliminate barriers to effective and efficient partnerships, response and recovery;
- Link businesses together with government resources to create a resource network for emergency events to enable a channeling of resources; and
- Encourage business emergency/disaster, mitigation, and resumption. (Big City Partnership—Arlington County, VA 2011)

In addition to a full-time staff, Arlington has 120 emergency management professionals from the private sector (profit and nonprofit) and public-sector organizations that have shown a desire to be informed about partnership activities. There are also 20 members of their partnership task force along with various subject-matter experts who are brought in as needed to address any given situation.

Summary

This section addressed specific partnerships and pointed out a difference in thinking and engaging partnerships through a series of different frameworks (FEMA) or through a single framework (DHS). The section concluded by describing the current BEOC phenomena and its potential value in reaching business through a distributed nodal network communication model.

Major Private-Sector Requirements

During a series of private-sector conferences held by the BEOC Alliance such as the Private Sector Summit (September 2009) and the Private Sector Symposium (May 2010), attendees identified a series of private-sector requirements. In addition, they collected data from the private sector as part of HS exercises, and the results of both are listed below. It is important to note that the partnership that arose between the private and public sectors benefits both sectors in protecting the critical infrastructure. However, the private-sector side can receive greater benefits from partnering with the public sector in HS.

Hank Straub, a retired US Air Force colonel, the executive director of NJ Business Force, and the vice president of the BEOC Alliance, developed the following list of data points regarding private-sector information and critical infrastructure protection:

1. Changes in the Homeland Security Alert System or information available through the new National Terrorism Advisory System (NTAS)
2. Increases/decreases in MARSEC (Maritime Security) levels
3. Changes in Continuity of Government Conditions (COGCON)
4. Initial activation and subsequent changes in the operational status/ staffing of state emergency operation/fusion centers
5. Area evacuation notifications and warnings
   - Buildings
   - Residential areas
6. Prioritization of the restoration of critical utilities/lifeline sectors like water, natural gas, and electricity during system outages

7. Permit and regulatory waiver application procedures and issuance of same (primarily affects transportation and transportation infrastructure)
8. Shipments and allocation of gasoline and diesel fuel during emergencies and national/regional shortages
9. Debris clearance prioritization and status
10. Credentialing
11. Transportation system closures/shutdowns (e.g., stoppage of all rail shipments, closure of ports to Liquid Natural Gas [LNG] shipments, airports, etc.)
    - Road closures/available open routes of travel
    - Mass transit disruptions
12. Roadway conditions during weather events
13. Weather conditions during HAZMAT incidents
14. Border closings and blockades imposed by executive decree
15. Strategic National Stockpile (SNS) distribution and activation of Points of Distribution (PODS)
16. Mandatory quarantines during health emergencies or infectious disease outbreaks among animals (Foot and Mouth Disease)
17. Employee absentee tracking and reporting
18. Building lockdowns
19. Security environment assessment/access to security alerts
20. Operating radio frequencies
21. Available Internet connections and functionality
22. Restrictions on the use of the commodity Internet during emergencies
23. Location/availability of recharging stations for batteries, cell phones, and laptop computers
24. Recommended inoculations for entry into disaster areas
25. Lodging and staging sites for incoming teams
26. Rules of Engagement (ROE) for deployed military during states of emergency or martial law
27. Specific provisions affecting the Private Sector within Emergency Declarations or States of Emergencies
28. Expectations held toward the Private Sector including role as resource provider
29. Suspicious activity reporting procedures and trends

Many items on this list suggest the need by the private sector for timely and accurate data to support business decision making and continuity of operations decisions. Such items as 1–4 suggest that these types of alerts have the potential to trigger certain behaviors in the organization. A review of these items should help the reader to understand the approach taken by the private sector as part of its emerging role within HS.

Summary

This section listed the overall requirements and data needs of the private sector. Understanding them will go a long way toward understanding the private sector and its role in effectively contributing to the DHS mission.

Conclusion

Since the tragic events of 9/11, we have seen the integration of the private sector within the DHS, FEMA, NORTHCOM, and public-sector jurisdictions at the state level and local (county, municipality) levels. These formalized efforts have been addressed within the context of a "top-down" model. We have also witnessed private-sector partnerships surfacing from the "bottom up" based upon the COI and COP models described in this chapter. The thrust moving forward is to integrate both models within the four major dimensions of emergency management. There is indeed strength in preparedness, prevention and mitigation, response, and recovery when linking the private sector and public sector together within the HS and HD mission space.

NOTES

1. See also *DHS/DOJ Fusion Process Technical Assistance Programs and Services*, May 2010, http://www.fema.gov/pdf/about/divisions/npd/cpg_502_eoc-fusion_final_7_20 _2010.pdf.

2. HSPDs and PDDs are explained in more detail in Chapter 2.

3. FEMA, NIMS Resource Center, accessed July 1, 2011, http://www.fema.gov /emergency/nims/.

4. DHS, *National Infrastructure Protection Plan*, accessed July 1, 2011, http://www .dhs.gov/xlibrary/assets/NIPP_Plan.pdf.

5. FEMA, *National Response Framework*, accessed July 1, 2011, http://www.fema.gov /pdf/emergency/nrf/nrf-core.pdf.

6. See also ibid.

7. DHS, "State and Major Urban Area Fusion Centers," accessed July 1, 2011, http:// www.dhs.gov/files/programs/gc_1156877184684.shtm.

8. DHS, "Critical Infrastructure Sector Partnerships," accessed July 1, 2011, http:// www.dhs.gov/files/partnerships/editorial_0206.shtm.

9. FEMA, on its Public Private Sector Partnership Models page, contains links to files that further explain what the PPP is and what its goals and objectives are (FEMA 2011b).

10. FEMA, "Training Opportunities," accessed July 1, 2011, http://www.fema.gov/privatesector/training.shtm.

11. See also http://www.njbf-beoc.com/, accessed July 1, 2011.

REFERENCES

Big City Partnership—Arlington County, VA. 2011. http://www.fema.gov/pdf/privatesector/safer_arlington_partnership.pdf.

Chumer, M., and S. Egan. 2011. "The Business Emergency Operations Center (BEOC): A Model for Inter-Agency and Inter-Sector Communication and Collaboration." Paper presented at the Sixteenth Meeting of the ICCRTS, Quebec, Canada.

Chumer, M., and M. Turoff. 2006. "Command and Control (C²): Adapting the Distributed Military Model for Emergency Response and Emergency Management." Paper presented at ISCRAM, Newark, NJ.

DHS OIP. 2011. http://www.dhs.gov/xabout/structure/gc_1185203138955.shtm.

DHS PSO. 2011. http://www.dhs.gov/xabout/structure/gc_1166220191042.shtm.

DOD Directive 8320.2. 2004. "Data Sharing in a Net-Centric Department of Defense" and 8320.02-G (Implementation Guide). http://www.dtic.mil/whs/directives/corres/pdf/832002p.pdf.

FEMA. 2010. "Public Private Partnerships: A Team Approach to Emergency Management." http://www.fema.gov/privatesector/ppp.shtm.

———. 2011a. "About FEMA Private Sector Division." http://www.fema.gov/privatesector/about.shtm.

———. 2011b. "Public Private Partnership Models." http://www.fema.gov/privatesector/ppp_models.shtm.

PDD-8. 2011. National Preparedness. http://www.dhs.gov/xabout/laws/gc_1215444247124.shtm.

PS-Prep. 2009. http://www.fema.gov/news/newsrelease.fema?id=49867.

Sector Partnership Model. 2009. http://training.fema.gov/EMIWeb/IS/IS860a.asp.

Techguide. 2004. http://metadata.dod.mil/mdr/ns/ces/techguide/community_of_interest_coi.html.

Wegner, E. 2006. http://www.ewenger.com/theory/.

PART II

Homeland Security Resources

This part is a discussion of what critical resources are necessary to defend America on a battlefield. Those resources will always start with the US military services, forces that are without equal. But when the conversation moves to key domestic resources, the place to start is not as obvious. As mentioned in the earlier chapters, there is a shared responsibility between the government and private industry. There are also key roles that are assumed by law enforcement and first-responder personnel, the military, and the National Guard, as well as other agencies.

Chapter 4: Critical Infrastructure Protection

The first step in protecting America's critical infrastructure is to identify what key resources compose it. The authors discuss the vast and diverse nature of our infrastructure and its growing significance to US national security strategic planning. The need to pursue the field of critical infrastructure and its protection (CIP) is based on Homeland Security Presidential Directive 7 and is explained in the National Infrastructure Protection Plan. The key is to understand the many interconnected systems and subsystems within our infrastructure. Consider, for example, how the following sectors merge: energy, finance, communications, technology, food, water, transportation, and the government. As the threat environment continues to change, the target attractiveness of the US infrastructure changes with it. As a result, there are now eighteen sectors labeled as "critical." The authors will identify physical-property and environmentally based aspects, people-based aspects, and cyber-based aspects of CIP and then connect each of them to US national security strategy planning and homeland security objectives and goals.

Chapter 5: Homeland Security Intelligence

As a result of the 9/11 attacks, the president established the National Commission on Terrorist Attacks upon the United States. The 9/11 Commission's findings reflected a need to improve intelligence collection, analysis, and communication. This chapter focuses on intelligence intended to improve the US homeland security enterprise. Homeland security intelligence is the key to improving our counterterrorism efforts, where counterterrorism in this case refers primarily to efforts to detect terrorist plans for attacks against the US homeland. Good intelligence about terrorist capabilities and intentions can increase the effectiveness of policies to prepare for, prevent, protect against, defend against, and respond to terrorist attacks. Good intelligence cannot guarantee that officials will make wise choices, but the absence of good intelligence about terrorist designs on the homeland is certain to degrade the quality of resulting policies and actions.

Chapter 6: Defense Support of Civil Authorities

This chapter focuses on the interaction of the military with civil authorities in preparing for and responding to threats to homeland security. The author addresses the traditional ethos behind the military's deliberate support status in these functions and the distinction between the federal and state components of that support. The author draws on his experience to examine how the military's support plays out directly in disaster preparation and response, whether those disasters are natural or man-made. He will also address specific situations to support law enforcement functions and in response to civil disturbances. Until the request comes from civilian authorities, the military units will remain a force in readiness. When the requests come, the first units to respond will be those of the National Guard, most familiar with the state and local agencies they will be supporting and most familiar with the requirements at hand. As additional requirements arise due to the scope or duration of the crisis, the active-component military is prepared to provide additional support, bringing added capacity to the appreciable capabilities already introduced. The author notes that from beginning to end, the military, in support of our civilian authorities, will neither seek nor assume "command." Rather, it will attempt to perform as the forefathers intended: always as the servant of the people, never as their overseers.

Chapter 7: Homeland Security Technology

As the threats to homeland security change, technologies must evolve to meet those challenges. There is an ever-increasing demand for new security technologies. From smuggling interdiction and border control to planning for and dealing with emergency situations, governments and industries are looking for security solutions. As this author explains, security technology can act as a force multiplier and a productivity tool to make security manpower more efficient and effective. But even the most advanced technology cannot eliminate the human element. The author notes that one of the major challenges to a security system is that it must be transparent to law-abiding citizens and not restrict their freedom of movement. These systems must block access to sensitive areas while maintaining privacy. This chapter increases the understanding of the fundamental and basic operating principles of current security systems used by homeland security agencies, by professionals, and within the various related industries. Some of the systems discussed in this chapter include X-rays, T-rays, metal detectors, infrared sensors, biometrics (fingerprints, iris recognition, and palm-vein authentication), smart cards, radio-frequency identification (RFID), electroshock weapons, the Active Denial System (ADS), the Long Range Acoustic Device (LRAD), and the Unmanned Aerial System (UAS).

Chapter 8: Environmental Security and Public Health

It is important to understand the many interconnected components of the environment, global environmental change, and US National Security considerations. The authors demonstrate how environmental security (ES) is a key component of US national and homeland security strategy planning that goes well beyond a traditional understanding of what most individuals believe constitutes homeland security. Through a presentation of a brief history of ES, they discuss how various ES researchers have examined relationships between the impacts of environmental phenomena and resulting security issues. ES manifests itself in the developing nations as a contributor to geopolitical instability, while in the developed nations ES has important linkages to critical infrastructure issues. Given the interdependencies of energy and food security, economic impacts from natural disasters, the possible security implications from global climate change, and the potential for radicalization in populations whose environmental living conditions are becoming increasingly desperate, it is very important to articulate a post-9/11 construct of ES in a way that allows it to be integrated into both national and homeland security strategy planning.

CHAPTER 4

Critical Infrastructure Protection

STEVEN D. HART and JAMES D. RAMSAY

Consider the morning routine of a typical household: turn on the lights, shower, eat breakfast, listen to the radio or television, check e-mail, recycle, take out the trash, and go off to work. Now consider the systems, from consumption back to source, that make this routine possible. Electricity arrives at the home after traveling through distribution lines, transformers, transmission lines, and generation plants. Generation methods include coal, natural gas, nuclear, hydro, wind, and solar. Before coming out of a tap, clean drinking water is extracted from ground or surface water sources, treated, pressurized, and distributed through a network of pipes that is often older than the consumers of the water. Many elements of the water system, including treatment and distribution, also rely on electricity. Before being cooked, the breakfast foods were in the grocery store, and before that in processing plants, distribution trucks, and farms. Without petroleum products, which are refined into fuel using electricity, food does not move and breakfast does not happen. Radio and television signals rely on electricity and satellites. Recycled materials are collected because there is a market for their resale, and it is good for the environment. Trash moves in petroleum-powered trucks. This simple scenario begins to describe the complex systems that make the typical morning routine possible.

These complex systems are collectively referred to as infrastructure. The *National Infrastructure Protection Plan* defines infrastructure as "the framework of interdependent networks and systems comprising identifiable industries, institutions (including people and procedures), and distribution capabilities that provide a reliable flow of products and services essential to the defense and economic security of the United States, the smooth functioning of government at all levels, and society as a whole," which is a fine textbook definition, but it is very impersonal.[1] "Infrastructure" puts food on our tables, keeps premature babies alive, keeps us healthy by transporting sewage away from homes and removing contaminants from drinking water, lets us call our family for less than five cents a minute, and allows intercontinental travel in a matter of hours. In short, our infrastructure defines our civilization.

Now consider what happens when elements of the infrastructure fail. When the sanitation workers strike, trash piles up on the curb. When the water treatment plant fails or a water main breaks, officials issue orders to boil drinking water. When the electrical grid fails, lights fail and traffic jams, Internet- and cable-based phones do not work, elevators stop working, homes go dark, and twelve hours later, frozen food starts to spoil. The failure of a critical infrastructure element usually serves to demonstrate society's typical interrelationships among our infrastructure; we do not notice it until it is gone, and then we clamor for its immediate restoration. The desire to ensure the continuous functioning of our infrastructure has been both a public and a private goal that has become increasingly prominent in light of historical and current events.

A Brief History of Infrastructure Protection

Over the past fifty years, as societies became more interconnected and interdependent, our government recognized the importance of protecting the parts of our infrastructure that are essential to the functioning of the nation. In 1963 President Kennedy established the National Communications System to ensure the federal government's ability to communicate in emergency situations, including nuclear attack. In 1979 the Federal Emergency Management Agency was established with responsibilities that included civil defense and hurricane- and earthquake-risk reduction. In the 1980s our current understanding of critical infrastructure began to evolve when President Ronald Reagan, in an executive order, charged the head of each federal department and agency with the responsibility of protecting essential resources and facilities within their organizations.[2]

The first World Trade Center bombing (1993) and the bombing of the Murrah Federal Building in Oklahoma City (1995) in the continental United

States together with the sarin gas attack in a Tokyo subway (1995); the bombings of the Nairobi, Kenya, and Dar es Salaam, Tanzania, embassies (1998); and the small-boat attack on the USS *Cole* (2000) all served to raise the awareness of acts of terror within the American people and government. Concurrent with these events, policy decisions were made by the federal government that began a coordinated effort to protect critical infrastructures. In 1996 President Bill Clinton established the Presidential Commission on Critical Infrastructure Protection. The work of the commission resulted in the definition of eight critical infrastructure sectors in Presidential Decision Directive 63 in 1998.[3]

The events of September 11, 2001, brought about a rapid expansion of critical infrastructure protection efforts. The *National Strategy for Homeland Security* was published in 2002 and was followed by the National Strategy for the Physical Protection of Critical Infrastructures and the Key Assets and Homeland Security Presidential Directive 7, which replaced PDD 63, in 2003. These documents expanded critical infrastructure to thirteen sectors, added five key assets, and led to the publication of the first NIPP in 2006.

In the aftermath of September 11, 2001, and the resulting wars, it is understandable that the nation was focused on protecting infrastructure from terrorist acts. However, the 2005 hurricane season, with widespread destruction, produced Hurricanes Dennis, Katrina, Rita, Stan, and Wilma, demonstrating that focusing on protection was not sufficient to ensure acceptable performance in the many aspects of the all-hazards environment. These events coupled with the fact that a viable economic case for the protection of most infrastructures from a terrorist act cannot be made have led to an expansion of focus from infrastructure protection to infrastructure resilience. The concept of a "resilient infrastructure" allows the aspects of the all-hazards environment—terrorism, earth effects and natural disasters, deterioration, and accidents—to be considered in light of how we want our infrastructure to perform under adverse conditions. This can be seen in that infrastructure resilience has become a central theme in both the 2009 NIPP and the 2010 National Security Strategy (NSS).[4]

Purpose and Use of This Chapter

Critical infrastructure protection and resilience (CIP/R) is an extremely complex, multidisciplinary problem that cannot be explained in a single chapter. Thus, rather than try to explain how to protect infrastructure or design a

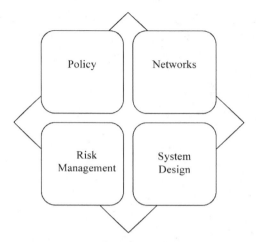

FIGURE 4.1 A framework for critical
infrastructure protection and resilience

resilient-infrastructure network, this chapter will provide a framework for understanding infrastructure protection and resilience, solving problems in this field, and assimilating new information.

A Conceptual Framework for Critical Infrastructure Protection and Resilience

The field of critical infrastructure protection and resilience seeks to protect those elements of the infrastructure "systems and assets, whether physical or virtual, so vital that the incapacity or destruction of such may have a debilitating impact on the security, economy, public health or safety, environment, or any combination of these matters, across any Federal, State, regional, territorial, or local jurisdiction."[5] Protection can include a wide variety of pre-, mid-, and postevent activities that deter threats, mitigate vulnerabilities, and minimize consequences. Resilience may be defined as "a capacity to absorb or mitigate the impact of hazard events while maintaining and restoring essential services."[6] It expands the concept of protection to encompass those activities necessary to restore the disrupted infrastructure. Whether the goal is protection or resilience, the topic is extremely broad and involves many perspectives and facets. Therefore, the framework in Figure 4.1 is useful for organizing and relating CIP/R information.

To borrow a mathematical term, each concept is necessary, but not sufficient, for an overall understanding of CIP/R. Together they allow for a holistic approach to this complex topic.

Policy

Critical infrastructure protection and resilience takes place in an environment of policy, strategy, plans, and law at the national, state, and local levels. Simply put, a law is the authority to do something, and the law that leads to all our efforts in CIP/R is the Homeland Security Act of 2002. This law established and organized the Department of Homeland Security, including its subordinate directorates. It also established a framework for the sharing, protection, and dissemination of critical infrastructure information.[7] Most of the agencies and departments working on CIP/R issues trace their origin to this law.

Homeland Security Presidential Directives are the documents that establish national policy. Of these, HSPD-7, Critical Infrastructure Identification, Prioritization, and Protection, is essential to understanding CIP/R. HSPD-7 "establishes a national policy for Federal departments and agencies to identify and prioritize United States critical infrastructure and key resources and to protect them from terrorist attacks." This document establishes policy; assigns roles and responsibilities to the DHS, sector-specific federal agencies, and other departments, agencies, and offices; and concludes with implementation guidance. Also related to overall CIP/R efforts are HSPD-8, National Preparedness, which requires establishing a national domestic all-hazards preparedness goal and improves federal, state, local, and tribal preparedness coordination, and HSPD-5, Management of Domestic Incidents, which establishes the National Incident Management System.[8]

From policy flows strategy, which may be defined as the direction and coordination of all national resources to achieve a national policy. Homeland security strategy is currently integrated with the National Security Strategy, most recently published in May 2010, where "Promote the Resiliency of our Physical and Social Infrastructure" is one of the seven major strategic themes.[9] This strategic theme is implemented through the National Infrastructure Protection Plan, most recently published in 2009.

Noting the most recent publication dates of these documents highlights a critical issue that complicates trying to understand their relationships. These documents are politically driven and change as the political climate and political leadership change. For instance, the current HSPDs were promulgated by the Bush administration, yet continue in force under the Obama administration until revised or rescinded. The NIPP should logically flow from the National Security Strategy, yet the current NIPP predates the current National Security Strategy. The process of establishing policies, strategies, and plans is often nonlinear, and a reader should always bear in mind publication dates when trying to resolve discrepancies.

The NIPP implements the infrastructure themes of the National Security Strategy by establishing a unifying framework for our national infrastructure protection efforts. In the public sector, the NIPP defines the roles and responsibilities of federal agencies and specific elements of the DHS. Because 85 percent of the infrastructure of the United States is privately owned, the NIPP establishes partnership frameworks to foster public-private cooperation to achieve common goals while addressing the need for maintaining the confidentiality of proprietary business information and federally classified information. Central to the NIPP is a six-step "Risk Management Framework" that provides a mechanism for prioritizing infrastructure protection efforts in a resources-constrained social and political environment. The six steps of the framework are as follows:

1. set goals and objectives
2. identify assets, systems, and networks
3. assess risks
4. prioritize
5. implement programs
6. measure effectiveness

These steps are applied across the physical, cyber, and human elements of infrastructures and are assessed through a continuous feedback loop. Another central theme of the NIPP is the definition of the thirteen critical infrastructures and five key resources (CI/KR) that make up the eighteen CI/KR sectors. These are shown in Table 4.1.[10]

Complementing the NIPP are the Sector-Specific Plans (SSPs), the National Response Framework, and NIMS. The Sector-Specific Plans are prepared though the cooperative efforts of CI/KR owners and operators and government officials and apply the NIPP risk-management framework to the specific characteristics of each sector. The National Response Framework establishes the principles that guide the national response to catastrophic events in the all-hazards environment. NIMS establishes a nationally unified approach to incident command, management, preparedness, and mutual aid.

TABLE 4.1 Critical Infrastructure/Key Resource Sectors

Critical Infrastructures	Key Resources
CIs are networked systems where failure of one element will typically impact other elements of that infrastructure sector and will, more than likely, impact other sectors.	*KRs tend to be discrete elements and failure of an element will probably not cause a cascading failure.*
Agriculture and Food	National Monuments and Icons
Defense Industrial Base	Nuclear Reactors, Materials, and Waste
Energy	Dams
Health Care and Public Health	Commercial Facilities
Banking and Finance	Government Facilities
Water	
Chemical	
Critical Manufacturing	
Emergency Services	
Information Technology	
Communications	
Postal and Shipping	
Transportation	

The National Security Strategy, NIPP, SSP, NRF, and NIMS documents establish the policy environment that surrounds all efforts for critical infrastructure protection and resilience (CIP/R). Homeland security CIP/R professionals must understand this environment before investigating the other three elements of the model.

Networks

Most CIs are actually working networks that are intradependent on critical assets within the network and interdependent on elements of other infrastructures. These interconnected infrastructures behave as networks according to certain principles, and these principles can reveal how the network will behave when degraded by random events or deliberate attack.

The components of a physical, human, or cyber infrastructure can be mathematically modeled as either nodes or links. A **node** is a virtual representation of a discrete element of interest within an infrastructure, whereas a **link** is a virtual representation of a connection between two discrete infrastructure elements. The degree of a node is the number of links that connect it to other nodes. For example, nodes may represent bridges, train stations, water-treatment plants, power-generation plants, water towers, or key individuals in an organization, whereas links may represent roads, rail lines, water mains, electrical transmission lines, or lines of organizational communication. Nodes of high degree will have large numbers of these connections, whereas nodes of low degree will have only a few connections. A network is a group of nodes connected by links that can be used to model the behavior of an actual network to determine vulnerabilities and predict behavior. Infrastructure networks can typically be classified as either random, small-world, or scale-free networks based on a nodal-degree histogram. Each type of network is described briefly below and shown graphically in Figure 4.2.

Random networks have nodes and a random distribution of links so that each node has an approximately equal number of links. The interstate highway system of the United States is an example of a random network. The nodal-degree histogram for a random network displays a Poisson distribution. A strength of a random network is that it tends to be resistant to both random and targeted node removal. Removing a node does not fragment the network; it is still possible to travel from node to node using an alternate path. A weakness is that it is very broad, and one must pass through many nodes and links to span the entire network.[11]

Many social and professional associations may be classified as small-world networks. A small-world network has many nodes of low degree and a few nodes of high degree. These highly connected nodes are called **hubs** and have great influence on the behavior of the network. Inspecting the nodal-degree histogram of a small-world network will clearly indicate the hubs. The loss of a hub or hubs in a small-world network tends to fracture the network into disconnected parts, whereas the loss of a node that is not a hub tends to cause only a localized effect. Another characteristic of small-world networks is that any item introduced into one node quickly communicates with many other nodes. This can be beneficial in terms of information distribution or situational awareness or detrimental in terms of a virus.[12]

The concept of scale-free networks emerged from the research of Albert László Barabási, Eric Bonabeau, Hawoong Jeong, and Réka Albert in deriving a network model of the Internet. Their research found that this network did not follow the expected patterns of a random network. Rather, they found that a few nodes were highly connected and that many nodes had only limited connections. The nodal-degree histogram of a scale-free network follows a power law, which accounts for a large number of minimally connected nodes and a small number of highly connected nodes. As with small-world networks,

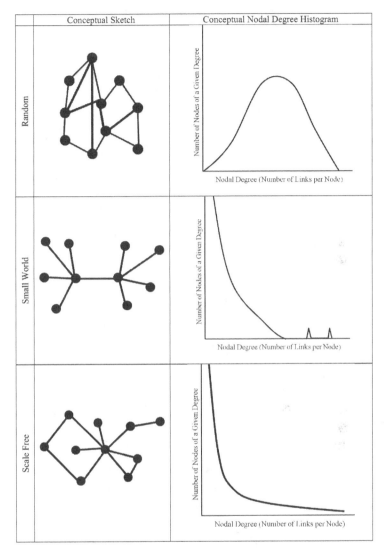

FIGURE 4.2 Network concepts

these highly connected nodes are called hubs; scale-free networks are also re-silient to random node removal, but are very vulnerable to the targeted re-moval of hubs.

The conceptual sketches and nodal-degree histograms shown in Figure 4.2 are easy to see in a plot for networks of forty or fifty nodes, but a challenge ar-rives when a network with 10^{12} nodes is considered. A network of this size cannot be drawn or analyzed by hand. Fortunately, with the use of a personal computer and statistical tools, networks of this size can be quickly analyzed. Given the proper data, a computer can produce the nodal-degree histogram that allows for the classification of the network and can provide additional statistical tools to describe and evaluate network behavior.

The purpose of abstracting physical, cyber, or human infrastructures as mathematical models is to properly characterize them and predict their behavior during adverse events. The principal question that a model can answer is, "Which nodes must be removed to impact or degrade the entire network?" The answer to this question tells us which of the nodes in the network must be protected to ensure overall network resiliency. It must be remembered that these mathematical abstractions are models; they are not the actual infrastructure. Decisions made in the modeling process can affect the behavior and predictions from the model. For example, when modeling a drinking-water distribution system, the water-treatment plant may be a node of low degree and therefore appear insignificant in the model when, in reality, it is crucial to the operation of the system.

Risk Management

Through a network analysis, the most important elements of an infrastructure system can be established. At this point, the next questions are obvious: "What can go wrong with those critical elements, and what should be done about it?" While the questions may be phrased and investigated separately, they are linked through the risk-management process. Understanding this process begins with these key definitions:

Risk: the potential for an unwanted outcome resulting from an incident, event, or occurrence, as determined by its likelihood and the associated consequence[13]

Risk Analysis: the process of determining relative levels of risk for a group of assets, generally a function of threat likelihood, asset value, and consequence[14]

Risk Management: the process of evaluating how changes in applied countermeasures affect risk levels and costs for the purpose of decision making[15]

"What can go wrong" is addressed through the all-hazards environment, "what can be done" is addressed through system design, and "what should be done" is addressed through the risk-management process, which considers the likelihood of adverse events and the costs and effectiveness of mitigation efforts.

The All-Hazards Environment

The NIPP defines the all-hazards environment as "a grouping classification encompassing all conditions, environmental or manmade, that have the potential to cause injury, illness, or death; damage to or loss of equipment, infrastructure services, or property; or alternatively causing functional degradation to social, economic, or environmental aspects."[16] One way to make this more manageable is to consider terrorism, earth effects and natural disasters, and accidents and deterioration separately.

Terrorism

The NIPP defines terrorism as a "premeditated threat or act of violence against noncombatant persons, property, and environmental or economic targets to induce fear, intimidate, coerce, or affect a government, the civilian population, or any segment thereof, in furtherance of political, social, ideological, or religious objectives."[17] The impact of terrorism has been a driving force in the need for improving critical infrastructure protection, but the threat of terrorism is not new. Many would agree with the statement that "the complexity of the modern world and the intricacy of international relations allow guerrilla warfare to be drawn out by new methods of deceit and subversion. In many causes the use of terrorism is regarded as a new way to wage war." However, most would be surprised that the source of this quotation is the Second Vatican Council in 1965.[18] Although large-scale terrorism may be a relatively new phenomenon for the United States, other areas of the world have been dealing with it for many years.

Terrorists have used a variety of weapons to attack civilian, political, military, and infrastructure targets. In 1995 the Aum Shinrikyo cult attacked the Tokyo subway using sarin gas, which resulted in 12 deaths and more than 500 hospitalized individuals. Also in 1995, Timothy McVeigh detonated a 7,000-pound bomb outside the Alfred P. Murrah Federal Building in Oklahoma City. The explosion resulted in the progressive collapse of the Federal Building, damage to 324 other buildings in a 50-block area, and 168 fatalities. In 1996 the arm of Hezbollah operating in Saudi Arabia detonated a large bomb concealed in a tanker truck outside of Khobar Towers, a US military housing area in Dhahran. The bomb was approximately 3,000 to 5,000 pounds and killed 19 service members and wounded 372 others. In 2000 terrorists used an explosive-laden small boat to attack and damage the USS *Cole* in the port of Aden, Yemen, resulting in 17 killed, 39 wounded, and extensive damage to the ship. In 2005 four British citizens became radicalized and detonated three bombs on subway trains and one on a double-decker bus, resulting in their deaths and the killing of 52 others and the wounding of more than 700 others.[19] In 2010 the Russian Federation reported two metro-station bombings in Moscow, by Islamic separatists, that resulted in the deaths of 38 individuals and dozens of injuries.[20] This list will continue to grow.

The terrorists have many advantages. They select target, method, and time and have to select only one each, while those engaged in protection must cover all possibilities. Although past events cannot predict future ones, understanding the historical impact, the development of terrorism, and the current trends, tactics, and targets of terrorism is essential background for executing the risk-management process subsequently discussed.

Earth Effects and Natural Disasters

Although terrorist events can be very devastating, they are extremely unlikely when compared to natural events, which are more common and can cause greater human and economic dislocation (the terrorist attacks of 9/11 being the one exception). Unlike terrorism, earth effects and natural disasters can be modeled probabilistically based on more than one hundred years of collected data. The principal hazards of interest are earthquakes, floods, snow, and wind. Depending on location, tsunamis, volcanoes, landslides, and hurricanes can also be hazards of interest. The risk of these hazards is measured probabilistically, explained below, and mitigated through the use of appropriate design codes, explained later.

Typically, facilities are designed to resist earthquakes based on ground acceleration. The design acceleration is the ground motion that has a 2 percent chance of being exceeded in a fifty-year period. This corresponds to an earthquake that would occur, on average, once in every twenty-five hundred years.[21] When considering atmospheric hazards such as wind, rain, snow, and the resulting floods, the design standard is the "one-hundred-year storm," a term that is often misunderstood. The "one-hundred-year storm" is not the largest storm that can occur once in a hundred-year period, but is properly defined as the event with a 1 percent probability of exceedance in a given year.[22] Because of the random nature of atmospheric events, the "one-hundred-year storm" could occur three times in ten years or once in only two hundred years at a given location. From a layman's perspective, perhaps a better way to explain it is to say that this is the largest event that could reasonably be expected to occur one or more times in any given one-hundred-year period. Standard design practices are based on these probabilities, but application of a risk-management process to a specific critical facility may indicate that a lower annual probability of exceedance that corresponds to a longer return interval may be more appropriate.

Accidents and Deterioration

Accidents and deterioration are evolving areas within the all-hazards environment and do not currently have the scholarly background and practical resources associated with terrorism and earth effects and natural disasters. It may be that events such as the I-35 bridge collapse, which was due to a design error so should be classed as an accident, and the Deepwater Horizons explosion with the resulting oil leak will lead to the establishment of centers to study these issues and design standards. Until then, it will be up to infrastructure owners and operators to consider the risks from accidents to specific facilities. Under some conditions, the best source of information on accidents may be in the insurance industry.

From the day a facility is placed into operation, it begins to degrade. Owners and operators must consider the effects of this degradation and develop an appropriate maintenance plan. Accidents can occur within a facility, and proper consideration of these potential accidents can lead to a redesign of processes and procedures so that a small accident does not cascade into a catastrophic failure. Another source of accidents can be infrastructure elements near a facility that have no connection to the facility except a common location. Consider, for example, the condition of a road that you travel every day to work; one week it is fine, then there is a depression, only to be followed the following week with a pothole. On a more significant level, consider a natural-gas main distribution line that runs under a city park. The park and the gas main are unrelated, but the deterioration of the gas main and a subsequent accidental explosion would have catastrophic results for the visitors to the park. A special case to be considered is "mutually hazardous sites," where two or more potential hazards are collocated and an accident in one site can cascade into an accident in the other. Under this condition, both infrastructure managers must consider the performance and risk profile of the adjacent infrastructure over which they have no control.

Levels of Protection

For many facilities, the level of protection or manner of performance in the design event is selected by the authors of the governing building code. For example, in a one-hundred-year storm with the accompanying wind, rain, or snow, a building should withstand the "loading" of these elements without structural damage. Facilities built outside of the one-hundred-year floodplain should not experience any flooding in a one-hundred-year storm. One drawback of the current code-based design philosophies is that they do not describe system performance beyond the design event. In loadings less than the design event, the system will perform acceptably. In larger events, the system will fail at some point, but the manner and mechanism of failure are not specified. Performance in the design earthquake is different. In the event of an earthquake, most buildings are designed to ensure the life safety of the occupants. This means that the building will not collapse during the earthquake, but may not be economically repairable after the earthquake. Better performance can be expected from critical facilities such as fire stations and hospitals.[23]

Although current municipal building codes do not address performance under terrorist-type loadings—explosions, weapons fire, or poison gas—information on these types of attack can be found in other sources. The Department of Defense has established a building-performance rating system in UFC 4-010-01, *Minimum Anti-Terrorism Standards for Buildings*. This manual establishes building-performance standards to prevent mass casualties in the event of a terrorist attack. Building owners could elect to apply these standards to their buildings if they felt there was a possibility of a terrorist attack of an unspecified nature. A challenge faced by facility owners, operators, and designers is what should be done when the facility is critical to the operation of an infrastructure, is a potential terrorist target, may be subjected to abnormal loadings, or happens to be across the street from the FBI Headquarters. This challenge of balancing a level of hazard with a level of protection is answered through the risk-management process.

Risk Management

Risk is the possibility that something bad will happen. When faced with risk, an individual or organization has three choices: reduce/mitigate it, shift it, or accept it. These three options are easiest understood with the analogy of an automobile. Every time we drive, there is a risk of an accident. We deal with (or manage) this in three ways. First, we attempt to reduce the risk by wear-

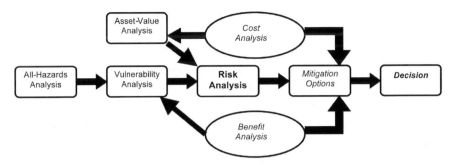

FIGURE 4.3 The risk-management process

ing seat belts and purchasing cars with airbags and other safety features. This "mitigation strategy" lowers the likelihood of a more severe incident occurring were the accident to actually happen. Second, we shift some of the financial risks to the insurance company by purchasing insurance so the insurance company pays the bills in the event of an accident. Shifting the economic impact also lowers the likelihood of increased severity were the accident to occur. Finally, we accept some of the risk; this acceptance is measured by the deductible amount on the insurance policy. Risk management is the process of deciding how much risk we mitigate, shift, and accept. The same applies to owners, operators, and managers of infrastructure, but the process can be much more complex.

The risk-management process shown in Figure 4.3 is the basic procedure used to mitigate risk to critical infrastructures. The first step is a "risk analysis" that establishes a relative value for risk. An "all-hazards analysis" is used to determine everything that can affect the infrastructure facility, from burglary to hurricanes to terrorist attacks. A "vulnerability analysis" determines the degree to which each adverse event could damage or degrade elements of a facility and the facility as a whole. An "asset-value analysis" determines the relative value of individual assets within a facility and the value of different facilities in an infrastructure. A "risk analysis" can then determine "risk" as a function of asset value, hazard, and vulnerability. Once a level of risk is established, mitigation options can be considered.

Mitigation includes all actions taken to reduce, shift, or accept risk. Risk-reduction strategies cost money, and the cost of the strategy must be weighed against the value of the asset. The benefit must also be assessed by measuring the reduction in vulnerability. Recall that vulnerability is the likelihood that a hazard will affect an asset. To be effective, the proposed action must reduce the risk, and it must do so at an acceptable cost. Once all risk-reduction strategies have emplaced, the residual risk that remains must be shifted through the purchase of insurance or accepted. Risk acceptance means that the infrastructure owner has either the cash on hand or a line of credit to restore the infrastructure in the event of a loss or is willing to live with the loss.

By way of example, consider an investment group that wants to build a hotel in an area where the first floor is likely to be inundated in a one-hundred-year flood. The risk that the structure will be damaged in the flood can be reduced by elevating the main structure using a sacrificial first floor. In the event of a flood, the first floor is lost, but it is designed to be lost for the protection of the rest of the building. The loss of income due to the flood can be insured, and the cost of restoring the sacrificial first floor can be accepted and the contingency included in the hotel's operating expenses. Taking this from example to concrete reality requires metrics to measure and quantify risk, risk-reduction strategies, costs, and benefits. Fortunately, a variety of these tools exist. But remember, protecting critical infrastructure based on national security considerations is more than just the dollar amount on an insurance policy.

The Risk Management Series from FEMA is an ongoing effort to publish techniques, tools, and guidance to reduce the impact of threats and hazards to society and the built environment. The *Reference Manual to Mitigate Potential Terrorist Attacks Against Buildings*, FEMA 426, is an excellent first reference for understanding counterterrorism risk management. The Maritime Security Risk Analysis Model is a tool used by the US Coast Guard to assess and manage critical infrastructure risk in our nation's ports.[24] The Transit Risk Assessment Methodology arose from the efforts of the Port Authority of New York and New Jersey to develop a risk-based funding-allocation strategy for the protection of transportation assets and has since been used by many regional transportation authorities.[25] RAMCAP (Risk Analysis and Management for Critical Asset Protection) is a product of the American Society of Mechanical Engineers–Innovative Technologies Institute (ASME-ITI). The current version, RAMCAP Plus, includes protection and resilience themes and can be applied to a wide range of facilities, from college campuses to industrial sites. ASME-ITI, together with the American Water Works Association, has recently adapted the RAMCAP methodology to publish a new American National Standards Institute standard, *J100 RAMCAP Risk and Resilience Management of Water and Wastewater Systems*.[26] These risk tools apply a risk-management process appropriate for managing risk in their discrete infrastructure elements and systems.

At the infrastructure-sector level, the application of the NIPP Risk Management Framework can be seen in the thirteen currently published CI/KR Sector-Specific Plans. For example, the Dam Sector-Specific Plan explains the Consequence-Based Top-Screen process used to conduct a sectorwide risk assessment and program prioritization.[27] In contrast, the Water Sector-Specific Plan applied the NIPP Risk Management Framework in the context of the Safe Drinking Water and Clean Water Acts to an infrastructure with more than 160,000 individual systems that are locally owned and operated yet highly interdependent with other infrastructures.[28] Sector-Specific Plans are also published for agriculture and food, banking and finance, chemical manufacturing, commercial facilities, communications, critical manufacturing, defense industrial base, energy, information technology, and national monuments and icons and demonstrate the application of the NIPP Risk Management Framework across different infrastructures.[29]

System Design

The design of protective systems is perhaps the broadest topic in the CIP conceptual framework. A complete protective system encompasses physical, human, and cyber dimensions (elements). The physical design of the facility tends to be the province of engineers and architects, whereas the equipment and procedures employed by the personnel using and securing the facility are typically addressed by physical security or law enforcement professionals. On top of these are the elements of cyber security, including information assurance (IA), information security, and control and defense of SCADA (supervisory control and data acquisition) systems. Since expertise in all of these areas is beyond most individuals, a complete design requires a team. A well-functioning team requires individuals who are both expert in their fields and familiar with other fields so that a complete, integrated design can be developed. Accordingly, this section briefly explains these three dimensions.

The Physical Dimension

Buildings and the people, processes, and equipment they house are a component of every infrastructure system, and they must be protected from terrorist attack and natural hazards. The goal of the physical design of these buildings is to keep the threats and hazards on the outside of the building. In many of these cases, particularly for human- and cyber-focused infrastructures, the purpose of the building is protection of the infrastructure. Design standards for environmental loads like earthquakes, wind, snow, and rain are contained in building codes. If a risk analysis determines that superior performance under higher loads is required, then this can be provided by an appropriate engineering design. The level of flood protection for a facility is typically established by the location of the facility relative to the floodplain (floodplains can be found on the Flood Insurance Rate Maps, available online).

Designing a building or other physical facility to resist a specific blast loading requires sophisticated engineering tools and experienced professionals. Unless there is a specific terrorist threat or risk of accidental explosion, specialized explosive-resistant design may not be appropriate for many structures. In this case, the procedures outlined in UFC 4-020-01, *DOD Security Engineering Facilities Planning Manual*, and the supporting manuals can be used to establish a minimum level of blast protection from typical but unspecified threats. This would be a decision made by the building owner, as it is typically not required by local building codes.

These design procedures typically protect the building from externally placed threats such as vehicle bombs. For small explosive devices, which are the most common, sufficient levels of protection can usually be achieved by providing sufficient standoff to keep the explosion away from the building and by moderate hardening or protection of the windows. If the threat is a larger explosive device, then the standoff requirements are usually too great, and the desired level of protection requires hardened construction.

The Human Dimension

If we keep everyone and everything outside of a facility, then we will not have internal threats, but this is not a very practical approach. When we let people and things into a facility, we must consider that they may bring threats with them. Accordingly, we establish policies and procedures to deter, detect, and defeat these threats. These approaches are commonly called "gates, guards, and guns" and are the province of law enforcement and physical security personnel.

The threats addressed by security procedures go beyond terrorism. The terrorist threat is very scary, but is also very unlikely. Accordingly, facilities are more likely to be faced with criminals, protesters, and disgruntled employees, and the threats could include theft, guns, knives, hand-carried explosives, chemical and biological hazards, and electronic surveillance. These are the individuals and techniques that physical security professionals must routinely address.

Facility security procedures must deter, detect, or defeat a threat and the threat vector. If the security procedures cannot do one of these, then the facility must be physically designed not to fail under the threat. Deterrence means that a facility projects an image that it is a hard target, and this image causes the individual to seek another target. This does not mean that the facility must look like a fortress; professional guards, state-of-the-art equipment, and consistent security policies can all serve to give the appearance of a "hard target." All detection procedures and equipment have a sensitivity, and the greater the sensitivity, the greater the intrusion to the building's occupants. For example, two and one-half pounds of C4 explosive is approximately twelve-by-two-by-two inches, and a physical search, designed to detect a charge (explosive) of this size, must look in all areas that contain at least forty-eight cubic inches. Charges smaller than this size will escape detection. Threats below the sensitivity of the detection system are dealt with in one of two ways. First, the security personnel within the facility must be able to deal with and defeat the threat. If a small handgun can be slipped through security, then the security personnel must have procedures and equipment to defeat a gunman. Second, the internal structure of the facility must be designed to withstand this threat, without failing catastrophically or causing mass casualties.

In summary, the physical envelope of the facility and the deterrent effect of the physical security procedures keep threats outside of the building. Detection procedures and equipment stop threats down to the level of the system's sensitivity. As a last line of defense, the procedures in place and the physical structure of the facility must defeat anything that penetrates these two barriers. Three layers of defense deal with physical threats, but what are the defenses against nonphysical threats?

The Cyber Dimension

Cyber systems typically fall into one of two categories. Information systems process information, such as credit card numbers, bank accounts, birth records, and family photos. Information assurance is a risk-management process that protects the use, transmission, and storage of this information and the hardware and software that enable these processes. Fundamental IA concepts include: (1) confidentiality—information is disclosed only to authorized users;

(2) integrity—data are complete and correct; and (3) availability—data are accessible when requested.[30] SCADA systems are supervisory, control, and data-acquisition systems. SCADA systems are essential to the operation of the infrastructure because they collect data, provide feedback, and allow for the control of distributed infrastructure elements. They allow operators in a centralized control facility to remotely operate pump stations, track movements of trains, monitor pressure in pipelines, and manage frequency and voltage in the electrical grid. Attacks on these systems can disable an infrastructure without physical contact and result in anything from complete destruction to no damage. SCADA systems must be protected from both deliberate sabotage and accidental failure. Cyber protective systems, when combined with personnel, procedures, and physical architectural and engineering design, provide a complete protective system for critical infrastructures.

Challenges in Critical Infrastructure Protection and Resilience

Because our infrastructure is so complex, the challenges in infrastructure protection and resilience are also extremely complex. Because critical infrastructures are so vast, establishing the limits of the infrastructure of interest results in a very large system. For example, the drainage basin and associated navigable waterways with their system of locks and dams for the Mississippi River cover about half of the country. This size leads to challenging interdependencies. Elements in an infrastructure are interdependent, as can be seen in the electrical infrastructure. For example, a coal-fired electrical plant depends upon water to boil into steam, the rail-transportation infrastructure to deliver the coal, and the mining infrastructure to extract the coal from the earth. This interdependency illustrates the challenge of conflicts in private ownership and public interests. About 85 percent of the infrastructures of the United States are privately owned and thus must operate profitably. Under this condition, the "best" decision may be a less expensive option of shifting risk to an insurance company and accepting a longer outage rather than a more expensive option of reducing the risk of a long outage. This conflicts with the public interest and desire of minimizing risk and the associated outages. All of these challenges taken together illustrate the complexity of critical infrastructure protection and resilience and the need for educated professionals, data collection, management, and accurate and accessible modeling tools. Solutions to infrastructure challenges may be characterized by three adjectives: *good, fast,* and *cheap.* Owners may pick two adjectives, and only two. They can have fast and cheap, but it will not be good. They can have good and cheap, but it will not be fast. Or they can have good and fast, but it will not be cheap.

Conclusion

This chapter provides an introduction to the field of critical infrastructure protection and resilience and a four-part framework for understanding this field. All CIP/R efforts take place in an environment of *policy* established by our federal, state, and local governments. Critical infrastructure systems are *networks,* and an application of network theory allows us to better predict the behavior of infrastructure systems. Because we do not have enough money or capacity to protect everything from every threat and hazard, a *risk-management* process is used to balance the level of threat and hazard with a level of protection in an economically viable manner. Finally, complete protective *system design* must account for the physical, human, and cyber elements inherent in an infrastructure. Through applying this framework for CIP/R, professionals can expand their knowledge, assimilate new information, and tackle this field's challenging problems. The result will be a nation with robust, redundant, and adaptive infrastructures that are better able to withstand the threats and hazards we will face in the future.

There are numerous online resources to expand one's knowledge and understanding of CIP. Many of these sites are sponsored by FEMA. The following are a few of those sources:

Policy, NIPP, and NIMS. The authors suggest students take the following free, online courses from the FEMA website: the National Response Framework—An Introduction; The National Infrastructure Protection Plan; and the National Incident Management System—An Introduction. All FEMA Independent Study courses can be found at http://training.fema.gov/is/crslist.asp ?page=all.

Networks. The Center for Homeland Defense and Security at the Naval Postgraduate School provides several online courses, including one on the behavior and vulnerability of infrastructure networks. Visit http://www.chds.us

/?special/info&pgm=Noncredit, apply for a user account, and access the course "Critical Infrastructure: Vulnerability Analysis and Protection."

Risk. Visit the website of the National Counter Terrorism Center (http://www.nctc.gov/) and review the annual reports on terrorism and the Worldwide Incident Tracking System, a searchable database of terrorist attacks throughout the world. Visit the website of the US Geological Survey Natural Hazards section (http://www.usgs.gov/natural_hazards/) to learn more about natural hazards and their effects. The FEMA Risk-Management Series is available at http://www.fema.gov/plan/prevent/rms/index.shtm#2. UFC 4-020-01, *DOD Security Engineering Facilities Planning Manual*, is the Department of Defense's planning manual for risk management of federal buildings and is available on the Whole Building Design Guide website at http://www.wbdg .org/ccb/browse_cat.php?o=29&c=4.

System Design. Learn more about site layout and designing for terrorist and environmental hazards on the resource pages of the Whole Building Design Guide, available at http://www.wbdg.org/resources/rpindex.php#. These articles provide an understanding of how engineers and architects approach protective design and the difficulties associated with this complex topic. Learn more about cyber security on the US Computer Emergency Response Team training home page, available at http://www.us-cert.gov/control_systems/cstraining .html.

NOTES

1. Department of Homeland Security, *National Infrastructure Protection Plan* (Washington, DC: Government Printing Office, 2009).

2. Ted Lewis, *Critical Infrastructure Protection in Homeland Security: Defending a Networked Nation* (Hoboken, NJ: Wiley-Interscience, 2006).

3. Ibid.

4. National Security Strategy Information page, 2010, http://www.whitehouse.gov /issues/homeland-security/.

5. Department of Homeland Security, *National Infrastructure Protection Plan.*

6. Infrastructure Security Partnership, "White Paper for the White House Office of Critical Infrastructure Protection and Resilience Policy and Strategy," March 9, 2010, http://www.tisp.org/index.cfm?pk=download&pid=10261&id=11968.

7. Homeland Security Act, 107th Congress, Public Law 107-296, November 25, 2003, http://www.cio.gov/documents/pl_107_296_nov_25_2003.pdf.

8. Homeland Security Presidential Directive 7 (2003), http://www.dhs.gov/xabout /laws/gc_1214597989952.shtm; Homeland Security Presidential Directive 8 (2003), http://www.dhs.gov/xabout/laws/gc_1215444247124.shtm; Homeland Security Presidential Directive 5 (2003), http://www.dhs.gov/xabout/laws/gc_1214592333605.shtm. A list of all HSPDs with links to the complete documents is available on the DHS website at http://www.dhs.gov/xabout/laws/editorial_0607.shtm.

9. National Security Strategy Information page.

10. Department of Homeland Security, *National Infrastructure Protection Plan.*

11. Albert-László Barabási and Eric Bonabeau, "Scale Free Networks," *Scientific America* (May 2003), http://www.scientificamerican.com/article.cfm?id=scale-free-networks.

12. M. E. J. Newman, "The Structure and Function of Complex Networks," *SIAM Review* 45 (2003), http://www-personal.umich.edu/~mejn/courses/2004/cscs535/review.pdf.

13. Department of Homeland Security, *National Infrastructure Protection Plan.*

14. Department of Defense, *DOD Security Engineering Facilities Planning Manual,* UFC 4-020-01 (Washington, DC: Government Printing Office, 2008).

15. Ibid.

16. Department of Homeland Security, *National Infrastructure Protection Plan.*

17. Ibid.

18. Second Vatican Council, Gaudium et spes [Joys and Hopes], Pastoral Constitution on the Church in the Modern World (1965), http://www.vatican.va/archive/hist_councils /ii_vatican_council/documents/vat-ii_cons_19651207_gaudium-et-spes_en.html.

19. Deputy Chief of Staff for Intelligence, US Army Training and Doctrine Command, *Terror Operations Case Studies in Terrorism,* Handbook 1.01 (Fort Leavenworth, KS: Command and General Staff College, 2007).

20. Andrea Peters, "Train Bombings in Moscow Kill Dozens," World Socialist Web Site, March 30, 2010, http://www.wsws.org/articles/2010/mar2010/russ-m30.shtml.

21. Building Seismic Safety Council, *The 2003 NEHRP Recommended Provisions for New Buildings and Other Structures,* FEMA 450 (Washington, DC: National Institute of Building Sciences, 2004), http://www.nibs.org/index.php/bssc/publications/2003/fema 450nehrp2003/2003.

22. US Geological Survey, "100 Year Flood: It's All About Chance," April 2010, http:// pubs.usgs.gov/gip/106/pdf/100-year-flood_041210web.pdf.

23. Building Seismic Safety Council, *2003 NEHRP Recommended Provisions.*

24. *Maritime Security Risk Analysis Model,* accessed September 5, 2011, http://aapa.files .cms-plus.com/PDFs/MSRAMBrochureTrifold.pdf.

25. Security Analysis and Risk Management Association, "Transit Risk Assessment Methodology (TRAM)," http://www.sarma-wiki.org/index.php?title=Transit_Risk _Assessment_Methodology_(TRAM).

26. American Society of Mechanical Engineers—Innovative Technologies Institute, RAMCAP Plus Process Home Page, accessed February 11, 2011, http://www.asme-iti.org /RAMCAP/RAMCAP_Plus_2.cfm.

27. DHS, Dams: Sector-Specific Plan, 2010, http://www.dhs.gov/xlibrary/assets/nipp-ssp-dams-2010.pdf.

28. DHS, Water: Critical Infrastructure and Key Resources Sector-Specific Plan as input to the National Infrastructure Protection Plan, 2007, http://www.dhs.gov/xlibrary/assets /nipp-ssp-water.pdf.

29. DHS, "Sector-Specific Plans," 2011, http://www.dhs.gov/files/programs/gc_117986 6197607.shtm.

30. Wikipedia, "Information Assurance," 2011, http://en.wikipedia.org/wiki/Information _assurance.

CHAPTER 5

Homeland Security Intelligence

WILLIAM J. LAHNEMAN

The role of intelligence is to provide policy makers and other government officials with processed information (i.e., intelligence) that helps them perform their jobs better. More precisely, "Intelligence is the process by which specific types of information important to national security are requested, collected, analyzed, and provided to policy makers; the products of that process; the safeguarding of these processes and this information by counterintelligence activities; and the carrying out of operations as requested by lawful authorities."[1]

This chapter focuses on intelligence intended to improve the US homeland security enterprise. Homeland security intelligence focuses on how intelligence can help counterterrorism efforts, where counterterrorism in this case refers primarily to efforts to detect terrorist plans for attacks against the US homeland. Good intelligence about terrorist capabilities and intentions can increase the effectiveness of policies to prepare for, prevent, protect against, defend against, and respond to terrorist attacks. Good intelligence cannot guarantee that officials will make wise choices, but the absence of good intelligence about terrorist designs on the homeland is certain to degrade the quality of resulting policies and actions.

Terrorism is a tactic that is practiced by groups that are weak compared to the government forces and other capabilities arrayed against them. Terrorists understand that, if they are discovered, government forces will have little difficulty in neutralizing them. As a result, terrorists operate in small groups under conditions of extreme secrecy, making them inherently difficult to detect. Since the 9/11 attacks, it has become clear that many terrorist groups are adept at exploiting gaps and weak spots created by today's rapidly globalizing world, which continues to experience increasing levels of global travel, communication, and financial flows. In addition, terrorists have great flexibility in choosing the time, place, and nature of their next attack. In fact, seemingly random attacks upon innocent civilians are an effective way for terrorists to further their immediate goal of terrorizing a target population in hopes of achieving their political goals. Terrorists want each member of a target population to believe that he or she might be the next victim of an attack, which spreads insecurity and mistrust in the government's ability to provide security.

Terrorists' tactics and their ability to choose the target of their next attack from among a virtually limitless set of potential ones make good intelligence a critically important component of a homeland security enterprise. For example, intelligence can provide warning of an impending terrorist attack, enabling the government to take steps to prevent it. If the intelligence enterprise can detect plans for a terrorist attack, then the relative weakness of terrorist groups virtually guarantees that government forces can prevent successful attacks through preemption. Even if intelligence provides warning too late to prevent terrorists from commencing an attack, good intelligence can still allow defense forces to defeat an attack in progress. Alternatively, undetected terrorist attacks have a much better chance of success, since terrorists are likely in any case to choose sites that are undefended and unprotected (i.e., sites that are not "hardened" by various security measures such as security checkpoints, fences, and other measures that make unauthorized entry difficult).

Intelligence can also provide more general information about what categories of targets a terrorist group might want to attack. Such information can increase the effectiveness of government and private-sector actions to reduce the vulnerability of the nation's critical infrastructure. It can also improve the preparedness of first responders and the overall resilience of the American people by providing information about the nature of terrorist threats to the homeland. As a result of these facts, it is difficult to overestimate the critical importance of good intelligence for effective CT efforts. In the absence of intelligence to guide CT actions, many have said that detecting terrorists is like looking for a needle in a haystack.

Before describing homeland security intelligence activities, it is important to understand that the missions of both the US intelligence enterprise and the US homeland security enterprise extend well beyond the CT mission alone.

US homeland security efforts include preparing for and responding to the effects of natural disasters, such as hurricanes and earthquakes, in addition to terrorist attacks. Although it is possible to provide warning of impending hurricanes and some other natural phenomena, doing so is not the job of the homeland security intelligence enterprise. Thus, when speaking about intelligence for homeland security, this chapter is referring specifically to activities pertaining to CT efforts.

Similarly, CT is just one of the principal missions of the US intelligence enterprise. There are many more. At the same time that it needs to provide intelligence to support CT efforts, the US intelligence enterprise must also produce intelligence about several traditional state actors of interest to policy makers, such as Iraq, Afghanistan, North Korea, and Iran. Increasingly, the intelligence enterprise must also provide policy makers with intelligence concerning nontraditional issues and trends, such as climate change, urbanization patterns, and the emergence of new ideologies. Even when considering their CT mission, intelligence activities aimed at preventing terrorist attacks against the US homeland are only a portion of the intelligence enterprise's overall CT mission. The intelligence enterprise is also responsible for detecting terrorist plans for attacks against American citizens and US interests throughout the world, and its liaison activities with foreign intelligence agencies contribute to detecting terrorist plans for attacks in other countries as well as in the US homeland. Importantly, the intelligence enterprise is also tasked with an *antiterrorism* mission. Whereas *counterterrorism* refers to efforts to prevent terrorist attacks, *antiterrorism* refers to efforts to understand the causes and effects of terrorism so that policies can be developed to diminish the appeal of terrorist movements.

Last, the intelligence enterprise encompasses activities that lie outside the boundaries of US national security affairs. Many government organizations at the federal, state, and local levels engage in intelligence collection and analysis concerning criminal and other illegal activities within the United States. These activities are referred to as "criminal intelligence" (CRINT) or "law enforcement intelligence" (LEINT). Five observations about CRINT/LEINT are in order. First, terrorism is a crime. CT is a legitimate and important area of focus for CRINT/LEINT efforts, and CRINT/LEINT is a vitally important contributor to the overall homeland security CT intelligence effort.

Second, since CRINT/LEINT is a US domestic law enforcement activity, CRINT/LEINT activities cannot violate US civil liberties and other laws. This is not true concerning US intelligence activities performed in other countries. Many common intelligence collection practices, such as espionage and wiretaps at overseas locations, are illegal in the countries where the US Intelligence Community conducts them (just as it is illegal for foreign intelligence agencies to perform such activities in the United States).

Third, CRINT/LEINT has traditionally been conducted with keen attention to future prosecution of offenders. This means that CRINT/LEINT activities must observe strict procedures so that the resulting intelligence products can be used in court.

Fourth, CRINT/LEINT tends to be reactive. Although there are exceptions, law enforcement agencies typically become focused on collecting intelligence about particular targets after individuals are already suspected of having committed a crime (normally, someone is not a criminal until they have committed a crime). One exception to this reactive bias is law enforcement efforts to map the occurrence of criminal acts in order to predict patterns that optimize placement of law enforcement assets to, it is hoped, reduce the commission of future crimes. Another is counterterrorism. According to US law, persons engaged in a conspiracy to commit a terrorist act are considered terrorists,[2] and law enforcement organizations can apprehend them to prevent a planned attack from occurring and later prosecute them in court.

Fifth, in today's interconnected world, developing CRINT/LEINT often involves intelligence collection and coordination efforts outside US borders, even though the goal is reducing the US domestic crime rate and prosecuting offenders. For example, the Federal Bureau of Investigation maintains legal attachés at many US embassies overseas, and the New York Police Department (NYPD) has stationed officers overseas in liaison roles with foreign law enforcement agencies. This move was a direct response to the 9/11 attacks; NYPD officers stationed outside the United States are there for CT intelligence gathering and coordination purposes. These kinds of actions blur the distinction between what used to be considered a relatively clear line between US intelligence activities directed at foreign entities and those directed against domestic ones.

Nowhere is this indistinct boundary more evident than when discussing intelligence for homeland security. Accordingly, this chapter will de-emphasize the differences between CRINT/LEINT and other types of intelligence in the interest of presenting as coherent a picture of the overall CT intelligence enterprise as possible. As this picture comes into focus, it will become clear that some activities are performed by law enforcement entities, while others are the domain of the organizations engaged in "foreign intelligence" collection, analysis, and production.

So far, the discussion has focused upon the first and second parts of the four-part definition of intelligence stated previously, that is, homeland security intelligence as a type of processed information and the resulting products that support efforts to counter terrorist activities against the US homeland. For the sake of completeness, it is necessary to address the last two elements of the intelligence enterprise and show how they relate to homeland security. These are covert actions and counterintelligence activities. Covert actions are "activities of the United States Government to influence political, economic or military conditions abroad, where it is intended that the role of the United States Government will not be apparent or acknowledged publically."[3] Covert actions can take the form of propaganda, political activity (such as clandestine financial support for foreign political campaigns), economic activities (e.g., secretly manipulating the price of important commodities in a country), supporting military coups, and conducting paramilitary operations. The practice of extralegal rendition is a recent example of paramilitary operations in which a suspected terrorist was apprehended outside of US territory by US intelligence officers and rendered to a third country for questioning, either with the tacit agreement of host-country officials or clandestinely.[4] In most cases, the purpose of these renditions was to obtain information about terrorist plans for attacks on the US homeland.

Counterintelligence refers to "actions taken to protect one's own intelligence operations from penetration and disruption by hostile nations or their intelligence services."[5] Effective counterintelligence is essential in CT efforts, just as it is in all areas of the intelligence enterprise. If terrorists learn that the government knows about their plans, they can change them, thus neutralizing the government's advantage. Terrorists who learn that an intelligence service has penetrated their organization can take more damaging actions as well. Knowledge about the kinds of information the intelligence organization has learned about the terrorist group might enable the terrorists to figure out how the intelligence organization learned such information. Maybe there is a spy in the terrorist organization, maybe satellite reconnaissance or surveillance by an unmanned aerial vehicle is responsible, or perhaps an intelligence service is intercepting terrorist cell phone calls. Armed with such information, terrorists could eliminate the leak by killing the spy, changing their location, or ceasing use of the tapped lines. However, they could also leave the intelligence service's assets in place and begin sending disinformation to deceive the intelligence agency concerning terrorist plans. For example, terrorists could deceive the intelligence agency into believing that a hospital is a secret factory for manufacturing improvised explosive devices in the hope that the US military will conduct missile attacks on the site.

Counterintelligence is clearly an important element of the homeland security intelligence enterprise. Of particular note, counterintelligence as broadly defined includes the many measures taken to protect the security of classified materials. These include both physical security and information security programs. These measures seek to restrict access to classified material to as small a number of personnel as possible—to those with a "need to know." This fact can create significant tensions in and among intelligence organizations when "connecting the dots"—sharing information among many organizations to maximize the chance of detecting terrorist plans—is the main priority. Information sharing is essential, but so is maintaining the security of the shared information.

In summary, intelligence for homeland security is a multifaceted enterprise performed by many actors. Given the nature of the terrorist threat to the US homeland, the ability of the intelligence enterprise to detect terrorist plans to attack the US homeland is critically important. At the same time, this mission is only one part of the much larger US intelligence enterprise, which must produce intelligence about a host of other potential threats and issues. The remainder of this chapter will explore how the intelligence enterprise produces intelligence products to detect terrorist plans to attack the US homeland. While the chapter refers to this mission as the "CT mission," readers should understand that, from the viewpoint of the US intelligence enterprise, its CT mission encompasses detecting plans for all terrorist attacks against US persons and other interests worldwide, not just within the US homeland.

It is also important to note that any successful homeland security intelligence enterprise must be accompanied by an effective counterintelligence effort. However, a detailed examination of this area is beyond the scope of this work. Similarly, certain types of covert action can contribute directly to the CT mission but will not be discussed further.

The Process of Producing Intelligence for Homeland Security

All parts of the US intelligence enterprise follow the same general process to gather raw intelligence and transform it into finished intelligence capable of being used by policy makers and other government officials in performing their duties. This process is known as the "intelligence process" or "intelligence cycle." Some variations of the process have five steps, including the one used by the Intelligence Community, but the seven-step approach described by Mark Lowenthal in *Intelligence: From Secrets to Policy* is more useful than the five-step process at detailing what must be accomplished to produce good intelligence.[6] Those seven steps are:

1. *Requirements*—Policy makers tell the intelligence enterprise the various issues and threats that it should target, along with priorities for each requirement. Providing intelligence for counterterrorism purposes has been one of the highest intelligence priorities since the 9/11 attacks. This circumstance should not obscure the reality that the intelligence enterprise cannot make up its own requirements, but must receive them from policy makers. This convention exists because the purpose of intelligence is to improve policy making and, as a result, the effectiveness of homeland security and other government efforts. Policy makers make the policies, with support from the intelligence enterprise. Also, in theory, policy makers know the kinds of intelligence they need to improve their policy making and are thus the correct agents to impose intelligence requirements. However, in practice, the relationship between policy makers and members of the intelligence enterprise is not so formal. Policy makers do not always know exactly what intelligence support they need (or are too busy to devote much time to such considerations). In such cases, intelligence officers can recommend that policy makers make certain requirements, as long as it does not appear that they are recommending that policy makers make certain policy choices.

2. *Collection*—The IC obtains information about the targets it is required to track through five collection mechanisms:
   A. Human intelligence (HUMINT)—Spy networks and other human assets, such as diplomats and military attachés, obtain information. In the law enforcement arena, informants would fall into this category.
   B. Signals intelligence (SIGINT)—The IC uses electronic means to collect signals of interest. These can consist of electronic communications

(called communications intelligence), electronic signals from various foreign weapons and other military and civilian systems (called electronic intelligence), and data from telemetry signals when weapons are tested (called telemetry intelligence). In the case of homeland security intelligence, various forms of communications intercepts would be examples of SIGINT.

C. Geospatial intelligence (GEOINT)—Satellites, manned and unmanned aircraft, and human agents take images of items of interest. These images derive from a range of techniques such as visual, infrared, acoustic, and radar imaging. GEOINT was formerly called imagery intelligence (IMINT). In the homeland security arena, any form of video surveillance against either domestic or foreign subjects would be examples of GEOINT. Also, GEOINT assets are now routinely used as a source of intelligence for major public events, such as the Super Bowl, and to provide intelligence concerning the progress of hurricanes and other major storms, as well as intelligence for directing response and restoration activities following a major disaster.

D. Measurement and signatures intelligence (MASINT)—MASINT employs a range of techniques such as multispectral analysis and imagery to discern the purpose of various facilities and installations (e.g., a facility producing chemical or nuclear weapons).

E. Open-source intelligence (OSINT)—OSINT is intelligence derived from nonsecret or "open" sources such as print media, news broadcasts, journals, books, and the Internet. In terms of homeland security, intelligence analysts monitor the websites of terrorist groups and use various financial and travel records to track potential terrorist activity (financial and travel records are not "open source" in the true sense of the term because they are not available to the public, but they are often categorized as OSINT since they are not government classified information either).

Collectively these five collection techniques are called the "INTs" for short. All but the last technique, OSINT, are designed to collect information that targets of collection efforts want to withhold—for example, the plans of foreign military installations, designs of foreign weapons, and private conversations—without US collection efforts becoming known to the targets. As a result, most intelligence consists of secret or "classified" information. Not only is the information itself often sensitive, but the IC must keep the sources and methods used to obtain sensitive information secret in order to preserve their effectiveness. As noted previously, if terrorists learn that intelligence agencies know certain pieces of information about them, they can mount denial and deception efforts in the hope that intelligence agencies will produce incorrect analyses.

3. *Processing and Exploitation*—A great deal of collected intelligence, particularly intelligence collected through SIGINT, GEOINT, and MASINT, is not useful until it has been processed by various techniques. For instance, encrypted information must be decoded, a foreign communications intercept must be translated, and satellite imagery must be interpreted before their full meanings can be known. Also, this step is where potentially useful pieces of information are sorted from the vast quantities of useless information that collection efforts also inevitably collect. When intelligence leaves this step of the process, it is called raw intelligence.

4. *Analysis and Production*—Analysts weigh all of the relevant raw intelligence about some requirement and construct conclusions concerning its meaning. Analysts and their managers then process the analysis into a product that summarizes their assessment. For the most part, these products are "classified," that is, they have a security classification of confidential, secret, or top secret. Only those with appropriate access—ideally those with a "need to know"—are allowed to view each product. Most CT-related intelligence products fall into this category. The intelligence enterprise also produces unclassified products for wide distribution. Intelligence regarding the likely track of a hurricane about to make landfall on a US coast and imagery detailing the extent of damage following such a storm are examples of unclassified intelligence products that pertain to the homeland security enterprise.

5. *Dissemination*—Intelligence products are distributed to consumers in various parts of the government as appropriate. The goal is to get an intelligence product to the right people in a timely manner. It does no good if warning of an attack does not arrive until after the attack is over. Intelligence products should be tailored to their consumers; they should minimize extraneous information while concisely expressing the intelligence that each consumer needs in a form that is easy for the consumer to use. Thus, dissemination takes many different forms depending on the audience.

6. *Consumption*—Policy makers weigh the contents of intelligence products and incorporate their conclusions to varying degrees into their policy making

and other efforts. This step emphasizes that intelligence does not serve any function if consumers ignore it.

7. *Feedback*—Consumers of intelligence analyze the value of the intelligence products they receive and provide this feedback to the IC to help improve subsequent products.

The intelligence cycle represents an ideal. In practice, all steps occur simultaneously, and there are many feedback loops that short-circuit the process (in a constructive way) as new intelligence is collected. However, the fact remains that the intelligence cycle remains an essential concept for analyzing problems and for understanding how the various parts of the IC fit together. When something is not going well within a particular area of intelligence, the intelligence cycle serves as a valuable troubleshooting tool. Are the collection efforts acceptable? Are we processing the information correctly so that no important pieces of raw intelligence are missed? Is the analytic process rigorous?

The Structure of the US Intelligence Enterprise for Homeland Security

The Pre-9/11 Intelligence Community

Prior to the 9/11 attacks, if someone were to ask how the US government went about producing intelligence, including intelligence about terrorist plans to attack US interests, the resulting explanation would have been limited to a description of the US Intelligence Community, where the IC referred to a number of agencies and offices of the federal government that existed in various different cabinet departments or as independent agencies. Two IC members, the Central Intelligence Agency and the FBI, maintained counterterrorism centers prior to 9/11. However, terrorism was assigned to the third and lowest tier of the IC's requirements.[7]

The activities of all but one member of the IC dealt with intelligence about foreign entities, primarily the activities of foreign states. The FBI was the only member of the IC with the mandate to perform intelligence activities domestically, and its intelligence-related missions included counterespionage, other forms of counterintelligence, and counterterrorism. As a law enforcement agency, the FBI was required to observe US laws, including those pertaining to civil liberties, at all times while pursuing its intelligence activities, just as it did when carrying out its other missions, which included investigating and apprehending violators of federal laws, usually crimes that crossed state lines such as the activities of organized criminal networks, kidnapping, and many others.

The remaining members of the IC were prohibited from performing domestic intelligence activities. As noted previously, many IC collection techniques (the INTs) are illegal in the countries where the IC practices them as well as in the United States. The prohibition against domestic activities for most IC members also had a historical basis. In the 1970s, the Church Commission had discovered plausible evidence that the CIA had performed illegal activities against American citizens. Subsequently, Congress initiated Intelligence Oversight Committees in both houses of Congress to provide focused oversight on IC conduct, and the IC's leadership enacted rigorous rules to preclude a repetition of such domestic activities.

This clear division of labor between foreign and domestic intelligence activities resulted in the erection of a virtual "wall" between the FBI and the other IC agencies. The concept of a wall was meant to serve as a metaphor for stressing that IC agencies engaged in foreign intelligence collection must meticulously respect the civil liberties of Americans. However, the wall came to represent the fact that the IC needed to be careful about how it shared information across this boundary lest it be accused of breaking US domestic laws, and this concern translated into reduced information sharing between the FBI and other members of the IC. For its part, the FBI, as a law enforcement agency intent on bringing criminals to justice, needed to exercise care when compiling intelligence to preserve its admissibility as evidence for prosecuting offenders, whether these criminals were Mafia bosses, foreign spies, or terrorists. This fact made the FBI reluctant to share pertinent information with the rest of the IC because it feared its evidence would become inadmissible if improperly handled. This bias was amplified by the reactive organizational culture of the FBI. In almost all crimes, a person does not become a criminal and liable for prosecution until *after* he or she has committed a crime. In contrast, it is vitally important to apprehend terrorists *before* they commit a terrorist act to prevent needless death and destruction. Accordingly, a reactive culture works well for most crimes, but not for terrorism. (Conspiracy to commit a crime is itself a crime, but law enforcement often tries to apprehend such criminals in the act of committing the planned crime to strengthen their case. This can be a good option because the cost of failure—that is, allowing the crime to occur—is often very low compared to the impact of a successful terrorist attack.)

While the existence of the wall detracted from information sharing within the IC and thus impaired the IC's chances of discovering al-Qaeda's plans for the 9/11 attacks, it is far from the only factor that degraded information sharing in the pre-9/11 IC. The IC's structure was also a major contributor. Figure 5.1 shows the structure of the IC on September 11, 2001.

Each IC member's mission is described below. The important point to observe is that there is no single, clear line of authority that guides IC actions. The Intelligence *Community* is aptly named. It is a confederation of various entities, each of which reports directly to different cabinet secretaries and a few other senior US officials rather than to a "chief of intelligence" with executive authority over all IC members.

This arrangement is not as odd or dysfunctional as a first glance might indicate. First, different parts of the IC perform specialized functions and contribute to various parts of the intelligence cycle. Each of these specialized areas requires employees with unique and highly developed skills to perform effectively. This means that, even if all of these functional areas were incorporated into one organization, considerable differences would exist in how various elements achieved their missions, resulting in variations in organizational cultures within the larger organization.

Second, since each cabinet secretary or other high-level executive requires intelligence to perform his or her job, each of these individuals demands that his or her organization has an office dedicated to producing intelligence tailored to the particular department's mission. In the event that all of the IC agencies were incorporated into one organization under the control of a director of intelligence, for example, each cabinet secretary would find the funds somewhere to reestablish an intelligence office under his or her direct control. This phenomenon actually occurred in 1962 when the Defense Intelligence Agency was formed. The DIA's purpose was to improve information sharing among the intelligence services of each branch of the armed forces (US Army, Navy, Air Force, Marine Corps), which had a terrible record in this regard. The intent was for the intelligence offices of each service to merge into the new DIA, but, fifty years later, each service still maintains its own separate, robust intelligence office dedicated to providing intelligence tailored to each service's missions. Meanwhile, the DIA provides intelligence about issues that affect joint operations, that is, military operations that require the participation of more than one branch of the armed forces in coordinated actions.

The missions of each IC member listed in Figure 5.1 are as follows:

1. National Security Agency—responsible for SIGINT, US encryption security, and foreign code breaking

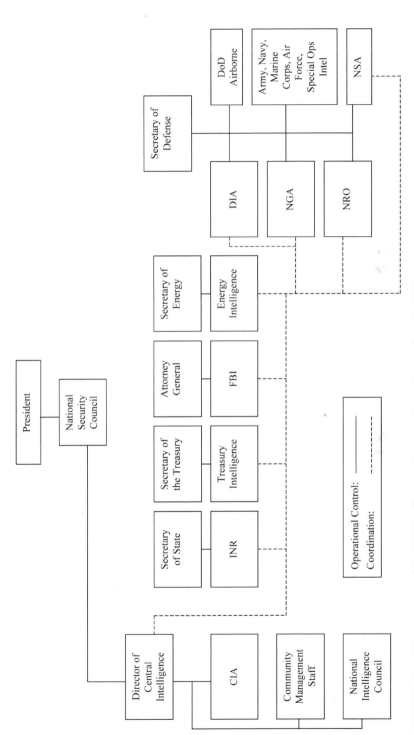

FIGURE 5.1 The structure of the US Intelligence Community on September 11, 2001.
Source: Adapted from Mark M. Lowenthal, *Intelligence: From Secrets to Policy,* 2nd ed. (Washington, DC: CQ Press, 2003), 26.

2. National Geospatial Intelligence Agency—responsible for GEOINT
3. Defense Intelligence Agency—responsible for defense analysis that transcends any one military service; contains the Central MASINT Office responsible for MASINT; an all-source analytic agency
4. National Reconnaissance Office—designs, builds, and operates US intelligence satellites
5. Defense Airborne—operates unmanned aerial vehicles (drones) that collect IMINT and SIGINT
6. Army Intelligence—develops intelligence specific to the US Army's mission
7. Navy Intelligence—develops intelligence specific to the US Navy's mission
8. Marine Corps Intelligence—develops intelligence specific to the US Marine Corps' mission
9. Air Force Intelligence—develops intelligence specific to the US Air Force's mission
10. Special Operations Intelligence—develops intelligence for Special Operations Command activities
11. Central Intelligence Agency—responsible for HUMINT collection; an all-source analytic agency
12. Department of Energy Intelligence—produces intelligence about foreign developments in nuclear weapons technology
13. Bureau of Intelligence and Research (State Department)—collects HUMINT and OSINT from US diplomatic posts around the world; an all-source intelligence agency
14. Department of the Treasury Intelligence—produces intelligence about currency and other financial flows (including terrorist financing operations)
15. Federal Bureau of Investigation—performs counterintelligence and produces CT-related intelligence

The first ten agencies are in the Department of Defense. The National Security Agency is the largest intelligence agency. The CIA is the IC's only independent agency. The remaining members of the IC fall under various cabinet departments.

Given the nature of the intelligence cycle, the segmented organizational structure used to perform it, and the fact that the IC must keep most of the knowledge it shares among its members secret from outsiders, IC members are naturally biased *against* sharing information. In fact, strict penalties exist for anyone found to have released classified information improperly. However, information sharing among agencies is essential for producing good intelligence about many threats, including the threat to homeland security posed by transnational terrorist groups.

The need to share information among the various members of the IC did not begin with the 9/11 attacks. In fact, three IC agencies—the CIA, DIA, and Bureau of Intelligence and Research in the State Department—are "all-source" analytical agencies, which means that they are responsible for performing analyses based on all available intelligence collected by the IC as a whole, not just by their own agency. All three agencies analyze the same issues in a process known as "competitive analysis." Competitive analysis is designed to ensure that the IC brings different perspectives to the same issues in the hope that multiple perspectives will produce the most complete, unbiased analyses. In addition to the competitive analysis process, the National Intelligence Council (NIC) brings members of all IC agencies together to produce National Intelligence Estimates (NIEs), which are the "most authoritative written judgments concerning national security issues. [NIEs] contain the coordinated judgments of the Intelligence Community regarding the likely course of future events."[8]

Despite these measures to ensure the proper level of information sharing while preserving the security of classified information, most agree that the IC and other government institutions failed to adequately share information about al-Qaeda and its plans prior to September 11, 2001. This apparent intelligence failure led to several intelligence reforms, which are described next.

The Post-9/11 US Intelligence Enterprise

In the wake of the 9/11 attacks, the IC was scrutinized by congressional and executive branch investigative bodies as well as by a host of private entities, such as foundations and think tanks, to discover why the IC had failed to warn of al-Qaeda's attack plans. These developments, particularly *The 9/11 Commission Report*, resulted in a series of intelligence reforms. These reforms were accompanied by a new awareness of the nontraditional nature of the threat that transnational terrorist groups posed to the US homeland. The IC's collection methods—the INTs described previously—had been developed during the Cold War and were optimized for collecting intelligence against the Soviet Union, a powerful state actor with large military forces and industrial capability. In contrast, terrorist groups were nonstate actors that possessed neither fixed territory nor traditional manifestations of power, such as large military forces or industrial facilities. As a result, while GEOINT reconnaissance satellites could readily identify a Soviet missile complex, it could not identify a small group of terrorists meeting in a safe house in a large city. This is just one example of the fact that if the IC were to detect terrorist activities, it needed different types of collection besides the INTs. Intelligence analysis would need to change as well to accommodate the new sources of raw intelligence.

As this awareness grew, it became clear that although the IC would remain vitally necessary for providing CT intelligence, the IC alone would not be sufficient. Rather, actors at the state and local levels of government, and even private-sector entities, would also be required. Many began to refer to this larger group as the US intelligence *enterprise*. The need for this larger group of partners to work together also necessitated the need for new and better information-sharing networks. The best way to understand the contours of this emerging intelligence enterprise is first to examine what has happened at the federal level and then look at developments at the state and local levels of government.

Federal Actions: "Reform" of the IC

Three pieces of legislation implemented the vast majority of the changes to the pre-9/11 IC. These were the USA PATRIOT Act, the Homeland Security Act of 2002, and the Intelligence Reform and Terrorism Prevention Act of 2004.[9] The USA PATRIOT Act, among other things, expanded the use of domestic surveillance activities for purposes of intelligence collection, including the government's ability to search various repositories of potentially useful information.

The Homeland Security Act transformed twenty-two existing government agencies with 180,000 employees into a new Department of Homeland Security. Among many other things, this new department was responsible for "information analysis" (i.e., intelligence production) directed at preventing terrorist attacks against the US homeland. The DHS incorporated a new Office of Information Analysis and Infrastructure Protection (IAIP) that performed this intelligence function as well as conducted programs to identify and harden the nation's critical infrastructure. A few years later, IAIP was divided into two offices. A new Office of Intelligence and Analysis (I&A) carried out the intelligence mission, and the Office of Infrastructure Protection concerned itself with critical infrastructure vulnerability issues. The Homeland Security Act gave IAIP (now I&A) two principal intelligence-related duties and responsibilities. First, I&A would receive and analyze law enforcement information, intelligence, and other information in order to understand the terrorist threat to the US homeland and to detect and identify potential terrorist threats within the United States. To empower this mandate, the act gave all executive agencies "an affirmative obligation to furnish I&A with the specified reports, assessments, and analytical information, even if no request was made for them." Thus, I&A would be an intelligence Fusion Center focused on homeland security CT issues. Second, I&A would exercise primary responsibility for issuing public threat advisories and providing specific warning information to state and local governments and the private sector.[10] This mandate implied a need to develop an effective information-sharing system among the many actors involved.

The DHS also contains several offices with highly developed intelligence collection and analysis activities of their own. These include the US Coast Guard, Secret Service, Immigration and Customs Enforcement, and Customs and Border Protection. The new department needed to establish methods for ensuring that this considerable amount of homeland security intelligence was properly shared within the department and with the IC and other organizations.

The third act, IRTPA, contained several elements that changed the structure of the IC. Prior to IRTPA, a director of central intelligence (DCI) performed three missions:

- coordinated the activities of the various IC agencies
- served as the president's senior intelligence adviser
- served as director of the CIA

After the 9/11 attacks, many believed that the DCI had spent too much time leading the CIA and advising the president, and accordingly too little time coordinating IC activities. IRTPA abolished the DCI position and created two new ones. A new director of national intelligence became responsible for the first two of the former DCI's responsibilities, and a new director of the Central Intelligence Agency was to perform the former DCI's third responsibility.

IRTPA provided the DNI with enhanced authority, intended to improve the position's ability to coordinate IC activities.[11] In addition, the DNI was provided with a staff—the Office of the Director of National Intelligence—to assist in managing IC activities. The DNI was given direct control over two new intelligence Fusion Centers, the National Counterterrorism Center and the National Nonproliferation Center, intended to provide the new position with assets focused toward preventing terrorist attacks upon the homeland. The DNI also has authority over the National Intelligence Council, which carried over from the DCI's old organization. The NIC coordinates the IC's analyses of and produces National Intelligence Estimates about the future trajectories of current and emerging threats. Thus, the DNI is well positioned to assess the future of transnational terrorism, including its threat to the US homeland (as well as the status of other threats and issues). The DNI also controls the National Counterintelligence Executive, which coordinates counterintelligence activities throughout the IC.[12]

There are two budgetary categories in the IC, the National Intelligence Program and the Military Intelligence Program. The NIP is almost three times bigger than the MIP. The NIP funds agencies that deal with strategic intelligence matters. The director of national intelligence oversees the NIP, but this command is sufficiently restricted so that the DNI does not have full budgetary authority. MIP programs deal with joint military and individual service intelligence matters. The secretary of defense controls the MIP.

Figure 5.2 shows the structure of the IC following implementation of the post-9/11 intelligence reforms. Except for the division of the DCI into two positions, none of the pre-9/11 IC organizations were abolished. The DNI and related organizations have already been discussed. The Drug Enforcement Administration and US Coast Guard intelligence both predated the 9/11 attacks and do not represent new IC capabilities. Since the attacks, they have been added to the "formal" list of IC agencies to acknowledge their continuing value as organizations that have historically contributed to homeland security intelligence.

The creation of a new National Security Branch (NSB) within the FBI is a new feature of the post-9/11 IC. The NSB

> was established on September 12, 2005, in response to a presidential directive to establish a "National Security Service" that combines the missions, capabilities, and resources of the counterterrorism, counterintelligence, and intelligence elements of the FBI under the leadership of a senior FBI official. In July 2006, the Weapons of Mass Destruction (WMD) Directorate was created within the NSB to integrate WMD components previously spread throughout the FBI. The NSB also includes the Terrorist Screening Center, which plays a crucial role in providing actionable intelligence to state and local law enforcement.[13]

The establishment of the NSB was the direct result of IRTPA's requirement for the FBI to "improve its intelligence capabilities through the development of

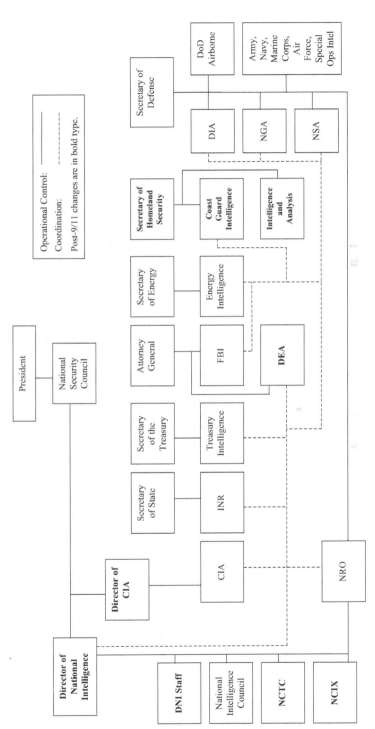

FIGURE 5.2 The post-9/11 Intelligence Community (as modified by the Homeland Security Act of 2002 and the Intelligence Reform and Terrorism Prevention Act of 2004).

Source: Adapted from Lowenthal, *Intelligence*, 4th ed., 32.

a national intelligence workforce," a step driven by the belief that the pre-9/11 FBI had been too dominated by a law enforcement organizational culture that elevated the status of the special agents who arrested criminals while diminishing the value of the bureau's intelligence analysts.[14] By concentrating all of the FBI's CT assets under one roof, the intent was to make CT efforts, including the CT intelligence function, equally important parts of the organization.

State, Local, and Private-Sector Responses

The 9/11 attacks brought to light the fact that state, local, tribal, and private entities are essential partners of the federal government in producing homeland security intelligence.[15] Local responders and other officials, as well as the public, are both *consumers* of intelligence and potential *collectors* of intelligence. As consumers of intelligence, it is vital that indications and warning of a terrorist attack get to the right people in a timely manner to prevent the attack if possible and, if not, to minimize the loss of life and property by optimizing the information available to first responders. As collectors of intelligence, local sources can be valuable collectors of information to help identify terrorist plots against the homeland. For example, since many of the individuals who carried out the 9/11 attacks were living in the United States legally under visas (some of which had expired), it became clear that police and other first responders would be the most likely ones to recognize suspicious behavior in their jurisdictions. Certainly, the federal IC was not in a position to do so. All IC members except for the FBI were prohibited from conducting operations domestically.

Joint Terrorism Task Forces. The FBI had operated a number of Joint Terrorism Task Forces from selected field offices prior to 9/11. JTTFs receive CT-related information from state and local law enforcement agencies, analyze this information, and send pertinent information to the FBI's CT Fusion Center. They are called "joint" because they include members of state, local, and federal law enforcement. Since 9/11 the bureau has expanded the number of JTTFs to about a hundred while increasing the emphasis on their intelligence function.[16]

Prior to 9/11, JTTFs had two problem areas. First, there were insufficient numbers of intelligence analysts in each JTTF. The FBI has since remedied this deficiency. Second, local law enforcement officials complained that, once they had sent a piece of potentially useful information to the JTTF, the FBI hardly ever provided feedback concerning the usefulness of the information.

This practice reduced local enthusiasm for passing information to the JTTFs. In the FBI's defense, when a piece of submitted information turned out to be useful, the FBI usually classified it in accordance with standard procedures. Since local officials rarely possessed the necessary security clearance, the FBI was not able to share intelligence information with them. Regardless of the reason, however, the damage was done, and local officials did not pass on as much information to the JTTFs as might have occurred had robust two-way information sharing been the norm. Since 9/11 there has been an effort to increase the number of police chiefs and other local officials who possess security clearances so that more information can be shared.

State and Local Intelligence Fusion Centers. At the time of the 9/11 attacks, two jurisdictions—New York City and Los Angeles Orange County—operated their own intelligence Fusion Centers. Both jurisdictions believed that their areas of responsibility were so complex that individual localities and each public safety organization (e.g., police, firefighting, emergency medical responders, public health) acting alone would not be able to produce intelligence about regional developments unless some kind of umbrella organization existed to fuse all of the available information. These centers were staffed by members drawn from the various law enforcement, firefighting, and other public safety organizations in the center's jurisdiction. They received information about potential terrorist activity, both from local police and other first responders as well as from the FBI's JTTFs and other members of the IC and analyzed it from their unique regional perspectives.

Today there are more than seventy state and local intelligence Fusion Centers. Many state centers have opened satellite offices to focus on intelligence fusion in different parts of their states. Although each center is somewhat unique because each was established by different states and cities with different needs, these Fusion Centers are now an essential ingredient in the homeland security intelligence enterprise. Fusion Centers receive intelligence from IC agencies (such as the JTTFs and the National Counterterrorism Center [NCTC]), from other Fusion Centers in their region, and from first responders in their jurisdiction. This enables the centers to develop their own independent analyses by "fusing" terrorist-related intelligence from all sources with a detailed knowledge of their jurisdictions. This capability did not exist on 9/11.

Since Fusion Centers are state or local government entities, the federal government has no authority to dictate how the centers will conduct their duties. However, in the years since 9/11, the Fusion Centers have come to interface with the federal government in four important ways. First, the DHS has assumed the role of collecting and disseminating Fusion Center best practices as a way to encourage Fusion Center effectiveness. This step holds the potential to develop new centers at a faster pace and generally improve effectiveness. Second, DHS grants are a significant source of funding for the Fusion Centers. It is uncertain whether many Fusion Centers could continue to operate in the absence of these funds. This reality has led many Fusion Centers to expand their missions from one of strict counterterrorism to an "all-crimes" or "all-hazards" approach. This is not meant to imply that funding concerns are the only reason to adopt such expanded charters; the Fusion Center model works quite well against such expanded sets of threats. Third, the DHS, CIA, and other IC agencies now routinely assign their analysts to Fusion Centers as a way of building professional cooperation and information sharing among federal, state, and local homeland security intelligence organizations. In fact, in some cases Fusion Center and JTTF personnel are collocated, which improves both information sharing and analytic capability. Most IC analysts assigned to state and local Fusion Centers continue to be paid by their parent agencies, which is another way of providing funding in kind for Fusion Center operations. Fourth, the DHS has developed the Homeland Security Information Network (HSIN) to connect the department with Fusion Centers and local jurisdictions. The HSIN and other information networks (discussed below) are vitally important if the kinds and levels of information sharing needed to produce good CT intelligence for homeland security are to become a reality.

Fusion Centers can perform two other important functions. First, they are the logical candidates to train state and local first responders about how to become effective collectors of CT-related intelligence in their localities in order to improve collection at these levels of government.[17] Second, they have proved to be an important link to the private sector. Since approximately 80 percent of the nation's critical infrastructure—likely targets of terrorist attack—is privately owned, it is important to train private-sector entities in relevant homeland security topics. This helps them to better protect their facilities. Proper training can also make them better intelligence collectors. Fusion Centers also are key to developing essential information-sharing networks between government and the private sector. In many jurisdictions, the local Fusion Center is the single point of contact that private firms call with information about suspicious activity or to ask a question relating to homeland security. Similarly, Fusion Centers usually run local telephone hotlines for reporting suspicious activity.

Sharing Information in the Post-9/11 Intelligence Enterprise

Networks for sharing CT-related intelligence information must move relevant information both "vertically," that is, up and down the line between local, state, and federal entities, and "horizontally," that is, among organizations at the same level. Vertical channels are usually managed by a federal government agency. For example, the HSIN has already been mentioned. In addition, the FBI manages a law enforcement information network (National Crime Information Center) that manages the sharing of various crime-related information in addition to CT information. The NCTC has developed a network for coordinating information sharing as well.[18]

Horizontal information sharing occurs at the federal, state, and local levels of government. At the federal level, the main participants in information sharing are the various IC agencies. Since 9/11 the IC has ramped up the volume and kinds of information it shares in recognition that the transnational terrorist threat requires CT analysts to have access to huge volumes of information that *might* prove useful, but the value of which cannot be known in advance.

The IC has emphasized making some of these networks into active analytic tools. Intellipedia, unveiled in 2006, is probably the best example. Using Web 2.0 technology, Intellipedia is interactive, which fosters collaboration within the IC.

> Its advocates claim Intellipedia . . . is producing results. The first time chlorine was used in an improvised explosive device in Iraq, someone created a wiki page asking what intelligence officers and others in the field should do to collect evidence of the usage. "Twenty-three people at 18 or 19 locations around the world chimed in on this thing, and we got a perfectly serviceable set of instructions in two days," says Tom Fingar, who headed the National Intelligence Council from 2005 to 2008. "Nobody called a meeting, there was no elaborate 'Gotta go back and check with Mom to see if this is the view of my organization.'" Last year [2007] traffic on Intellipedia became so heavy that the Office of the Director of National Intelligence had to find extra money to upgrade its servers.[19]

Innovations like Intellipedia are undoubtedly necessary to connect the dots for the homeland security intelligence enterprise. However, there is a downside anytime that classified material is made available to large numbers of users. The "WikiLeaks" compromise of huge volumes of classified information in July and November 2010 is a perfect example of this problem. A low-level intelligence analyst is alleged to have provided up to 340,000 classified US government documents dealing with the wars in Afghanistan and Iraq as well as various classified State Department cables to a nonprofit firm called WikiLeaks.org. Its website states that "WikiLeaks is a non-profit media organization dedicated to bringing important news and information to the public. We provide an innovative, secure and anonymous way for independent sources around the world to leak information to our journalists. We publish material of ethical, political and historical significance while keeping the identity of our sources anonymous, thus providing a universal way for the revealing of suppressed and censored injustices."[20]

Such a large amount of classified information could be pirated in this way only because each network user has access to vast amounts of information. There is no easy solution to this situation. After all, each user must have access to all available information because such access is necessary to produce good homeland security intelligence. However, the WikiLeaks compromise of information makes the vital importance of effective counterintelligence crystal clear.

At the state level, many Fusion Centers share information with each other, usually within a region. Take the National Capital District, for instance, which includes Washington, DC. Fusion Centers in the District of Columbia, Maryland, and Virginia must share information for there to be any hope of developing a coherent intelligence picture of potential terrorist activity in the region. In fact, given the relatively small geographic area involved, producing good regional CT intelligence also requires information sharing with the Fusion Centers in Pennsylvania, Delaware, New Jersey, and West Virginia. These kinds of information-sharing relationships around the country have generally emerged in an ad hoc manner. They are critically important for effective homeland security intelligence production.

In summary, there are several networks that, taken as a whole, permit information sharing both vertically and horizontally. A number of networks existed prior to 9/11, and several more, such as Intellipedia, have been added since then. The expansion in the number of JTTFs and, somewhat later, the establishment of the NSB by the FBI have helped to provide enhanced information sharing among local, state, and federal sources of CT intelligence information. In addition to the communications network used by the JTTFs, several different networks carry CT-related intelligence information. As mentioned previously, the DHS maintains its HSIN, and the NCTC has a separate channel for sharing information vertically. There are other networks that play a role in disseminating CT-related information, such as the High Intensity Drug Control Trafficking Areas network run by the Office of National Drug Control Policy in the Executive Office of the President.[21]

The proliferation of vertical information-sharing networks is understandable, but it has produced a situation in which state Fusion Center analysts, for instance, must monitor a large number of networks in order to extract all potentially relevant CT-related information available. This situation has resulted because detecting terrorist threats to the homeland became the number one priority immediately following the 9/11 attacks, but today's principal homeland security organizations did not emerge until 2003 (DHS) and late 2004 (DNI and NCTC). In the meantime, organizations such as the CIA and FBI made rapidly realigning themselves to the CT mission their first priority. Accordingly, they adjusted existing networks to handle the CT information-sharing mission. Later, when new federal actors, such as the DHS, were established, they formed their own information networks to have control over a critically important tool for carrying out their missions. The situation is not optimal, but, as WikiLeaks has shown, neither is a system that concentrates all relevant CT-related information into just one or two networks. In the final analysis, too many networks are better than not enough.

Conclusion

This chapter has outlined how intelligence for homeland security is produced. It has moved from the general to the specific, first defining intelligence and explaining what makes intelligence to support US homeland security unique—not only uniquely focused but also uniquely difficult because of the large number of sources of potentially valuable intelligence, none of which are conclusive by themselves. The chapter went on to describe the process of intelligence as summarized in the intelligence cycle. Although the intelligence cycle represents an ideal, it is nevertheless critically important for understanding how the intelligence enterprise collects information, processes some of this information into raw intelligence, and analyzes it to produce finished intelligence capable of providing warning of terrorist plans for attacking the US homeland as well as helping policy makers craft effective homeland security policies. After laying this groundwork, the chapter detailed the various parts of the intelligence enterprise that are devoted to producing intelligence for homeland security. In the process, it highlighted the changes to organizational structures and other intelligence reforms that have occurred in response to the 9/11 attacks. These steps have been intended to improve America's ability to provide good intelligence about terrorist threats to the US homeland and for other CT purposes.

Producing such intelligence is very difficult. Many actors at all levels of government as well as the private sector are involved. If these actors fail to cooperate with each other sufficiently, particularly in the area of information sharing, then the quality of the resulting intelligence products drops. Thus, large-scale information-sharing networks are essential for producing effective homeland security intelligence. However, much of the information flowing through these networks needs to stay secret. This means that only those individuals with a need to know can have access to it. This produces a tension that makes information sharing challenging, beyond the technical challenges of storing and moving such large volumes of data. The chapter has provided an overview of the kinds of information networks intended to create and facilitate appropriate sharing while preserving the security of classified information. The recent WikiLeaks episode has showcased how difficult meeting both standards—appropriate sharing and rigorous security—can be.

There might be a few things in the homeland security intelligence enterprise that can be streamlined. For instance, the various networks that carry information among federal, state, and local intelligence organizations might profit from a reduction in numbers. By and large, however, the enterprise is complex because transnational terrorism has many dimensions, which demands that the homeland security intelligence enterprise incorporate many unique personnel competencies spread across many jurisdictions. Additionally, in almost all cases, the different parts of the enterprise have other duties besides their CT-related ones, making combining agencies based solely on their CT missions inappropriate. Accordingly, making the many parts of this complex enterprise work together as seamlessly as possible must remain the highest priority to achieve the goal of producing effective homeland security intelligence.

NOTES

1. Mark M. Lowenthal, *Intelligence: From Secrets to Policy*, 4th ed. (Washington, DC: CQ Press, 2009), 8.

2. USA PATRIOT ACT, Public Law 107-296, 115 Stat. 224 (2001).

3. Excerpted from the National Security Act of 1947 in Lowenthal, *Intelligence*, 4th ed., 165.

4. Ibid., 169–170.

5. Ibid., 151.

6. Ibid., 55–67.

7. See William J. Clinton, "Remarks by the President at the 50th Anniversary of the Central Intelligence Agency," press release by the White House, Office of the Press Secretary, September 16, 1997. In these remarks, President Clinton referred to Presidential Decision Directive 35 (PDD-35) of March 2, 1995, which set out the administration's intelligence priorities. PDD-35 itself remains classified. In addition, the fact that, prior to the 9/11 attacks, the IC had not produced a National Intelligence Estimate on the issue of transnational terrorism since 1997 supports terrorism as a low-level intelligence priority. See *The 9/11 Commission Report: Final Report of the National Commission on Terrorist Attacks upon the United States* (New York: W. W. Norton, 2004), 343, http://www.911commission.gov/report/911Report.pdf.

8. http://www.dni.gov/nic/NIC_about.html, accessed March 6, 2011.

9. The Uniting and Strengthening America by Providing Appropriate Tools Required to Intercept and Obstruct Terrorism (USA PATRIOT) Act, October 24, 2001, http://epic.org/privacy/terrorism/hr3162.html; Homeland Security Act of 2002, http://www.dhs.gov/xabout/laws/law_regulation_rule_0011.shtm, accessed September 20, 2011; Intelligence Reform and Terrorism Prevention Act of 2004, http://www.gpoaccess.gov/serialset/creports/intel_reform.html, accessed September 20, 2011. A summary of the act's provisions is available at http://www.fas.org/irp/congress/2004_rpt/s2845-summ.pdf, accessed September 20, 2011.

10. Analysis for the Homeland Security Act of 2002, 3–4.

11. The DNI is responsible for coordinating the activities of IC agencies funded through the National Intelligence Program (NIP). The NIP includes IC activities that go beyond support to military forces. NIP-funded activities are either nonmilitary in nature or transcend the boundaries of a single agency. For a list of specific NIP programs, see Lowenthal, *Intelligence*, 4th ed., 50. The remainder of the IC's budget falls under the Military Intelligence Program (MIP). The MIP funds those portions of the IC that deal exclusively with military matters, such as the individual service intelligence offices. Specific details about the authority given to the DNI are available in the US Senate Committee on Governmental Affairs, *Summary of Intelligence Reform and Terrorism Prevention Act of 2004*, http://www.fas.org/irp/congress/2004_rpt/s2845-summ.pdf, accessed September 22, 2011. For more information, see Mark M. Lowenthal, *Intelligence: From Secrets to Policy*, 3rd ed. (Washington, DC: CQ Press, 2006), 29–54. Also visit the Intelligence Community's website at http://www.intelligence.gov. Adapted from Lowenthal, *Intelligence*, 4th ed., 32; National Security Branch website, http://www.fbi.gov/about-us/nsb/nsb_brochure.pdf, accessed March 6, 2011; and US Senate Committee on Governmental Affairs, *Summary of Intelligence Reform and Terrorism Prevention Act of 2004*, December 6, 2004, http://www.fas.org/irp/congress/2004_rpt/s2845-summ.pdf.

12. For more information, see Lowenthal, *Intelligence,* 3rd ed., 29–54. Also visit the Intelligence Community's website at http://www.intelligence.gov.

13. National Security Branch website, http://www.fbi.gov/about-us/nsb/nsb_brochure .pdf, accessed March 6, 2011.

14. US Senate Committee on Governmental Affairs, *Summary of Intelligence Reform and Terrorism Prevention Act of 2004.*

15. Native American reservations are considered semiautonomous governmental entities within the larger United States. Within certain limits, tribal governments make their own laws and enforce them within reservation boundaries. Thus, any effective homeland security effort must include tribal entities. This is particularly true when reservation boundaries extend to the US borders with Mexico or Canada.

16. Charles P. Nemeth, *Homeland Security: An Introduction to Principles and Practice* (London: CRC Press, 2010), 286–288.

17. Considerable controversy still surrounds what constitutes an "effective" intelligence collection effort at the federal level. In general, the more that police officers move toward the role of intelligence collectors, the greater the possibility that they will alienate the very communities capable of providing relevant intelligence. In the case of some first responders—health care workers, for instance—federal law imposes strict guidelines on what kinds of information can be shared. Finally, preservation of American civil liberties in the face of increased government prying is always a concern

18. National Counterterrorism Center, "NCTC and Information Sharing: Five Years Since 9/11: A Progress Report," September 2006, http://www.tc.gov/docs/report_card _final.pdf; Worldwide Incidents Tracking System, http://www.nctc.gov/wits/witsnextgen .html.

19. Massimo Calabresi, "Wikipedia for Spies: The CIA Discovers Web 2.0," *Time,* April 8, 2009, http://www.time.com/time/nation/article/0,8599,1890084,00.html#ixzz1G7W V7Qdi.

20. WikiLeaks, http://wikileaks.org, accessed March 8, 2011.

21. See http://www.whitehousedrugpolicy.gov/hidta/, accessed March 8, 2011.

CHAPTER 6

Defense Support of Civil Authorities

BERT TUSSING

A secure United States homeland is the nation's first priority, and is a fundamental aspect of the national military strategy.
–US Joint Chiefs of Staff, *Civil Support,* Joint Publication 3-28 (2007)

The sentiment of homeland defense being "job one" in the Department of Defense is a frequently espoused position . . . and genuinely held. However, one has to consider the paradigm of defense in the past century for the United States in order to clarify the real intent behind this sentiment. For most of the uniformed services, homeland defense is a function of national defense. Theirs is a position that precedes the country's emphasis on defense concerns within the territorial confines of the United States, recently reemphasized by the current administration in the president's first Presidential Study Directive: "My highest priority is to keep the American people safe. I believe that Homeland Security is indistinguishable from National Security—conceptually and functionally, they should be thought of together rather than separately. Instead of separating these issues, we must create an integrated, effective, and efficient approach to enhance the national security of the United States."[1]

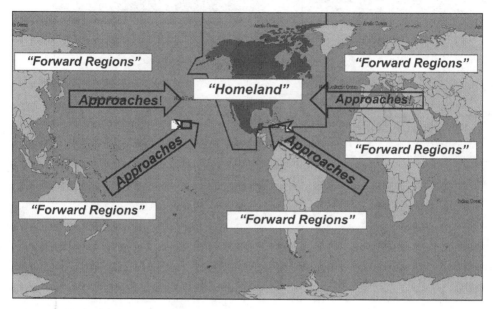

FIGURE 6.1 Active, layered defense

Indeed, one could argue that commencing in the twentieth century, the preponderance of the United States's concerns for defense were focused and played out *away* from the United States. The defense philosophy seems to have become one directed toward engaging the enemy as far away from the United States as possible. By assisting our allies in addressing shared concerns against a common enemy "over there," we precluded the requirement to face the same "over here." The events of 9/11, however, resulted in a violent shift of paradigms that caused us to at least temporarily turn our defense focus "inward." In the midst of that inward focus, however, the DOD still retained the twentieth-century perspective, calling in its *Strategy for Homeland Defense and Civil Support* for an "active, layered defense" of the country that begins in the "forward regions," continues in the "approaches," and finally plays out, as required, in the homeland itself (see Figure 6.1).

Defense, Security, and Civil Support

All of this strategy is interesting enough in discussing the defense dilemma, but defense is not the only element of our concern in providing for the *security* of our country. *Defense* and *security*, after all, are not synonymous. Indeed,

the DOD joins with the rest of the federal government in recognizing homeland defense and homeland security as related, but distinct, functions, and
goes further in delineating its own responsibilities as divided between homeland defense and defense support of civil authorities—also known as civil support. The challenge, therefore, comes from not only understanding the
distinction between homeland security, homeland defense, and civil support,
but likewise understanding why the distinctions are important.

Distinction in Definitions: Homeland Security, Homeland Defense, and Civil Support

We may begin to understand the distinctions through a basic examination of
definitions. The first of these, *homeland security*, has evolved over time. The
first "official" definition of the term was a clear reflection of the events of
9/11, which stimulated the development of the governmental sectors of the
homeland security enterprise. "Homeland Security is a concerted national
effort to prevent terrorist attacks within the United States, to reduce America's vulnerability to terrorism, and minimize the damage and recover from attacks that do occur."[2] This definition, of course, is "terrorism centric," as were
many of the motivations in establishing the Office and then Department of
Homeland Security. Those motivations were, perhaps, understandable, but
ultimately flawed, as highlighted by the first great test of the Department of
Homeland Security: Hurricane Katrina. In spite of the fact that the actual
definition did not change (as portrayed in the 2007 revision of *The National
Strategy for Homeland Security*), the DHS clearly acknowledged that "security"
implied more than preventing, protecting against, and recovering from terrorist attacks:

> The human suffering and staggering physical destruction caused by Kat-
> rina were a reminder that threats come not only from terrorism, but also
> from nature. Indeed, certain non-terrorist events that reach catastrophic
> levels can have significant implications for homeland security. The result-
> ing national consequences and possible cascading effects from these events
> might present potential or perceived vulnerabilities that could be exploited,
> possibly eroding citizens' confidence in our Nation's government and ulti-
> mately increasing our vulnerability to attack. This *Strategy* therefore rec-
> ognizes that effective preparation for catastrophic natural disasters and
> man-made disasters, while not homeland security *per se*, can nevertheless
> increase the security of Homeland.[3]

To be sure, emergency management was a part of the DHS's responsibility from its inception. Borne primarily on the back of the Federal Emergency Management Agency in terms of response and recovery, the function nevertheless has been spread across multiple elements of the DHS in terms of preparedness, prevention, and protection. The latest "definition" of *homeland security*, offered in the *Quadrennial Homeland Security Review*, plainly recognizes as much: "Homeland Security describes the intersection of evolving threats and hazards with traditional governmental and civic responsibilities for civil defense, emergency response, law enforcement, customs, border patrol and immigration."[4]

This is all important to our discussion, because the slow acknowledgment of emergency management in the DHS's strategy documents has been mirrored in a fashion by the DOD's approach to homeland security. The dual path to domestic operations for the DOD is delineated by its own characterization of the same: "The Department of Defense protects the homeland through two distinct but interrelated missions: Homeland Defense and Civil Support."[5] The DOD's definition of *homeland defense* is what one might expect of the Pentagon: "the protection of United States sovereignty, territory, domestic population and critical defense infrastructure against external threats and aggression or other threats as directed by the President."[6]

There is some room for interpretation (and thoughtful debate) over a clear delineation between "external" and "internal" threats. The distinction may be a reflection of the DOD's intent to leave "internal" domestic threats under the purview of federal, state, and local law enforcement, while reserving response to "external" aggressors for the military. But the nuances of that definitional division are beyond the scope of this chapter. For our purposes it is important to note only that the claim to "defense" as a mission falls exclusively under the *lead* of the DOD.

The emphasis here is deliberate—because in nearly all other functions of domestic operations within the territorial confines of the United States, the DOD casts itself in a *support* role. Once again, the DOD's definition of terms attempts to remove all doubt in this regard. "Civil Support is that support provided in response to requests for assistance from civil authorities for special events, domestic emergencies, designated law enforcement support and other domestic activities."[7] The divisions of support—emergency response and (as directed) support to law enforcement—encompass a potentially wide range of activities that will be addressed in this chapter. The underlying philosophy of the DOD is to complement civilian capabilities, on the one hand, and supplement them, on the other. But under no circumstances will the DOD seek to gain charge of civil emergency management functions, either in preparedness and prevention or in response and recovery. The very term *defense support of civil authorities* is an indication of the new sensitivity in the DOD's mindset. In the past, the terminology was "defense support *to* civil authorities." *To* was abandoned in favor of the word *of* in order to indicate less of a directive and more of a supporting stance. In a recent symposium hosted by the US Army War College's Center for Strategic Leadership, the Honorable Paul Stockton, assistant secretary of homeland defense and America's security, reemphasized this position:

> We understand all disasters are local. From that, we get a second thing that is good about the National Response Framework: we understand the distribution of roles and responsibilities—between federal agencies, and between the federal, state and local authorities. We understand that ultimately we are supporting first responders, throughout the system. . . . We know what first responders do. We support them.
>
> [As for the] States; Governors are sovereign. They are responsible for the public safety of their citizens. They are the independently elected Chief Executives of their states—they don't work for the President . . . and they are in position to take the lead in their states when a catastrophe rises to a certain level. We understand their special role.
>
> And then [as for the] federal family . . . We're in support of FEMA and the Department of Homeland Security. The Department of Defense is *not* going to be in the lead for catastrophic response.[8]

The philosophical underpinnings of this marked reticence are twofold. From the perspective of the DOD itself, it is not indicative of an intent to escape responsibility. It is reflective of an internal tension in the DOD between its charge (and desire) to perform domestic support operations and its ultimate responsibility to fight and win the nation's wars. The leadership of the Pentagon is not being disingenuous behind the previously cited euphemism of homeland defense (and, by implication, civil support) being "job one." But another commonly held euphemism is one connoting the military's "day job"—fighting and winning the nation's wars, or at least being prepared to do so—which also has a compelling hold on the armed forces' leadership. Only recently in the military have forces been organized, trained, and equipped specifically—and in some cases exclusively—for civil support missions. Balancing the inevitable restraints of constrained resources, in terms of equipment, expertise, and manpower, is a challenge faced by both the Office of the Secretary of Defense and the chairman of the Joint Chiefs of Staff. It is a balance that must be approached carefully.

Trust at Arm's Length

This heading describes the Pentagon's reticence—but it is, figuratively, only one-half of the issue. Arguably, there is an equal if not greater reticence to the military's role in domestic operations, held by the very civil authorities envisioned to receive that support. At every level of government—federal, state, and local—there is a hesitance emanating from the perception that the DOD's uniformed forces will, indeed, "take charge"—a charge that civil authorities are not inclined to surrender. All protests from the Pentagon to the contrary, civil officials are frequently concerned that the qualities we admire most in those forces on the battlefield will surface as unwelcomed intrusions on the home front.

Precedents from the earliest days of our nation's history may help to explain the American trust of its military "at arm's length." Colonial umbrage over the British military asserting itself as an occupying force, through mechanisms like the Quartering Acts,[9] left a spirit of distrust for military power and the Third Amendment to the Constitution. These misgivings may have been made manifest in the forefathers' deliberate design in our Constitution to contain the notion of expanding the federal army and to balance (and keep in check) the same by establishing and maintaining the sovereign states' militias.

This attitude continued throughout our history, surfacing again in the oft-cited Posse Comitatus Act (PCA): "Whoever, except in cases and under circumstances expressly authorized by the Constitution or Act of Congress, willfully uses any part of the Army or Air Force[10] as a posse comitatus or otherwise to execute the laws shall be fined under this title or imprisoned not more than two years, or both."[11] Many aspects of this act are misunderstood. Misconceptions include a belief that all military forces are prohibited from performing law enforcement functions (untrue for either the Coast Guard, authorized to perform law enforcement functions under Title 14 of the United States Code, or the National Guard, serving in anything other than a federalized status).[12] Likewise, this misperception fails to take into account the occasions when the PCA was suspended by either the executive branch or congressional order.[13] Finally, detractors fail to understand that support to law enforcement entities by means *other* than arrest, apprehension, incarceration, or interrogation is not prohibited by either the provisions or the interpretations of this legislation. Operation Jump Start[14] in the last administration and similar activities authorized by the Obama administration in support of customs and border patrol along the southwestern border of the United States are both examples of military forces supporting law enforcement agencies logistically, in training, in information operations, in specialized equipment operation, and otherwise.

Having said all that, it is the *spirit*, if not the letter, of the law that defines the value of Posse Comitatus in portraying the American ethos. Reminiscent of the reaction against British overlords and the army in the Reconstructionist South, the nation's attitude is one set against employing our soldiers as policemen. Even today, in the atmosphere of confidence and esteem the armed forces enjoy from our citizenry, the American psyche is still set on retaining its military as its servant—not its overseer. Fortunately, those sentiments have no greater set of supporters than the leadership of the nation's military. In the all-volunteer force that has characterized our military since the elimination of the draft in 1973, one may safely contend that the world has never seen a military more clearly "of the people, by the people," and therefore emphatically "for the people."

Beyond Philosophy to Application

All of the preceding discussion could be ascribed to lofty-sounding rhetoric, were it not for the fact that our strategies and doctrine within the military, and statutes and policy without, ensure the practical manifestation of the erstwhile philosophy. Moreover, this manifestation is provided for at every level of government.

The Robert T. Stafford Act, cited elsewhere in this book, outlines the conditions and limitations by which the interagency components of the federal government will be applied in response to requests for assistance from sovereign states and territories of the United States. In consonance with the Federal Response Plan, the National Response Plan that followed it, and what has since evolved to become the National Response Framework, the Stafford Act is founded upon the expectation that federal assistance following a major disaster will be rendered only after the affected state and local government capabilities have been stressed or exceeded. Even then, said assistance will most frequently be held until specifically requested by those states.

The most visible manifestation of the federal response, when requested, is the military. Likewise, it is the clearest depiction of the federal employment philosophy that calls for its resources to be "last in, first out." The Advisory Panel on Department of Defense Capabilities for Support of Civil Authorities After Certain Incidents exemplifies this notion in its report *Before Disaster Strikes: Imperatives for Enhancing Defense Support of Civil Authorities*, when it notes succinctly: "As the Federal Response Plan was replaced by newer plans and, most recently, the National Response Framework (NRF), the Department of Defense was still considered a resource of last resort, to be called on when alternative federal response assets were depleted or unavailable."[15]

Homeland Security Presidential Directive 5, Management of Domestic Incidents, addresses the role of the active component directly, but recognizes both the domestic and the international responsibilities of the DOD. Early in the HSPD, the primacy of the DHS in coordinating federal resources in response and recovery operations is reinforced: "The Secretary of Homeland Security is the principal Federal official for domestic incident management. Pursuant to the Homeland Security Act of 2002, the Secretary is responsible for coordinating Federal operations within the United States to prepare for, respond to, and recover from terrorist attacks, major disasters, and other emergencies. The Secretary shall coordinate the Federal Government's resources utilized in response to or recovery from terrorist attacks, major disasters, or other emergencies." Five paragraphs later, however, the directive notes, "Nothing in this directive impairs or otherwise affects the authority of the Secretary of Defense over the Department of Defense, including the chain of command for military forces from the President as Commander-in-Chief, to the Secretary of Defense, to the commanders of military forces. . . . The Secretary of Defense shall provide military support to civil authorities for domestic incidents as directed by the president. . . . [The] Secretary of Defense and the Secretary [of Homeland Security] shall establish appropriate relationships and mechanisms for cooperation and coordination between their two Departments."[16]

Accordingly, the military component of the federal response is reasonably well understood. Moreover, the application of the military component of the federal response at the state and local levels of government is also well understood, under the guidance of the National Response Framework. Facilitated by the National Incident Management System, the NRF provides the structure and mechanisms for federal policy involving incident management. The tenets of the same apply, therefore, to all federal activities, including the DOD.[17] In attaining that compliance, the military has aligned itself directly with the five key principles of the NRF (see Figure 6.2).

1. Engaged Partnership
2. Scalable, Flexible and Adaptable Operational Capabilities
3. Unity of Effort through Unity of Command
4. Readiness to Act
5. Tiered Response

FIGURE 6.2 Key principles of the NRF

1. **Engaged Partnership**—As a support function of the federal response, the DOD will consistently seek out opportunities with other elements of the interagency to ensure that both complementary and supplementary requirements are met in preparing for, and responding to, incidents.

2. **Scalable, Flexible, and Adaptable Operational Capabilities**—The DOD is dedicated to providing support to civil authorities at all levels of government (federal, state, local, tribal, or territorial) when required, and with the required assets. Utilizing both active and reserve components, to include the National Guard, the military can scale its response to meet the need of the moment, without wasting limited resources. Conversely, the DOD will not impose itself upon the civil authorities until requested, and as directed by the president.

3. **Unity of Effort Through Unity of Command**—The purpose of unity of command, as defined by the DOD, is to "ensure unity of effort."[18] In a strictly military environment this is relatively easy to achieve, as responding forces are, more often than not, under one continuous chain of authority. In a civil-military environment, however, this cut-and-dried construct is far more elusive, as the disparate responders and stakeholders are seldom, if ever, under one command, and may in fact be from many different agencies and organizations. Accordingly, recognizing the need to arrive at unity of effort from a variety of different perspectives, and in recognition of its support status in serving those perspectives, the military has shifted its traditional focus away from "command and control," to more of an attitude of "collaboration and coordination."[19]

4. **Readiness to Act**—Traditionally a hallmark of the military, this principle is effectively unattainable without an engaged partnership and a clear understanding of how unity of effort is attained in response to disaster or other support to civil authorities. Readiness, however, is not attained in response; it is attained through preparation. In that light, the department looks for opportunities to first plan for responses requiring civil-military integration and then exercise the plans.

5. **Tiered Response**—The NRF is structured on the concept of tiered response to emergencies and disasters. Expectations are that emergency management begins at the local level of government. As a crisis begins to exceed both the capabilities and capacities of the local elements, response elements from the state, tailored for the requirement, will reinforce and strengthen the local response. If this new combination of state and local resources is further stressed, the affected governor may turn to other states for assistance thorough the Emergency Management Assistance Compact,[20] or request federal disaster assistance through the Stafford Act. At each level of response, the military may (as required) be a part of the supplementary or complementary reinforcement addressing the needs of the state. The states' National Guard forces serve as the de facto first responders of the military's forces. Not only is the National Guard, with thirty-two hundred units positioned nationwide, likely to be the military force in closest proximity to the problem, but it is also the force most associated with (familiar with) civil authorities charged with meeting those requirements. By extension, National Guard forces from adjoining states are most likely to be a vital component of a supporting states' EMAC response. And as the additional capacities and capabilities of the federal government are introduced to support a state in crisis, the appreciable resources and manpower of the active component military can be tapped as an emergency measure.

Long-held and still-evolving initiatives between the National Guard and their fellow stakeholders in a state's domestic security make introduction of its forces a seamless, if not integrated, transition during crisis. The greater challenge, encumbered by the lack of familiarity and relationships enjoyed by the National Guard, is folding federal military forces into the plans and operations of disparate states and localities. In meeting that challenge, the DOD has taken deliberate measures to integrate strategy, planning, and operational capabilities for homeland defense and civil support missions more fully into its

• Aviation	• Medical Support
• Engineering	• Communications
• Ground Transportation	• CBRN
• Logistics	• Security
• Maintenance	• Command and Control

FIGURE 6.3 The National Guard's ten essential capabilities

extant processes. (Some specific measures devoted to these ends will be addressed later in this chapter.)

The distinction between capabilities and capacities in these discussions is an important one. Many of the same capabilities that reside in the military are contained in the civilian world, in both the public and the private sectors. However, in times of crisis, capabilities are only the first part of the equation; having enough capability is the deciding factor. Accordingly, emergency managers, law enforcement officials, and other civil authorities are well served by understanding the strengths and limitations of their own capabilities and prepared—as required, available, and permitted—to supplement them through the military.

The nature and depth of these capabilities are extensive, and certainly deserving of consideration in preparing for and responding to a crisis. The National Guard, in fact, has identified ten essential capabilities[21] that may be vital in both crisis management and consequence management in their states (see Figure 6.3). Of course, these capabilities would apply equally to recommending federal military forces, as a crisis expands in scope or severity.

An *Aviation* capability is liable to exist to a certain extent among some civil authorities—federal, state, and local—but nothing like the requirements the country has witnessed in response to hurricanes in the Gulf, wildfires in the West, and so on. *Engineering* assets certainly reside outside of the military, but the uniformed services' rapid response in supplementing the same has proved essential in stemming floods, clearing blocked lines of communication, and a host of other situations. Similarly, military augmentation in *Ground Transportation* and *Logistics and Maintenance* may be intuitive to crisis planners. Less intuitive, perhaps, is additional capacity attainable through the military in *Medical Support. Communications*, including the capacity to frequently link diverse systems that cannot otherwise attain interoperability, may not be a unique capability of the military, but is certainly a valuable one. The threat of a *CBRNE* (chemical, biological, radiological, nuclear, or high-yield explosive) incident, whether accidental or deliberate, highlights a widely enhanced capability available through the military, but those military capabilities are genuinely unique to the US military in that many of them are *not* "dual-use," that is, they are not readily available for both overseas and home missions. Rather, such military capabilities are trained, organized, and equipped primarily, and in some cases exclusively, for domestic response. Also intuitive, though absolutely essential, is the inherent *Security* capability provided by the introduction of a military force. History has consistently demonstrated the best and worst of human behavior in times of crisis. Frequently, no other facet of response and recovery may be introduced until a secure environment is established. Disciplined forces, schooled in the appropriate application, and suspension of force are the surest means of providing that environment. Finally, *Command and Control*, as previously noted, may be unattainable beyond the military element of disaster response. However, the construct and mechanisms that provide for that command and control may further lend themselves to "collaboration and coordination" in the combined civil-military response.

Beyond these "ten essentials" may be the most important capability the armed forces bring to the civil-military team: their core competency in *planning*. The more familiar one grows with the military, the more impressed one may become with its ability to first define, and then clarify, mission requirements. Having done so, the military can assist in coordinating the means to meet those requirements in mobilizing, deploying, and employing a host of diverse units and their accompanying resources to effectively and efficiently accomplish the task at hand. This planning capacity is developed over years of progression from tactical application of small units to operational coordination of combined arms and accompanying logistics and finally to an appreciation of the role and utility of the military in a strategic environment. That environment spans the gamut from interagency to intergovernmental and international.

In working through this progression from tactical to operational to strategic, the military is trained in contingency planning—a process that is highly structured, supports iterative concurrent and parallel planning activities, and produces thoroughly and fully coordinated contingency plans (CONPLANs). By extension the armed forces are equally schooled in "crisis action planning" that allows them to draw from the CONPLAN product to support the dynamic requirements of changing events.[22]

This is not to imply, even momentarily, that the military seeks to "take charge" of plans devoted to civil security. It is, however, an acknowledgment of potential synergies to be drawn from the civil authorities' knowledge of their requirements—along a spectrum of routine to emergency to crisis response—and the military's ability to integrate its efforts, and those of its civil superiors, in meeting those requirements.

A formal example of the envisioned civil-military planning partnership is seen in the Task Force for Emergency Readiness (TFER) initiative,[23] a program that enlisted National Guard officers to work with state emergency managers in writing comprehensive "state" homeland security plans to address specific catastrophic scenarios.[24] FEMA is currently funding five pilot states (Hawaii, Massachusetts, South Carolina, Washington, and West Virginia) through the initiative, with the intent of expanding TFER to all states.

In all of these affairs, however, it is important to keep in mind the "organizational construct" delineated by the DOD in approaching homeland defense and civil support. As outlined in the *Strategy for Homeland Defense and Civil Support*, the DOD's activities to secure the United States generally fall under three categories: lead, support, and enable.

- **Lead** has to do with those activities dedicated to defending the homeland. In this regime the DOD is decidedly the lead federal agency. The missions associated with the department's lead responsibilities include those actions taken to dissuade, deter, and, as necessary, defeat attacks upon the United States, our population, and our critical infrastructure.
- **Support** actions are those taken, at the direction of the president or the secretary of defense, in support of civil authorities. When responding as a part of a federal component, DOD forces would fall under the direction of a designated lead federal agency. In the federal capacity, the military is listed as being in support of every Emergency Support Function (ESF) of the NRF, except Emergency Support Function 3, Public Works and Engineering. The ESF alone lists the DOD as the coordinator and primary agency, under the auspices of the United States Army Corps of Engineers.
- **Enable** indicates the DOD's desire to enhance and improve the internal defense and security capabilities and capacities of its domestic and international partners. In the domestic environment, for instance, the

DOD has supported the DHS in initiatives such as intelligence analysis, training, infrastructure support, and more.

Evaluation Criteria for DOD Support

For all of the DOD's willingness to engage in civil support missions, the previously described "internal tension" borne of its domestic and overseas missions forces the DOD's commitments to civil support to be measured and occasionally constrained. Moreover, the restraints a free people would predictably want to see over a marshal force may also recommend a balanced application of power, especially when placed among the citizenry the military is sworn to serve. As a function of the same, six "evaluation criteria" have been established by the department to evaluate all requests by US civil authorities for military assistance (see Figure 6.4).[25]

> - Legality   • Cost
> - Lethality   • Readiness
> - Risk   • Appropriateness

FIGURE 6.4 Evaluation criteria

- **Legality**—examining whether the requested support would be in compliance with laws and presidential directives
- **Lethality**—questioning whether the use of force, by or against DOD personnel, is likely or expected
- **Risk**—ensuring the mission can be accomplished safely, in terms of both the members performing the mission and those for whom the mission is launched, and if there are concerns from either perspective, determining whether they can be mitigated by equipment or training
- **Cost**—raising the unfortunate questions of who will be paying for resource expenditures and what impact those expenditures will have on the Defense Department's budget
- **Readiness**—questioning the short-term and longer-term impact on the department's ability to perform its "primary mission" of defending the United States
- **Appropriateness**—addressing the question of who normally performs and is best suited to perform the mission at hand

Assuming that these "tests" are met, the DOD is prepared to support the homeland security mission through its homeland defense and civil-support missions. It approaches the support through an operational framework constructed around the concepts of Prepare, Detect, Deter, Prevent, Defend, and Respond and Recover.

- **Prepare**—The military prepares across a wide range of activities, beginning with planning, continuing to conduct exercises to validate the plan, organizing training and equipping to provide for the ways and means to support the civil-support ends, and so on. Another notable aspect of the DOD's preparation is found in its various assessment capabilities, working both independently and with civilian counterparts. These capabilities allow for gathering, analyzing, and disseminating information in order to assist in the identification of threats and hazards. Having done so, they can then contribute to the determination of vulnerabilities and mitigation of their effects.

- **Detect**—In domestic operations, the DOD maintains a judicious balance between detecting and monitoring potential threats against our people and observing the rights of those people to be free of illegal intrusion. On the one hand, for example, the DOD is charged with leading the US government's efforts in detecting and monitoring aerial and maritime transit of illegal drugs into the United States.[26] On the other hand, the DOD is explicitly forbidden by its own regulations from gathering and maintaining information on US persons or their activities.[27] Between these two standards lies the DOD's ability to routinely support federal law enforcement agencies and border-monitoring operations using capabilities and capacities almost unique to the military.[28]

- **Deter**—The mere presence of uniformed forces may have a calming effect in certain domestic crises and a deterring effect in others. This effect may be deliberate in design or inadvertent, but the end results remain the same. Referring again to Operation Jump Start and support missions that have followed it along the southwestern border of the United States, a residual effect of having troops engaged in engineering, monitoring, and detection missions was an accompanying deterrent value against illegal trafficking across the border.

- **Prevent**—Prevention, as it pertains to US military federal force operations in a domestic environment, is deliberately constrained. Nevertheless, the DOD is empowered to support federal law enforcement, primarily through intelligence analytical support, whereby it may detect threats and provide for their intediction. This interdiction may be accomplished by US law enforcement agencies or those of partner nations in a common pursuit. By way of example, these capabilities are rendered routinely by the DOD as members of the Joint Terrorism Task Forces, led by the Federal Bureau of Investigation.

- **Defend**—Simply stated, defense is the raison d'être of the DOD. By far the vast preponderance of its forces and their resources are devoted to it. Civil support missions are most often performed by units whose equipment and expertise have been temporarily tailored to meet the requirements of an emergency response but whose primary function is combat, combat support, or combat service support. Nevertheless, defense actions may be either passive—such as seen in the construction of obstacles or barriers—or through the traditional notion of closing with and destroying an adversary.

- **Respond and Recover**—DOD defines *response*, as it relates to civil support, as "the ability to rapidly and effectively support civil authorities in providing appropriate support to law enforcement agencies, and assistance in managing the consequences of disasters and catastrophes, including natural, man-made or terrorist incidents."[29] The DOD's focus in response operations is in saving lives, reducing further suffering, and preventing and mitigating greater property damage in support of emergency management officials. Likewise, the DOD is devoted to the support of law enforcement agencies in preventing terrorist incidents. In either instance, introduction of military forces for civil support, whether federal or state resources, implies that there is a requirement for either the unique capabilities or additional capacities that reside therein. Said introduction is envisioned as "an essential, decisive, time critical contribution."[30] It is not envisioned to be a sustained commitment of resources, employed beyond immediate response requirements, as part of a long-term recovery effort. With the exception of the United States Army Corps of Engineers, the DOD's role is one more inclined in these endeavors toward emergency response and stabilization—not rebuilding.

Consequence Management and Crisis Management

It is important, therefore, to understand the nature and limits of the military's use in domestic operations. An overview depicts military support operations falling generally under two broad concepts: consequence management and crisis management. The DOD's definition of *consequence management* is "actions taken to maintain or restore essential services and manage and mitigate problems resulting from disasters and catastrophes, including natural, man-made or terrorist incidents."[31] This definition should remind us that actions can, and should, be taken ahead of emergencies, disasters, or catastrophic incidents to ensure that "essential services" are preserved in order to better manage the suffering and destruction predictably associated with these events. Once an incident has occurred, maintenance, restoration, and mitigation should come as functions of civil-military preparations, including plans that have been drawn together under civil authorities. They should incorporate insights and concerns, requirements, and responsibilities of all stakeholders, from both the public and the private sectors. Plans developed should be run in an exercise to identify weaknesses to be overcome and to instill a cooperative understanding of roles and responsibilities in response and recovery operations.

Crisis management is focused on the terrorist threat. According to the DOD, crisis management includes "measures to identify, acquire, and plan the use of resources needed to anticipate, prevent, and/or resolve a threat or act of terrorism. It is predominantly a law enforcement response, normally executed under federal law."[32] As the definition implies, the federal lead agency in crisis management operations will be the Department of Justice. Even more than consequence management, the success of crisis management hinges upon preparations and actions taken before an incident occurs, with the intent that the incident will be precluded. Because we can never assume perfect success, however, the military response to a credible threat or act of terrorism may require both crisis management and consequence management operations, which may overlap in the process.[33]

It may be important to note that both HSPD-5 and the NRF combine these concepts under the broader concept of incident management. The DOD continues to hold them separate and distinct for purposes of planning and conducting military operations. *Joint Publication 3-28* explains this apparent departure from a common federal approach:

> The application of crisis management and consequence management is unique and separate in the context of planning and conducting military operations with non-DOD actors, including local civil authorities and first responders, that are generally not familiar with US military terms, definitions, and doctrine. When working with non-DOD actors/partners,

especially in an emergency situation, clear, effective, and mutually understandable communication is essential. DOD elements will be able to work much more seamlessly, efficiently, and productively by employing operational concepts and terms that other departments, agencies, and authorities already understand.[34]

Categories of Civil Support

Under this consequence management–crisis management overview, the DOD divides civil support into three categories, already seen in its definition: domestic emergencies, designated law enforcement support, and other activities. Most of the focus of this chapter so far has been devoted to the first category, as it pertains to civil-military preparations for and response to natural and man-made disasters. Within potential man-made disasters, an area of great concern is CBRNE incidents. These may be deliberate (a major source of our terrorist concerns) or accidental; Chernobyl (Russia) and Bophal (India) are both examples of horrific accidents, sometimes referred to as "technological disasters," which resulted in massive loss of life, environmental destruction, and human suffering.

Because of the pronounced concern over employing US military forces in law enforcement functions, support to law enforcement entities will always be approached warily. Generally designed to support and restore public health services and civil order, DOD support may take form in augmenting federal, state, or local officials in terms of personnel, equipment, expertise, or any combination of the three. As in all civil-support activities, these personnel and resources would be placed under the primary jurisdiction of the affected state and local governments, or in support of federal law enforcement agencies in the execution of their own missions. Support in these regards can span from animal- and plant-disease eradication to postal support, but for our purposes the following areas of particular support are highlighted.

Border Security and Immigration Enforcement Support

Recent operations in support of the Customs and Border Protection Division of the DHS have highlighted the role, and potential, of the military in these endeavors. Operation Jump Start (cited previously) saw more than twenty-nine thousand National Guardsmen supporting border-patrol operations, logistically and administratively, by operating detection systems, providing communication support, analyzing border-related intelligence, providing additional aviation assets, and through various other activities that allowed the

CBP to "return badges to the border."[35] This is in perfect consonance with the DOD's tradition of providing technical assistance, services, and facilities support in this regime, if only on a temporary basis. It is important to note, however, that this support does not extend to actual service in traditional law enforcement functions. As noted by the Honorable David V. Aguilar, chief of the border patrol, "Law enforcement along the border between the ports of entry will remain the responsibility of Border Patrol agents. The National Guard will play no direct law enforcement role in the apprehension, custodial care or security of those who are detained."[36]

Equipment and Other Support for Law Enforcement

By far the majority of requests coming to the military for support of law enforcement officials are connected with borrowing or maintaining military equipment or the information obtained from the use of that equipment. As noted above, a significant amount of the support that has gone to the CBP fits this description. But even in this support, the military must remain judiciously aware of the extent of, and the limitations to, its support, particularly as it pertains to the rights and privacy of our citizenry. For example, if operating equipment in support of law enforcement officials, the military may be more constrained in its use than the agencies they are supporting. DOD intelligence components may provide law enforcement officials "incidentally acquired information" reasonably believed to indicate violation of federal, state, or local laws, but they may not actively plan for and pursue that information or continue to collect the same beyond the incidental acquisition.[37] Likewise, support of law enforcement activities beyond information collection will generally follow the letter and intent of the Posse Comitatus Act, to wit:

> The prohibition on the use of military personnel "as a *posse comitatus* or otherwise to execute the laws" prohibits the following forms of direct assistance:
> . . . Interdiction of a vehicle, vessel, aircraft, or other similar activity.
> . . . A search or seizure.
> . . . An arrest, apprehension, stop and frisk, or similar activity.
> . . . Use of military personnel for surveillance or pursuit of individuals, or as undercover agents, informants, investigators, or interrogators.[38]

Counterdrug Operations

DOD resources were used frequently in the late 1980s in support of counterdrug operations. In 1989, in fact, the secretary of defense announced the activation of Joint Task Force Six (JTF-6), specifically devoted to counterdrug missions in support of federal, regional, state, and local law enforcement agencies throughout the United States.[39] With the activation of the United States Northern Command, JTF-6 was redesignated Joint Task Force–North (JTF-N), and their mission focus shifted from counterdrug to counterterrorism. Nevertheless, the military retains its role in counterdrug support in missions that include transportation (ground and air), training, detecting, monitoring and communicating the movement of traffic, communications, linguistics support, intelligence analysis, and more.[40]

As with all functions surrounding domestic law enforcement functions, the military remains in a deliberate support stance—never taking a role until called upon at the request of the duly constituted civilian authority. Moreover, even the roles that the military assumes at the behest of the civil authority in counterdrug operations will not deviate from the *posse comitatus* restrictions held in every other aspect of its support to civil law enforcement. As such, the military will not arrest, apprehend, detain, or interrogate. Likewise, ensuring against inadvertent violations of privacy and civil liberties remains at the forefront of the DOD's thinking. As if to reinforce this notion, the secretary of defense himself expressly reserves approval authority for requests for listening and observation posts and mobile patrols or requests to target or track suspicious buildings, vehicles, vessels, and persons in the United States.[41]

Counterterrorism Operations

In spite of the potential ramifications of terrorist attacks against the "sovereignty, territory, [and] domestic population" of the United States—the definitional focus of homeland defense—the DOJ is without question the lead federal agency in matters of preventing, protecting against, and responding to terrorist attacks. As stated in *Joint Publication 3-28, Civil Support:* "The Attorney General, acting through the FBI and in coordination with the heads of other federal departments . . . , coordinates domestic intelligence collection and the activities of the law enforcement community to detect, prevent, preempt, and disrupt terrorist attacks, and to identify the perpetrators and bring them to justice in the event of a terrorist attack."[42] The publication goes on to describe a potential "overlap" in dealing with terrorist activities between crisis management functions and consequence management functions. In the former, the DOJ (through the FBI) is the primary agency involved in preventing or resolving terrorist threats. In the latter, the DHS (through FEMA) assumes the lead in emergency response or mitigation activities to lessen the consequence of attacks or incidents. In both cases, through activities already described in this chapter, the DOD may anticipate involvement through direct support activities.

Civil Disturbance Operations

When requested by a state or territorial governor or its legislature, or when in the estimate of the president the authorities of a given state are incapable of protecting its citizenry or infrastructure through maintenance of public order, the armed forces of the United States (to include the National Guard) may be deployed to restore law and order. Under the auspices of the Insurrection Act of 1807, this authority has been used a number of times in US history.[43] Most recently, the act was exercised in 1992 in response to a request from the governor of California to quell riots in Los Angeles.[44]

As in all activities wherein the military is called upon to take over traditional civil functions, the focus on military assistance in civil disturbance missions is to provide whatever assistance is required only when requested, and only for as long as it takes for duly constituted civil authorities to regain control. Accordingly, the DOD directive that regulates these missions rests on a philosophical foundation that the primary responsibility for protecting life and property and maintaining law and order is vested in the state and local governments and that any employment of military forces in support of law enforcement operations shall maintain the primacy of civilian authority. The DOD directive regulating the employment of military forces in these circumstances makes the issue clear: "The DOD Components shall not take charge of any function of civil government unless absolutely necessary under conditions of extreme emergency. Any commander who is directed, or undertakes, to control such functions shall strictly limit military actions to the emergency needs, and shall facilitate the reestablishment of civil responsibility at the earliest time possible."[45]

Other Activities

A number of other examples of military support to civilian events fall outside of what might be considered the normal scope of DOD activities. Many of these are undertaken as a public service, as a function of availability, appropriateness, and other factors alluded to earlier in the chapter. Many of the activities are at once familiar and understated, such as the military's support to special security requirements surrounding "National Special Security Events" (e.g., political conventions, the presidential inauguration, state funerals, and so on). Likewise, periodic planned support can be garnered from the military

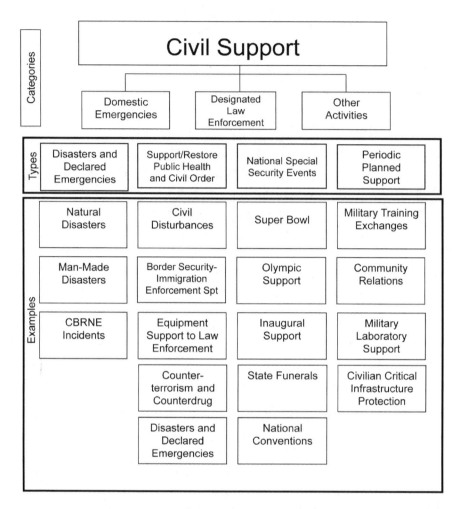

FIGURE 6.5 Civil-support operation categories and operational types

to enhance civil-military relations within local communities. Activities of this sort include military training exchanges (e.g., training support to local first responders) and community relations (public affairs activities featuring organizations like the Blue Angels, the US Navy's Flight Demonstration Squadron, the US Army's Golden Knight parachute team, or the US Marine Corps Silent Drill Team).

Figure 6.5 provides a graphic depiction of the types of civil support missions the military will routinely support. The forces that respond to these missions will be described in the next section.

Military Forces in Support of Civil Authorities

In the most general sense, military forces that may be assigned to support civil authorities may be from either the active or the reserve components. The active component refers to those forces serving full-time duty in the active military service of the United States.[46] The reserve component of the military is generally divided between the Armed Forces Service Reserves and the National Guard. The Guard, then, is further divided into the states' Army National Guard and the Air National Guard.[47]

As previously described, the National Guard is the military component most frequently associated with civil-support operations. In all but the most extreme circumstances, the Guard is the force of choice for civil support: it is literally and figuratively the closest force to the civil authorities that would require the support and is more likely to have an established relationship with their agencies. The states' adjutants general, who command the Guard's forces, respond directly to their respective governors in most operations. Their forces are most familiar with their localities and, therefore, the localities' requirements in times of duress.

An adjutant general once helped to characterize the requirement for military forces in response to state and local requirements. He noted that 94 percent of the time, local governments were capable of taking care of emergencies that strike their areas. In 4 percent of the remaining time, additional assistance provided by the respective state—to include its National Guard—would fulfill the requirements. In only 2 percent of the time were capabilities and capacities beyond those contained in state and local governments required in response to major disasters or catastrophic events. At that point, the additional capacity of the federal government, to include the active-duty military, would be called upon to complement or supplement the extant capabilities responding to and through state and local governments.[48]

The Combatant Command responsible for conducting civil-support operations is NORTHCOM.[49] NORTHCOM is in charge of the military's active component in both civil-support and homeland defense operations. Its area of operations (AOR) includes the continental United States, Alaska, Puerto Rico, and the US Virgin Islands. Its naval component, in cooperation with the US Coast Guard, is responsible for civil-support activities in the waters surrounding its AOR out to approximately five hundred nautical miles. Whereas the command maintains a robust cooperation with the National Guard, particularly through its association with the National Guard Bureau,

FIGURE 6.6 US Northern Command

it does not exercise command over those forces. NORTHCOM, rather, is charged with the creation and maintenance of plans that will supplement and complement those of the states and territories (see Figure 6.6).

NORTHCOM organizes and executes its missions through its assigned service components, its designated functional components, and its subordinate standing joint task forces. The service components are: the United States Army North, located in Fort Sam Houston, Texas; the 1st Air Force, headquartered at Tindall Air Force Base in Florida; the US Fleet Forces Command out of Norfolk, Virginia; and the 4th Marine Division out of New Orleans, Louisiana. There are currently five standing JTFs:

- **Joint Force Headquarters–National Capital Region (JFHQ-NCR):** responsible for land-based homeland defense, defense support of civil authorities, and incident management in the National Capital Region
- **Joint Task Force–Alaska:** charged with, in coordination with other government agencies, deterring, detecting, preventing, and, as necessary, defeating threats within the Alaska Joint Operations Area in order to

protect US territory, citizens, and interests and, as directed, conduct civil support
- **Joint Task Force–Civil Support (JTF-CS):** anticipates, plans, and integrates US NORTHCOM chemical, biological, radiological, nuclear, and high-yield explosive consequence management operations; when directed, JTF-CS commands and controls designated DOD forces to assist federal, state, local, and tribal partners in saving lives, preventing further injury, and providing critical support to enable community recovery
- **Joint Task Force–North:** tasked with supporting our nation's federal law enforcement agencies in the interdiction of suspected transnational threats within and along the approaches to the continental United States; as previously noted, JTF-N was originally established as Joint Task Force Six (JTF-6), but was redesignated in 2004, as its primary mission focus shifted from antidrug to antiterrorism activities
- **US Northern Command Standing Joint Force Headquarters (NC/SJFHQ):** provides the commander of US NORTHCOM with the scalable capability to form the core of a joint task force or to augment multiple organizations in order to anticipate and conduct homeland defense and civil-support missions anywhere in the US NORTHCOM area of responsibility during planned or crisis operations; it should be noted that this headquarters is equally dedicated to augmenting states' National Guard headquarters, as required, to provide for the integration of additional units and assets, active and reserve, in responding to natural or man-made disasters

It is important to note that all of these JTFs are composed of active, reserve, and National Guard members from the US Army, Navy, Air Force, and Marines. Moreover, in the execution of their mission, both JTF-CS and NC/SJFHQ are prepared to fall in support of states' units already engaged in response and recovery operations following a major disaster or catastrophic event.

Title 10, Title 32, and State Active-Duty Forces

The choice of military forces to respond to disasters is more than a matter of convenience. Indeed, the choice, and authorities over the chosen force, is tied to tenants of federalism that are embedded in the earliest concerns surrounding the Constitution of the United States. Application of military force, even in planning for or responding to disaster, raises questions over the limits of federal power against state sovereignty, on the one hand, and the authority

FIGURE 6.7 The National Guard

and responsibility of the president in providing for the protection of the citizenry, on the other.

It should come as no surprise that the fifty-four governors of the states and territories of the United States would want control of military forces in their own regions. They are, as Secretary Stockton assessed, "the independently elected Chief Executives" of what we recognize as separate sovereignties and feel immediate responsibility to their citizenry in times of trial. In the vast majority of cases, they retain control of the immediate military response to urgent requirements, through the adjutants general of their respective National Guard (see Figure 6.7). Those National Guards, however, may be mobilized and employed pursuant to three separate authorities, based upon circumstances surrounding the emergencies or other events in question.

Under normal circumstances, the Guard is activated under what is commonly called "state active-duty status." In this status, the forces are under the control of the governor through the adjutant general, and all costs for activation, mobilization, and employment are incurred by the state or territory. There are conditions, however, under Title 32 of the United States Code, wherein state National Guard forces may be employed under the authority of the governor but paid for by the federal government (through the Department of Defense).[50] This status was formerly reserved to fund annual training requirements for the members of the Guard (e.g., inactive-duty training and annual training). However, in the aftermath of 9/11, there have been many instances wherein National Guard units and members were placed in Title 32 status while performing missions in airport security, critical infrastructure protection missions, and (in some cases) disaster response. A significant amount of the National Guard response to Hurricane Katrina, for instance, was executed under Title 32 status. It is currently the DOD policy that such operations are unauthorized unless specific authority is provided by Congress or directed by the president.[51] Nevertheless, the appeal of this status for the states is obvious.

National Guard units that have been federalized for overseas missions, such as those currently employed in Iraq and Afghanistan, are under Title 10 authorities. In this status, the federal government is, indeed, paying for the forces, but they are responding to the president of the United States, not their respective governors. In rare circumstances, this same authority can be exercised in the United States, with National Guard forces federalized, responding to the president, and falling under the Department of Defense's chain of command. A potential benefit in employing the Guard under this status is a strengthened chain of command, with both active and Guard components responding to a single Title 10 authority. A disadvantage (beyond predictable political friction from the states' chief executives) is that, once federalized, National Guard forces fall under the same *posse comitatus* restrictions as their active-duty counterparts. Until such federalization, the National Guard *can* perform law enforcement functions, as deemed prudent by their governors. The importance of this capability was played out poignantly in the wake of Hurricane Katrina. National Guard forces were judiciously applied to law enforcement situations as required on their own right. In addition, however, individual National Guardsmen were occasionally attached to active-component forces in order to provide the latter with a degree of law enforcement capabilities, as requirements demanded. The Guardsmen were effectively a law enforcement detachment, paralleling similar constraints and solutions worked out between the US Navy and the US Coast Guard.

Special Units for Special Challenges

In trying to anticipate threats that could result in the gravest consequences to the states and localities they serve, the National Guard and the United States Northern Command have developed forces specially organized, trained, and equipped to meet domestic emergencies. While an "all-hazards" approach holds the greatest aesthetic appeal to most state emergency managers, the military must be prepared for very specialized hazards that could likely outstrip the means of state and local emergency management personnel in terms of capacities, if not capabilities. In that light, perhaps the most pronounced preparations undertaken by the Guard for catastrophic events surround those having to do with CBRNE threats to our people, known in the DOD as the

CBRNE Enterprise. These preparations have advanced over time from a matter of analysis to a robust, integrated response.

- **Weapons of Mass Destruction–Civil Support Teams (WMD-CST):** In 1998 the president of the United States announced the establishment of ten WMD-CSTs, for each FEMA region. These teams were envisioned as the first elements of the DOD's response to a WMD attack. Composed of twenty-two highly skilled US Army and Air National Guardsmen, the units are operated under Title 32 and are federally funded, trained, equipped, and sustained. In execution the teams are dispatched to support civilian authorities by identifying CBRNE agents and substances, assessing current and projected consequences, advising on response measures, and assisting with appropriate requests for state support to facilitate additional resources.[52] Indicative of the value these teams hold in the eyes of emergency managers is the fact that the original ten teams envisioned in the 1998 presidential mandate grew to twenty-seven by the end of 2002 and on to their current number of fifty-seven distributed across the states and territories of the United States. In addition to their numbers, the mission of the WMD-CSTs has also expanded. The National Defense Authorization Act of 2007 authorized operations for the units to include response to both intentional and unintentional release of nuclear, biological, radiological, toxic, or poisonous chemical materials. Moreover, the act provided for the employment of these units in response to both natural and man-made disasters in the United States that result in, or could result in, catastrophic loss of life or property.[53]
- **CBRNE Enhanced Response Force Package (CERFP):** In spite of the impressive capabilities residing in the WMD-CSTs surrounding detection, identification, analysis, and advice, the twenty-two-man units are limited in both capabilities and capacities. Following the example of the US Marine Corps' Chemical and Biological Incident Response Force (CBIRF),[54] the National Guard sought to increase its means and competencies for responding to CBRNE incidents, as required. Accordingly, in 2007, seventeen CERFPs were established around the United States, with at least one in each FEMA region. Deployed alongside WMD-CSTs, these 186-man units add capabilities in command and control, decontamination, medical support, casualty search and rescue, and fatality search and recovery. Beyond responding to CBRNE incidents, the packages provide governors of the states and territories with a means to mitigate risks associated with col-

lapsed structure rescue, enhance medical triage and stabilization, affect mass decontamination, and recover fatalities following a disaster.[55]

- **Homeland Response Forces (HRF):** The pattern for enhancement in capabilities and capacities designed for CBRNE response is continued in the National Guard through their Homeland Response Force. By the end of fiscal year 2012, one of these units will be stood up across each of the ten FEMA regions. Composed of 566 soldiers and airmen of the US Army and Air National Guard, these units will possess an expanded range of life-saving capabilities to include search and rescue, decontamination, emergency medical capabilities, command and control, and security for all disaster-response endeavors. When combined with the CERFPs, the HRFs are envisioned as being the first military response to a CBRNE incident.[56]

- **Title 10 Forces Devoted to CBRNE Operations:** HRFs are envisioned as providing a bridge between initial National Guard response and Title 10 capabilities.[57] Each progression through the units discussed so far has resulted in greater capabilities in the states' and territories' National Guards and greater operational flexibility. Through the progression, the governors of the respective states and territories have retained control of response to incidents occurring in their states. Still, the possibility of these impressive resources being strained beyond their means in the face of catastrophic events, or even a series of major disasters, cannot be ignored.

  - **CBRNE Consequence Management Response Forces (CCMRF)—** In order to address this potential requirement, the Department of Defense has established a CBRNE Consequence Management Response Force (CCMRF). The military's most robust assemblage of resources and capabilities in one unit dedicated to disaster response, the CCMRF brings together approximately 4,700 personnel to provide additional capacity in all of the capabilities delineated in the previously described units. In addition, the force contains personnel and equipment dedicated to engineering, ground and aviation medical and casualty evacuation, enhanced medical and surgical capabilities, and other logistical support to complement and supplement the civil requirements.[58] The DOD's original plan was to develop three of these forces. The first, as described, is predominantly constructed of active component forces; the second and third would have been drawn predominantly from the National Guard.

  - **Defense CBRNE Response Force (DCRF)**—In an effort to "field faster, more flexible consequence management response forces," however, the CCMRF concept is being restructured.[59] The first CCMRF will be replaced by a Defense CBRN Response Force. The DCRF will add 500 personnel beyond the CCMRF capacity and will be configured to provide for greater lifesaving capabilities, faster than the timelines envisioned for the CCMRF. This additional speed in response will be facilitated by dividing the DCRF into two force packages. The first, envisioned to be deployed within twenty-four hours of activation, will consist of 2,100 personnel. The second, composed of the remaining 3,100 personnel of the DCRF, will deploy no later than forty-eight hours after activation.

– **Command and Control CBRNE Response Elements (C²CRE)**— Following the resource management decision that came out of the Department of Defense's *Quadrennial Defense Review* of 2010, plans for establishing two more CCMRFs were abandoned. In their stead, the department is calling for the establishment of two robust command elements, each with appreciable capabilities in CBRNE assessment, search and extraction, decontamination, and emergency medical and other functions important to immediate response and recovery missions. Building upon this foundation, other units could be attached to round out a capability similar to that one afforded by the DCRF. The C²CRE, therefore, provides an economy of force solution to potential requirements beyond a single catastrophic event, and it does so while simultaneously ensuring a degree of preparation and expertise that raises our level of response to additional requirements, beyond the "ad hoc," to planned, deliberate, and focused.[60]

All of these units, of course, represent the lead elements of what would, as necessary, be a prolonged response to any given disaster. Follow-on forces, taking advantage of additional resources traditionally associated with combat support and combat service support, could also be introduced as an element of support to civil authorities. But the special units described above are important not only for their capabilities but likewise for the deliberate focus that will make them both effective and responsive. The military is now configured to deploy in response to requests and direction from civil authorities in a matter of hours rather than a matter of days (see Figure 6.8). When they arrive, they will come with personnel, expertise, and resources tailored for the requirement, rather than making do with what was available from a set of missions designed for warfare.

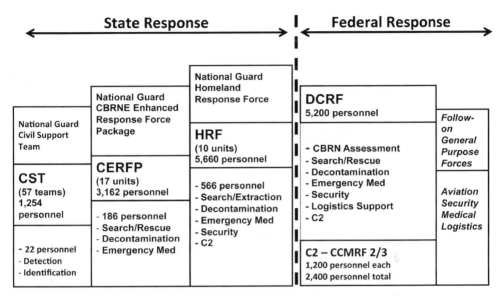

FIGURE 6.8   The evolving CBRNE enterprise

Conclusion

In many ways, the CBRNE enterprise is a perfect reflection of the military's ethos as it pertains to defense support of civil authorities. The employment of these forces will begin with a request to complement or supplement the capabilities of a civil infrastructure under strain due to emergencies, major disasters, or catastrophic events. Until the request comes, the units will remain a force in readiness. When the requests come, the first units to respond will be those of the National Guard—most familiar with the state and local agencies they will be supporting and most familiar with the requirements at hand. As additional requirements arise due to the scope or duration of the crisis, the active component military is prepared to provide additional support, bringing added capacity to the appreciable capabilities already introduced. The military, at this juncture, would be a part of the federal response—which, in turn, would be introduced in support of the states and localities under duress. From beginning to end, the military, in support of our civil authorities, will neither seek nor assume "command." Rather, it will attempt to perform as the forefathers intended: always as the servant of the people, never as their overseers.

NOTES

1. Barack Obama, *Organizing for Homeland Security and Counterterrorism,* Presidential Study Directive 1 (Washington, DC: White House, February 23, 2009).

2. George W. Bush, *National Strategy for Homeland Security* (Washington, DC: White House, July 2002), 2.

3. George W. Bush, *National Strategy for Homeland Security* (Washington, DC: White House, October 2007), 3.

4. Department of Homeland Security, *The Report of the Quadrennial Homeland Security Review* (Washington, DC: Department of Homeland Security, February 2010), 11.

5. US Joint Chiefs of Staff, *Civil Support*, vii.

6. Department of Defense, *Strategy for Homeland Defense and Civil Support* (Washington, DC: Department of Defense, June 2005), 5.

7. Ibid.

8. The Honorable Paul Stockton in an address at the US Army War College, Carlisle Barracks, Pennsylvania, November 17, 2010.

9. The first Quartering Act (May 1765) provided that Great Britain could house its soldiers "in inns, livery stables, ale houses, victualling houses, and the houses of sellers of wine and houses of persons selling rum, brandy, strong water, cider or metheglin" and, if numbers required, in "uninhabited houses, outhouses, barns, or other buildings." It further required any inhabitants (or, in their absence, public officials) to provide food and alcohol for the soldiers "without paying anything for the same." A second Quartering Act (June 1774) was designed to restore imperial control over the American colonies. This became part of what the colonists would refer to as the Intolerable Acts. See David Ackerman, "The Tea Crisis and Its Consequences Through 1775," in *The Blackwell Encyclopedia of the American Revolution*, edited by Jack P. Greene and J. R. Pole (Malden, MA: Blackwell, 1999).

10. Originally enacted in response to federal force employment in the Reconstruction Era following the Civil War, the statute's dictates were extended from the US Army to the US Air Force when those services divided. Whereas not specifically delineated in the act, policy and practice have applied it to the US Navy and the US Marine Corps.

11. Section 1385 of Title 18, United States Code (USC).

12. Distinctions between the National Guard in federalized status, under Title 32, USC, and in State Active Duty Status, will be examined later in this chapter.

13. A notable example of Congress calling for exceptions to Posse Comitatus was seen in congressional support of the use of the military in counterdrug operations in the 1990s as depicted in the National Defense Authorization Act of 1991 (Public Law 101-510, Section 1004). The legislation opened the way to direct DOD support to state and local law enforcement agencies. An extension of this thinking occurred in 1997, when the House of Representatives passed a resolution calling for the deployment of ten thousand additional troops in support of counterdrug operations on the southwestern border.

14. US Customs and Border Protection Fact Sheet, *Operation Jump Start*, March 21, 2008, updated May 10, 2010, https://help.cbp.gov/app/answers/detail/a_id/1021/~/fact-sheet-operation-jump-start.

15. Advisory Panel on Department of Defense Capabilities for Support of Civil Authorities After Certain Incidents, *Before Disaster Strikes: Imperatives for Enhancing Defense Support of Civil Authorities* (Washington, DC: Advisory Panel on Department of Defense Capabilities for Support of Civil Authorities After Certain Incidents, September 15, 2010), 10.

16. George W. Bush, *Management of Domestic Incident*, HSPD-5 (Washington, DC: White House, September 18, 2009), 1, 2.

17. US Joint Chiefs of Staff, *Civil Support*, viii.

18. National Defense University, Joint Forces Staff College, *Joint Staff Officers Guide, 2000*, Joint Forces Staff College Publication 1 (Norfolk, VA: Joint Forces Staff College, 2000), 3–16.

19. Use of this very phrase was attributed to Lieutenant General Keene, deputy commander of the US Southern Command, in a presentation delivered by Michael Byrne, FEMA IMAT-East, at the US Army War College in November 2010. General Keene was referring to international civil-military response and recovery operations in Haiti, following the earthquake of January 2010.

20. EMAC, the Emergency Management Assistance Compact, is a congressionally ratified organization that provides form and structure to interstate mutual aid. Through EMAC, a disaster-impacted state can request and receive assistance from other member states quickly and efficiently, resolving two key issues up front: liability and reimbursement. All fifty states are signatories of the EMAC. See *The Emergency Management Assistance Compact* (Public Law 104-321, October 1996.

21. Craig R. McKinley, *National Guard Posture Statement, 2010: America's Indispensable Force*, posture statement presented to the 111th Congress (Washington, DC: US National Guard Bureau, 2010), 10.

22. See Department of Defense Joint Publication 5-0, *Joint Operation Planning*, December 2006.

23. McKinley, *National Guard's Posture Statement, 2010*, 25.

24. Among these were earthquakes, pandemics, and hurricanes.

25. US Joint Chiefs of Staff, *Civil Support*, II-4.

26. Title 10, USC, Section 124.

27. See US Department of Defense, *Under Secretary of Defense for Intelligence*, DODD 5143.01 (Washington, DC: US Department of Defense, November 2005); US Department of Defense, *Assistant to the Secretary of Defense for Intelligence Oversight*, DODD 5148.11 (Washington, DC: US Department of Defense, September 2010); and US Department of Defense, *Department of Defense Intelligence Activities*, DODD 5240.01 (Washington, DC: US Department of Defense, August 2007).

28. See US Department of Defense, *DOD Cooperation with Civilian Law Enforcement Officials*, DODD 5525.5 (Washington, DC: US Department of Defense, January 1986).

29. US Joint Chiefs of Staff, *Civil Support*, I-5.

30. Ibid., I-6.

31. Ibid., GL-6.

32. Ibid., GL-7.

33. Ibid., III-7.

34. Ibid., I-9.

35. McKinley, *National Guard's Posture Statement, 2010*, 26.

36. David V. Aguilar, *National Guard and Border Security: Testimony of David V. Aguilar, Chief, Office of Border Patrol, U.S. Customs and Border Protection, Department of Homeland Security*, 109th Cong., 2nd sess. (Washington, DC: US Department of Homeland Security, May 24, 2006), 4.

37. US Department of Defense, *Procedures Governing DOD Intelligence Activities That Affect U.S. Persons*, DODD 5240.1R (Washington, DC: US Department of Defense, December 1982), 56.

38. US Department of Defense, *DOD Cooperation with Civilian Law Enforcement Officials*, 15–16.

39. *Joint Task Force North Home Page*, accessed April 14, 2011, http://www.jtfn.northcom.mil/subpages/history.html.

40. US Joint Chiefs of Staff Instruction, *DOD Counterdrug Support*, CJCSI 3710.01B (Washington, DC: US Joint Chiefs of Staff, January 26, 2007, updated January 28, 2008), A2–A3.

41. Ibid., A1.

42. Ibid., III-5.

43. Title 10, USC, Sections 331–335.

44. Jennifer K. Elsea, *The Use of Federal Troops for Disaster Assistance: Legal Issues* (Washington, DC: Congressional Research Service, September 16, 2005), CRS-3.

45. US Department of Defense, *Military Assistance for Civil Disturbances (MACDIS)*, DODD 3025.12 (Washington, DC: US Department of Defense, February 4, 1994), 5.

46. US Joint Chiefs of Staff, *Joint Mobilization Planning*, Joint Publication 4-05 (Washington, DC: US Joint Chiefs of Staff, March 2010), GL-4.

47. Ibid., GL-9.

48. Attributed to Major General Timothy W. Lowenberg, adjutant general of the State of Washington, in a brief delivered to a Dual Status Commanders Course conducted by the US Northern Command in October 2010.

49. The same responsibilities held by Northern Command are held by the US Pacific Command for their area of operations (which include Hawaii and several US territories).

50. Title 32, USC, Section 325.

51. Department of the United States Army, *Domestic Operational Law: Handbook for Judge Advocates* (Charlottesville, VA: US Army Judge Advocate General's Legal Center and School, September 2010), 154.

52. National Guard Bureau, National Guard Fact Sheet, National Guard Weapons of Mass Destruction Civil Support Teams (WMD-CSTs), *2012 National Guard Bureau Posture Statement* (Washington, DC: Army National Guard, December 2010), http://www.ng.mil/features/ngps/default.aspx.

53. US Congress, House Armed Services Committee, *John W. Warner National Defense Authorization Act of 2007* (Washington, DC: House Armed Services Committee, 2007), Section 527.

54. The CBIRF, established in 1996 in response to Presidential Decision Directive 39, is trained, organized, and equipped to respond to a credible threat of a nuclear or high-

yield explosive incident. It is designed to assist local, state, or federal agencies and designated combatant commanders in the conduct of consequence management operations. Disciplines embodied in the unit include detection and identification of agents, search and extraction, personnel decontamination, technical rescue, medical augmentation, explosive ordnance disposal, and communications. The force consists of approximately 350 marines and sailors and possesses the potential to add an additional 200 marines for security purposes, as required.

·55. National Guard Bureau, National Guard Fact Sheet, National Guard CERFP Teams, *2012 National Guard Bureau Posture Statement* (Washington, DC: Army National Guard, December 2010), http://www.ng.mil/features/ngps/default.aspx.

56. Department of Defense, *Homeland Response Force Fact Sheet* (Washington, DC: Department of Defense, June 2010), http://www.defense.gov/news/d20100603HRF.pdf.

57. McKinley, *National Guard Posture Statement, 2010*, 27.

58. Ibid., 23.

59. Robert M. Gates, *Quadrennial Defense Review Report* (Washington, DC: Department of Defense, February 1, 2010), 19.

60. Major Scott Zimmerman, Army National Guard Operations Division, Current Operations Branch, telephone interview by author, July 29, 2011.

Homeland Security Technology

RANDY R. GRIFFITH

The mission of the Department of Homeland Security is to ensure that the United States is safe, secure, and resilient against terrorism and other hazards. This chapter discusses some of the technologies that are used by the DHS to achieve its mission. Homeland security technologies continue to evolve as the threats to national security change. This chapter focuses on applications that fall into the following areas:

- **Detection:** This is an area with a wide array of technologies and potential technologies. Technologies include new X-ray systems such as backscatter or millimeter-wave machines. There are also numerous chemical, biological, and radiation detectors.
- **Identification:** Biometrics—identification using a person's unique physical characteristics—is increasingly being used in a number of security-related fields. Fingerprints, still the most common biometric identifier, are used as identity verification for foreign travelers arriving in the United States. The United Kingdom's registered traveler program uses an iris-scan identification system to allow passengers to pass more quickly through automated barriers at certain airports. Other biometric identifiers currently

in use include retina scans, face recognition, voice analysis, hand geometry, and palm-vein authentication.

- **ID Cards:** Improved identification cards can provide a number of security benefits. Under the REAL ID program, the DHS requires that state-issued ID cards contain codes to verify authenticity. Some nations have begun placing radio-frequency identification tags in passports, while other ID cards verify authenticity through the use of an embedded biometric identifier.

- **Less Lethal Weapons:** At one time, the search for nonlethal weapons was considered a search for an alternative to deadly force. Now, it is viewed as an effort to find tools or devices that subdue subjects without harm. Although these tools can be lethal if used inappropriately or in unusual circumstances, they are not considered weapons in the usual sense, nor are they seen as alternatives to deadly force. To distinguish between "less lethal" and "nonlethal," the latter refers to a device that cannot cause death no matter how it is used.

- **Surveillance:** Closed-circuit television has proved to be an invaluable investigative tool. The presence of surveillance cameras can also help to prevent a crime. Computer programs that help to identify suspicious behavior have been developed. These programs can detect intruders, loiterers, or people moving against the flow of pedestrian traffic (for instance, walking into the exit of a secure area). Unmanned surveillance aircraft are being used by Customs and Border Protection to help provide aerial surveillance video. Smaller surveillance drones are being developed for use in crowded urban environments.

This chapter addresses the DHS structure and how it procures new technologies. The DHS has a science and technology directorate tasked with overseeing research and implementation. The DHS strategy for this outlines several steps to develop improved expertise in the field, both in government laboratories and in universities.

Detection

X-rays

X-rays, named that by Wilhelm Conrad Röntgen when he first discovered the unknown rays in 1895 because *X* was the symbol for "unknown," are a form of electromagnetic radiation, similar to light and radio waves. X-rays have

TABLE 7.1 Electromagnetic spectrum

Region	Wavelength (cm)	Frequency (Hz)	Energy (eV)
Radio	> 10	$< 3 \times 10^9$	$< 10^{-5}$
Microwave	10–0.01	$3 \times 10^9 - 3 \times 10^{12}$	$10^{-5} - 0.01$
Infrared	$0.01 - 7 \times 10^{-5}$	$3 \times 10^{12} - 4.3 \times 10^{14}$	0.01–2
Visible	$7 \times 10^{-5} - 4 \times 10^{-5}$	$4.3 \times 1014 - 7.5 \times 10^{14}$	2–3
Ultraviolet	$4 \times 10^{-5} - 10^{-7}$	$7.5 \times 10^{14} - 3 \times 10^{17}$	$3 - 10^3$
X-rays	$10^{-7} - 10^{-9}$	$3 \times 10^{17} - 3 \times 10^{19}$	$10^3 - 10^5$
Gamma Rays	$< 10^{-9}$	$> 3 \times 10^{19}$	$> 10^5$

Source: NASA.gov.
Note: Wavelength is the inverse of frequency ($\lambda = 1/f$). An electron volt (eV) is a measure of energy. It is very a small amount of energy similar to the amount of energy possessed by a single photon of light.

high energy and short wavelength and are able to pass through tissue. On their passage through the body, the denser tissues, such as the bones, will block more of the rays than will the less dense tissues, such as the lung.

Not all of the X-ray energy passes through the body; some is deposited in it, and it is this deposited energy that causes the biological effects of X-ray radiation. X-ray pictures are recorded on a special kind of photographic film. The more X-ray energy that reaches the film, the darker that region will be. Bones will be shown as "white" because less X-ray energy passes through them, while soft tissue such as lungs will be shown as "darker" because more energy passes through.[1]

For many years dental and other X-rays have been used by law enforcement to help identify unknown crime victims. In recent years, especially at airports, X-rays have been used to help detect dangerous substances in luggage items. X-rays are also used in courthouses, jails, and hospitals to search for objects that might be a weapon, and many schools use them to prevent students from bringing weapons into buildings. X-ray machines used to screen luggage at airports and student baggage at schools are very low dose and are considered safe for people to be near. An X-ray Baggage Inspection System consists of an X-ray generator, a sensor to detect radiation after passing through the baggage, a signal processor (usually a computer) to process the signal from the detector, and a conveyor system for moving baggage into the system. The scanner operator is able to distinguish items in baggage because materials pass or absorb X-rays at different levels. Based on the energy that

FIGURE 7.1   X-ray scan of a truck showing a person hiding behind the cab.
Source: http://borderbeat.azstarnet.com.

passes through the items, the display shows various colors to indicate three main categories: organic, inorganic, or metal.

Among manufacturers various colors are used to display "inorganic" and "metal," but because most explosives are organic, all X-ray systems represent "organic" in shades of orange. Scanner operators must look for any suspicious item that could part of an explosive and not focus solely on obvious items like guns or knives. Some airports use a backscatter X-ray device to screen passengers. With a backscatter device, low-energy X-rays that come into contact with the body do not penetrate but are mostly scattered back to detectors. Although most of these low energy X-rays are scattered off the skin, they can penetrate clothing, and some can penetrate beneath the skin. In just a few seconds a body-outline image is created that may show explosives or drugs. However, because they do not penetrate, these rays cannot detect anything deep inside the body. Also, due to their inability to penetrate, two scans are needed—front and back—which takes about ten seconds.[2] There are also portable backscatter devices that can be used to scan trucks for smuggled contraband and people.

There is some concern about the exposure to X-ray radiation. The **sievert** (Sv) is the International System of Units unit of dose-equivalent radiation. As an example, the typical dental X-ray is 0.005 mSv, while the typical mammo-

TABLE 7.2   Radiation symptoms

Radiation Dose (within one day)	Symptom
0–250 mSv	None
250–1,000 mSv	Some people feel nausea and loss of appetite; bone marrow, lymph nodes, spleen damaged.
1,000–3,000 mSv	Mild to severe nausea, loss of appetite, infection; more severe bone marrow, lymph node, spleen damage; recovery probable, not ensured.
3,000–6,000 mSv	Severe nausea, loss of appetite; hemorrhaging, infection, diarrhea, peeling of skin, sterility; death if untreated.
6,000–10,000 mSv	The previous symptoms plus central nervous system impairment; death expected.
Above 10,000 mSv	Incapacitation and death.

Source: National Institutes of Health.

gram is around 4 mSv. The typical backscatter X-ray scan would equal one hundred chest X-rays or seven hundred abdominal X-rays. Or to put it another way, to accumulate a dose that will cause a clinically observable effect (not harmful, but observable) would require more than one million scans in a relatively short period of time.[3]

Air travel exposes people on aircraft to increased radiation from space as compared to sea level, including cosmic rays and from solar-flare events. For example, a dose of 6 mSv per hour was measured from London Heathrow to Tokyo Narita on a high-latitude polar route. For a typical commercial cross-country flight in the United States, an air traveler is likely to receive 0.02 to 0.05 mSv of radiation. The Federal Aviation Administration (FAA) requires airlines to provide flight crews with information about cosmic radiation, and the International Commission on Radiological Protection recommends the general public be exposed to no more than 1 mSv per year. In addition, to comply with a European directive, many airlines do not allow pregnant flight-crew members. The FAA has a recommended limit of 1 mSv total for a pregnancy, and no more than 0.5 mSv per month. (Information originally based on *Fundamentals of Aerospace Medicine* published in 2008).

There are advantages and disadvantages to using X-rays for detection. X-ray advantages include the following:

- 2-D and 3-D imaging capability
- well established in the marketplace, so equipment is readily available
- technicians can operate equipment after some training
- X-ray equipment can be made mobile
- effective at determining various items such as smuggling, contraband, weapons, and explosives (switches, detonators, and the like)
- backscatter X-rays can reveal fine details and materials discrimination
- backscatter X-rays do not have the same safety issues as standard X-rays; a passenger would need to be scanned using a backscatter scanner, from both the front and the back, about two hundred thousand times to receive the amount of radiation equal to one typical CT scan[4]

X-ray disadvantages include the following:

- X-rays require high voltages (140 to 160 kilovolts) to penetrate materials
- X-rays cannot discriminate between materials
- X-rays do not have a definite range; the intensity of radiation transmitted through a material falls exponentially with the thickness of the material
- X-rays cannot find objects hidden within dense materials
- X-ray systems raise health issues because they emit ionizing radiation
- X-rays cannot distinguish between two materials of the same density
- the devices that generate X-rays are not efficient and still quite expensive
- backscatter X-rays require multiple scans to get a complete view of the subject

T-rays

Terahertz or T-rays lie between microwaves on the low end and infrared radiation (IR) on the high end in the electromagnetic spectrum. Terahertz waves, like infrared waves, can be used to form images of people and objects. T-rays do not have enough energy to damage cells, unlike X-rays, which can cause cell damage that can lead to radiation sickness or cancer. And although T-rays cannot see through metals or water, they can pass through materials such as clothing, packaging, and certain building materials. T-ray scanners also have "standoff capability," meaning they can scan from a few meters away. Full-body T-ray scanners sweep a beam across a person and then use sensors to detect the reflected radiation. Because substances will reflect the radiation differently, each one will have a different terahertz spectrum, or fingerprint, that can be classified by software.[5]

FIGURE 7.2
Terahertz scan of a briefcase
showing a gun and a knife.
Source: http://spectrum.iee.org.

Privacy concerns have been raised regarding the use of T-ray technology. Because it allows the operator to see through clothes, some believe it effectively implements virtual strip searches. The operator sitting directly in front of the machine does not see the image; that screen only shows confirmation that the passenger has cleared. Conversely, the person viewing the image does not see the person the device is scanning. To help address these privacy concerns, it has been proposed that only people who are independently detected to be carrying contraband are scanned, or software could mask genitals and other private areas. In some locations, travelers have the choice between the body scan or a traditional "pat down." In the UK and some other countries, the scans are mandatory. The Transportation Security Administration issued a statement saying it had taken steps to address privacy objections and claimed that the images captured by the scanners were not stored. However, the US Marshals Service admitted that it had saved thousands of images captured from a Florida courthouse checkpoint.[6]

Health concerns regarding terahertz radiation have been raised. Unlike high-frequency ultraviolet and X-rays, T-rays do not pass through the body and cannot cause cancer, as mentioned earlier, though there is conflicting research over whether they can interfere with gene expression and DNA replication.[7]

Although terahertz scanners hold much promise, there is an ongoing debate about their current effectiveness versus cost. To date, there have been no reports of a terrorist capture as a result of a body scanner, although such scanners

FIGURE 7.3
X-ray of pistol showing
rounds in magazine
and chamber.
Source: http://thefull
enchilada.com.

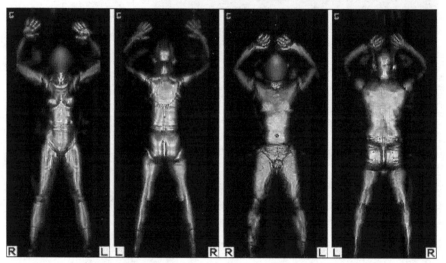

FIGURE 7.4   T-ray full-body scan.
Source: L3 Communications.

may have deterred some attempted attacks. Further, in a series of repeated tests, the body scanners were unable to detect a handgun hidden in an undercover agent's undergarments.[8]

There are advantages and disadvantages to using T-rays for detection. T-ray advantages include the following:

- Unlike X-rays, terahertz is nonionizing and safe
- no need for operator interpretation because software will automatically recognize the material's terahertz fingerprint

- technicians can operate equipment after minimal training
- T-ray scanning is quite fast, offering the possibility of real-time imaging
- T-ray machines are more compact that X-ray devices

T-ray disadvantages include the following:

- not a mature technology compared to other techniques and thus more expensive
- more spectra need to be added to database to allow more applications
- water vapor absorbs strongly in the terahertz region, which could lead to the possibility of spurious or tainted measurements
- T-ray technology produces images at a lower resolution than X-ray backscatter systems
- T-ray devices have a narrow field of view

Metal Detectors

Metal detectors can be used for a number of purposes, such as security, item recovery, archaeological exploration, and geological research. Development of the modern metal detector began in the 1920s. Metal detectors have been a major element of airport security for decades. Public access to an airport is channeled so that every person must walk through a metal detector, and all items go through an X-ray machine. Most walk-through metal detectors used in airports use pulse induction (PI) metal detectors. In this system, a coil of wire on one side of the arch acts as both the transmitter and the receiver. The system sends pulses (short, powerful bursts) of current through the coil, which generates a brief magnetic field. When the field collapses, the coils create what is called a *reflected pulse*.[9]

The pulse creates a magnetic field in any metal object that passes through the detector. When the pulse's magnetic field collapses, the object's magnetic field delays the time it takes for the reflected pulse to completely disappear. This process is similar to an echo. In a PI metal detector, the presence of a metal object causes the reflected pulse to last just a bit longer because the magnetic field of the object adds its "echo" to the reflected pulse. The *sampling circuit* of the metal detector monitors the length of the reflected pulse. The circuit can determine if another magnetic field has delayed the pulse decay by comparing it to the expected decay time. It then converts these signals into tones that change whenever a metal object is detected. A handheld detector, using the same PI principle, is used to isolate the location if the metal detector continues to indicate its presence.

Newer *multizone* metal detectors have entered the market. This device has multiple transmit and receive coils, each at a different height. In effect, it is several metal detectors in a single unit. Most airport metal detectors will not catch all the metal that passes through them. This is due to the sensitivity of the metal detector being slightly reduced. Without this reduction, alarms would be set off due to metal teeth fillings and metal jean rivets and metal zippers. However, this also reduces the effectiveness of the metal detectors. While smaller metal items may not be detected, the settings are always set high enough that most items considered dangerous will set off the alarm (although this means that most metal orthopedic implants will also set it off).

There are advantages and disadvantages to using metal detectors. Metal detector advantages include the following:

- metal detectors can deter someone from carrying a weapon and find it if they do
- metal detectors can find hidden objects
- little training is necessary to operate the detector
- handheld detectors reduce the need for pat downs during weapon screening

Metal detector disadvantages include the following:

- privacy concerns: for the system to be effective, security will still have to inspect some of the people who pass through the detector to see if they have any dangerous or prohibited objects on their person
- there are false alarms, such as those set off by some surgically implanted metal devices
- the electromagnetic field the metal detector creates is small, whereas the size of the walk-through device can create large magnetic fields, which can interfere with electronic devices in the vicinity of the metal detector, including medical devices

Infrared

Electromagnetic radiation is often categorized by wavelength. Short-wavelength radiation has the highest energy and can be dangerous—gamma, X-rays, and ultraviolet are examples of short-wavelength radiation. Longer wavelength radiation is of lower energy and is usually less harmful—examples include radio, microwaves, and infrared. Thermal imaging cameras, using infrared en-

Black hot - Target range = 52.1 M / 10.02.2002 / Batt= 37%

FIGURE 7.5   Infrared photo of suspect in total darkness.
Source: Sierra Pacific Innovations.

ergy, capture the inherent heat radiated by objects: warm objects stand out well against cooler backgrounds. Humans and other warm-blooded animals become easily visible against the environment, day or night.

This makes infrared cameras very useful for finding people who are lost at night or lost at sea. The warm body heat from a person will cause them to glow brightly in the infrared. Police can use infrared cameras to find criminals hiding in the dark. Because infrared light can travel through thick smoke and visible light cannot, infrared cameras are used by firefighters to find people and animals in smoke-filled buildings, as well as hot spots in the fire. Also, because infrared light can travel through thick fog, it is very useful to have infrared cameras on ships and airplanes to help in navigation. An infrared image can also reveal differences in temperature, which help find leaks in walls, lack of insulation, or even electrical circuits that are overloaded. Satellites also use infrared cameras to measure the temperature of the oceans, to study the earth's weather during the day and at night, and to study the infrared light from outer space.

Infrared detectors cannot sense heat through glass, which is why the lens of an infrared camera is made of exotic material. There are materials that block, reflect, absorb, or emit infrared light. One common material that blocks IR is

Plexiglass, which is what NASA uses to demonstrate infrared radiation and the greenhouse effect. Water is a good absorber of IR, which is why most infrared astronomy measurements are done above the atmosphere's water-vapor level. Infrared light can be reflected by any good mirror. Finally, thermal IR is a measure of heat, and *any* object above absolute zero (−273°C) emits infrared radiation. The hotter a source, the more IR light it emits.

Infrared devices have advantages and disadvantages when used for detection. Infrared detector advantages include the following:

- infrared detectors can be applied to large areas
- infrared detectors operate in real time
- the detectors can be used to detect heat sources that would otherwise not be seen
- the detectors require less calibration and are relatively maintenance free

Infrared detector disadvantages include the following:

- infrared detectors cannot detect temperature differences in objects that have a similar temperature range
- infrared detectors are expensive
- dust and dirt can coat the sensor and impair its response
- humidity can interfere with infrared systems because it can absorb infrared frequencies
- moisture in the path between the sensor and the target can disrupt the infrared beam

Identification

On September 11, 2001, nineteen terrorists boarded aircraft in Boston, Massachusetts, and Dulles Airport in Virginia, and changed our world. All had successfully passed through security screening prior to boarding the aircraft and, previously, had also successfully passed through immigration screening while entering the country. A suspected twentieth terrorist had been refused entry by a suspicious immigration inspector at Florida's Orlando International Airport the previous month. Of the remaining nineteen terrorists, eighteen had been issued US identification documents. The Global War on Terror had reached American soil, and the terrorists had already realized how important a false identity could be in avoiding security systems.[10]

Biometrics

Biometrics are automated methods of recognizing a person based on a physiological or behavioral characteristic. Among the features measured are face, fingerprints, hand geometry, handwriting, iris, retina, palm vein, and voice. Biometric technologies are becoming the foundation of an extensive array of highly secure identification and personal verification solutions. As the level of security breaches and transaction fraud increases, the need for highly secure identification and personal verification technologies increases.[11] Biometrics are used in confidential financial transactions and to protect personal data. The technology is currently being used in network security, government IDs, retail sales, electronic banking and other financial transactions, law enforcement, and health and social services.

Fingerprints

Governments have been using fingerprints as a means of accurate identification worldwide for more than one hundred years, and it is still the most common biometric in use today. Other visible human characteristics change, but fingerprints do not. Barring injuries, surgery, or diseases such as leprosy damaging the layers of skin, finger- and palm-print features have never been shown to change as a person ages.

A fingerprint is made of a number of ridges and valleys on the surface of the finger. The ridges form so-called minutia points: ridge endings, ridge bifurcations, dots (very small ridges), islands (ridges slightly longer than dots), and others. The uniqueness of a fingerprint can be determined by the pattern of ridges and furrows as well as the minutiae points.[12]

FIGURE 7.6
Fingerprint characteristics.
Source: ROSISTEM.

The technique of fingerprinting is known as **dactyloscopy**. Until the advent of digital scanning technologies, fingerprinting was done using ink and a card.[13] Unfortunately, the ink fingerprint system was quite cumbersome. When fingerprints came in, they would have to be manually compared with the fingerprints on file—if there were prints on record. This process could take hours or even days and did not always produce a match. By the 1970s, with the advent of computers, the FBI realized it had to automate the process of classifying, searching for, and matching fingerprints. The Japanese National Police Agency paved the way for this automation, establishing the first electronic fingerprint-matching system in the 1980s. Their Automated Fingerprint Identification Systems (AFIS) eventually enabled law enforcement officials around the world to cross-check a print with millions of fingerprint records almost instantaneously.[14]

AFIS uses sophisticated computer software that looks for patterns and minutiae points to find the best match in its database. The first AFIS system used in the United States was faster than manual systems, but there was a lack of coordination among different agencies. Because many local, state, and federal law enforcement departments were not connected to the same AFIS system, they could not share information. This changed in 1999 when the FBI's Criminal Justice Information Services Division introduced Integrated AFIS (IAFIS). This system can categorize, search, and retrieve fingerprints from virtually anywhere in the country in as little as thirty minutes. It also includes mug shots and criminal histories on some 47 million people. IAFIS allows local, state, and federal law enforcement agencies to have access to the same huge database of information. The IAFIS can compare results with automated fingerprint systems in countries around the world and has the fingerprints of more than 250 million people on file. The IAFIS system operates twenty-four hours a day, 365 days a year.[15] It is estimated that one in six Americans has fingerprints on file with the FBI. Not all the fingerprints are related to criminal investigations, however. People need to have their fingerprints taken for many other reasons, including employment, licenses, and adoption—any situation where someone needs to be checked for a possible criminal background.

There are advantages and disadvantages to using fingerprints for identification. Fingerprint advantages include the following:

- relatively easy to use with some training
- most systems are small and take up little space

- large existing database readily available to allow background and watch-list checks
- proven effective over many years of use
- unique to each finger of each individual and unchanged during one's lifetime

Fingerprint disadvantages include the following:

- an individual's age and occupation may cause some electronic sensors difficulty in capturing a complete and accurate fingerprint image
- collecting high-quality, nail-to-nail images requires some training and skill (but new scanner technology is proving very accurate and robust)
- negative public perceptions (privacy concerns of criminal implications and health or societal concerns associated with touching a sensor used by countless individuals)

Iris Recognition

Newer biometric recognition security systems can use the unique characteristics of the iris to identify persons. Virtually any asset that requires a unique identification or verification can use an iris-recognition system, such as controlling access through specific doors or entrances to authorized individuals. Currently, buildings or offices that have sensitive or classified materials use these systems. They are also used at border crossings and in frequent-flyer passenger screening at airports.

The iris is an ideal biometric measurement because iris patterns tend to stabilize shortly after birth. There are no two irises alike, even in identical twins, and a person's right iris differs from the left. The iris is protected by a clear crystalline lens (the cornea) and is not subject to the variations of aging or physical changes that are common to some other biometric measures, such as the hand, fingerprints, and the face. There are some limited natural changes that occur with time, but these changes generally affect only the eye's color and not its individual patterns. Also, because iris scanning uses black-and-white images, these color changes will not affect the scan. Thus, barring specific injuries or certain rare surgeries directly affecting the iris, the iris's unique patterns remain relatively unchanged over an individual's lifetime.[16]

An iris-recognition system utilizes a black-and-white video camera that uses both visible and near infrared light to take video of an individual's iris. Video is used rather than still photography, in part to confirm the continuous

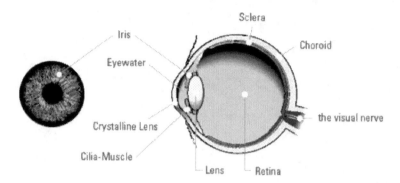

FIGURE 7.7   Iris recognition.
Source: IDTEK.

fluctuations of the pupil as the eye focuses to ensure that the scan is of a living human being and not a photograph. Using a device called a "frame grabber," a high-resolution image of the iris is extracted. The unique characteristics of this image are then converted into a numeric code and stored as a "template" for that user.[17]

The process by which an individual has his or her iris information scanned and stored in the iris-recognition system is referred to as *enrollment*. A trained operator is necessary to correctly enroll each person. To enroll in the system, a template of the user's iris is made by the camera scanning the iris.[18]

False acceptance rates (FARs) and false rejections rates (FRRs) are the measurements used to determine the accuracy of a biometric security system. False acceptance occurs when a biometric security system incorrectly makes a match, resulting in an unauthorized individual gaining access to a secure area. False rejection occurs when a biometric security system incorrectly prevents an authorized individual from gaining access to an asset.[19] Each submission for recognition has inherent variability. That is, all biometric recognition systems produce small differences between a user's stored template and subsequent scans due to slight differences in the environment when each was taken.

In general, when compared to other biometric recognition systems, iris-recognition systems are highly accurate. Independent studies of iris-recognition technology have found false acceptance rates of approximately 1 in 1.2 million.[20] This is far lower than most other forms of biometric recognition. For instance, most fingerprint scanners have a false acceptance rate of 1 in 10,000, and facial recognition systems typically have false acceptance rates of 1 in 1,000. It is more difficult to determine false rejection rates for iris recognition, but it is generally recognized to be lower than other forms of biometric security.[21] In addition, consistent operation and user training may do more to reduce the false rejection rate than improving the system equipment.

There are several advantages and disadvantages of iris recognition. Iris advantages include the following:

- iris scans can be accomplished without the subject's iris needing to touch the camera
- patterns are individual (even in identical twins)
- iris is believed to be highly stable over a lifetime
- the scanning process is quick and does not cause injury
- imitation is almost impossible

Iris recognition disadvantages include the following:

- the iris is difficult to capture for some individuals
- iris may be obscured by eyelashes, eyelids, lenses, and reflections from the cornea
- public myths and fears about "scanning" the eye with a light source
- acquisition of an iris image requires some operator training and attentiveness
- lack of existing data deters ability to use for background or watch-list checks
- cannot be verified by a human

Palm-Vein Authentication

Palm-vein authentication has a high level of authentication accuracy due to the uniqueness and complexity of vein patterns of the palm. Because vein patterns are internal to the body, they are difficult to forge. Also, the system is contactless and hygienic for use in public places. Palm-vein authentication uses the vascular patterns of an individual's palm as personal identification data. Compared with a finger or the back of a hand, a palm has a broader and more complicated vascular pattern and thus contains a wealth of differentiating features for personal identification. The palm is an ideal part of the body for this technology; it normally does not have hair, which can be an obstacle for photographing the blood-vessel pattern, and it is less susceptible to a change in skin color, unlike a finger or the back of a hand. See Figure 7.8. When the infrared ray image is captured, unlike the image seen in (a), only the

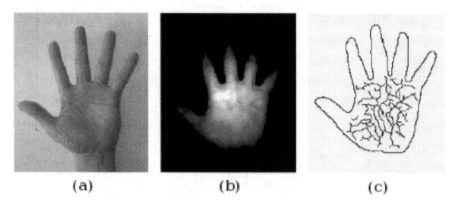

FIGURE 7.8   Palm-vein authentication: (a) visible image, (b) infrared image, (c) palm blood-vessel pattern.
Source: Fujitsu.

blood-vessel pattern is visible as a series of dark lines (b). Based on this feature, the vein-authentication device matches this pattern (c) with the previously registered blood-vessel pattern of the individual.

An individual's palm-vein image is registered along with the other details in his profile as a reference for future comparison. Each time a person attempts to gain access by a palm scan to a particular bank account, secured entryway, and so on, the newly captured image is similarly processed and compared to a bank of stored files for verification, all in a matter of seconds. Numbers and positions of veins and their crossing points are all compared, and, depending on verification, the person is either granted or denied access.[22]

Palm-vein technology has many applications, such as a secure system for ATMs and banking transactions; a PC, handheld, or server log-in system; an authorization system for schools, hospital wards, storage areas, and high security areas in airports; and even facilitating library lending. Manufacturers are continuing to develop uses for palm-vein technology and are working to shrink the scanner to fit a mobile phone.

There are several advantages and disadvantages of palm-vein authentication. Palm-vein advantages include the following:

- nonintrusive—there is no physical contact between the user and the system
- it is difficult for intruders to forge because the blood vessels are hidden within the body

- not affected by skin dryness or roughness or by physical injury to the surface of the hand
- palm-vein recognition has an FRR of 0.01 percent and an FAR of 0.00008 percent[23]

Palm-vein disadvantages include the following:

- numerous factors can affect the quality of the captured image, including body temperature, ambient temperature, camera calibration, and focus
- public myths about palm-vein scanning process being painful
- equipment is relatively expensive and not yet in mass production
- lack of existing data deters ability to use for background or watch-list checks
- cannot be verified by a human

Smart Cards

A smart card is a plastic card that contains an embedded computer chip—either a memory or microprocessor chip—that stores and transacts data via a reader. There are a number of smart cards applications, including health care, banking, entertainment, and transportation. US consumers use the cards for everything from visiting libraries to buying groceries to attending movies. Several states have integrated chip cards for government applications, ranging from the Department of Motor Vehicles to electronic benefit transfers.

Currently, the Subscriber Identity Module (SIM) is the most common application of smart card technology. A SIM is required for all phone systems under the Global System for Mobile Communication standard, which accounts for more than half of all smart cards consumed each year.[24] Smart cards generally fall into two categories: contact and contactless.

The most common type of smart cards is a contact card. Electrical contacts located on the outside of the card connect to a card reader when the card is inserted. Transmission of commands, data, and card status takes place over these physical contact points. The cards do not contain batteries; power is supplied by the card reader. The chips on contact smart cards that contain both memory and a microprocessor are similar in size to a DVD, except they contain a controller to securely add, delete, change, and update information contained in the memory. The more sophisticated microprocessor chips have security features built in to protect the contents of memory from unauthorized access. Contact smart cards are used in a wide variety of applications, including

FIGURE 7.9
Smart card construction.
Source: CardLogix.

network security, vending, electronic cash, IDs, e-commerce, and health cards, among others.

Contactless smart cards are similar to contact smart cards, except contactless cards do not have to be inserted into a device. Instead, contactless smart cards contain an embedded antenna for reading and writing information contained in the chip's memory. They need only be passed within range of a radio-frequency acceptor to read and store information in the chip.[25] Contactless smart cards are used in many of the same applications as contact smart cards, especially where the added convenience and speed of not having to insert the card into a reader is desirable. Student identification, electronic passports, vending, parking, and tolls are common applications for contactless cards.

Digital identification is a rapidly growing smart card application. When the card combines a personal identification number with biometrics such as fingerprints, iris scans, or palm-vein patterns, the cards can provide two- or three-factor authentication. Smart cards are also beginning to be used in emergency situations. Emergency response personnel are starting to carry smart cards that contain additional personal information, such as medical records

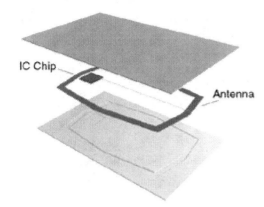

FIGURE 7.10 Contactless smart card.
Source: IDWholesaler.

and skills, so that they can be positively identified in emergency situations. These cards provide immediate access to information that will allow first responders to bypass organizational paperwork and focus more time on the emergency at hand.

There are several smart card advantages and disadvantages. Smart card advantages include the following:

- they can be readily reconfigured and are reusable
- smart cards are much more durable and reliable than magnetic strips
- multiple applications can be stored in one card
- data can be encrypted to give more security, thus reducing the risk of transaction fraud
- information cannot be accidentally erased by electrical or magnetic means
- the card can contain emergency information

Smart card disadvantages include the following:

- potential of cards to be hacked or subjected to a virus attack
- contactless cards may be read from a distance without the owner knowing
- liability issues if card is lost or stolen
- cards are still expensive and have compatibility issues across manufacturers

Radio-Frequency Identification

Radio-frequency identification is a technology that connects an object to the Internet so it can be tracked. A transponder (a microchip with an antenna) is placed on an item, and then a reader (a receiver with one or more antennas) is used to read the data sent by the microchip. The reader then passes the information to a computer. The most common RFID tags or transponders (the term *tags* is often used when referring to transponders) store their information, including their particular serial number, on a microchip.

There are two general classes of RFID systems—*passive* and *active*. Passive RFID tags do not have a transmitter; the energy from the reader is simply reflected back. Active tags have a transmitter and a power source—most commonly a battery, but they can get their energy from other sources. They send the information on their microchip in a broadcast signal. Active tags are most often used on large assets, such as cargo containers and railcars that need to be tracked over long distances.[26] Active tags can be further divided into general types: *transponders* and *beacons*. An active transponder must receive a signal from a reader in order for it to "wake up." These are commonly used for toll collection, checkpoint control, and similar applications. The reader at the tollbooth transmits a signal to the active transponder in the windshield of the car as it approaches, causing it to wake up and broadcast its special ID to the reader. The battery life of the tag is increased by having the transponder broadcast its tag only when it is within range of the reader.

A real-time locating system (RTLS) uses beacons when the precise location of an item is required. In an RTLS, the beacon transmits its identifier at preset intervals (the interval varies depending on how important it is to know the location of the item at any given moment—the more important it is, the more often the beacon will transmit). At least three antennas positioned around the tracking area will pick up the beacon's signal. Automakers use RTLS in their distribution yards and manufacturing facilities to track parts bins.

Passive RFID tags do not have a power source or transmitter. They do not require maintenance and are cheaper than active tags, which is why manufacturers and retailers use them in their supply chains. They have a much shorter read range than active tags (a few inches to thirty feet). A passive RFID transponder is basically a microchip and an antenna. There are many different ways to package the transponder depending on the application. For instance, they can be mounted on a substrate or sandwiched between an adhesive layer and a paper label to create a printable RFID label, or "smart label." They can also be embedded in a plastic card, a key fob, or the walls of a plastic container.[27]

RFID can be used in access control, personnel tracking, and location systems to help ensure the security of restricted areas in airports, maritime ports, and other transportation hubs. These systems are completely hands-free, so

FIGURE 7.11
E-passport with RFID symbol.
Source: US Passport Service.

they have minimal interference with the work and flow of employees and passengers. An active RFID access control and tracking system can ensure that only authorized personnel can enter restricted areas. To enable rapid response during an emergency, the system can quickly identify the location of key personnel and continuously track employees working in critical or sensitive areas. In the United States, the Enhanced Border Security and Visa Entry Reform Act of 2002 states that smart card identity cards may be used in lieu of visas. If a foreign passport was issued on or after October 26, 2006, that passport must be a biometric passport. The chip on a US passport stores the photograph, passport data, and personal data of the passport holder; it also has the capacity to store additional data,[28] such as fingerprints and retina scans. Data in a passport chip can be scanned by readers, a capability intended to speed up immigration processing. Like toll-road chips, data in passport chips can be read when passport chips are in proximity to readers, though the cover must be opened for the data to be read, as it acts as a radio-frequency shield to prevent unauthorized access to the data.

According to the Department of State, the Basic Access Control (BAC) security protocol prevents access to the data on the chip unless the printed information within the passport is also known or can be guessed.[29] But according to some privacy advocates, the BAC and the shielded cover are ineffective when a passport is open, and a passport may have to be opened for inspection in a public place such as a hotel or bank. An open passport is subject to illicit reading of chip data.[30]

There are advantages and disadvantages to RFID technology. RFID advantages include the following:

- RFID tags are very simple to install or inject in items as well as animals
- RFID technology is better than bar codes because it cannot be easily replicated
- RFID tags can be read through cardboard, plastic, wood, and even the human body
- RFID systems help manage updates of stocks, transportation, and logistics of products
- RFID tags can be placed inside jewelry and other high-priced items to prevent theft
- RFID tags can store up to two kilobytes of data

RFID disadvantages include the following:

- potential of cards to be hacked or subjected to a virus attack
- contactless cards may be read from a distance without the owner knowing
- liability issues if card is lost or stolen
- cards are still expensive and have compatibility issues across manufacturers
- RFID technology raises privacy concerns about buying habits, tracking, and data theft
- tag collision and reader collision when too many of each occupy the same space, resulting in signal interference and multiple reads of the same tag
- RFID reader has problems with tags installed in liquids and metal products
- devices such as forklifts, walkie-talkies, and mobile phone towers can interfere with RFID radiowaves
- there are no global RFID standards, requiring vigilance from international firms using the technology

Less Lethal Weapons

Less lethal weapons were developed to provide law enforcement, corrections, and military personnel with an alternative to lethal force. They are designed to temporarily incapacitate, confuse, delay, or restrain an adversary in a variety of situations. They have been used primarily in on-the-street confrontations and suicide interventions, but have also been applied in prison disturbances and hostage rescues. Less lethal weapons are most often used when lethal force is not appropriate, justified but not required, or justified but could result in injury to bystanders or unacceptable damage to property and environment. The principal requirements for any less lethal weapon are *safety* and *effectiveness*, although there is a natural tension between the two.[31] As the safety of a less lethal weapon is maximized, the weapon's ability to incapacitate is degraded. Similarly, if effectiveness is maximized, then there is a higher safety risk.

Electroshock Weapons

There are two types of electrical shock devices. The first is a handheld direct-contact weapon that has two probes that are pressed against the skin (or clothing) of an aggressor. When the operator presses a switch, the skin contact completes a path for current, and the subject receives a paralyzing and painful electrical shock. The second device fires two barbs connected to trailing wires that lead back to the operator. When the barbs penetrate the subject's skin or clothing, an electrical circuit is completed and an electrical discharge automatically results. This device is commonly referred to by the name of the manufacturer: "Taser." These devices work by disrupting the nervous system, which is essentially an organic electricity grid. The resulting state is technically called neuromuscular incapacitation (NMI). While in the state of NMI, the "stunned" individual experiences an inability of the brain's electrical signals to reach and control body muscles, with the overall effect of being involuntarily immobilized and incapacitated. The initial sensation to the electric charge is pain, but this quickly turns into an awkward and possibly alarming condition of muscle spasms, confusion, and involuntary movement. Typical reactions include falling to the ground, screaming, and vertigo. When used appropriately, all these effects of an electroshock weapon dissipate in a matter of seconds or minutes.

The typical Taser device is not without limitations. Because the barbs are connected to the firing mechanism through wires, the typical Taser has a range limited to the length of the wires—about thirty-five feet.[32] And while a Taser works well for controlling a single subject, a fired Taser device is not easy or quick to reload—something the situation may not permit. With these limitations in mind, Taser introduced the eXtended Range Electronic Projectile (XREP), a small, self-contained Taser device that can be fired from a standard 12-gauge shotgun. The XREP uses a special transparent shotgun shell casing to make it easier to load the shotgun with the correct shell. The XREP propels the shell with gunpowder and ejects the casing just as it would a normal shot-gun round. But instead of firing a slug or round of shot, the shotgun fires an electronic projectile divided into two main sections: the nose and the electronics.[33] The nose contains four sharpened electrodes designed to penetrate the clothing and skin of the target and is the main point of contact for the electric charge. Before striking the target, the two sections travel as a single unit and are connected through a pair of Kevlar-coated wires. The electronics portion of the XREP projectile, which contains a battery, a transformer, and a microprocessor, delivers the voltage to a target.[34] When contact is made with the target, six electrodes unfold from the projectile body. The base also has three spring-loaded fins that deploy when fired to help stabilize flight.

Taser's website says that after suffering a blunt impact, most people tend to react the same way: they instinctively reach for the impact site. That is not a good idea with the XREP. If the subject's hand makes contact with the XREP's reflex-engagement electrodes, the effect of the XREP is spread through more of the subject's body. If the only contact with the subject is through the nose of the XREP, the subject's body will be subject to a smaller NMI effect. The twenty seconds of charge allow enough time to close the distance to the subject and restrain him or her. It would also allow enough for a second round to be loaded into the gun if necessary. There are other varieties of electroshock weapons available commercially.

Stun Belts

A stun belt is a device most often used with prisoners. It carries a battery and control pack and is fastened around the subject's waist, leg, or arm. It contains features to stop the subject from unfastening or removing it. A remote-control signal tells the control pack to give the subject an electric shock. Some models are activated by the subject's movement. One manufacturer markets its device under the Band-it brand, which consists of a sleeve with electrodes that is placed on the prisoner's leg or arm. When activated, the sleeve delivers a high-voltage, low-current shock. The sleeve can be set to discharge automatically on movement or manually with a wireless remote up to 175 feet away.[35]

Electric-Shock Stun Batons

A stun baton is similar in design to an electric cattle prod. It typically has two thin projecting metal electrodes about an inch apart at the end of a shaft containing the batteries and mechanism. At the other end of the shaft are a handle and a switch. Both electrodes must touch the subject. In some types the sides of the baton can be electrified to stop the subject from grasping the baton above the electrodes. Some of these devices are disguised as other objects, such as umbrellas, cell phones, or pens. They may also have an option to make a noisy, visible electric arc between the electrodes to warn potential victims. The same shocking mechanism can be installed on an antiriot shield. The electrodes are mounted on the outside, and the batteries and switch are on the inside. The officer can push the shield against the target and deliver a shock when the electrodes are touching the target or make a visible arc as he or she approaches the target.

Of the three, the Taser has the widest application. Taser sales have increased from $2.2 million in 1999 to $86 million in 2010.[36] The increasing popularity and use of electroshock weapons such as Tasers have raised safety issues, however. Critics maintain that such devices can lead to cardiac arrest and—if not treated immediately—to sudden death. People vulnerable to this outcome may be otherwise healthy and unaware of their susceptibility. The proximate cause of death of some of these individuals may be medical conditions or illegal drug use; the electric charge from one of these devices can significantly heighten the risk for vulnerable subjects. This suggests that the use of electroshock weapons on people with certain medical conditions can be dangerous, yet, since a person's medical history or possible drug use is typically unknown, there is a risk of death with virtually any suspect. Taser instructions explicitly state that it is not to be used where flammable liquids or fumes may be present, such as gas stations or methamphetamine labs, because, like other electric devices, Tasers have been found to ignite flammable materials, including CS gas, a component of some tear gas. This poses a problem for law enforcement, because some departments approve the use of tear gas before the use of a Tasers.[37]

Proponents of electroshock weapons such as Tasers claim they are more effective than other means such as pepper spray, batons, or other conventional ways of inflicting pain and handguns at bringing a subject down to the ground with minimum physical exertion.

There are advantages and disadvantages to electroshock weapons. Electroshock weapon advantages include the following:

- a Taser can stun a subject from about thirty-five feet away with a jolt of electricity
- stun guns like Tasers are easy to use, offer better user control, and present less danger to both the officer and the target

- Taser International tries to restrict sales of Tasers outside the law enforcement arena

Electroshock weapon disadvantages include the following:

- they may lead to cardiac arrest, especially if the victim suffers from heart problems; an Amnesty International study found 351 Taser-related deaths in the United States between June 2001 and August 2008[38]
- the operator needs a clear shot at the target, during which time the operator may have to expose himself to the target; the operator of this weapon may have to find a suitable angle to fire at an armed suspect
- if one Taser shot fails, the next one cannot be fired from the same weapon instantly; the wire has to be repacked and the gas cartridge replaced

Active Denial Systems

The Active Denial System is a less lethal, directed-energy weapon that was created for the US military by Raytheon. It is a strong millimeter-wave transmitter mainly deployed for crowd control. It is sometimes colloquially referred to as the "pain ray." The Active Denial System functions by directing electromagnetic radiation at the targets. Similar to a microwave oven, the waves excite the water and fat molecules in the body and cause a painful sensation of extreme heat on the epidermis. The burning sensation that is experienced has been described as almost identical to the feeling of pressing an incandescent lightbulb against the skin, though it does not burn the skin during regular usage. The temperature will continue to rise as long as the beam is applied, but dissipates, along with any pain, as soon as the target leaves the beam. The beam that is emitted can be pointed at targets at a range in excess of 2,300 hundred feet (700 meters). The device is capable of penetrating thick clothing, but it is not yet able to penetrate the thickness of a wall.[39]

The ADS, like any focused energy system, will illuminate all matter in the target area, including everything beyond that is not shielded, without discrimination among individuals, objects, or materials. Highly conductive materials such as aluminum foil should reflect this radiation and could be used to make clothing that would be protective against this radiation. Demonstrations have shown that all living things in the target area receive a similar dosage of radiation.[40] Critics of the ADS have expressed health concerns for those exposed to the beam, but the independent, nongovernment Human Effects Advisory Panel (HEAP)—established in 1998 to provide an independent

FIGURE 7.12 Active Denial System mounted on a Humvee.
Source: Raytheon.

human effects review of DOD nonlethal weapon efforts—has reviewed the ADS research program three times, in 2002, 2004, and 2007, and has consistently concluded that ADS is safe for use. Their findings show:

- no significant effects for wearers of contacts or other eyewear (e.g., night vision goggles)
- skin applications, such as cosmetics, have little effect on ADS's interaction with skin
- no age-related differences in response to ADS exposures
- no effect on the male reproduction system
- developing cancer from exposure is "very unlikely"
- no deleterious effect on fetal development
- the worst injuries recorded were pea-sized blisters in less than 0.1 percent of exposures

HEAP concluded that the ADS is a nonlethal weapon that has a high probability of effectiveness with a low probability of injury.[41] Currently, the ADS is available only as a vehicle-mounted weapon, though there are reports the US Marines and police are working on portable versions. The Los Angeles

County jail has installed an ADS unit on the ceiling. The unit is being evaluated by the National Institute of Justice for use in jails countrywide.[42] Raytheon has developed a smaller version to protect assets from theft and ships against pirates.[43]

There are advantages and disadvantages to the Active Denial System. Active Denial System advantages include the following:

- the ADS can be used to disperse a crowd or to move them from an area without damage to personnel or the environment
- despite the sensation, the beam does not cause injury because of the shallow penetration and the low energy levels used; it exploits the human natural defense mechanism that induces pain as a warning to help protect from injury
- the system allows the operator to see the entire beam path and target area and requires no adjustments for ballistics or windage; it also incorporates (hardware and software) computer systems that limit shot duration and beam power to achieve a safe and effective, nonlethal repel effect

Active Denial System disadvantages include the following:

- as of 2010, each system costs $5 million
- there is the possibility of burns resulting from prolonged beam exposure; a technical device that prevents retriggering would prevent this potential injury
- rain, snow, and fog hamper its effectiveness, and it can be blocked by highly reflective materials such as aluminum foil
- in some situations—particularly in busy crowds—working out the right range can be complicated, and there is the possibility of targets unable to move out of the beam's path

Long-Range Acoustic Devices

The American Technology Corporation developed the Long Range Acoustic Device following the bombing of the USS *Cole* in October 2000. Designed to enforce safe zones around US military vessels, the device can be set at a frequency up to 120 decibels (dB) to first warn any craft approaching a military vessel to change course. If the craft does not comply, then the frequency can be increased up to 151dB, producing a loud, irritating, and potentially painful noise. The idea is to act as a deterrent and avoid employing lethal force. The LRAD can emit sound fifty times greater than the human threshold for pain and can cause permanent damage.[44]

The LRAD uses an array of piezoelectric transducers to produce sound. A transducer is simply a device that changes energy from one kind to another, which in this case changes electrical impulses into sound. All of these transducers are attached to a mounting surface. Identical waves emerge from the transducers, and their amplitudes combine to help the LRAD create very loud sounds. The LRAD uses the phase of the sound waves, the size of the device, and the properties of air to create more directional sound. Essentially, it is a loudspeaker that receives input from a range of devices and amplifies the signal, enabling the operator to send the target a clear message—painful or not. The high directivity of the LRAD device reduces the risk of exposing bystanders or people in the vicinity to excessive audio levels. Sound behind the LRAD unit is more than 40dB, less than the forward output.[45] Major LRAD characteristics include the following:[46]

- the LRAD has a range of about three city blocks over land or five over water
- it has a beam width of about thirty degrees
- though they can vary, typical LRADs are roughly thirty-three inches in diameter and five inches thick and weigh around forty-five pounds
- input signals can be anything from a microphone, laptop, MP3 player, or translation device
- the LRAD has a maximum volume of 120dB at 1m in normal operation, 146dB sustained, or 151dB burst at 1m with override

On November 7, 2005, the LRAD was first used to foil a pirate attack on a Seabourn Cruise Line luxury cruise. The system was installed as a part of the ship's defense systems and was activated when pirates attacked the ship off the Somali coast. Although the effectiveness of the LRAD during the attack is not completely clear, the pirates did not succeed in boarding the vessel and eventually fled.

On November 28, 2008, the Liberian vessel MV *Biscaglia* was attacked. The ship's security detail claimed to have used an LRAD device in an effort to repel attackers, but the ship was seized and the security team abandoned ship, leaving the ship and crew to the pirates.[47] The incident called into question the usefulness of LRADs. In January 2011, the *Spirit of Adventure*, a cruise ship

Decibel (dB) Range Chart

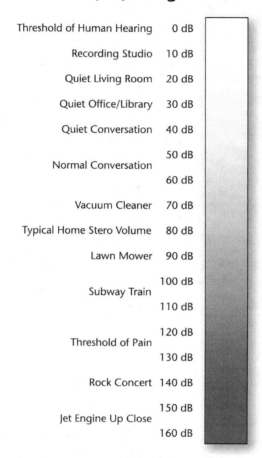

Threshold of Human Hearing	0 dB
Recording Studio	10 dB
Quiet Living Room	20 dB
Quiet Office/Library	30 dB
Quiet Conversation	40 dB
Normal Conversation	50 dB
	60 dB
Vacuum Cleaner	70 dB
Typical Home Stero Volume	80 dB
Lawn Mower	90 dB
Subway Train	100 dB
	110 dB
Threshold of Pain	120 dB
	130 dB
Rock Concert	140 dB
Jet Engine Up Close	150 dB
	160 dB

FIGURE 7.13   Decibel scale.
Source: Neoseeker.

sailing through the Indian Ocean, deployed an LRAD system as part of its defensive measures when being pursued by pirates. The pirates broke off their pursuit before directly engaging the ship.[48]

Human rights groups and hearing specialists have raised concerns about the LRAD. According to the National Institute on Deafness and Other Communication Disorders, any sound over 90dB can damage a person's hearing. So the LRAD can threaten the hearing of anyone in its path, regardless of whether there is any wrongdoing, even when used only for communication. Ultra Electronics manufactures the HyperShield, a polycarbonate riot shield that incorporates an acoustic cannon with a 140dB peak acoustic output at 164 feet (50 meters) to penetrate high noise environments. It can broadcast commands and authoritative messages or sound a piercing 2 kHz alert tone. It is also equipped with an SD memory card to record custom messages, warnings, and announcements.[49]

The Long Range Acoustic Device has several advantages and disadvantages. LRAD advantages include the following:

- the LRAD has the potential to prevent violence without endangering personnel
- the LRAD can be used to issue a verbal challenge with instructions in excess of 1,640 feet (500 meters) and can follow up with a warning tone to influence behavior or determine intent
- the LRAD is highly directional and can be effective at 3,200 feet (1,000 meters)

LRAD disadvantages include the following:

- the LRAD may cause permanent hearing damage to those within its range
- the LRAD can be counteracted through the use of earplugs or other ear protection
- sounds emitted from the LRAD can be reflected back by using a flat solid object

Surveillance

Within the DHS aerial assets are operated by the US Customs and Border Protection's Office of Air & Marine. The CBP utilizes technology to augment its US Border Patrol agents' ability to patrol the border. The technologies used include, but are not limited to, sensors, light towers, mobile night-vision scopes, remote video surveillance systems, directional listening devices, and unmanned aerial vehicles. These "force multipliers" allow the USBP to deploy fewer agents in a specific area while maintaining the ability to detect and counter intrusions and are increasingly becoming a part of the USBP's day-to-day operations. Increasingly, the DHS has explored the use of UAVs to augment USBP agents' ability to patrol the border. There are two different types of UAVs: drones and remotely piloted vehicles (RPVs). Both drones and RPVs are pilotless, but drones are programmed for autonomous flight. RPVs are actively flown—remotely—by a ground-control operator. UAVs are defined as a powered aerial vehicle that does not carry a human operator, uses aerodynamic forces to provide lift, can fly autonomously or be piloted remotely, can be expendable or recoverable, and can carry lethal or nonlethal payloads.[50] The Customs and Border Patrol currently operates three UAVs: the Hermes 450, Predator XP, and Global Hawk. Each is described briefly below.

Hermes 450

The Elbit Systems Hermes 450 is a medium-size (20 feet long with a wingspan of roughly 34 feet) UAV supplying real-time intelligence data to ground forces. The UAV was designed for tactical long endurance missions. It has an endurance of more than 20 hours and range of 124 miles, with a primary mission of reconnaissance, surveillance, and communications relay. The Hermes 450 employs an ElectroOptical/Infrared/Laser Designator Sensor System that enables the UAS operator, along with other networked elements, to have real-time "eyes" as it patrols and make real-time decisions regarding detection, location, and prosecution of threats, day or night. The Hermes Universal Ground Control Station (UGCS) is common to all Hermes UAV platforms and can be mobile or fixed.

The UGCS is built to enable the full control of the UAV. It provides full mission debriefing and simulation as well as in-flight mission editing and payload control. Capable of simultaneously controlling two parallel UAV missions, each mission managed by a single operator, the UGCS enables advanced mission performance, automatic taxiing, autonomous flight, and automatic takeoff and landing systems.[51]

Predator XP

The CBP is replacing the Hermes 450 with the Predator XP, which is larger (36 feet long with a 66-foot wingspan) and has a longer flight endurance (28 hours), wider range (3,682 miles), a higher ceiling and operating altitude (50,000 feet and 25,000 feet, respectively, versus 18,000 and 9,500 for the Hermes 450), and faster maximum and cruising airspeeds (300 mph and 175 mph versus 125 mph and 90 mph).[52]

The Predator XP is a long-endurance, medium-altitude unmanned aircraft system for surveillance and reconnaissance missions. Surveillance imagery from synthetic aperture radar, video cameras, and a forward-looking infrared can be distributed in real time both to the frontline officer and to the operational commander via satellite communication links. The Predator XP employs sensors to automatically find, fix, and track critical targets. The ground-control segment consists of a launch-and-recovery element (LRE) and a mission-control element (MCE) with embedded line-of-sight and beyond-line-of-sight communications equipment.

Global Hawk

The Global Hawk is a high-altitude, long-endurance unmanned aircraft system with an integrated sensor suite that provides intelligence, surveillance, and reconnaissance, or ISR, capability worldwide. It is roughly 44 feet long with a wingspan of about 166 feet. It has a ceiling of 65,000 feet, operational altitude of 60,000 feet, and a maximum airspeed of just under 500 mph with a cruising speed of about 400 mph. Its range exceeds 15,000 miles and it can remain airborne for up to thirty-six hours. Global Hawk's mission is to provide a broad spectrum of ISR collection capability to support joint combatant forces in worldwide peacetime, contingency, and wartime operations. The Global Hawk provides near-real-time coverage using imagery intelligence sensors. The IMINT uses radar, electro-optical, and infrared sensors.[53] The Global Hawk system consists of the aircraft with an integrated sensor suite, launch-and-recovery element, mission-control element, sensors, communication equipment, mission-planning equipment, support element, and trained personnel. The LRE are located at the aircraft bases that include one pilot station that provides the capability to operate one aircraft with no sensor operations. It can launch, recover, and operate an aircraft while en route to or from the target area. The MCE controls the Global Hawk for the bulk of the ISR mission. Like the LRE, the MCE is manned by one pilot, but adds a sensor operator to the crew. Command and control data links enable complete dynamic control of the mission aircraft. The pilot workstations in the MCE and LRE are the control and display interface (cockpit), providing aircraft health and status, sensors status, and a means to alter the navigational track of the aircraft. From this station, the pilot communicates with outside entities to coordinate the mission (air traffic control, airborne controllers, ground controllers, and other ISR assets).

The sensor operator workstation provides capability to dynamically update the collection plan in real time, initiate sensor calibration, and monitor sensor status. The sensor operator also assists with image quality control, target prioritization, and scene tracking to ensure smooth operations.

The Global Hawk wide-area moving-target indicator (MTI) can detect moving targets within a radius of 62 miles. In the search and rescue (SAR) mode, the MTI strip provides 20-foot resolution over a swath 23 miles wide at ranges from 12.4 to 68 miles. The SAR spot mode can provide 6-foot resolution over 3.8 square miles, as well as provide a sea-surveillance function. If a Global Hawk were flown out of San Francisco, it would be able to operate in Maine for 24 hours, observe a 230 x 230 mile grid, and then fly back home.

FAA Regulations

The FAA's main concern about UAV operations in the National Airspace System (NAS) is safety. The NAS encompasses an average of more than 100,000 aviation operations per day, including commercial air traffic, cargo operations, and business jets. Additionally, there are more than 238,000 general aviation aircraft in the system at any time. It is critical that aircraft do not endanger other users of the NAS or compromise the safety of persons or property on the ground.[54]

The FAA generally limits recreational use of UAVs to below 400 feet above ground level and away from airports and air traffic.[55] The FAA expects the use of small UAVs in civil and commercial applications to continue to grow, principally because of their relatively low purchase price, low operating cost, and versatility. There has been a great deal of public comment submitted to the FAA on small UAVs, from both proponents who feel minimum regulation is required because of their small size and those concerned about hazards to general aviation aircraft and the safety of people and property on the ground. The FAA has chartered an Aviation Rulemaking Committee to examine these operational and safety issues and make recommendations on how to proceed with regulating small UAVs.

Microdrones

Microdrones are miniature UAVs. Microdrones do not typically require specially trained operators or complicated ground-control stations. The purpose of UAVs is to provide real-time images and intelligence to ground personnel. Below are a few examples of typical microdrones.

The Skate

The Skate is designed for use in cluttered environments. It uses nearly silent electric power on long endurance autonomous flights and easily fits into a standard military backpack. The Skate, sometimes referred to as the "Flying

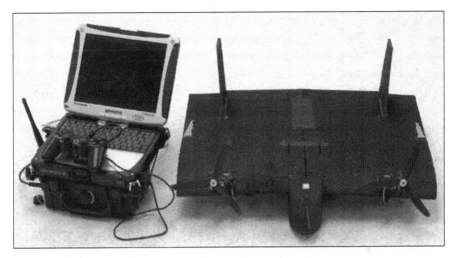

FIGURE 7.14 Skate UAV and mobile command center.
Source: Aurora Flight Sciences.

Pizza Box," weighs just two pounds, can carry a payload up to a half pound, and has a maximum speed of about 57 mph.[56] The Skate combines the simplicity and endurance of a fixed-wing aircraft with the maneuverability of a vertical takeoff and landing craft. Independently articulating motors allow the Skate to quickly transition between vertical and horizontal flight, which increases its endurance and range. The Skate is extremely maneuverable due to the thrust vectoring of its motor pods. The ability to fly both vertically and horizontally allows the Skate UAS to navigate in cluttered environments such as city streets or even inside buildings. The Skate's modular airframe provides a substantial sensor payload capability, as well as quick deployment and easy field repair.[57]

WASP III
With a weight of less than one pound and a wingspan of less than three feet, the hand-launched WASP III drone is the smallest unmanned aerial vehicle in production.[58] It can fly for up to forty-five minutes from 50 to 1,000 feet aboveground at speeds between 25 and 40 mph and is equipped with cameras that can pan, tilt, and zoom. The WASP is now flown by Air Force Special Operations Command for use in tracking and targeting. It can either fly a preprogrammed route or be controlled by a remote pilot.[59] The WASP is ruggedized for use on land and sea and incorporates a global positioning system and an altimeter as part of its autonomous navigation system.

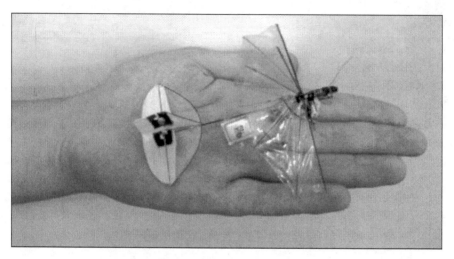

FIGURE 7.15 DelFly Micro.
Source: http://www.delfly.nl.

DelFly Micro

Built by Delft University of Technology in the Netherlands, the DelFly Micro is the world's smallest ornithopter. The flapping robot weighs 0.1 ounces, has a 4-inch wingspan, and includes a camera that broadcasts real-time wireless video. The ultimate goal is for this mechanical flying insect to fly autonomously, guided by global positioning or other navigational systems.[60]

Conclusion

As a nation, we must be prepared not only to react to acts of terrorism, but also to take proactive measures necessary to stop a terrorist threat in its tracks. The devices and technologies discussed above represent the "tip of the spear" of available homeland security technologies. There is considerable research that is ongoing at government labs, in research facilities, and under classified contracts that are not even hinted at in this chapter. Hence, for technology to help professionals do their jobs, and to stay current and useful, continuous funding for homeland security technology is essential. Homeland security professionals know that technology is not a panacea. Rather, in order to safeguard all the complex and critical infrastructure in the United States, as well as the sheer size of our borders and of the economy, security professionals must rely on technology. Even though working with technology is critical to our ability to cost-effectively preserve and protect the United States, it's only as good as the training and education and professionalism of the people using it.

NOTES

1. Dr. Sarah Burnett, "X-rays," Net Doctor, May 10, 2005, http://www.netdoctor.co .uk/health_advice/examinations/x-ray.htm.

2. "Airport X-ray Scanners," Radiation Answers, 2007, http://www.radiationanswers.org /radiation-blog/Airport_xray_scanners.html.

3. "Radiation Risk from Full-Body Airport Scanners Very Low, New Analysis," *Medical News Today*, March 29, 2011, http://www.medicalnewstoday.com/articles/220470.php.

4. Stephen Reinberg, "Airport Full Body Scanners Pose No Health Threat: Experts," *BusinessWeek*, January 8, 2010, http://www.businessweek.com/lifestyle/content/healthday /634724.html.

5. K. Hosako Fukunaga, "Terahertz Spectral Database for Expanding Applications," Infrared, Millimeter, and Terahertz Waves, 2009, IRMMW-THz 2009, 34th International Conference, September 21–25, 2009, updated November 10, 2009, http://ieeexplore.ieee .org/Xplore/login.jsp?url=http%3A%2F%2Fieeexplore.ieee.org%2Fiel5%2F5306513%2F 5324588%2F05324909.pdf%3Farnumber%3D5324909&authDecision=-203.

6. Declan McCullagh, "Feds Admit Storing Checkpoint Body Scan Images," Privacy Inc., *CNET News*, August 4, 2010, http://news.cnet.com/8301-31921_3-20012583-281.html.

7. B. S. Alexandrov, "DNA Breathing Dynamics in the Presence of a Terahertz Field," October 28, 2009, http://arxiv.org/abs/0910.5294; Eric S. Swanson, "Modelling DNA Response to THz Radiation," March 30, 2011, http://arxiv.org/abs/1012.4153.

8. Grant Stinchfield, "TSA Source: Armed Agent Slips Past DFW Body Scanner," NBC DFW, February 21, 2011, http://www.nbcdfw.com/news/local/TSA-Agent-Slips-Through -DFW-Body-Scanner-With-a-Gun-116497568.html.

9. "Security Scanners," 2008, http://www.security-facts.com/security-scanners.

10. "Biometrics Overview," Biometrics.gov, August 7, 2006, p. 1, http://www.biometrics .gov/Documents/BioOverview.pdf.

11. "An Introduction to Biometrics," Biometric Consortium, February 17, 2006, http:// www.biometrics.org/html/introduction.html.

12. "Fingerprint Biometrics, " Biometric Newsportal, accessed May 20, 2011, http:// www.biometricnewsportal.com/fingerprint_biometrics.asp.

13. "Recording Legible Fingerprints," Federal Bureau of Investigation, accessed May 18, 2011, http://www.fbi.gov/hq/cjisd/takingfps.html.

14. Kenneth R. Moses, "Automatic Fingerprint Identification Systems," National Criminal Justice Reference Service, chap. 6, 2010, http://www.ncjrs.gov/pdffiles1/nij/225 326.pdf.

15. "Integrated Automated Fingerprint Identification System," Federal Bureau of Investigation, accessed May 18, 2011, http://www.fbi.gov/about-us/cjis/fingerprints_biometrics /iafis/iafis.

16. "Biometric Overview: Iris Recognition," US Environmental Protection Agency, June 6, 2011, http://cfpub.epa.gov/safewater/watersecurity/guide/productguide.cfm?page=biometricoverviewirisrecognition.

17. Ibid.

18. Ibid.

19. Ibid.

20. "Iris Recognition," Biometricsinfo.org, accessed May 14, 2011, http://www.biometricsdata.com/irisrecognition.htm.

21. "Biometric Overview: Iris Recognition."

22. T. Rao, "Future of Human Security Based on Computational Intelligence Using Palm Vein Technology," *Global Journal of Computer Science and Technology*, p. 70, September 2010.

23. Ishani Sarkar, "Palm Vein Authentication System: A Review," *International Journal of Control and Automation* 3, no. 1 (March 2010): 32.

24. "Smart Card Overview," Smart Card Basics, 2010, http://www.smartcardbasics.com/smart-card-overview.html.

25. "Storing Data on ID Cards," ID Learning Center, 2011, http://www.idwholesaler.com/learning-center/articles/id-cards/data-storage.htm.

26. "Active RFID Tags," Sage Data Learning Centre, accessed May 18, 2011, http://www.sagedata.com/learning_centre/active-rfid-tags.html.

27. "The Basics of RFID Technology," *RFID Journal*, accessed May 17, 2011, http://www.rfidjournal.com/article/view/1337/2.

28. "The U.S. Electronic Passport," US Department of State, accessed May 14, 2011, http://travel.state.gov/passport/passport_2498.html.

29. "The U.S. Electronic Passport Frequently Asked Questions,." US Department of State, accessed May 14, 2011, http://travel.state.gov/passport/passport_2788.html.

30. Bruce Schneier, "Renew Your Passport Now!," Schneier On Security, September 18, 2006, http://www.schneier.com/blog/archives/2006/09/renew_your_pass.html.

31. The Honorable Sarah V. Hart, Director, National Institute of Justice, Statement Before the Subcommittee on Aviation, Committee on Transportation, US House of Representatives, May 2, 2002, http://www.nij.gov/speeches/aviation.htm.

32. "TASER Cartridges," Law Enforcement and Corrections, TASER, 2011, http://www.taser.com/products/law-enforcement/taser-x26-ecd#features.

33. "TASER eXtended Range Electronic Projectile (XREP) Cartridge," Law Enforcement & Corrections, TASER, 2011, http://www.taser.com/products/law-enforcement/taser-xrep.

34. "TASER eXtended Range Electronic Projectile (XREP) Cartridge," Law Enforcement & Corrections, TASER, 2011, http://www.taser.com/products/law-enforcement/taser-xrep#features.

35. "Stinger Systems," NIOA Defence, 2008, http://www.nioa.net.au/Defence/Suppliers/Stinger%20Systems/Default.aspx.

36. "TASER International (TASR)," Wikinvest, 2010, http://www.wikinvest.com/stock/TASER_International_%28TASR%29.

37. Nick Paton Walsh, "Safety Flaw in Police's New Gun," *Guardian*, December 9, 2001, http://www.guardian.co.uk/uk/2001/dec/09/ukcrime.nickpatonwalsh.

38. Daniel Tencer, "Analysis: Taser-Related Deaths in US Accelerating," Raw Story, September 5, 2010, http://www.rawstory.com/rs/2010/09/05/taser-related-deaths -accelerating/.

39. "Vehicle-Mounted Active Denial System (V-MADS)," Globalsecurity.org, July 29, 2010, http://www.globalsecurity.org/military/systems/ground/v-mads.htm.

40. Jürgen Altmann, "Millimetre Waves, Lasers, Acoustics for Non-Lethal Weapons? Physics Analyses and Inferences," printed in Germany, Deutsche Stiftung Frieden-forschung, p. 27, 2008.

41. Dr. John Kenny et al., "A Narrative Summary and Independent Assessment of the Active Denial System," Human Effects Advisory Panel, February 11, 2008.

42. John Adams, "New 'Laser' Weapon Debuts in LA County Jail," NBC LA, August 23, 2010, http://www.nbclosangeles.com/news/local/New-Laser-Weapon-Debuts-in-LA -County-Jail-101230974.html.

43. David Hambling, "'Pain Ray' First Commercial Sale Looms," Wired Danger Room, August 5, 2009, http://www.wired.com/dangerroom/2009/08/pain-ray-first-commercial -sale-looms/.

44. "Long Range Acoustic Device," Tec-FAQ, accessed May 16, 2011, http://www.tech -faq.com/long-range-acoustic-device.html.

45. "LRAD Product Overview," LRAD Corporation, accessed May 17, 2011, http://www.lradx.com/site/content/view/15/110/.

46. David Grieg, "The Long Range Acoustic Device: Pirate Deterrent, Crowd Con-troller or Soft Drink Seller?," *Gizmag*, April 10, 2009, http://www.gizmag.com/lrad-long -range-acoustic-device/11433/.

47. Martin Fletcher, "British and Irish Anti-piracy Experts Rescued—After Pirate At-tack," *Times*, November 29, 2008, http://www.timesonline.co.uk/tol/news/world/africa /article5253731.ece.

48. Gene Sloan, "Report: Cruise Ship Blasted Pirates with Sonic Wave," *USA Today*, January 18, 2011, http://travel.usatoday.com/cruises/post/2011/01/pirate-cruise-ship -spirit-adventure-indian-ocean-saga/138838/1.

49. "HyperShield Acoustic Riot Shield," Ultra Electronics, accessed May 16, 2011, http://www.ultra-hyperspike.com/hypershield.html.

50. US Department of Defense, *Dictionary of Military and Associated Terms*, Joint Pub-lication 1-02, April 12, 2001, p. 557.

51. "Hermes 450-Tactical Long Endurance UAS," Elbit Systems, 2011, http://www .elbitsystems.com/elbitmain/area-in2.asp?parent=3&num=32&num2=32.

52. "MQ-9 Reaper," US Air Force, August 18, 2010, accessed June 2, 2011, http:// www.af.mil/information/factsheets/factsheet.asp?id=6405.

53. "RQ-4 Global Hawk," US Air Force, November 19, 2009, accessed June 2, 2011, http://www.af.mil/information/factsheets/factsheet.asp?fsID=13225.

54. "Fact Sheet: Unmanned Aircraft Systems," Federal Aviation Administration, De-cember 1, 2010, http://www.faa.gov/news/fact_sheets/news_story.cfm?newsId=6287.

55. Ibid.

56. "Skate UAS Factsheet," Aurora Flight Sciences, June 2010, http://www.aurora.aero /Common/Images/ResearchDevelopment/RDfact.pdf.

57. "Small Unmanned Aerial Systems," Aurora Flight Sciences, 2011, http://www.aurora .aero/ResearchDevelopment/SUAS.aspx.

58. "UAS: Wasp, Data Sheet," AeroVironment, 2011, http://www.avinc.com/downloads/ Wasp_III.pdf.

59. "UAS: Wasp," AeroVironment, 2011, http://www.avinc.com/uas/small_uas/wasp/.

60. "DelFly Micro," DelFly, accessed May 16, 2011, http://www.delfly.nl.

CHAPTER 8

Environmental Security and Public Health

TERRENCE M. O'SULLIVAN AND JAMES D. RAMSAY

This chapter will enable the reader to think about a planning process in a way that allows complex environmental security linkages to be considered at the level of strategic national and international policy making and long-range human security. Environmental security is presented both as a concept that should be a key component of US national and homeland security strategy planning, as well as a major, growing, and complex global problem. This chapter provides a summary of weather and climate, global warming, and a brief history of ES; describes the meaning and context of security at various levels; and examines the relationships between the impacts of environmental phenomena and resulting global political and security issues. Just as important, it examines the current and likely future *health* impact of the environment on *human security*. It also makes a direct linkage between ES and both *national* and *homeland security* strategies in developing as well as developed countries.

Weather, Climate, and a Definition of ES

Weather is not the same as climate, though it is commonly mistaken to be. The clearer relationship is that long-terms trends in weather come over time to characterize a region's climate. Weather, and therefore climate, has always been primarily a cyclic natural phenomenon. The earth has had periods of great cooling and great heating, and today, we find ourselves in the midst of a heating period. Many people have heard of "global warming," but the debate has become massively political. Although human science cannot say with unequivocal certainty what all the causes of natural phenomena like weather are, there is a lot of peer-reviewed science (including a Nobel Peace Prize for Science) behind the argument that there is a discernible man-made contribution to climate. Generally, the scientific community is not suggesting that greenhouse gases (GHGs) from human activity cause the earth to warm, as if the earth would not warm without those human activities; rather, the scientific community has measured and believes that human (or anthropomorphic) contributions have made naturally occurring weather cycles worse. To put it simply, human activities exacerbate the natural cycles of climate; put another way, human activities are helping to cause hotter hots, drier dries, wetter wets, and colder colds. This chapter will discuss this and related issues that threaten the security of all peoples.

Global warming and the resulting varying climate change around the world are among the biggest challenges humanity faces. Global warming should not be considered a distant or abstract problem, but rather a challenge we need to all participate in solving. And taken together with various other related problems—especially *peak oil* (and related energy-resource pressures), growing water and food shortages, and population growth—global warming *is expected to become a more significant human security challenge*. This concern is recognized by governments and militaries around the world, including the US Pentagon. For example, hunger is already a rising global problem, reducing decades-long improvements. This has been caused in part by rising food and fuel prices, which will vary, but worsen overall with reduced oil and gas supplies caused by drops in "peak oil" production. Rising hunger has been the cumulative result of several factors, among them are: crop failures and water shortages due to climate change, local growth in population, and a growing demand for high-quality, high-energy input foods like meat (the latter related to rising wealth in countries like India, Brazil, and China). Many food-, water-, and oil-stressed poorer nations are reaching political and social tipping points that culminate in mass migrations or social and political unrest that can eventually lead to their governments failing (i.e., *failed states*).

The main goals of environmental security include stabilizing natural systems that ultimately impact national security, including those systems affected by global warming. Hence, the concept is that sustainable natural systems lead to sustainable security. Hunger, water and fuel shortages, and disease all breed misery and political instability, and such political instability breeds disruptive, expensive terrorism, wars, and other political violence and economic distress, as seen in many of the conflicts in northern Africa and the Middle East. Central challenges of environmental sustainability include: reducing population growth rates as much as possible; eliminating or reducing poverty, which would help stabilize population growth; stabilizing and restoring the earth's critical environmental systems, such as forests, soil, oceans and fisheries, and freshwater supplies; reducing greenhouse gas emissions, to reverse the rising atmospheric levels from their current, and future, unsustainable levels; and achieving sustainable energy policies, including improved *energy efficiency* (better use of energy consumed) and *alternative energy* sources (such as solar, wind, geothermal, biofuels, and the like) to replace the fossil fuel shortages already looming.

What are the expected short- and long-term manifestations of warmer global temperatures? First, these changes will not just occur slowly and incrementally, but some will happen relatively quickly when ecological "tipping points" have been reached (points beyond which stressed natural systems are not able to recover). Among the important climate change–related occurrences will be increasing extreme weather events, including greater heat waves, heavier snowfall and blizzards (in winter), heavier rains, and hurricanes and cyclones and related coastal flooding. The warming of oceans will alter land and water ecosystems and ice melt in land- and sea-based glaciers—especially in the two greatest "canaries in the coal mine" regions of Greenland and the Antarctic that have already led to rising sea levels. Second, other negative impacts will occur with passing time, including the following: bleaching of ocean coral reefs, altered land ecosystems from drought, and water loss from the heat; animal and plant population changes, including increasing and potentially massive species extinctions; and the health effects due to worsening spread of infectious disease agents among humans.

How have we been making the observations about the changing climate? Many top scientists from around the world and from a variety of disciplines (such as meteorology, physics, geology, biology, chemistry, and so on) have been researching various aspects of global warming and climate change for decades—some from as far back as more than one hundred years ago. Global warming and the science behind it are not new, and warnings about the impact of greenhouse gas emissions on climate have been issued by multiple American presidents, including Lyndon B. Johnson, Bill Clinton, and Barack Obama (and vice presidents, such as former US vice president and Nobel Prize winner Al Gore). Climate change is accepted as a reality by every Western major political party in the world (conservative to liberal), with the exception of a few within American politics. But the scientists who know the most about these issues have reached consensus on the fact that anthropogenic (human-caused) greenhouse gas emissions have been and will continue to be the cause of worsening global climate change.[1]

The most respected source for systematic analysis of global warming and its effects has been the Intergovernmental Panel on Climate Change (IPCC), which also won the Nobel Prize for its work.[2] The IPCC has assembled the evidence from thousands of sources and released periodic reports that lay out the best estimates of the evidence for global warming, its current and likely future impacts, and what might be done to reduce or reverse the levels of atmospheric carbon dioxide and other GHGs. The IPCC has taken a cautious approach to its conclusions, and a few of its projections have been revised downward (notably, the speed of Himalayan glacier melt), but many have been exceeded (shown to be worse) by subsequent evidence and actual events. However good the science is, there are several problematic challenges to our understanding of natural systems. For example, scientists do not know how much carbon dioxide the oceans are ultimately able to absorb. Further, even with the best estimates available to measure ozone depletion over the Antarctic or of glacial retreat in the western Antarctic and in Greenland, observations consistently show that the ozone is depleting more quickly than our estimates indicate[3] and that the glaciers have appeared to be both retreating more quickly than we predicted and slower than predicted.[4]

Environmental security is, in many regards, the ultimate *transnational security* problem, since it addresses the fate of the world as a complex physical, economic, and political *ecosystem*. Because of this, ES is a very complex global security policy problem, requiring the participation of governments and transnational organizations, as well as many other global, regional, and local groups. To illustrate the complex and dynamic nature of ES, consider that environmental security manifests itself differently depending on where one is; that is, as mentioned above, security tends to be context specific. For example, in the *developing world* ES manifests as a contributor to geopolitical instability, failed states, and human suffering and ultimately as a significant input into the radicalization process. However, in the industrialized *developed world* ES has important linkages to *critical infrastructure* issues, as well as strategic security issues related to resource supplies and related military and diplomatic relations with resource-exporting nations.

Given the interdependencies of energy, water, and food security, and the economic impacts from natural disasters, the possible security implications from global climate change reveal the distinct possibility of subsequent security challenges for the United States and the West. For example, disruptions in the political economies of developing nations may lead to or enhance the potential for radicalization in populations whose environmental living conditions are becoming increasingly desperate. Environmental security is also an international security problem, in which all nations will be affected by the outcomes, and for which solutions will require the cooperation of many, if not all, national governments, including the largest economies and the largest greenhouse gas contributors, such as the United States, Europe, China, and India.

Human security addresses the safety and well-being of individuals and populations of people versus traditional security's focus on states. Human security includes not just military security or protection from attack, but also freedom from want; it encompasses issues as diverse as public health, infectious diseases, housing, nutrition/food and water (basic needs), and other human needs and quality-of-life issues. Why is this important for climate change and public health? Among the most important solutions to reduction of GHG-producing fossil fuels and *sustainable growth* is *reducing population growth rates*. The best way to accomplish this is by improving the human security of the global population—reducing poverty, improving education, and providing basic human needs, as well as basic family-planning resources.

Ultimately, ES straddles the realms of traditional international and national security. ES and public health policy formulation is also relevant to both traditional security and human security. ES policy formation is highly decentralized and includes many congressional committees, environmental regulatory agencies, and intergovernmental organizations, as well as individual and nongovernmental organization interests. In other words, ES is itself complex and dynamic and can be greatly influenced by the values of individuals, groups, companies, and nations.

Environmental Health, Global Warming, and Climate Change

It is very important to distinguish climate from weather. Weather is a highly variable, not very easily predictable phenomenon that occurs every day. Climate is the overall longer-term weather patterns year to year. While "weather" tends to be naturally variable, "climate" tends to be more stable over time. When scientists use the term *climate change*, they are really referring to per- turbations in the otherwise more stable patterns of climate due to human ac- tivities. Hence, a cold January day in Wisconsin followed by a very warm forty-degree day is not an example of "global climate change." Rather, longer- term trends seen globally that are changing at rates that exceed the historic rates of change are more the point of "climate change." For example, average global temperatures have risen at least 1.4 degrees Fahrenheit since the begin- ning of the twentieth century.[5] To the average person, this may seem signifi- cant. However, the reason that so many nations in the world as well as the majority of the global scientific community are concerned about *global warm- ing* and *climate change* is because of the disruptive, dangerous, and unhealthy results that have come from it. Although some of the details, such as the rate and extent of changes, and some as yet unforeseen consequences have not all been precisely determined, there is a powerful *scientific consensus* that *anthro- pogenic climate change* is occurring. This consensus shows conclusively that human-caused global warming and climate change are occurring. While human activities are affecting the earth's temperature and therefore its envi- ronment due to the release of tremendous amounts of greenhouse gases (GHGs) into the atmosphere, particularly carbon dioxide (CO_2), it is the nat- ural phenomenon called the *greenhouse effect* (discussed below) that actually enables GHGs to warm the earth.

GHGs come from a variety of sources that are, not surprisingly, related to the types of energy consumed by organizations, people, and the government. According to the US Energy Information Administration, in 2010, 21 percent of the energy consumed in the United States was from coal, 37 percent from petroleum, 25 percent from natural gas, and 17 percent from nonfossil fuels.[6] This correlates directly to carbon dioxide emissions as follows: 35 percent of the CO_2 emissions is from coal, 23 percent from natural gas, and 42 percent from petroleum fuels.[7]

Biogeochemical Cycling and Human Activity

The current amount of carbon in the earth's atmosphere is above 390 parts per million (ppm). National Aeronautics and Space Administration scientists stated in 2008 that CO_2 concentrations above 350 ppm are "not compatible with the planet on which civilization developed and to which life on Earth has adapted."[8] The last time the earth's atmospheric carbon levels were as high as they are now was three million years ago; during the Pliocene Epoch the temperature was a full four degrees Celsius higher and the ocean levels seventy-five feet higher. Scientists today predict that ocean levels are expected now to rise one meter (more than three feet) by 2100.[9]

Among the central climate effects on ecological systems is the earth's natural *carbon cycle*, called "the earth's thermostat," in which carbon is cycled through geological processes such as plate tectonics, volcanic activity (which releases carbon and other GHGs into the atmosphere), absorption of airborne carbon by plants and the ocean, and subsequent recycling of carbon into the earth's crust again through dead plants and animals (from which coal, oil, and gas are derived) and other processes on the land and sea. The irony of human-caused or *anthropogenic climate change* from carbon and other GHG emissions is that they are supplementing the already natural carbon cycles that have made life on earth possible. Not all atmospheric carbon is bad. Indeed, the *greenhouse effect* is a natural phenomenon that serves to allow life to exist by trapping sufficient warmth from the sun's radiation and to help in maintaining the earth's atmosphere as a protection from solar radiation and as a nurturing environment for plant growth and all life on earth (see Figure 8.1). Humans have substantially mitigated (that is, influenced) this natural carbon cycle by artificially extracting and burning carbon-emitting fossil fuels, upsetting carbon's natural cycle on a scale not seen for many millions of years. Hence, regarding mitigations in the carbon cycle, the principle of human-caused exacerbation is the focus of environmental scientists who strive to understand the complex interplay between human activities and the natural world.

Rules of Thumb for Environmentalism

There are many biological and chemical laws that govern nature. We mean to suggest below a few "rules of thumb" that students need to keep in mind when learning about how human activities may mitigate natural chemical cycles. These rules are as follows:

1. "What is demanded is supplied." This rule refers to the nature of human economic systems and how a market economy influences nature. Most companies do not set out to negatively influence or pollute nature. It may be safe to say that most people don't either. However, when the supply process erodes or diminishes resources or nature in order to meet demand from the marketplace, the root cause is ultimately the

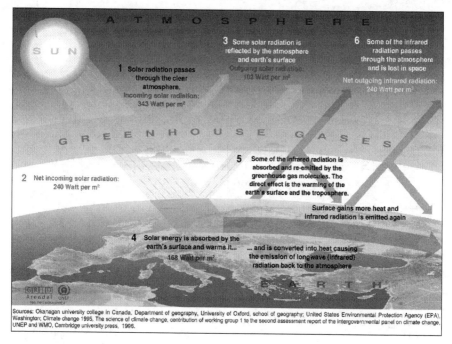

FIGURE 8.1   The greenhouse effect.
Source: http://maps.grida.no/go/graphic/greenhouse-effect.

demand for the good or service, as well as the production or delivery process. Hence, it is incorrect to place blame only on companies when their production, distribution, or storage methods are found to be environmentally harmful.

2. Environmentalism is about relative rates. This rule refers to the fact that humans can demand more of a resource than nature is able to provide, even though that resource may naturally regenerate itself, as water does in the water cycle. When the rate of extraction and use exceeds the recharge rate, the aquifer runs dry.

3. Environmental sustainability does not imply a static condition. This rule refers to the need to allow nature the capacity to change over time in order to meet the stresses placed on it by changes in the chemical or physical environment. In other words, we cannot preserve an ecosystem by placing it in a sealed container. Further, we must recognize that change is one of nature's constants.

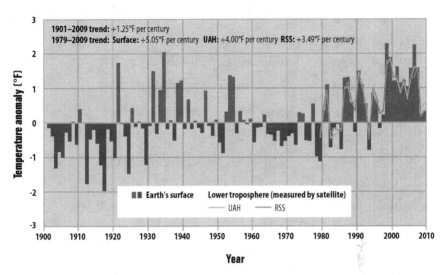

FIGURE 8.2 Temperatures in the Lower 48 States, 1901–2009.

Source: National Oceanic and Atmospheric Administration. 2010.
www.ncdc.noaa.gov/oa/ncdc.html.

Biogeochemistry is the scientific study of the various processes and *systems* that contribute to and regulate the earth's environment. As the name indicates, this includes the biological, geological, and chemical processes, as well as the physical aspects of the earth's environment and interactions, from the *atmosphere* (including the upper layer, the stratosphere, and the lower layer in which we live), the *lithosphere* (the earth's surface and land), the *hydrosphere* (the oceans), the *cryosphere* (the ice), and the *biosphere* (all living systems, and their plants, animals, microbes, and so forth). Biogeochemistry particularly concentrates on the natural cycles of chemicals essential to the fabric of life on earth, such as the cycles of carbon, sulfur, phosphorus, water, and nitrogen. We will exemplify the critical contributions of these chemicals by examining in more detail the carbon cycle below.

Carbon cycles through the environment in a variety of chemical forms. Of these, carbon dioxide is perhaps its most important form. Carbon dioxide is considered the most important "anthropogenic" (that is, coming from human activity) greenhouse gas since it is a key regulator of the earth's surface temperature. Temperature regulation is an interesting characteristic of carbon, since CO_2 is only a trace gas in the atmosphere. The percentage of CO_2 in the atmosphere is only about .037 percent, while nitrogen, argon, and oxygen together constitute more than 99 percent of the atmosphere.[10] Interestingly, using trapped atmospheric gases in ice core samples that can be dated back 650,000 years, scientists know that the level of carbon dioxide exceeds by far the natural levels (180 ppm to 300 ppm).[11] Figure 8.2 indicates the relationship between CO_2 accumulation and average surface temperature. Between 1990 and 2006, the EPA estimates carbon emissions in the United States went up almost 15 percent, with CO_2 from automobiles, coal-fired power plants, and agrobusiness being among the largest sources.[12] With the help of global information system mapping techniques, biogeochemists have now better determined where the balance of US CO_2 emissions is coming from. Scientists have finally started to determine which parts of the country are pumping out the most CO_2 and have been surprised at what they have found.[13] According to the US Energy Information Administration, in 2010, coal is used to produce about 48 percent of the electricity used in the United States, compared to 19 percent from natural gas, 1 percent from petroleum, and 31 percent from nonfossil fuels.[14] As one might expect, 81 percent of the CO_2 arising from electricity production comes from coal, while only 18 percent comes from natural gas and 1 percent from petroleum.[15]

Acid Deposition and Ocean Acidification

As part of the carbon cycle, CO_2 naturally becomes dissolved in the earth's oceans that are able to absorb large amounts of carbon dioxide. The good news is that this has slowed the effects of atmospheric carbon levels, but the bad news is that scientists believe that the oceans may be able to absorb only a finite amount of CO_2 without significantly reducing the acidity level. That is, as oceanic carbon levels increase, it lowers the pH (pH is a measure of the acidity of a solution) of the ocean, or acidifies it.[16] In addition, as a normal part of the carbon cycle, atmospheric CO_2 combines with atmospheric water to form carbonic acid. Carbonic acid then falls in rain into the oceans. This, in addition to the oceanic absorption of CO_2, is acidifying the oceans. If the oceanic pH falls too low, the very bottom of the food chain could be so badly deteriorated so as to be unable to support the oceans' ecosystems.[17]

Ocean acidification only recently came to the full attention of climate scientists and ecologists. The bleaching of coral reefs was among the early warnings of this growing problem. Without a healthy coral reef, the breeding ground for many primary producers is limited. Hence, the very basis of the oceanic food chain is in jeopardy. Given the fact that a large percentage of the world's population depends on the oceans for food and economic vitality, and the speed with which acidification is occurring is increasing, there is enormous stress on the oceans to continue to be able to produce food. In addition, once levels reach dangerous levels, it could be several thousands of years before recovery could occur. Many species will not have enough time to evolutionarily adapt to ocean acidification, leading to extinctions. In the past, much slower geologic historical climate changes have allowed species to adapt to changes in climate. The comparatively rapid, unprecedented pace of changes occurring now will not allow such adaptation and will eventually lead to massive ocean (as well as land) species extinctions; this has occurred only a handful of times over hundreds of millions of years of geologic time.

The Science of Global Warming and Climate Change

Among the many physical manifestations of climate change have been nonpolar glacier retreat, reduction in Arctic sea ice extent and thickness in summer, reduced thickness of Antarctic sea ice, and breaking off and disintegration of large whole ice sheets.

Changes in Sea Level, Ice Melt, and Uncertainties

Among the major trends in climate change is the rise in sea levels and the increasingly disturbing modeling that projects a significant increase in sea levels over the course of the twenty-first century. Sea levels have already risen for four main reasons, including the following:

1. Melting of land-based ice held in year-round high-altitude and mountain glaciers
2. Thermal expansion of the seawater due to ocean warming (water naturally expands with heat)
3. Melting of the polar ice sheets in the Arctic (northern polar region)
4. Melting of ice in Greenland and the Antarctic ice sheets

Because of the effects of heat, ocean water will likely eventually rise from a handful of inches to up to one foot in the next eighty years, depending on the extent of average global temperature increases.

Arctic Sea Ice

Among the many early indications of dramatic change from global warming and climate change is the increasing seasonal (summer) melting of the Arctic sea ice. If current trends continue, the Arctic sea ice may disappear to such an extent in summer that the Arctic becomes navigable to standard oceangoing ships for the first time in human history. This has implications not only for sea-level rise, but also (along with Greenland ice melt) for the amount of cold meltwater that infiltrates into the northern Atlantic Ocean. This ice melt could help disrupt the ocean conveyor belt in that region and, if so, have both weather and longer-term climate cooling effects on Europe. Last, Arctic Sea ice melt will effect both shipping and the strategic security calculations of the world's navies, especially if the "northern passage" significantly opens for several months of the year.

Greenland and West Antarctica: The Canaries in the Coal Mine

It is the potential for the melting of the Greenland and Antarctic ice—the two "canaries in the coal mine"—that is the most troubling. These two regions collectively hold a vast majority of the world's freshwater, frozen in the *cryosphere*. The south polar region (Antarctica) holds 90 percent of the earth's ice and 70 percent of the earth's frozen freshwater.[18] If only the West Antarctic ice sheets, which hold less than 10 percent of the Antarctica's ice, were to melt, sea levels would eventually rise around an estimated seventeen feet—inundating most current major coastal cities in the world. If both Greenland and all Antarctic ice were to melt, sea levels would eventually rise almost two hundred feet, according to estimates.

If either the Greenland or the West Antarctic ice sheet was to even partially melt, global sea levels would rise catastrophically. Even a few feet of rise will do significant damage to coastal cities and lowlands. It is too early to know if, and how fast, these regions might see such melting. But increasing evidence, from observed melting and various geological history investigations of past carbon levels correlated with global temperature, shows that such melting could be happening much more easily and faster than believed only a few years ago.

Overall, the rise in sea level from eventual land-based glacial melt, ocean expansion, and even conservative estimates of glacial melt from Greenland and Antarctica, all from climate change–related temperature increases, could be seven to twenty-three inches above today's level by 2100. This is significant on its own, as it would mean extensive flooding in Southeast Asia, Florida, and

Louisiana and devastation to many South Pacific Island nations.[19] Given that more than half the earth's population lives within 120 miles of the ocean, living on 10 percent of the land's surface,[20] security impacts are predictable due to mass migrations and food shortages, and subsequent disruption in the economic and political structures of these regions would logically ensue.

Hurricanes, Drought, Floods, Blizzards, and Heat Waves

Higher global temperatures are going to lead to a number of increasingly severe swings in weather events (short-term storms and medium- to longer-term patterns and weather extremes). The following are among various severe weather events expected, all of which are already occurring at various levels:

1. An *increase in maximum temperatures* in most land areas on earth, including more hot days and severe *heat waves*. The 2007 *IPCC Report* asserted with very high confidence that heat waves will continue to occur. In turn, heat waves will lead to increased heat-related deaths in *urban heat islands*, which can be seven to twelve degrees Fahrenheit hotter than rural or even suburban residential areas.[21] Even now, on average, heat events kill more Americans than tornadoes, hurricanes, and other extreme weather events combined (and such deaths tend to be underreported). More than half the world's population lives in urban areas (up from 30 percent in 1950), which are much hotter than rural areas, given the lack of cooling foliage and an environment of heat-absorbing concrete, dark roofs, stone, and street tarmac. In recent history, major heat disasters have already occurred. One heat wave killed more than thirty-four thousand Europeans, including fourteen thousand in France in August 2003.[22] Other negative results of increasing heat events will be greater damage to crops and heat stress among livestock, resulting in economic damage and loss of food sources, rising food prices, and so on.
2. Climate change could lead to *higher minimum temperatures* over nearly all land areas on earth, leading to fewer cold days (as well as frost and cold episodes). This will reduce heating requirements, but will also extend the range of pests and *disease vectors* such as mosquitoes and ticks and various related tropical diseases—such as malaria, yellow fever, and dengue fever—that do not flourish in colder climates. Warmer minimum temperatures could also lead to the loss of some fruit crops dependent on

frosts and cooler weather and damage or destroy local weather-sensitive industries, such as wine production, in many areas.

3. Climate change will bring more intense *high precipitation–related weather events* over many land areas. This means heavier rainfall and even heavier snowstorms in winter. Such extreme events will lead to more landslides and mud slides, heavy flooding, and increasing economic and insurance losses from life and damage to property. Worsening flooding and extreme storms are predicted to occur in places like the United States, where many regions are expected to have rising average precipitation and temperatures attributed to climate change.

4. *Drought* and increasing *seasonal summer drying* is another consequence in midlatitude continental interiors (such as the American Midwest). This would reduce agricultural productivity and land available for grazing, increase the risk of wildfires, reduce water available for human and animal use, and reduce the output of hydroelectric dams in affected areas.

5. Climate change and global warming will likely *increase the intensity of tropical hurricanes and cyclones*. Damage to cities, coastlines, agriculture, and delicate natural ecosystems could be caused by increased peak wind intensity and increased average and peak precipitation intensities. In addition, there will likely be increased numbers of higher category (more severe) storms during the Atlantic hurricane season, which, in combination with rising ocean levels, could imperil Gulf and Atlantic coast states as well as poorer nations in Central America and South America.

"Global Cooling" and Ocean Currents

Global cooling refers to two phenomena: that the upper atmosphere—the troposphere—is cooling because the greenhouse effect is preventing heat from reflecting back up into it from the earth, and that there is the possibility that regional climates could actually cool in some places, rather than warm, due to overall climate change effects that would disrupt current heat exchange patterns.

The *ocean conveyor belt* works, most simply, by circulating warm and cold water and nutrients in currents around the world. The ocean also absorbs and stores carbon dioxide from the atmosphere, acting like a sponge for up to one-third or more of atmospheric carbon dioxide. Thus, the oceans regularly help to reduce the impact of anthropomorphic emissions of GHGs on the global climate. However, the degree to which the oceans can continue to absorb GHGs is unclear. The ability to absorb GHGs can be disrupted by ice melt runoff and the introduction of huge amounts of cold freshwater into the oceans in the North Atlantic. According to scientific modeling, melting Arctic and Greenland ice could disrupt the ocean conveyor belt that transfers warming water from the Gulf Stream current, to the south, from the Gulf of Mexico and the Caribbean, through the Atlantic up past the British Isles, and into the Nordic seas of northern Europe. Without the Gulf Stream waters' heat transfer, the European continent would experience (and has before, in geologic history) a climate much cooler than it is at present.

"Global Dimming" and the Prospect of Rapid Warming

The idea of global dimming is one that has been reported off and on for the past several years. One of the ironies of high-level particulate pollution (for example, sulfur and nitrogen oxides, coal particulates like soot, and photochemical smog) is that in many areas of the world, there has been a "dimming" effect that is actually partially offsetting some of the negative effects of GHGs. High-altitude particulates (soot), water vapor, and other gases from pollution are reducing the amount of sunlight or heat energy that reaches the earth. Global dimming is akin to polluting your way to cooler temperatures. The notion that catastrophes (such as 9/11) can add to air-pollution levels was confirmed during the days immediately after the 9/11 terrorist attacks, according to an EPA study.[23]

International Treaties and the Environment

Since environmental issues gained prominence on the international stage in the 1970s, there have been attempts to curb environmental degradation and destruction through the international treaty structure. These have met with limited success, at best, as this section will review.

Ozone Diplomacy

In 1987 most of the world's nations signed the *Montreal Protocol*, an international treaty regulating the production of *halogens/halocarbons*, such as chlorofluorocarbons, freons, and halons, which are the main culprits in the damage to the earth's protective ozone layer.[24] Among the reasons for the success of the Montreal Protocol was the ability to replace these chemicals with acceptable (e.g., cheap and effective) alternatives. Without this replacement technology, restriction of these ozone depleting chemicals would have been very difficult. Despite the successful reductions in these destructive compounds, there is a lag period of a number of decades before which they will dissipate, meaning that the risk of ozone depletion from halocarbons will continue for at least a generation. According to the latest international report assessing the state of the ozone layer, ozone should recover its pre-1980 levels around 2045–2060 over the South Pole and probably one or two decades earlier over the North Pole.[25]

Climate Negotiations Stalemate: From Rio to Kyoto and Beyond

The first major climate breakthrough followed the UN Framework Convention on Climate Change (UNFCCC), negotiated at the 1992 Earth Summit in Rio de Janeiro.[26] There the participating nations pledged to create and execute climate-related measures appropriate for and specific to each of the contributing members present. The industrialized nations present agreed to voluntary reductions in their respective GHG emissions down to 1990 levels, ostensibly by 2000.[27] The convention was ratified by 186 countries, including the United States. However, in ensuing years very few developed, industrialized nations met these voluntary targets. According to the *Fifth US Climate Action Report*, GHG emission levels increased 17 percent between 1990 and 2007.[28] During the same time, the US population increased 21 percent and the US gross domestic product increased 65 percent,[29] showing how tightly connected population growth and economic activity are to GHG emissions and climate change.

The 1997 *Kyoto Protocol*, the protocol to the UNFCCC (a.k.a. "Rio+5"),[30] attempted several improvements over the original Rio convention. Each of these improvements was based in the economics of free trade, innovation, and market interactions. In other words, the Kyoto Protocol recognized that there are solid business principles behind "going green" and attempted to initiate those principles into each signatory's economy. Briefly, the market-based mechanisms included: emissions trading (a.k.a. the "carbon market"), clean development of green technologies, and joint implementation, which allows a nation to meet its emissions targets by removing older and dirtier technologies or by renovating existing technology. By establishing absorptive GHG "sinks" such as forests and farmland, the Kyoto accords allowed that nations could reach their emissions targets by reducing six different GHGs.

The protocol also aspired to set up strict monitoring and reporting elements and sought to begin establishing a more stringent compliance regime to pressure noncompliant nations to fulfill their commitments. While admitting that the United States was "hooked" on Middle Eastern oil, President Bush did not sign the Kyoto accords, claiming doing so would hurt the US economy.[31]

More recently, in Cancún, Mexico, far more modest progress has been made in working out compromises aimed at carbon emission regulation.[32] But major breakthroughs have not subsequently occurred, and the United States continued to reject the stricter, more comprehensive Kyoto Protocol provisions even under the Obama administration. In addition, congressional efforts in the United States to achieve a climate bill, which might have included a broad "cap-and-trade" (for carbon emissions) market-based provision, were blocked in the US Senate by a coalition of Republicans and some Democrats.

Climate-Denial Politics

It is believed by some people in the United States that there is still a scientific "debate" about whether global warming and climate change are occurring. From a scientific standpoint, there is a consensus among climate experts that such changes are occurring and human greenhouse gas emissions are measurably contributing to it. The only real "debate" now is based upon discussing how fast these changes are occurring, how bad they will be, and what might be done to mitigate or reverse them. Most of the false debate that has been promoted is by those with an economic interest, including corporations, states, or regions that rely on income from energy (oil, gas, and coal) industries. The evidence supporting climate change is advanced, multifaceted, overwhelming, and represents the consensus of thousands of scientists from more than eighty-five nations who have studied, researched, and debated this topic over the past forty years and submitted their findings to the peer-review process. Nevertheless, not everyone agrees. There are several organizations based in the United States that attempt to subvert the climate change debate, most of which are funded by large corporations.[33] Among such climate-denial organizations is the Heartland Institute, which makes claims directly counter to climate scientists, but with either false information or distorted logic.[34] Another is the Competitive Enterprise Institute, funded up until 2005 by the largest corporation in the world, Exxon-Mobil, which, along with other major oil companies, still supports climate-denial organizations.[35]

Global Water Politics: Shortages in the United States and the World

Illustrating the environmental principle that what is demanded is supplied, among the most significant problems that will result from climate change is growing water shortages around the world. This situation is made worse by growing populations and water overuse (and misuse) patterns. Already there are many regions where "water politics" have been simmering, and the future is bleak for those areas in the world already stressed by simultaneous diminishing *supply* and growing *demand* for water. Several factors are contributing to the water-shortage issue, but they all add up to tremendous problems for the standard of living, and even survival, of affected populations.

- Climate change has contributed to melting high-altitude glacial ice in mountain ranges; disappearing year-round glaciers will eliminate dry-season melt flows to lower-altitude areas. Some of the most critically affected regions will be the Indian subcontinent. India will be particularly hurt, since it has a double water crisis occurring—both a rapidly growing population (and rising consumption demands from industry, farming, and direct consumption by people) and a soon-to-be diminishing water supply coming from the Himalayas.

- Climate change is also contributing to rising average global temperatures that will *deplete* the amount of moisture in soil, particularly in farmland, reducing crop yields and increasing crop-failure rates. This will also lead to soil-wind erosion and potential "dust bowls," similar to those that occurred in the central US states, such as Oklahoma, in the early twentieth century. The drier topsoil will blow away more easily and erode faster overall.

- The overuse of water sources will result in excess *diversion*. Many rivers and lakes in the world have been increasingly diverted for water use in cities and agriculture. Once the largest freshwater lake in Asia, the Aral Sea in Kazakhstan has been virtually drained dry because of diversion of its source rivers for irrigation (note that this is an application of the second rule in environmentalism, "relative rates"). It is now a huge bowl of toxic dust blowing up from the former lake bottom. In the western United States, growing populations have caused increasing water diversion, and reduced rainfall averages (increasing drought years) have diminished the flow of rivers such as the Colorado River. In California, Owens Lake, once among the largest freshwater lakes in the western United States, has been drained by diversion to Southern California and nearby agricultural irrigation. And diminishing Himalayan mountain glacial runoff and population growth in those areas are causing rising water-politics tension. China is discussing diversion of Brahmaputra River water, much to the consternation of India, which is downstream.

- Drilling for water for farming and other uses has been increasing, leading to dropping levels in *water aquifers*. In particular, water "mining" of deep underground *ancient aquifers*, such as the Ogallala in the United States, has permanently depleted these sources of water in many nations. In concert with exponentially increasing population, *depletion* via extraction has been occurring around the world, particularly when shallower rechargeable aquifers are depleted first. Even if natural resources naturally recharge, as water does, society can deplete them by using them at rates that exceed nature's ability to recharge. The US Ogallala aquifer is being tapped aggressively for agricultural irrigation. The irrigation "crop circles" visible from the air as one flies over the plains and Midwest are often tied to deep underground aquifers. Ultimately another application of the second rule of environmentalism, the depletion of these ancient reservoirs is an example of how society is able to destroy a shared public resource predicted by *The Tragedy of the Commons*.

Failed States and Environmental Security

Among the biggest risks from climate change and related resource shortages, as well as growing "peak oil" (see below) energy shortages, will be the security instability presented by states (nations) that will devolve into weakened, and even chaotic, "failed," states. The concept of a *failed state* arises from political science and security studies and refers to governments that have either lost the ability to adequately govern their territory or dissolved entirely. The economic and political implications of climate change, rising populations, and energy, food, and water resource shortages in already stressed regions will lead to more examples of the failed-state phenomenon. And with that will come increasing situations of civil war, "warlord" rule, and havens for international terrorism. A *stable state* has the comparative ability to control borders, enact and enforce national laws, put policies into effect, maintain an effective judiciary and police capability, collect taxes, and so on. A *weak state* lacks some of these capabilities and often is in a situation in which its policies are not in effect across the entire nation (often limited to major cities, for instance) and lacks political legitimacy. Although the definition is not absolute, a state that has "failed" is one in which there is little or no government legitimacy or authority; there is anarchy and often civil war on the streets, and political and military control is divided and controlled by warlords. The classic case of this was Somalia in the 1990s, when the Clinton administration intervened to provide humanitarian relief and finally withdrew after the disastrous *Blackhawk Down* incident.

Among the variables that can lead to failed states are the following: humanitarian and refugee crises from mass migrations, population pressures, violent political schisms, significant economic decline and poverty, widening income disparities, erosion of public services, corruption and criminalization of government, military violence against civilians, and declarations of "martial law" (suspensions of legal rights) and other human rights oppression. In a primary planning document of the US military, the *QDR*, each of these causal contributing variables can be triggered or worsened by natural disasters and resource shortages, many of which will arise as global warming causes cascading economic, political, and social system failures.

Meanwhile, as both oil-producing and -consuming nations confront global production shortages and rising prices, the combined impact of energy- and climate-related environmental and economic disruptions will continue to weaken already susceptible countries and increase the threat from terrorism and spillover conflicts. Without intervention to prevent these failures, the security threat will grow. Historically, the United States has intervened to prevent failed states in dozens of instances. The largest such programs in human history, the Marshall Plan, helped save post–World War II Europe (and Japan) from state failures.

Energy Shortages, "Peak Oil," and Political Crisis

Energy is an absolute requirement for most human development and well-being. As if the problems of greenhouse gases, anthropogenic climate change, growing global populations, and the attendant demand on resources were not bad enough, there is a looming crisis in the global supplies of energy of all kinds. Oil and gas reserves are declining, now past their "peak," and increasingly expensive and energy-intensive to extract from the ground. Even without a reduction in GHG emissions due to burning fossil fuels, unless there are miraculous advances in new energy-generation technologies (such as cold fusion), the growing global energy demand will lead to energy shortages, rising prices, and political and security tensions. There is a growing recognition that energy will be an issue with considerable *international security* implications for all nations. The US military and security institutions around the world have recognized the need to better prepare for this. They are beginning to invest in fuel-efficient and non-fossil-fuel energy technologies to reduce dependency on dwindling global oil and gas supplies.

Peak Oil: Dwindling Supply, Rising Demand

Peak oil refers to the concept that there is a finite amount of it available, so there is a point where the maximum amount of oil that can be extracted is extracted. Oil extraction after that point continues to dwindle. Of course, the challenge peak oil presents is twofold: most of the world's economies are directly dependent on oil, and the earth's population continues to increase. As such, the "peak oil" point is a looming crisis that has increased the urgency of both finding alternative energy technologies to replace oil as well as finding ways to reduce demand. As indicated earlier, oil and gas use has been the central driver of global economic development in *all* nations. Even if climate change were not such a pressing crisis by itself, peak oil complicates the *supply and demand* dynamics immeasurably, unless alternative technologies and efficiencies in use are accelerated during the next few decades. The world's use of nonrenewable fossil fuels has depleted the supplies of oil and gas such that production is decreasing as demand increases. As such, many nations have been replacing or increasingly supplementing oil and gas energy with coal, an even dirtier source of energy. About half of the United States's electricity supply is produced by the burning of one billion tons of coal per year.[36] The average American household uses almost ten tons of coal for electric power annually. China alone uses coal in massive amounts, depending on coal for about 80 percent of its electricity.[37]

Peak oil and gas, and associated growing energy supply and demand problems, should not be underestimated as a cause of future global security instability and human misery. Access to, and control over, oil was the crux of political tensions for much of the twentieth century and will be so for the twenty-first century, as supplies drop in the face of ever-growing demands.

Oil and the Pending Global Food Crisis

Climate change, population growth, peak oil, and other anthropogenic variables influence food supply and demand and, as such, are examples of interactive and potentially cascading global crises. If population growth continues to outpace food production and if food distribution is hampered by climatic, economic, and political reasons, experts expect there to be a pending food-shortage crisis that will be caused by the following:

Peak oil: Energy use and inputs in the form of oil- and gas-related products (e.g., nitrogen fertilizers, fuel for farming), machine production, and transportation of food to distant markets have become very important for modern agricultural productivity and distribution. The rising price of oil is thought to be at least in part caused by a combination of the inevitable depletion of oil and gas reserves (supply) and rising global demand for energy. Since food production in the developed world is energy intensive, as the price of oil increases, the price of food follows. Rising food prices will be particularly traumatic for the poor. Consequently, as food becomes increasingly expensive, mass migrations of populations seeking better opportunities can be expected. Such migrations will add stress to the economies and governments of both receiving nations and the nations who are losing the skills and talents of their populace.

Population increase and pressure for rising standards of living: As with all economic patterns in global free markets, both the supply of a product and the demand for it interact to influence prices and availability. Even if there was no pressure on current food supplies from climate, energy inputs, and land use, the demand for food must inevitably rise as the global population grows. The world population, currently at 7 billion,[38] is projected to be anywhere from 7.4 to more than 10.6 billion by 2050.[39] Further complicating the stresses, about 70 percent of the earth's population exists in either a developing or a less-developed nation.[40] Expanding populations in cities and in the countryside most often take over land that had been among the most fertile, removing it from agricultural production use. In addition, demand for food has been rising because all nations aspire to raise their overall economic growth rate and standards of living. China and India, the two most populous nations, have rapid growth rates, and their per capita use of resources, including food, has been rising accordingly. The increased consumption of meat, for instance, takes much greater energy and resources per calorie consumed than other agricultural products.

Land use: One of the negative effects of a growing population is changing, often destructive, land use. Land previously used for food crops is increasingly taken outside urban areas to develop housing for rapidly expanding populations. In addition, a number of other land-use patterns have reduced the availability of arable and fertile land, reduced productivity per acre farmed, or simply destroyed forests that are important for capturing and storing atmospheric carbon. One of the effects of rising food prices worldwide has been a growing incentive to cut down forests—know as *deforestation*—to plant various profitable crops. As the food crisis grows, so will deforestation pressures, just at a time when more, not less, forest is needed to help offset anthropogenic carbon and climate change. *Overfarming* is another problem, especially in developing, poorer nations, and this is leading to mineral-depleted soil with reduced or no ability to produce crops. Even in the developed Western nations, soil depletion is avoided mostly by the addition of supplemental fertilizer—made from oil and gas fossil fuels. *Soil depletion* will then interact with rising temperatures that lead to the loss of soil moisture; all of this inevitably leads to *topsoil loss*, further reducing the amount of agricultural land available to farm.

Climate change: Global warming and climate change will lead to rising temperatures and climate disruptions in food-production areas. Desertification, drought, and extreme weather, especially flooding, will all reduce agricultural productivity in many areas of the world. In other areas, food-crop productivity will improve (Canada, for instance), but will not make up for lost acreage and *extreme weather*-related crop failures elsewhere. Certain areas of the world, parts of Africa and South America, for instance, may become virtually uninhabitable because high heat and arid climates prevent local food production.

Adequate global food production and distribution are among the biggest challenges in the coming decades, worsened by a combination of climate change, population pressures, energy-input shortages (peak oil), land-use patterns, and unstable political environments. From a *human security* standpoint, food shortages would be a major problem. But food shortages themselves will also be an important causal variable in worsening overall *global security*, through political instability and a rise in *failed states*. People who are hungry are more vulnerable to disease and public health problems, but also more likely to rebel against their governments. Food and other resource shortages lead to everything from the overthrow of governments to wars with other nations and terrorism. This is among the many reasons *climate change is a homeland security problem*.

Infectious Diseases and Public Health Security

Climate change will be a causal variable in rising global infectious disease risks. However, infectious disease *biological security* risks are rising for other reasons as well. Not only are they, in part inadvertently, related to the economic system created by globalization, but they are also related to *bioterrorism* risks as a result of rising biological technological capabilities.[41]

Globalization and disease risk: Global economic integration and trade have led to rising incomes, standards of living, life expectancy, medical care, sanitation, and a host of other factors that have contributed to improvement in the overall health of the world's populations. However, many nations are still very poor and have not benefited as much; on the other hand, dozens of emerging nations have undergone rapidly rising living standards because of world trade, travel, and economic interdependency—that is, *globalization*. There have been unanticipated, unintended side effects of globalization. Vulnerability to infectious disease outbreaks is one of these results. Several aspects of globalization are implicated in infectious disease vulnerability. First is *trade* in goods, which has exploded over the past forty years. Extensive trade in goods of all kinds allows for a free ride for infectious disease agents or their insect and animal *vectors* (intermediary disease carriers) to distant locations, on ships, planes, trains, trucks, and so on. Infectious disease outbreaks have been traced to tainted food and water transported by ships. One of the worst cholera pandemics in the twentieth century was originally thought to be linked to cholera bacteria in seawater picked up in the Indian Ocean bays. Ships would intake ballast water and then dump it offshore in South America. But that outbreak, which killed more than ten thousand people, was subsequently traced to strains of cholera from Africa, showing that such disease "migration" can be difficult to pin down.[42] Various species of mosquitoes can carry diseases such as malaria, yellow fever, and dengue fever and are transported in the holds of ships and aircraft, allowing for the geographic spread of such diseases. This is made worse by warming temperatures worldwide that allow a greater range for tropical diseases.

Travel is also implicated in the rising risk of globalization-related infectious disease. Hundreds of millions of passenger flights occur every year; global airline travel is rapidly increasing. Someone who is sick can spread that illness just about anywhere in the world within forty-eight hours. This means that it is far more difficult to prevent the spread of transmissible, highly infectious diseases such as influenza. For instance, the 2003 SARS outbreak was made worse by its rapid spread from China to other cities, such as Toronto, Canada. Other globalization-related public health and infectious disease risk factors include rising *urbanization*, migration, and even population growth itself. More than half the world lives in cities. This is comparatively good for access to medical care, but much of the developing world's populations increasingly live in megacity slums in countries like India, Nigeria, and Mexico, where the necessary medical care is not provided. Many infectious diseases thrive when people are in close proximity; migration and urbanization have worsened this vulnerability, just as rising overall populations have stressed public health infrastructures.

Antimicrobial drug resistance: Among the most troubling, growing dilemmas for global public health is the rise in *antimicrobial resistance*, described as the declining effectiveness of antibiotic (antibacterial), antiviral, and other drugs that have revolutionized medicine since the discovery of penicillin in the early twentieth century. Among the reasons for the rise in antimicrobial resistance are misuse of these drugs, either for inappropriate reasons (e.g., using an antibiotic drug for a viral infection against which it has no effect) or not using it for a sufficient length of time to kill the infectious disease organism; overuse in people, but particularly overuse in agrobusiness on animals used for food (cattle, pigs, chickens, and more), in which 70–80 percent of all US antibiotics are used; and, related to use of antibiotics in agrobusiness or animal husbandry, the significant runoff of animal waste from farms into the environment (soil, rivers, and lakes), which raises the antibiotic resistance of bacteria such as E-coli. E-coli has been implicated in many severe food-borne disease outbreaks, in the United States and elsewhere, including the infamous 2011 German-based European case in which a newer, more deadly O104:H4 strain emerged that killed scores of people and crippled hundreds of others.

Economic, legal disincentives for drug and vaccine development: Part of the problem with rising antimicrobial resistance to *existing* drugs is the fact that *new* drug development is not keeping pace to replace the losses. Among the reasons for the failure of pharmaceutical corporations to keep pace with the reduction in antibiotic effectiveness, or to invest more in development of new vaccines, is that companies do not see either as sufficiently profitable to pursue. This is caused in part by concern for consumer legal liability lawsuits that have historically been aimed at vaccine and drug manufacturers and to a comparative economic incentive system in which research, development, and marketing of other drugs are far more profitable. This is especially true for infectious diseases primarily associated with the poorer, developing world, where there is less of a profitable market to tap.

The interaction of public health and climate change: Climate change is expected to lead to regional increases in *arboviruses*, such as mosquito-borne and other vector-borne diseases that thrive in warmer climates. Many diseases are carried by biting insect vectors, and their range and persistence will increase the incidence of infectious diseases that are carried by them. Extreme weather, from droughts to hurricanes and floods, will also increase the risks from infectious disease. For instance, the infectious disease effects of massive flooding were seen in 2010 in Pakistan.[43] Subsequent public health surveys conducted six months later showed that 25 percent of children under five were malnourished, due to the destruction of crops and the failure of sufficient aid to reach the affected areas; future seasons' crops were also jeopardized by destruction of irrigation systems from flooding.[44] Droughts reduce availability of water for drinking and sanitation, as well as contributing to crop failure and resulting malnutrition and hunger—all of which increase disease susceptibility.

Global public health governance: Among the obstacles with addressing global public health problems is the lack of strong international institutions to manage and regulate cross-border infectious disease and other health risks. The main institution for global public health is contained within the UN's World Health Organization (WHO), which represents hundreds of nations, but does not have much power to influence change. WHO is limited by a number of variables, including its decentralized (regional) power structure, which is far less effective than the equivalent economic and trade organization, the World Trade Organization, and some other international treaty organizations, and by larger Western nations' unwillingness to let WHO regulate national public health–related policies, including patent laws that affect the global "free markets" in which large private corporations (such as biotechnology drug manufacturers) operate.

Economic implications of public health security issues: There will be rising costs from public health–related problems in a world with various climate change– and resource-related stresses. Although it is difficult to predict just how costly they will be, it is certain that they will cumulatively strip trillions of dollars from the global economy over the course of this century.

Public health implications of biotechnology- and biological defense–related research and development: Among the most pressing "double-edged swords" in the twenty-first century will be the rise in biological technology (*biotech*) and related technologies that will revolutionize everything from medicine to industry. The emergence of microbiological techniques and devices has opened the door for breakthroughs in genetic mapping, vastly increasing humanity's understanding of the genetic makeup—the genomes—of humans, animals, plants, and microbial organisms. Advances in *bioengineering* have already led to novel versions of plants and even animals, the rise in gene therapy for individuals, and the promise of treatments and cures for cancer, heart disease, and other chronic diseases. *Nanotechnology*, the manipulation of materials at the microscopic *nanometer* level, is also a related area that combines multiple converging technologies and fields, including biotech, chemistry, physics, biology, engineering, and materials sciences, among others. Biotech and associated nanotech are already rapidly growing areas of economic investment, research for pharmaceutical and medical companies, and a host of other product-development sectors. Nonetheless, with the good often comes the bad. With the proliferation of biological and nanotech research worldwide comes a rising risk from accidental release of dangerous organisms or materials and environmental contamination from unknown risks.

Biological accidents: Already, there have been troubling accidents related to civilian biotech and government "biodefense" research. In the United Kingdom there was an outbreak of the highly contagious animal disease known as foot-and-mouth disease (FMD), traced back to a Surrey biotech research facility that was working on ways to minimize those very same FMD risks. And among the risk variables is that much of the work being done in these fields is increasingly in developing nations, with less oversight than would be provided by Western regulatory agencies.

Bioweapons: Many of the same rising technologies might, in the very near future, be used for development of weapons that could do harm. A number of government commissions and civilian scientific organizations have warned of the coming threats from unregulated *biotech* and *nanotech* capabilities falling into the wrong hands. It will be easier for would-be terrorists, or national militaries, to develop bioweapons that might be even more deadly than existing infectious diseases. And it all may have started with research to engineer a vaccine, but results in drug-resistant pathogens that could render standard public health and medical response measures ineffective.

Conclusion

This chapter presented several different perspectives of homeland security, human security including environmental security, and public health; in particular, we addressed many aspects of environmental health and how it relates to US security concerns. For example, we connected the principles of environmental and public health to climate change in order to illustrate the need to include the precepts of ES in our national security strategic planning process. If the precepts of ES are left out of the national debate on homeland security policy and out of the national security strategic planning process, our national security strategy will itself be deficient. In effect:

1. Failure to secure our environment acts as a threat multiplier, especially in fragile nations or regions with pervasive conflict, so knowing how to avoid or offset catastrophic environmental changes is in the nation's vital interest. This reflects the need to consider ES as an objective of homeland security policy.
2. ES may act differentially across nations; that is, failure to secure the environment may destabilize the political economy of less developed countries, potentially leading to radicalization; however, it may instead act to create vulnerabilities in critical infrastructure in more developed countries. This indicates the need to consider ES in strategic policy

making in order to diffuse transnational asymmetric terrorism as well as to make the US infrastructure more resilient to catastrophic disasters.

3. As a result, ES can be used as a nexus for both an overseas-focused counterterrorism strategy as well as a long-term homeland security strategy.

Figure 8.3 demonstrates the many impacts of global warming.

Better integration of ES principles into national security strategic planning leads us to consider how ES might be integrated in transnational security as well as homeland security. That is, we should thoroughly examine environmental threats and hazards transnationally in order to determine how these threats become HS issues for the United States and its allies. Further, we need to better examine domestic environmental threats and hazards in order to understand the degree to which these threats become infrastructure security issues for the United States. Several examples follow:

1. ES can employ environmental science and health principles such as sustainability and carrying capacity to analyze and evaluate environmental vulnerabilities to natural disasters or prolonged climatic anomalies in areas of US security interest. Considering that the United States has eighteen sectors of critical infrastructure and the world's largest economy, it is logical to assume that it can afford to protect everything all the time from all hazards. ES principles may enable a better use of risk-management methodology to help the United States and its allies better understand how to sustainably protect enormous amounts of critical infrastructure and thereby better safeguard the economy.

2. ES principles can be connected to HS strategic planning by using the same types of vulnerability analysis and assessment tools used to evaluate risks to local or regional populations from natural disasters and to build resiliency and sustainability.

3. The US national security strategy should reflect the fact that environmental effects can cause security impacts in areas already stressed by resource scarcity, overpopulation, deforestation and land overuse, population migration, and political instability, such as in the Middle East and sub-Saharan Africa.

Ultimately, a large part of homeland security seeks to protect and promote smooth economic functioning that leads to political stability. Since

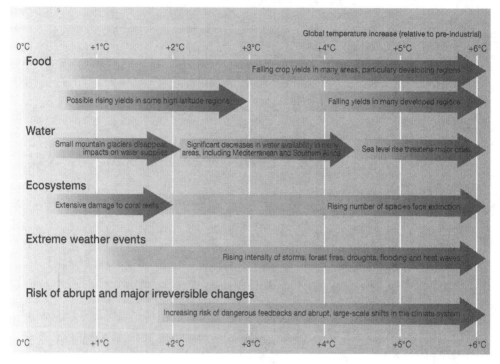

FIGURE 8.3A   Projected impacts of climate change.
Source: Stern Review, 2008.

use of fossil fuels is the primary energy basis of the US economy, as well as the economies of all nations of the world, the degree to which nations have become so dependent upon fossil fuels implies that change to new energy use and consumption habits is a daunting prospect—but one that is critical to long-term energy security. When one considers all the externalities of the use of oil, including GHG emissions, rising food and energy prices, and disputes over its production and control, in the midst of increasing pressure from a growing population, it is clear why environmental security needs to be a key element in homeland security strategic planning.

NOTES

1. W. R. L. Anderegg, J. W. Prall, J. Harold, and S. H. Schneider (2010-06-21), "Expert Credibility in Climate Change," *Proceedings of the National Academy of Sciences of the United States of America* 107, no. 27 (2010): 12107–12109.

Phenomenon[a] and direction of trend	Likelihood of future trends based on projections for 21st century using SRES scenarios	Examples of major projected impacts by sector			
		Agriculture, forestry, and ecosystems	Water resources	Human health	Industry, settlement, and society
Over most land areas, warmer and fewer cold days and nights, warmer and more frequent hot days and nights	Virtually certain[b]	Increased yields in colder environments; decreased yields in warmer environments; increased insect outbreaks	Effects on water resources relying on snowmelt; effects on some water supplies	Reduced human mortality from decreased cold exposure	Reduced energy demand for heating; increased demand for cooling; declining air quality in cities; reduced disruption to transport due to snow, ice; effects on winter tourism
Warm spells/heat waves. Frequency increases over most land areas	Very likely	Reduced yields in warmer regions due to heat stress; increased danger of wildfire	Increased water demand; water quality problems, e.g. algal blooms	Increased risk of heat-related mortality, especially for the elderly, chronically sick, very young, and socially isolated	Reduction in quality of life for people in warm areas without appropriate housing; impacts on the elderly, very young, and poor
Heavy precipitation events. Frequency increases over most areas	Very likely	Damage to crops; soil erosion, inability to cultivate land due to waterlogging of soils	Adverse effects on quality of surface and groundwater; contamination of water supply; water scarcity may be relieved	Increased risk of deaths, injuries, and infectious, respiratory, and skin diseases	Disruption of settlements, commerce, transport, and societies due to flooding: pressures on urban and rural infrastructures; loss of property
Area affected by drought increases	Likely	Land degradation; lower yields/crop damage and failure; increased livestock deaths; increased risk of wildfire	More widespread water stress	Increased risk of food and water shortage; increased risk of malnutrition; increased risk of water- and food-borne diseases	Water shortage for settlements, industry, and societies; reduced hydropower generation potentials; potential for population migration
Intense tropical cyclone activity increases	Likely	Damage to crops; windthrow (uprooting) of trees; damage to coral reefs	Power outages causing disruption of public water supply	Increased risk of deaths, injuries, water- and food-borne diseases; post-traumatic stress disorders	Disruption by flood and high winds; withdrawal of risk coverage in vulnerable areas by private insurers; potential for population migrations; loss of property
Increased incidence of extreme high sea level (excludes tsunamis)[c]	Likely[d]	Salinization of irrigation water, estuaries, and freshwater systems	Decreased fresh-water availability due to saltwater intrusion	Increased risk of deaths and injuries by drowning in floods; migration-related health effects	Costs of coastal protection versus costs of land-use relocation; potential for movement of populations and infrastructure; also see tropical cyclones above

FIGURE 8.3B Global warming and temperature-related effects.

Source: Joel Benoit, ed., "Projected Impacts of Climate Change," *UNEP/GRID: Arendal Maps and Graphics Library,* 2009, http://maps.grida.no/go/graphic/projected-impacts-of-climate-change.

Notes: a) See Working Group I Table 3.7 for further details regarding definitions. b) Warming of the most extreme days and nights each year. c) Extreme high sea level depends on average sea level and on regional weather systems. It is defined as the highest 1% of hourly values of observed sea level at a station for a given reference period. d) In all scenarios, the projected global average sea level at 2100 is higher than in the reference period. The effect of changes in regional weather systems on sea level extremes has not been assessed.

2. The Intergovernmental Panel on Climate Change is found at: http://www.ipcc.ch/.

3. W. Feng, M. P. Chipperfield, S. Davies, G. W. Mann, K. S. Carslaw, and S. Dhomse, "Modeling the Effect of Denitrification on Polar Ozone Depletion for Arctic Winter/Spring 2004/05," *Atomic Energy and Physics Discussion* (2011): 3857–3884.

4. "Greenland, West Antarctic Ice Caps Melting at Half the Speed Previously Predicted," Science 2.0.com, September 6, 2010, http://www.science20.com/news_articles/greenland _west_antarctic_ice_caps_melting_half_speed_previously_predicted.

5. From the US EPA, accessed July 2, 2011, http://www.epa.gov/climatechange/science /index.html.

6. US Energy Information Administration, *Monthly Energy Review* (March 2011).

7. Ibid.

8. J. Hansen et al., "Target Atmospheric CO_2: Where Should Humanity Aim?," *Open Atmospheric Science Journal* 2 (2008): 217–231, http://www.moraymo.us/2008 _Hansenetal.pdf.

9. International Polar Year–Oslo Science Conference (June 10, 2010). Sea levels may rise by as much as one meter before the end of this century. *Science Daily*, accessed July 2, 2011, http://www.sciencedaily.com/releases/2010/06/100610095043.htm.

10. *Scientific American* (July 24, 2006).

11. IPCC, "Summary for Policymakers," in *Climate Change, 2007: The Physical Science Basis; Contribution of Working Group I to the Fourth Assessment Report of the Intergovern-mental Panel on Climate Change*, edited by S. Solomon et al. (Cambridge: Cambridge University Press, 2007).

12. EPA, accessed June 7, 2011, http://www.epa.gov.

13. "Tracking CO_2? Biogeochemists Map Out Carbon Dioxide Emissions in the U.S.," *Science Daily News*, December 1, 2008, http://www.sciencedaily.com/videos/2008/1209 -tracking_co2.htm.

14. US Energy Information Administration, *Monthly Energy Review* (March 2011).

15. Ibid.

16. R. Feely, C. Sabine, and V. Fabry, "Carbon Dioxide and Our Ocean Legacy," National Atmospheric and Oceanic Administration, accessed June 29, 2011, http://www .pmel.noaa.gov/pubs/PDF/feel2899/feel2899.pdf.

17. Ibid.

18. R. Britt, "Antarctica Losing Ice; Contrary to Expectations," Live Science, March 2, 2006, http://www.livescience.com/7074-antarctica-losing-ice-contrary-expectations.html.

19. National Geographic Global Warming Fast Facts, June 14, 2007, http://news.national geographic.com/news/2004/12/1206_041206_global_warming.html.

20. Ibid.

21. M. L. Parry et al., eds., *2007 IPCC Report: Contribution of Working Group II to the Fourth Assessment Report of the Intergovernmental Panel on Climate Change* (Cambridge: Cambridge University Press, 2007).

22. J. M. Robine et al., "Report on Excess Mortality in Europe During Summer 2003," February 28, 2007, http://ec.europa.eu/health/ph_projects/2005/action1/docs/action1 _2005_a2_15_en.pdf.

23. US EPA Office of the Inspector General, "EPA's Response to the World Trade Center Collapse: Challenges, Successes, and Areas for Improvement," Report No. 2003-P-00012, August 21, 2003, http://www.epa.gov/oig/reports/2003/WTC_report _20030821.pdf.

24. Richard Elliot Benedick, *Ozone Diplomacy: New Directions in Safeguarding the Planet* (Cambridge, MA: Harvard University Press, 1991).

25. Centre National de la Recherche Scientifique, "Record Ozone Loss over the North Pole," *ScienceDaily*, April 2011, http://www2.cnrs.fr/en/1848.htm?debut=24.

26. The 1992 UN Conference on Environment and Development, http://www.un.org /geninfo/bp/enviro.html.

27. Ibid. And for a nice review of the 1992 summit, see http://dsp-psd.pwgsc.gc.ca /Collection-R/LoPBdP/BP/bp317-e.htm.

28. From the US EPA, accessed June 29, 2011, http://www.epa.gov/climatechange /emissions/index.html.

29. Ibid.

30. Found at UNFCCC, http://unfccc.int/kyoto_protocol/items/2830.php.

31. "Bush: Kyoto Treaty Would Hurt the US Economy," June 30, 2005, http://www .msnbc.msn.com/id/8422343/ns/politics/t/bush-kyoto-treaty-would-have-hurt-economy/.

32. Learn more at: http://cc2010.mx/en/.

33. Naomi Oreskes and Erik Conway, *Merchants of Doubt: How a Handful of Scientists Obscured the Truth on Issues from Tobacco Smoke to Global Warming* (London: Bloomsbury Press, 2010).

34. Heartland Institute, accessed July 7, 2011, http://www.heartland.org/environment andclimate-news.org/index.html.

35. See the Competitive Enterprise Institute at http://cei.org/.

36. US Energy Information Administration, http://www.eia.gov/cneaf/electricity/epm /epm_sum.html.

37. "China Outpaces US in Cleaner Coal-Fired Plant," *New York Times*, May 10, 2009, http://www.nytimes.com/2009/05/11/world/asia/11coal.html.

38. According to the US Census Bureau, accessed July 7, 2011, http://www.census .gov/population/international/.

39. UN Department of Economic and Social Affairs Population Division, "World Population to 2300," 2004, http://www.un.org/esa/population/publications/longrange2 /WorldPop2300final.pdf.

40. United Nations Population Fund, *Special Bulletin on the Population Dynamics in Least Developed Countries*, accessed May 6, 2011, http://www.unfpa.org/webdav/site /global/shared/documents/publications/2011/LDC_Fact_Sheet.pdf.

41. National Research Council, *Globalization, Biosecurity, and the Future of the Life Sciences* (Washington, DC: National Academies Press, 2004), http://www.nap.edu/catalog .php?record_id=11567#toc.

42. Connie Lam et al., "Evolution of Seventh Cholera Pandemic and Origin of 1991 Epidemic, Latin America," *Emerging Infectious Diseases* 16, 7 (2010), http://www.cdc .gov/eid/content/16/7/pdfs/1130.pdf.

43. "Millions of Pakistan Children at Risk of Flood Diseases," BBC News, August 16, 2010, http://www.bbc.co.uk/news/world-south-asia-10984477.

44. Declan Walsh, "Pakistan Flood Crisis as Bad as African Famines, UN Says: Survey Shows Almost a Quarter of Children Under Five Are Malnourished in Sindh Province, Six Months After Floods," *Guardian*, January 27, 2011, http://www.guardian.co.uk/world/2011/jan/27/pakistan-flood-crisis-african-famines

PART III

Homeland Security Strategies

As the previous authors have explained, homeland security is anything but a simple process. These next chapters will not dispute that notion, but they will improve our understanding of homeland security. These authors examine homeland security from a different perspective. The first chapter addresses the critical area of emergency management, followed by chapters on strategic communications and strategic planning. The last chapters for this part are examinations of terrorism, first with an analysis of what terrorism is, followed by a review of what is involved with addressing counterterrorism.

Chapter 9: Emergency Management

Homeland security calls upon the efforts of diverse organizations to address diverse problems. In this chapter, the author surveys the types of hazards that homeland security professionals must consider. It is in this discussion of hazards that the intersection of homeland security and emergency management becomes clear. The chapter introduces key concepts from the study of emergency management, including the phases of emergency management. The chapter concludes with a survey of the actors and institutions central to emergency management and homeland security, including federalism, the Incident Command System, the National Incident Management System, and various sectors of society.

Chapter 10: Strategic Communication

This chapter provides an overview of strategic communication and related communication topics. In 2009 the Office of the President issued the *National Framework for Strategic Communication*. In this document, strategic communication is defined as the synchronization of words and deeds and how they will be perceived by selected audiences, as well as programs and activities deliberately aimed at communicating and engaging with intended audiences, including those involved in public affairs and public diplomacy as well as information operations professionals. Instead of focusing on the tactical, short-term elements of communication, strategic communication aims to align an agency's communication activities to achieve the nation's homeland security goals. A well-designed strategic communication process helps an organization manage its communication resources and evaluate the effectiveness of communication tactics. Strategic communication is proactive rather than reactive. Therefore, an important element of the strategic communication planning process is the analysis of the environment that allows an organization to anticipate events. Another critical element of the strategic communication process is stakeholder analysis. The author includes a description for developing a strategic communication planning process, including an analysis of the environment, stakeholders, themes and messages, choice of channels, use of credible sources, and metrics for measuring effectiveness. Several key subjects included in this chapter are the definitions and principles of strategic communication, the strategic communication planning process, aligning strategic communication with national security goals, measuring the effectiveness of the agency's communication activities, and risk communication.

Chapter 11: Strategic Planning

This chapter addresses strategic planning for homeland security and the challenges at all levels of government and for each jurisdiction, agency, and department. At the federal level, legislation dictates strategic planning activities. At the state and local levels, particularly in the homeland security arena, planning is tied to receiving grant funding from the DHS. This author offers a view of the conventional strategic planning process and presents some considerations on how to gain more effectiveness with limited resources. As knowledge increases, uncertainty is reduced. By reducing uncertainty, planners have more insight into reducing risk, an important element in homeland security planning.

Chapter 12: Terrorism and Counterterrorism

This chapter provides an overview of terrorism and the impact it has had, and the role it has played in homeland security, including both domestic terrorism in the United States and also the international terrorist threat facing the United States. The author describes a variety of definitions, followed by a discussion of the notion of "old terrorism" versus "new terrorism." He also addresses the subject of domestic terrorism, including a typology of orientations (e.g., extreme Right, anarchist, ecoterrorists, and others) and the government response. The author pays particular attention to the international terrorist threat facing the United States, with a special focus on radical Islamist groups and on the US Global War on Terror.

Chapter 13: America and Terrorism in the Twenty-First Century

Defending our homeland against the destructive goals of terrorists is the central tenet to ensuring the safety and security of our country. As terrorist groups and individual extremists develop tactics and technologies to achieve their destructive goals, our public and private services and our citizens must develop and integrate new tactics to counter them in equal measure. This chapter highlights a homeland security strategy using a local hometown-team perspective as a counterterrorism strategy. This chapter will provide new insight for a more holistic approach to countering terrorist activity.

Chapter 14: Foundations of Homeland Security Education

Finally, Part III includes a short history of homeland security education. This chapter will reflect on how homeland security education as we now see it emerged over the past eight to ten years. The chapter will explore how and why focus areas of homeland security education have emerged, what those skills and competencies are across some exemplary programs, and what knowledge and skills homeland security students will need to know upon graduation.

Epilogue

Homeland security is a complex and dynamic enterprise. It consists of hundreds of players in the public sector, private sector, and the military all working together to identify and contain threats to our society and to our economy. With a plethora of threats to our nation, both man-made and natural, homeland security has been in nearly a constant state of flux and development. However, ten years after the terror attacks of September 11, 2001, the author identifies and describes three main themes that characterize the nature and practice of homeland security that have emerged. These include the concept that change is constant, which causes continual evolution in strategies and tactics and the need for practitioners to be flexible and adaptive. A second theme concerns the rise of academic homeland security and its role in the field. The last theme to emerge is the ever-evolving role that homeland security plays in protecting our nation's critical infrastructure and strengthening the economy.

CHAPTER 9

Emergency Management

SCOTT ROBINSON

A great deal of attention in homeland security is focused on how to prevent extreme events, ranging from terrorist attacks to the accidental release of noxious chemicals. Recent attention has also integrated efforts to prepare for and respond to natural disasters (hurricanes, earthquakes, flooding, and so on) into the domain of homeland security. What unites these extreme events is the inability of local jurisdictions to fully handle the consequences of the events. A major flood may exceed the capacity of a city to respond. A major hurricane may exceed the capacity of various states impacted by the event. A major terrorist attack may exceed the capacity of local first responders to provide care and call for the expertise of national-level actors such as the Federal Bureau of Investigation or the Centers for Disease Control.

For years before the emergence of homeland security, scholars studied the variety of extreme events, including natural disasters, chemical spills, and other damaging emergencies. Over those decades, emergency management grew as a field with its own key concepts and lessons. Given the importance of extreme events (and their prevention) to the field of homeland security, these key concepts and lessons are also of vital importance to those seeking to understand homeland security in general. The inclusion of the Federal Emergency Management Agency within the Department of Homeland Security drives home the point that emergency management is an important component of homeland security.[1]

This chapter provides a brief overview of key concepts and lessons from emergency management that will serve to support homeland security operation. We start with a discussion of how one understands hazards and the types of hazards one faces in emergency management and homeland security. From there, the chapter introduces key concepts such as the emergency management cycle and reviews the various stakeholders with which one interacts in dealing with emergency management.

Risks, Hazards, and Vulnerability

Emergency management, not surprisingly, begins with careful consideration of what constitutes an emergency. A highly powerful storm that passes over an uninhabited island is not generally considered an emergency. A much less powerful storm that passes over a highly populated area may, on the other hand, create a dramatic emergency. What matters most are the consequences of the event. Accordingly, emergency management emphasizes that consequences are the product of two factors: hazards and vulnerability (Turner et al. 2003). A small hazard that strikes a particularly vulnerable community may create large negative consequences. Similarly, a large hazard that hits a well-protected community may not create large negative consequences. Events with consequences large enough to exceed a community's capacity to respond are what we call disasters (Lindell, Prater, and Perry 2007, 3). We will consider each of the components of the model individually before returning to the most important lesson of the model.

Types of Hazards

Hazards are events that may create negative consequences to society. These hazards come in a variety of forms (Flynn 2007) and are typically categorized by the frequency with which they occur (often versus rare) and by their relative destructiveness (e.g., how bad they are when they occur).

Magnitudes of Hazards

The most fundamental distinction between hazards is between those of different magnitudes of potential consequences. Hazards may threaten thousands of lives or only a few. Media attention focuses on a small number of hazards—but often on those that threaten a large number of lives or property. Examples are easy to think of: hurricanes, earthquakes, tsunamis, radiological (dirty) bombs, pandemic influenza, or a chemical weapon release. These are not the only, or the most common, hazards, though. On a daily basis, emergency management officials deal with smaller hazards as well. Forest and household fires, industrial accidents, and tornadoes affect smaller numbers of people but occur with a greater frequency than the larger hazards.

A significant question for homeland security and emergency management professionals is how best to prioritize the preparation for a catastrophic but rare event (e.g., a terrorist attack with a nuclear weapon), as opposed to a less disruptive but highly likely event (e.g., winter storms). Homeland security in particular wrestles with how to allocate resources when we can imagine—but have not yet seen—extremely damaging terrorist attacks using nuclear or biological weapons, but we also see a steady stream of smaller terrorists attacks using conventional explosives as well as regional natural disasters. Such questions of priority become politically sensitive, particularly during periods of tight budgets. Should we invest in programs to prepare for events that could be catastrophic but that have not yet been seen (e.g., a dirty bomb attack on a major urban center) or the events we face on a regular basis (e.g., hurricanes)? Should we send a disproportionate amount of funding to large urban centers because these locations are thought to be more attractive targets for terrorists? These issues have made homeland security funding decisions sensitive to a variety of political forces.

Intentional Versus Unintentional Hazards

The second fundamental distinction among hazards is between intentional and unintentional hazards. We think of threats from individuals or groups who are trying to cause harm as intentional. Clearly, terrorist attacks fall into this classification. We do not, alternatively, think of a hurricane as choosing its point of landfall or an earthquake of waiting until it can cause the greatest amount of damage. Even when people are involved, hazards may be unintentional. A chemical spill involves humans and possibly human error or neglect, but is not generally timed or targeted for maximum effect.

Threats or hazards to people, property, or the environment that are not natural (e.g., storms, weather) or technologically based (e.g., a failure in a bridge or power grid) are labeled as "intentional." Terrorism is a good example of an intentional threat. Intentional threats have important distinguishing characteristics for purposes of homeland security and emergency management professionals; that is, terrorists choose their targets. Intentional actors (like terrorists) may pass over well-protected communities to target other communities. Or intentional actors may time their attacks to maximize damage by attacking during major sporting events, heavy traffic periods, or the like. Furthermore, it is possible to directly intervene against intentional hazards (and, to a lesser degree, accidental but technological hazards) to reduce their intensity. Intelligence officials may, in some sense, prevent a terrorist attack by arresting suspected terrorists, for example (Haddow, Bullock, and Coppola 2008). This is simply not an option for unintentional hazards. One cannot prevent a hurricane from emerging. A hurricane will form or not regardless of our wishes on the matter.

All-Hazards Planning

Despite the diversity of hazards that a community may face, the current strategy for emergency management is to adopt an "all-hazards" approach (Schwab, Eschelbach, and Brower 2007). Such an approach emphasizes the overlapping threats posed by a diverse set of hazards. Some basic functionality is important regardless of the hazard type. If there is an evacuation, there are specific housing and sheltering needs regardless of whether the reason for the evacuation is an accidental chemical release, a severe winter storm, or a terrorist act.

An all-hazards approach raises key questions of emergency preparedness and homeland security strategy. The all-hazards approach emphasizes the most likely hazards a community may face. A good place to start is FEMA's "Multi-hazard Identification and Risk Assessment" (FEMA 1997). This document provides information on the likelihood that communities will face various hazards based on their geographic location. The emphasis in an all-hazards planning process is on building capacity that will be repeatedly useful—and thus useful in commonly occurring events. Critics allege that this approach deemphasizes very important hazards, particularly terrorist attacks, because of the historical association of "all-hazards" planning and traditional emergency management (as seen in FEMA's "Multi-hazard Identification and Risk Assessment" planning documents referenced above).[2] If preparation for terrorist attacks requires a quite different set of capabilities than natural hazards, the all-hazards approach may privilege the preparation for natural hazards that occur with regularity and are altogether more familiar to community leaders. Alternatively, focusing resources on rare (though, possibly, more destructive) hazards may leave the community relatively unprepared for more predictable hazards. The trade-off between preparing for frequent, low-intensity hazards as opposed to rare but high-intensity hazards is a continuing challenge for professionals in the fields of homeland security and emergency management. (Discussion on this point is also addressed in the critical infrastructure probabilistic risk-assessment chapters.)

Vulnerability Assessment

The complement to hazard assessment is vulnerability assessment. Just as we need to understand the threats that we face, we must understand the vulnerability of each community to these hazards. Even once we understand the hazards that a community faces, we need to understand the various elements of the community that may be vulnerable to each of these hazards. Most basically, one must consider the physical environment of the community to identify points of vulnerability. Beyond this, one must consider vulnerability of people within the community; in other words, one must consider "social vulnerability."

Critical Infrastructure

Hazards can create problems for the built infrastructure of a community. One must assess how vulnerable each of the critical elements of this infrastructure is to the various hazards that the community is likely to face. The DHS provides some guidance in these efforts through its National Infrastructure Protection Plan.[3] Within this strategy, officials are tasked with the identification of "critical infrastructure and key resources,"[4] as well as establishing priorities for protection. Supporting documents provide sector-specific advice to provide a tailored infrastructure analysis and protection plan.

It is important to note that the NIPP and other such documents provide only a framework and process for community vulnerability assessments. The hard work still resides at the community level. Broad information, like that contained in the NIPP, must be supplemented with information specific to one's own community. One needs to identify, for example, where large amounts of potentially toxic or volatile chemicals are stored and transported through the community. Next, one can start to inventory the community to identify key structures such as government buildings, health facilities, and the like. Having a strategy and a procedure is only the start.

Social Vulnerability

Focusing on the built infrastructure is clearly important, but it does not tell the whole story. An intact road system, for example, is not much good to the members of the community that lack access to transportation. Losing access to electricity or natural gas may impact different segments of the community differently depending on each person's access to additional resources, insulated housing, and so forth. The individual members of the community that face greater or unique challenges in the event of a hazard make up the social vulnerability of the community (Cutter, Boruff, and Shirley 2003).

Within social vulnerability research, the emphasis has been on the role of poverty in disaster preparedness (Cutter, Boruff, and Shirley 2003). Households in poverty have few resources to devote to disaster preparedness and fewer resources to call upon in the event of a disaster. Households in poverty are unlikely to be able to afford simply moving to a hotel in the event that their house is damaged, for example. Households in poverty have less access to resources through family and neighborhood ties as a safety net because their friends and family are also likely to be in poverty. Planning for hazards in a community with a great deal of social vulnerability requires special care and outreach.

It is important to emphasize that social vulnerability is not limited only to poverty. There are other forms of social vulnerability that require attention on the part of emergency planners. A community may include closed-language communities—that is, communities in which many of the community's members do not speak the same language as the majority of residents. Such a language barrier may present difficulties in communicating important warning messages and information about preparedness within the community (Lindell and Perry 2004). One must also consider the social vulnerability represented by residents of advanced age and those who possess special needs (such as vision or hearing impairment, mobility limitations, cognitive limitations, and so on) (Cutter, Boruff, and Shirley 2003). The strategies for communicating with and protecting those who are moderately affluent, well educated, and socially integrated may differ from those who possess special needs, in terms of access to resources or accommodation of special needs. Understanding the vulnerability in one's community requires understanding these social elements of vulnerability, as well as the vulnerability of the built environment.

Fundamentals of Emergency Management

Understanding the hazards and vulnerabilities that a community faces is an important first step. Preparing for and responding to emergencies based on this knowledge is the next step. Emergency management scholarship provides some key tools in understanding how to carry out these important tasks, including mitigation, preparedness, response, and recovery.

Phases of Emergency Management

The tasks necessary to protect our communities from the range of hazards that threaten them are numerous and complicated. To help organize the various demands on those involved in emergency management and homeland security, scholars and practitioners have developed a simple way to organize these activities by phase (Haddow, Bullock, and Coppola 2008).

The phase-based approach to emergency management implies a specific chronology—but this should not be taken too literally. The phases of the EM cycle are as follows: mitigation, preparation, response, and recovery. The first two phases take place, in some sense, before a specific hazard and involve elements of preparation. The third and fourth phases deal with posthazard response. However, readers should note that the phases of EM are not discrete; that is, one phase does not end in order for the "next phase" to begin. In addition, all of the phases in the cycle take place in the context of previous disasters. Furthermore, one can move quickly from pre-event preparations to response depending on the occurrence of a hazard. Hazards do not appear on our schedule.

Mitigation

The first phase of the emergency management cycle is mitigation. Mitigation involves the reduction of vulnerability through investments in the built environment (Haddow, Bullock, and Coppola 2008). Mitigation really refers to long-term strategies to reduce vulnerabilities. Examples of mitigation activities are easy to come by. To mitigate damage caused by potential flooding, one can build levees. To mitigate earthquake damage, one can require that new buildings be built to specific codes. The goal is to develop passive structures to reduce vulnerability (Lindell, Prater, and Perry 2007, 193). Once you build a levee, it requires little more than regular maintenance. Without this maintenance, even mitigation is not effective protection.

Three major tools are common in mitigation strategies (Schwab, Eschelbach, and Brower 2007). The first is the public building and support of mitigating structures. Levees, channels, and similar structures serve as accessible examples of these efforts. Both levees and channels mitigate flooding risk through building large structures. The goal is to create an infrastructure that will prevent flooding by channeling water through and past a community or by creating a larger holding capacity for local bodies of water.

A second major tool of mitigation is land-use planning. Here emergency management officials use the regulatory authority of government to guide where new structures are built within a community. If a particular area of a community is prone to flooding, one may prevent the building of new structures in that area. The goal of such policies is to reduce vulnerability by preventing the development of housing or other structures in areas most likely to suffer hazards. The most common example of this approach is the prevention of building in flood zones.

The third major tool is the use of building-code regulations to reduce vulnerability in new structures. Whereas the first strategy relied on government building large structures, the employment of building codes uses government's regulatory authority to shape how the private sector builds structures. These codes may require windows that are resistant to high winds in a tornado-prone community, specific construction practices and materials needed to make a building more stable during an earthquake, or a specific driveway approach to reduce a building's vulnerability to car bombs. It is not the government actually doing the building. Instead, these codes provide rules for how the private sector must build in an effort to ensure that all such buildings will be less vulnerable.

As emphasized above, while mitigation is the first phase of the emergency management process, it occurs within the context of previous events. In this sense, mitigation never really ends as a phase; it is always ongoing. As an example, it is not uncommon for mitigation spending to be required as a part of response and recovery funding from previous events (Haddow, Bullock, and Coppola 2008). The logic of such requirements is clear. One hopes that investments following an event will make the consequences of similar events less dire or severe. Each investment will then reduce the need for such investments in the future. One does not want to create a system where the government funds rebuilding a community that flooded in exactly the same way, only to find that community floods again (and, naturally, asks to be rebuilt). Mitigation funding is intended to reduce vulnerability in the process of rebuilding a community.

Preparedness

The second pre-event phase of the emergency management cycle is preparedness (Perry and Lindell 2007). This phase involves the active participation of community members, emergency management professionals, and other community members. Preparedness activities among emergency management officials involve a great deal of planning. The first goal is to engage the broad range of stakeholders in the planning and preparedness processes. The expertise to plan for emergency situations does not reside solely within a single organization—including the emergency operations center. Response to a large-scale disaster will involve participation from public health officials, transportation officials, public works officials, law enforcement officials, and many others. If it is likely that an organization will be needed in an emergency response, they need to be involved in the planning process.

Plans should emerge organically from the efforts of the various participating organizations. However, there are some common elements recommended for all community plans. The most prominent common element is the Incident Command System (Haddow, Bullock, and Coppola 2008). Each community planning process involves adapting an ICS plan for local conditions, organizations, and personnel. However, the ICS framework provides a common vocabulary and expectations that can help people unfamiliar with the local plan to participate productively in response activities.[5]

Response

The third phase of the emergency management cycle, response, includes the activities most commonly associated with organizations such as FEMA—emergency response. Although it is the most familiar phase of EM, this phase still includes a great many different activities. It is worthwhile to break this phase, itself, into two components.

Immediately following a hazard event, one begins early-phase response activities. At this point in the development of an event, information is at a premium. It is vital to gather information on the scope and nature of the hazard. If the event is localized (for example, in an explosion), one needs to know how accessible that location is. If the event is spread out over a large area (say, in the path of a hurricane), one needs to know the extent of the damage. This sort of basic information is the precondition of any other actions.

This initial assessment will provide the information one needs to take an active stance. The assessment may reveal the presence of victims trapped within the impact area of the hazard. The assessment will have to proceed along with search-and-rescue activities (Lindell, Prater, and Perry 2007). Such operations involve a delicate balance between assessing the situation, sending responders into the impact zone itself, and the removal of victims from harm's way.

At the same time that assessment and search-and-rescue activities proceed, response activities must have a central location for coordination (Haddow, Bullock, and Coppola 2008). This site may be located safely near the impact area, or it may be remote (especially when coordinating activities related to a geographically dispersed event). The key is to follow the plan negotiated among the various local stakeholders in the planning phase. Response activities involve the coordination of a large number of different organizations with the highest of stakes.

Recovery

Recovery is the final phase of the emergency management cycle and is often forgotten, or at least neglected. After emergency response activities, one has to start the process of long-term recovery (Lindell, Prater, and Perry 2007). The priority of getting people out of harm's way in the response phase is obvious. The recovery phase involves returning a community and its members to a pre-event state, that is, returning community and business operations to the status they were before the incident or hazard occurred.

Depending on the nature of the event, the recovery may not begin until people have started to return to the community. This process may involve people returning from local shelters, from hotels, or from family members with whom evacuated people have stayed during the response phase. Of course, the community must be made safe and fit to accommodate residents. Making the community fit for habitation may involve assessing the safety of buildings, the removal of debris from the community, and the reestablishment of basic utility services like power, water, and the like.

Getting people back into the community may be only the beginning of the recovery process. The hazard may have closed down businesses, forced the permanent relocation of some portion of the population, or damaged key elements of the infrastructure. Recovery will involve overcoming all of these challenges.

Resilience: A New Framework for Emergency Management

Emergency management practitioners and scholars have begun to integrate the lessons of the phase-based approach into a focus on community resilience

(Manyena 2006). As an approach to EM, resilience is still taking form but offers important insights that supplement the phases discussed earlier. Resilience seeks to integrate activities and processes across the various phases—particularly mitigation and recovery—to develop a better, broader understanding of the needs of community.

Resilience emphasizes two elements: measurability and inclusiveness. Resilience approaches recommend a broad view of what constitutes a community recovery. This makes developing indicators of successful recovery quite difficult. For example, is the return of the population of New Orleans to pre-Katrina levels a necessary part of a full recovery?

The second emphasis is on including a broad range of stakeholders in emergency management activities. Whereas prior efforts had often discussed the need for collaboration across different government organizations, contemporary reliance approaches emphasize the need to engage all of civil society in emergency management. The next and final section will provide a sense of what the inclusion of a broad range of stakeholders can mean to emergency management and homeland security.

Stakeholders in EM

Relations with Stakeholders

The contemporary resilience approach argues that one should include a wide range of stakeholders (that is, the various groups and people with shared or mutual interest in effective homeland security) in emergency management processes. This chapter will conclude with a survey of the various types of stakeholders that one should consider along with the participation of these groups.

Communication

When one considers the engagement of various types of organizations, the first step is communicating with the various groups (Lindell and Perry 2004). Every group presents a unique communication challenge—some of which will be discussed in relation to specific stakeholder groups below. However, there are also some general challenges to communication that deserve special attention.

Like many areas involving various organizations and policies, emergency management and homeland security have developed their own vocabulary that can be confusing. In addition to acronyms with which people are likely familiar

(FEMA, DHS, and so on), EM policies and documents routinely refer to other documents and policies that people will not immediately recognize, such as ICS (Incident Command System)[6] or FEMA's *CPG* (the *Comprehensive Preparedness Guide*). The first step in communicating with organizations and individuals unfamiliar with emergency management is to eliminate or minimize the reference to such jargon. (See also Chapter 10, "Strategic Communication.")

It is also important to remember that one cannot take communication for granted in emergency management contexts. Hazards may interfere with traditional means of communication. If power is interrupted, one cannot simply check e-mail or turn on a television for news. In the field, security concerns motivate many organizations to keep their communication channels private. Establishing a plan that ensures communication will be possible between important parties under a variety of hazard circumstances is essential.

Coordination and Collaboration

Moving beyond communication requires the integration of organizations into the various phases of emergency management through coordination and collaborative practices. These collaborative practices are essential, given the diversity of actors involved in effective emergency management. The remainder of the chapter will serve to emphasize the various actors that are important to emergency management and some of the challenges to collaboration between the relevant actors.

Government: Federal Actors

The federal agencies involved in emergency management are among the most familiar to the average American. Most people are familiar with the DHS and FEMA. People are less familiar with the role that a variety of other federal agencies play in EM, or the collaborative role that these agencies have with either the DHS or FEMA. A key effort over the past decade has been to create a national-level plan for integrating the efforts of various organizations into a single EM effort. For example, the Department of Agriculture plays a role in emergency management, though it is not known as an emergency management organization. Similarly, the Department of Health and Human Services is a lead agency on matters of public health and medical services. The current plan for integrating all of these various organizations is the National Response Framework and its associated Emergency Support Function (ESF) annexes. Within the ESFs, one can find the specific agencies and groups by functions such as transportation or medical and public health support.

The large number of federal agencies taking primary responsibility for various emergency support functions in the NRF raises many questions related to how one should organize federal emergency management operations. The creation of the DHS indicated an interest in centralizing our federal efforts on matters of homeland security and emergency management—though many key agencies, like the FBI and CIA, were kept as separate agencies. Debates continue as to whether FEMA should also be an autonomous agency separate from the DHS (Waugh and Streib 2006, 132).

Homeland Security Presidential Directive 5 (Management of Domestic Incidents) called for the creation of a national plan to integrate federal and nonfederal actors in emergency management efforts. A main result of HSPD-5 is the current National Incident Management System.[7] The purpose of NIMS is to clarify what roles various organizations should take in EM. Designed to work along with the NRF, NIMS provides a series of principles and values that guide the management of emergencies. NIMS provides a shared vocabulary, terminology for incidents, common communication techniques, frequencies and ideologies, and a uniform understanding of the chain of command; this leaves no doubt as to who is ultimately in charge when many agencies respond to an incident.

NIMS clarifies terms such as *preparedness* and provides a review of the various actors present within the federal preparedness system. The intent is to create a scalable strategy for incident management that can guide efforts related to everything ranging from a local grass fire to a massive hurricane. Consistent language and clear principles to guide the efforts of the various participating organizations is essential to the general nature of the strategy. NIMS seeks to avoid a situation where local officials do not understand the language and assumptions of the federal officials they may call on for assistance. Similarly, the standard language and assumptions should help federal officials predict and understand what local officials are doing at any given time.

A significant part of this plan is the standardization of the ICS—the approach for management of incidents on-site (as in the immediate vicinity of the hazard) (FEMA 2008, appx. B). The ICS implements the principles of NIMS on either the smallest levels or the largest as the emergency situation grows. Hence, the ICS is considered "scalable." The goal is to inspire each community to define its strategy for dealing with local hazards. Each community needs to know who is in charge in the event of a grass fire or a chemical spill. The lines of communication and authority have to be absolutely clear to everyone involved, regardless of what organization or township sent them to the incident. This plan needs to connect to the national strategy, NIMS, to ensure the smooth transition of authority and resource sharing across levels of government.

A key assumption of the ICS is that each community's strategy for incident response may appear a little different—but each should have a common framework and connect to the national system. This approach leaves considerable autonomy, or choice, to local officials to define a system that works best within their community. However, the common language of the ICS and NIMS provides some predictability and transparency among the responders and how they act. As the incident grows, the plan will include a strategy for how to add people without disrupting lines of communication and authority, eventually handing off responsibility to state and federal officials if necessary.

Government: State and Local Actors

State and local governments are also key actors in the area of emergency management. Historically, most emergency management efforts have been focused on the local and state levels. The national strategy for dealing with emergencies is to allow the hazard to be handled at the lowest level that can possibly deal with the problem (Lindell, Prater, and Perry 2007). Consider the case of a community experiencing flooding. The event is not considered an emergency warranting the use of state-level resources unless the local resources are insufficient to deal with the hazard. In a sense, the event escalates from the local to state level through the failure of the local officials to contain the hazard. The flooding event would then be a state matter unless the flooding exceeded state resources to handle. State officials would then have to appeal to federal officials for additional resources. Acceptance of a need for federal resources is an indication that the state resources are insufficient to contain the hazard. Again, the hazard has forced a failure upward to the federal system.

This strategy of "failing upward" places critical importance on the capacity of local officials. The local officials have control of the situation until the hazard has clearly exceeded their capacity. The first crucial hours of many emergency situations are centrally guided by local offices. Strategies to expand resilience since 2001 have involved increasing the resources available to local officials as a means of strengthening this first line of defense against many hazards (Haddow, Bullock, and Coppola 2008).

This simple ladder of escalation has been challenged in recent years in two ways. First, terrorist and other intentional (man-made) hazards involve an investigative component that complicates the ladder of escalation. Most of these hazards involve interstate movement of resources and the involvement of federal-level investigative expertise in the form of the FBI, Joint Terrorism Task Forces, and other similar units. These organizations do not wait for local and state officials to escalate an emergency to begin their investigation. Second, recent experiences with large, predictable hazards (notably, hurricanes and other large meteorological hazards) have led to the development of instruments by which states can ask for federal assistance on the prediction that a hazard will exceed its capacity to respond. As a hurricane bears down on Alabama, say, the governor may ask for the federal government to prepare efforts to respond (and to preposition federal resources, including some funding) before the hazard has actually struck the state. This effort has facilitated the escalation of emergencies, but has made the escalation process more complicated.

As federal, state, and local agencies sort out a new strategy through such policies as NIMS, some efforts are emerging to create regional emergency management coordination and collaboration organizations (Gerber and Robinson 2009). Recognizing that hazards do not respect jurisdictional boundaries, some state and large metropolitan areas are joining together to create regional coordinating bodies. The role of these regional bodies (and whether they will predominantly coordinate activities between local agencies or between state agencies) is still being worked out, as the responsibility and capability of different agencies are rapidly evolving.

Nongovernmental Organizations

Watching media reports of disasters, it is easy to imagine that the work of emergency management is done entirely within government organization. However, this view neglects the vital role played by nonprofit organizations in the emergency management process (Simo and Bies 2007). We can divide the participating nonprofit organizations into two types: traditional and nontraditional participants.

Traditional nongovernmental organizations have been heavily involved in the emergency management process for decades. The American Red Cross, for example, was written into the NRF by name for its vital role in organizing sheltering during evacuations. It is simply impossible to understand the current sheltering plan for the country without understanding the role of the

American Red Cross in these activities. Other major nongovernmental organizations have participated in national emergency management efforts for years, including the Salvation Army, Catholic Charities, Southern Baptist Disaster Relief, and others. Many of these organizations have united to create a national structure of VOADs (Voluntary Organizations Active in Disaster), including local and state chapters along with the national organization (NVOAD).

In addition to these long-standing participants in emergency management, there are a number of nongovernmental organizations that play important—though often overlooked—roles (Robinson and Gerber 2007). When a disaster strikes a community, organizations that have little to do with emergencies most of the time stand up to provide supporting services. Local churches are integral parts of most communities' efforts at sheltering dislocated people. Local charities may provide food or clothing to victims. Less obviously, the local animal shelter may coordinate activities to house lost or abandoned pets. These services fill gaps in the sorts of activities provided by government organizations and the more traditionally disaster-oriented nongovernmental organizations.

Public Health Organizations

Emergency management organizations face a wide variety of hazards, many of which include potential impacts on the health of a community's residents. A quick look at the National Planning Scenarios—the scenarios that EM and homeland security organizations are to use when gauging their levels of preparedness—reveals that a large proportion of the threats involve obvious connections to public health (e.g., pandemic influenza, chemical release, and so on). Clearly, hazards such as pandemic influenza or any large-scale or weapon of mass destruction attack, such as a chemical weapon attack, will certainly require coordination between emergency management and public health officials.

Parallel to the federalized system of emergency management lays a similarly massive, complicated system of public health organizations. Public health organizations have their own local, state, and federal organizations along with complicated partnerships with local political officials, hospitals, clinics, and others. The parallel nature of the organizations has predisposed each of these systems to keep to themselves, remaining in their particular silo. Even funding has generally funneled through either emergency management or public health systems with too little effort to improve coordination between these offices. Integrating public health and emergency management systems promises to be a key challenge for the next decade in the fields of emergency management, homeland security, and public health.

Private-Sector Organizations

The recently expanding view of community resilience has renewed interest in the engagement of the private sector in emergency management efforts. Like engagement with other nongovernmental organizations, these efforts involve partnerships that cross the traditional boundaries separating state from non-state actors. There are two major purposes for which private-sector entities are brought into emergency management efforts.

First, private-sector organizations are greatly impacted by any community emergency. And as a direct result, businesses can be greatly interrupted or even taken off-line due to a disaster. Not only does this greatly disrupt the flow of commerce, but it may also negatively impact the availability of supplies and even employee benefits. In addition, the workforce may be unavailable, as may the transportation and operation of critical infrastructures such as the water system, the health system, the energy systems, or manufacturing. Businesses need to plan for such potential disruptions. Such planning efforts on the part of private-sector businesses are known as "continuity of operations" (COOP) plans (Perry and Lindell 2007). Government emergency managers have a role in facilitating the development of such COOP plans. (See also Chapter 11, "Strategic Planning.") COOP plans, otherwise known as business continuity plans, are designed to keep businesses afloat in the face of catastrophic loss. As such, they are often developed in conjunction with comprehensive emergency management plans. COOP plans need to be aware of local governmental plans (and, hence, the participation of the local government EM organizations) so that businesses will better be able to withstand the disruptions of disasters, thus contributing to the resilience of the community as a whole.

Second, having a prepared business community can also help in periods of emergency response and recovery. As was the case with other nongovernmental organizations, businesses often provide essential services—sometimes called "wraparound services"—supporting governmental response activities. For example, local restaurants may assist in providing food and shelter for first responders. The materials for rebuilding likely come from local home improvement stores. Households staying home during a winter storm (and needing water and food in case of a utility disruption) are going to buy materials from their local grocery store. These businesses are involved in emergency activities. Bringing these businesses into emergency management activity can help these organizations provide those important but often forgotten supporting services in emergency situations while also ensuring that businesses can prepare themselves for emergencies.

The Public

To this point, the focus has been on collaboration between emergency managers and other formal organizations—some routinely focused on emergency management and some not. However, the biggest impact an emergency management organization can have in supporting community resilience is in its relationship with the members of the public (Lindell, Prater, and Perry 2007). In the pre-event period, the emergency management organization must support household-level preparedness for events. Immediately before an event, the emergency management organization plays a vital role in providing warning about the hazard.

For all that emergency managers can do in their offices and in coordination with other organizations, the best preparedness starts at home (Haddow, Bullock, and Coppola 2008). Households can prepare in a variety of ways, including storing food and water for periods of disrupted utility services, ensuring communication between members of the household, having appropriate material for cold or hot weather without utilities, and ensuring access to information about current events related to the emergency (say, through a radio that does not require active electricity service to a location). Despite the importance of household-level preparedness to community resilience, very few households have made basic preparations (Tierney, Lindell, and Perry 2001). To make matters worse, those who respond to surveys that their house is prepared often turn out not to have provided for even the basics of survival, such as at least three to five days of food, water, as well as communication equipment and the like when asked about specific preparedness activities. A great challenge for EM organizations is educating the public about the steps each household should take to prepare for emergency events.

The experience with the DHS's color-coded warning system has revealed how much there is still to learn about how to create effective warning systems (just see recent efforts to replace the system). We must understand the public if we hope to design systems to effectively warn them about a pending emergency. A warning that is not understood by the public is not useful. This places severe limitations on traditional systems such as warning sirens. Having a complex system of short and long blasts from the siren that indicate different types of hazards may not be effective if the public does not understand the differences between different signals.

New technologies have created new opportunities for warning systems—though not without complications. Reverse-911 systems can push phone calls and even text messages out to telephones registered in their databases, as well as target specific geographic locations. More recently, jurisdictions are experimenting with dedicated e-mail and SMS/text-messaging notification services as methods for sending easily understood messages about matters such as evacuation, sheltering announcements, and so forth. Although these tools seem promising, considerable work remains in how to implement the systems and how to overcome disparities in access to these communication channels. The best bet is to have multiple and redundant emergency notification systems and to have complete agreement with the organization for who crafts and sends out the emergency message.

Special-Needs Populations

It is worth emphasizing that planning must accommodate members of the public with a variety of special needs. FEMA has recently offered guidance to emergency management officials using the more informative term *functional-need support services*. This reframing of special needs serves to emphasize the variety of needs in the population.

To build on the previous section, recall that warning systems are an important part of the relationship between EM organizations and the public. Warning systems require that the public perceives and understands the warning. As complicated as this can be in the best of circumstances, one must raise a variety of questions related to members of the public with special functional needs. A warning siren is not useful for members of the public with hearing disabilities. Warning systems relying on text messages will require coordination with services to convert text to audio messages for those with vision impairments. Many communities also include members that cannot read the majority language. In these cases, care must be taken to ensure that warning information is available in other languages and through media outlets where people who speak those languages are likely to see it (Lindell and Perry 2004).

Evacuation and sheltering activities face a variety of other complications related to the accommodation of community members. The experience with Hurricane Katrina made clear that emergency managers must plan for members of the community lacking access to personal transportation (GPO 2006). Other members of the community may face great difficulty with mobility—including those requiring the assistance of a wheelchair or those of an age or disposition where mobility is otherwise limited. Evacuating and sheltering these populations may be a challenge. Active coordination with nursing homes and with organizations that serve populations with mobility limitations is essential to incorporating residents with these needs into emergency management.

One can think of a variety of other special needs, and this is a worthy exercise for those interested in matters of emergency management. The purpose here is not to document even the range of such planning. Instead, it is to emphasize that the incorporation of representatives of residents with a wide variety of functional needs is essential to effective emergency management.

Conclusion

Emergency management is clearly a robust, dynamic, and rapidly evolving area within homeland security. With a decades-long tradition of scholarship and practice, and contributions to society, emergency management has developed a number of vital strategies for dealing with many and various hazards. Most important, it has become clear that the capacity to manage the diverse array of emergencies our communities face does not reside with any particular organization—or even industrial or governmental sector. Rather, emergency management thrives when all sectors plan and act in a cohesive and well-coordinated manor. As such, emergency management offices have to rely on a variety of other organizations across every phase of the emergency management process. Some important expertise resides in local public health offices, while other expertise lies in federal law enforcement and investigative organization. Some of the expertise and capacity lies in state government agencies, while other expertise and capacity lie in nonprofit and private-sector organizations.

The challenge for EM and homeland security moving forward is how to integrate the efforts of these diverse organizations, sectors, and agencies. Separately evolving public health and emergency management organizations will need to work together to prepare for and respond to pandemic influenza outbreaks and other mass-casualty events. Historic tensions and information-sharing capabilities between federal and local law enforcement agencies will need resolution to integrate intelligence gathering more effectively. Emergency managers will need to better understand how best to engage community members as partners in preparation. Strategies for building these connections are emerging but are relatively untested. The future of EM lies in how well we can connect the great capacity for emergency management residing in each of these various elements of the community to create a resilient community.

NOTES

1. See also Presidential Policy Directive 8, National Preparedness, accessed July 1, 2011, http://www.dhs.gov/xabout/laws/gc_1215444247124.shtm.

2. FEMA Library, accessed July 4, 2011, http://www.fema.gov/library/viewRecord .do;jsessionid=ACF913615B6D4C5D85AC5BB63ACAC614.WorkerLibrary?action=back &id=2214.

3. NIPP, accessed July 4, 2011, http://www.dhs.gov/xlibrary/assets/NIPP_Plan.pdf.

4. See also PDD-8, National Preparedness.

5. See also FEMA, NIMS, accessed July 1, 2011, http://www.fema.gov/emergency /nims/.

6. FEMA, ICS, accessed July 1, 2011, http://www.fema.gov/emergency/nims/Incident CommandSystem.shtm.

7. FEMA, NIMS, accessed July 1, 2011, http://www.fema.gov/emergency/nims/.

REFERENCES

Cutter, Susan L., Bryan J. Boruff, and W. Lynn Shirley. 2003. "Social Vulnerability to Environmental Hazards." *Social Science Quarterly* 84, no. 2: 242–261.

FEMA. 1997. "Multi-hazard Identification and Risk Assessment: A Cornerstone of the National Mitigation Strategy." http://www.fema.gov/library/viewRecord.do?id=2214.

———. 2008. "National Incident Management System (NIMS)." http://www.fema.gov /pdf/emergency/nims/NIMS_core.pdf.

Flynn, Stephen. 2007. *The Edge of Disaster*. New York: Random House.

Gerber, Brian J., and Scott E. Robinson. 2009. "Local Government Performance and the Challenges of Regional Preparedness for Disasters." *Public Performance and Management Review* 32, no. 3: 345–371.

Government Printing Office (GPO). 2006. *A Failure of Initiative: Final Report of the Select Bipartisan Committee to Investigate the Preparation for and Response to Hurricane Katrina*. Washington, DC: GPO.

Haddow, George D., Jane A. Bullock, and Damon P. Coppola. 2008. *Introduction to Emergency Management*. 3rd ed. New York: Elsevier.

Lindell, Michael K., and Ronald W. Perry. 2004. *Communicating Environmental Risk in Multiethnic Communities*. New York: Sage.

Lindell, Michael K., Carla Prater, and Ronald W. Perry. 2007. *Introduction to Emergency Management*. Hoboken, NJ: Wiley.

Manyena, Siambabala B. 2006. "The Concept of Resilience Revisited." *Disasters* 30, no. 4: 434–450.

Perry, Ronald W., and Michael K. Lindell. 2007. *Emergency Planning.* Hoboken, NJ: Wiley.

Robinson, Scott E., and Brian J. Gerber. 2007. "A Seat at the Table for Nondisaster Organizations." *Public Manager* 36, no. 3: 4–7.

Schwab, Anna K., Katherine Eschelbach, and David J. Brower. 2007. *Hazard Mitigation and Preparedness.* Hoboken, NJ: Wiley.

Simo, Gloria, and Angela L. Bies. 2007. "The Role of Nonprofits in Disaster Response: An Expanded Model of Cross-sector Collaboration." *Public Administration Review* 67, Issue Supplement s1: 125–142.

Tierney, Kathleen J., Michael K. Lindell, and Ronald W. Perry. 2007. *Facing the Unexpected: Disaster Preparedness in the United States.* Washington, DC: Joseph Henry Press.

Turner, B. L., II, Roger E. Kasperson, Pamela A. Matson, James J. McCarthy, Robert W. Corell, Lindsey Christensen, Noelle Eckley, et al. 2003. "A Framework for Vulnerability Analysis in Sustainability Science." *Proceedings of the National Academy of Sciences of the United States of America* 100, no. 14: 8074–8079.

Waugh, William L., and Gregory Streib. 2006. "Collaboration and Leadership for Effective Emergency Management." *Public Administration Review* 66, Issue Supplement s1: 130–140.

CHAPTER 10

Strategic Communication

GAIL FANN THOMAS

Across all of our efforts, effective strategic communications are essential to sustaining global legitimacy and supporting our policy aims. Aligning our actions with our words is a shared responsibility that must be fostered by a culture of communication throughout the government. We must also be more effective in our deliberate communication and engagement, and do a better job understanding the attitudes, opinions, grievances, and concerns of peoples—not just elites—around the world. Doing so is critical to allow us to convey credible messages, develop effective plans and to better understand how our actions will be perceived.

—*2010 National Framework for Strategic Communication*

This quote comes from a national study that aimed to clarify the importance and need for strategic communication across US government agencies. The result of the study was the creation of a national framework for strategic communication. This framework explains how US government agencies, including those within the Department of Homeland Security, should work together to achieve higher-order strategic goals through communication.

This chapter provides an introduction to strategic communication, including definitions, basic concepts, planning techniques, and assessment approaches.

We will also look at related topics such as risk and crisis communication and explore the role of the media.

Why Strategic Communication Now?

In a world of 24/7 news, the Internet, blogging, Twitter, and other social media, communication is becoming more central in our everyday lives. Within minutes, a teen in rural Kansas can Skype a teen in Cairo, Egypt. A college student can develop a podcast that explains how to make a bomb. The Federal Emergency Management Agency can launch a mobile website that allows people to use their smart phones to immediately access emergency-preparedness information. As people around the world become more connected, the government must rethink how it communicates, both internally in the DHS and its component parts and externally with others stakeholders, including other government agencies, the private sector, the public, and the media. The DHS needs to become more strategic, more deliberate, and more participative in its communication. Strategic communication is an emerging big-picture approach for addressing communication in a more global and technologically advanced world.

Definitions of Strategic Communication

Strategic communication is a term that is used in both the private and the public sectors. In the private sector, strategic communication has been defined as "communication aligned with the company's overall strategy, to enhance strategic positioning" (Argenti, Howell, and Beck 2005, 83). In the US Department of Defense, it is defined as "focused United States Government efforts to understand and engage key audiences to create, strengthen, or preserve conditions favorable for the advancement of United States Government interests, policies, and objectives through the use of coordinated programs, plans, themes, messages, and products synchronized with the actions of all instruments of national power" (US Joint Forces Command 2010, xi–xii). The National Framework for Strategic Communication defines it as "the synchronization of our words and deeds as well as deliberate efforts to communicate and engage with intended audiences" (White House 2010, 2).

These definitions focus on three key elements:

1. *They focus on the big picture and align strategic communication with strategic intent.* The definitions take a big-picture view of communication.

Strategic communication is aligned and linked to a nation's, agency's, or organization's strategic intent. For the DHS, this would mean that strategic communication would be aligned to the National Security Strategy and to the DHS's strategic guidance. For an agency such as the US Coast Guard, strategic communication would help align words and deeds to higher-level guidance as well as the USCG's strategic intent. A strategic communication program would provide guidance for day-to-day tactical communication both internally and externally.

2. *They affirm that strategic communication engages with the stakeholder.* Strategic communication is stakeholder-centric rather than sender-focused. An audience-focused approach helps an agency better understand the needs and concerns of its constituents. Engaging with stakeholders is a better approach than simply broadcasting directives.

3. *They indicate that strategic communication is an intentional, choice-based process.* Strategic communication uses a systematic planning process. Those people who are engaged in the planning process devise alternative strategies and allocate communication resources to achieve desired results.

Principles of Strategic Communication

In 2008 the educators and practitioners from the joint forces and other agencies of the US government developed a set of nine principles for strategic communication (US Department of Defense 2008). All of these principles would apply to strategic communication for homeland security:

1. *Leadership driven.* If strategic communication is to succeed, leaders must make it a top priority. Leaders drive the strategic communication process within an agency. Without their support, the process is ineffective.

2. *Credible.* Communication must be perceived as consistent and credible. Stakeholders must believe that communication is accurate, truthful, and respectful. Words and actions should be congruent. When words and actions are not aligned, people will believe actions more than they believe words. Inconsistencies between words and actions create cynicism and distrust.

3. *Understanding.* Effective strategic communication requires a deep comprehension of the stakeholders' attitudes, culture, identities, behavior,

history, perspectives, and social systems. A stakeholder determines the meaning of a message through these lenses.

4. *Dialogue.* Successful communication requires active listening, engagement, and pursuit of mutual interest. These processes usually develop over time.

5. *Pervasive.* Every action, image, and word sends a message. Even inaction and no communication send a message. All personnel within an agency are communicators. With the advent of social media, even the most junior employee's words can have strategic effects.

6. *Unity of effort.* Effective strategic communication is accomplished through vertical and horizontal integration. It flows from the strategic level to the tactical level and horizontally across all stakeholders. Communication strategies are aligned with higher levels and are nested throughout the organization.

7. *Results based.* Strategic communication is outcome or results based. Communication goals are determined that align with strategic intent. Communication is assessed over time to determine how communication strategies are working.

8. *Responsive.* Feedback loops should be included in the strategic communication process. The strategic communication process should be sufficiently flexible to incorporate the feedback.

9. *Continuous.* Strategic communication is a continuous process of research, analysis, planning, execution, and assessment. This dynamic process is sensitive to the environment and the various stakeholders and is able to make adjustments as needed to accomplish the desired results.

Strategic Communication as Risk Mitigation

Strategic communication serves as a risk-mitigation and resource-management tool. An agency's strategic initiatives are often analyzed for technical, financial, and economic risk. Rarely do managers or administrators analyze the social, political, or cultural risks associated with a strategic initiative. Yet these people-centered risks are often the ones that cause an initiative to fail. Social, political, and cultural risks can often be mitigated with effective stakeholder communication. By assessing the impact and probability of social, political, and social risks, administrators can be more efficient in allocating communication-related resources.

A Move Away from One-Way, Conduit Communication to More Participative Communication

In the past, communication has been more top-down and one-way. Organizational leaders often espoused a communication philosophy that was more push and less pull, using a one-size-fits-all formula (Mefalopulos 2003). The dominant communication metaphor was the conduit where a "correct" message was injected or transferred from the sender to the receiver (Axley 1984). This type of communication used a sender-message-channel-receiver model, or what some have referred to as the hypodermic-syringe approach (DeFleur and Dennis 1994).

Today, communication professionals understand that communication is interpretive. An interpretive approach to communication asserts that the meaning of a message is determined by the receiver. Unlike the conduit or injection metaphor, communication is now recognized as a process of creating shared understanding beween the sender and receiver. To better understand how people will respond to a message, senders must determine how communication will be filtered through various experiences, attitudes, beliefs, and values. This interpretive approach points to a more participative, two-way model of communication. It requires the sender (the DHS and its subcomponents) to listen carefully to its various stakeholders—both internally and externally.

Internally, the goal is to engage department or agency employees. Engaged employees are more likely to be committed to an organization's strategic goals and able to contribute in significant ways to problem analysis and resolution (Fleming, Coffman, and Harter 2005). Externally, the department and its subcomponents are able to better understand the attitudes, opinions, grievances, and concerns of the US public and other people beyond our borders. A better understanding of these critical stakeholders makes credible messages more likely.

The two-way, interpretive model assumes a more participative approach. The participation "ladder" is illustrated in Table 10.1, with the lowest level of participation on the bottom and the most participative approach on the top. Although the more participative approach requires more time up front, research shows that it can be an effective method for gaining stakeholders' acceptance and involvement. It is also a good strategy for building sustainable change (Arnstein 1969; Dietz and Stern 2008).

TABLE 10.1   A typology of participation

Type of Participation	Description
Inform	We will keep you informed.
Consult	We will keep you informed, listen to you, and provide feedback on how your input influenced the decision.
Involve	We will work with you to ensure your concerns are considered and reflected in the alternatives considered and provide feedback on how your input influenced the decision.
Collaborate	We will incorporate your advice and recommendations to the maximum extent possible.
Empower	We will implement what you decide.

Source: Adapted from the International Association for Public Participation's "Spectrum of Public Participation," http://www.iap2.org/associations/4748/files/IAP2%20Spectrum _vertical.pdf.

Strategic Communication for the Department of Homeland Security

The 2008–2013 DHS Strategic Plan is titled "One Team, One Mission: Securing Our Homeland." This unity of mission is also emphasized in the following quote: "We are a unified Department with a shared focus: strengthening our Nation—through a partnership with individual citizens, the private sector, state, local and tribal governments, and our global partners" (i). Robust strategic communication programs and plans are a means to achieving this goal. Strategic communication provides a big-picture, deliberate, and participative approach to achieving unity of focus within the DHS and its various subcomponents. Strategic communication programs and plans also provide a deliberate, participative approach for protecting our nation in concert with the US public, the private sector, and other federal, state, and local governments. Likewise, with a goal of protecting the United States and contributing to international security, strategic communication programs and plans provide a road map for working in concert with our global partners. Examples of specific DHS initiatives that might benefit from a strategic communication plan include global aviation security, cargo screening, national emergency preparedness, and border management, just to name a few.

Strategic Communication for Agencies Within Homeland Security

Similarly, nested strategic communication processes can help the various DHS subcomponents at the federal, state, and local levels achieve their strategic goals. Agency-level strategic communication programs, plans, and processes provide a horizontal integrative mechanism across the other subcomponents, align with DHS and national security goals, and ultimately provide direction for the day-to-day communications that are conducted by subcomponent employees.

Strategic Communication Planning Process

Strategic communication planning is not a linear, onetime, one-size-fits-all process. It is dynamic, iterative, and adaptive to fit specific circumstances. Each strategic initiative generally requires an associated strategic communication plan. The plan should be integrated with the strategy or operational plan. The desired outcome of the planning process is not simply a piece of paper; it is an approach and a way of thinking. With that in mind, there are some clear elements that require thoughtful analysis. The following strategic communication planning guidance helps achieve this goal. The planning process is best achieved by a small team of individuals who have key insights and different perspectives about the strategic initiative.

1. **Strategic Initiative and Risk Assessment**—What higher-level strategic initiative will be the focus of the strategic communication planning? The initiative should have strategic consequences for DHS subcomponents, the DHS, or the United States. Provide a description of the initiative. What are the consequences of failure? What are the risks your organization will face in achieving this initiative?
2. **Policy and Guidance**—With which higher-level policies or guidance is your strategic initiative aligned?
3. **Strategic Considerations**—What contextual factors, history, or other issues are important to know about this initiative? Why is this strategic initiative a priority now?

4. **Objectives and Director's Intent**—What is the guidance from the director regarding this initiative? Are there any constraining factors?

5. **Results**—What are the results this strategic initiative is intended to create?

6. **Strategic Communication Planning Goals**—What do you hope to accomplish with your strategic communication planning process?

7. **Stakeholder Analysis**—Who are the internal (to your agency) and external stakeholders who will be impacted by this initiative? Note that these groups may change over time. Who are the most influential actors?

8. **Research and Analysis**—What information would you want to have to better understand the factors (political, economic, social, infrastructural, and informational) that would impact the success or failure of this initiative? What information is already available to you? What would you need to gather this information?

9. **Overarching Themes**—Themes will be developed for this initiative using the supporting policies, department or agency strategy and guidance, agency themes, and director's intent.

10. **Key Messages**—These are the specific messages that flow from the themes. Their impact may vary by stakeholder group, but always assume all stakeholder groups will see all messages. Consistency is key.

11. **Assessment**—How will you measure the overall success of your strategic initiative? What baseline measures would you want to have? What measures of performance and effectiveness will you use to measure the success of your strategic communication objectives and more specifically interactions with your stakeholders?

12. **Resources**—What resources (manpower, equipment, and the like) are required to accomplish this strategic communication plan? What special expertise will be needed? What cultural, linguistic, and measurement expertise will be required? Who should be on your strategic communication planning team?

13. **Process**—How will the strategic communication planning process be integrated with existing planning processes? What role will leadership need to play to make this effort successful? (Thomas 2008)

Table 10.2 is an example of a strategic communication planning template. The detailed strategic plan might be lengthy, but the executive summary could be provided in a one-page brief.

TABLE 10.2 Strategic communication plan executive summary

STRATEGIC COMMUNICATION TEMPLATE

Strategic Context
Frame the strategic initiative and describe the critical contextual elements that will influence the issue.

Themes
List the overarching themes associated with the strategic objective.

Strategic Objective
Describe the objectives of the strategic initiative and desired end results.

Messages
List messages that could be associated with the various stakeholders.

Communication Goals
Describe the overarching communication goals that will allow you to achieve the strategic initiative.

Assessment
Describe how you will measure progress toward your communication goals. What methods will you use?

Key Stakeholders
List the key internal and external stakeholders who will impact the achievement of the strategic goal.

Next Steps
What is the way ahead?

Context Analysis

Communication is context driven. Therefore, it is critical to monitor and assess the environment to inform the strategic communication process. Conditions that might influence communication include technology, regulations, history, politics, the economy, society, demographics, and culture. Often referred to as environmental scanning, this process allows an agency to analyze trends to know what conditions might affect communication in the future.

Understanding the environment is critical for three reasons:

1. *It alerts you to the facts on the ground.* For instance, an environmental assessment would let you know which media are used most frequently by a particular community. It could also alert you to particular social norms or mores that might influence how the public hears your communications.

2. *It provides information about trends.* By assessing trends in the environment, you can better anticipate the future. An example of this would be

the understanding of changing infrastructure in a community. A better grasp of infrastructure trends could help the DHS better communicate in future emergencies.

3. *It helps you be proactive.* Understanding the environment helps you anticipate likely scenarios. It allows you to "look around the corner" to see what is coming. It also helps you lean forward rather than constantly be in a reactionary mode.

Scanning the environment can be accomplished by gathering information from sources such as publications, conferences, personal and organizational networks, think tanks, experts, and scholars. Once these data are gathered, strategic communication planners interpret the data and determine the implications for strategic communication programs and plans.

Stakeholder Identification and Analysis

Stakeholder thinking is an increasingly important concept in the public and private sectors. The term was developed in the private sector to challenge traditional shareholder-centric management (Parmar et al. 2010). Rather than focusing solely on a healthy return to shareholders, the stakeholder approach factors in the concerns of a broader set of constituents. In public administration, stakeholder thinking is applied to the implementation of an agency's strategy, policies, or other strategic initiatives (Bryson 2004). Ultimately, public agencies such as the Department of Homeland Security and its subcomponents must demonstrate that they are able to create public value by meeting public mandates and fulfilling their missions. If they are not able to do so, they will face diminished budgets and possible extinction.

In his classic text *Stakeholder Management: A Stakeholder Approach*, Freeman defines a stakeholder as "any group or individual who can affect or is affected by the achievement of the organization's objectives" (1984, 4). Today agencies cannot solve public problems independently. Instead, multiple organizations must solve problems interdependently. Solving interorganizational problems means identifying stakeholders who have a "stake" in the problem and solution. Research shows that when stakeholders' concerns are not factored into strategic decision making, the result is often poor performance, failure, or disaster (Burby 2003; Nutt 2002). On the other hand, when key stakeholders are engaged in the problem definition and search for solutions, implementation is more successful. It is important to note that stakeholder analysis does not mean addressing all stakeholders' concerns equally. Instead, it requires astute judgment in deter-

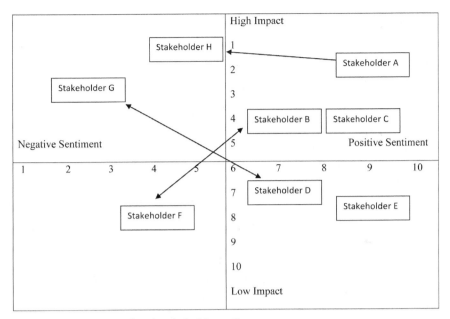

FIGURE 10.1   Completed stakeholder-influence map

mining which stakeholders are most important in achieving the agency's goals, determining the priority of concerns that should be addressed, and anticipating the consequences of concerns that are not addressed.

Stakeholder identification and analysis are essential steps to developing a strategic communication plan. Ideally, this process is conducted by a small team of individuals who have insights into the strategic initiative, using the following steps:

1. Prior to the stakeholder identification session, create a large stakeholder chart (approximately four feet by six feet). See Figure 10.1.
2. Ensure that every one of the team members is clear about the key objectives of the initiative.
3. Have each person on the team identify key stakeholders who can affect or are affected by the achievement of the objectives. One technique is to have each member of the team write single stakeholder names on small Post-it notes. In other words, if a team member identifies sixteen key stakeholders, she would have sixteen Post-it notes with sixteen stakeholder names.

TABLE 10.3   Stakeholder-engagement plan

STAKEHOLDER	3 months	6 months	9 months	12 months
A	Inform	Consult	Involve	Collaborate
B	Collaborate	Collaborate	Collaborate	Collaborate
C	Involve	Involve	Inform	Inform
D	Inform	Inform	Inform	Inform
E	Consult	Inform	Inform	Inform
F	Collaborate	Involve	Inform	Inform
G	Inform	Inform	Inform	Inform
H	Inform	Inform	Inform	Inform

4. Have each person place the Post-it notes on the stakeholder chart. Each note should be positioned to indicate the level of potential impact on the vertical axis and sentiment (positive, neutral, or negative) on the horizontal axis.

5. Once all the Post-it notes have been positioned, team members reconcile their differences. This part of the exercise helps uncover assumptions about various stakeholders and draws on various knowledge that the team members have about each stakeholder.

6. When complete, the chart will have only one Post-it note per stakeholder. This set of stakeholders represents a stakeholder network as related to your objective.

7. The next phase is to create an influence network. Draw arrows showing which stakeholder will influence whom in the network.

Stakeholder Engagement

Once the stakeholders have been identified, the next step is to determine the level of engagement. Table 10.3 provides an example of a stakeholder-engagement plan.

Synchronizing Words and Actions

Agencies and their leaders communicate with their stakeholders through words and actions. Formal communication includes mission statements, leaders' speeches, and websites. While these communications are important, ultimately it is the agency's actions that test its credibility. Credibility, according to Kouzes and Posner, is the foundation of leadership. Based on their leadership study that has spanned more than twenty-five years, gathering data from tens of thousands of people, they ask how one recognizes credibility. Comments included "They practice what they preach," "They walk the talk," "Their actions are consistent with their words," and "They do what they say they will do" (2007, 40). Credibility is granted when words are consistent with actions. When they are not consistent, stakeholders experience a "say-do" gap that diminishes trust, creates cynicism, and destroys credibility. Sopow (1994) offers a diagnostic for closing the say-do gap:

1. *Assess your performance gap*—Compare corporate mission, action plans, values, and policy announcements with actual performance reviews, actions taken, and management updates. This gap is the difference between what you said you would do and what in fact you are doing.
2. *Assess your communication gap*—Compare what you are actually doing with what external and internal stakeholders see you doing. This gap can be measured through opinion polls, surveys, and media content analysis.
3. *Assess the expectation gap*—Compare data on what you are seen doing with what the public thinks you should be doing. Obtain this information through surveys, customer feedback, and other research.

Choosing Appropriate Channels and Using Credible Sources

Media and source choices are tactical considerations that should be driven by the strategic analysis. While aligning with strategic guidance, tactical decisions about communication channels and sources are generally accomplished through such agency offices that deal with public affairs, intergovernmental affairs, legislative affairs, employee communications, and community engagements.

Choices about various media channels should be based on research and past experience. A question one might ask is "What media channel or channels will best help me achieve this objective? Based on factors such as timing, stakeholder preferences, and accessibility, should we use face-to-face communication, television, radio, print media, and/or social media?"

Regarding sources of the communication, who will have the most credibility with the audience: an expert, a peer, a senior leader? Importantly, tactical communication plans and programs should aim at developing communication plans that will accomplish the operational goals and objectives. One way of ensuring the effectiveness of the communication is by developing an assessment strategy.

Assessing the Effectiveness of Strategic Communication

More organizations are requiring staffs to produce a return on investment for their strategic communication programs (World Bank 2008). In the past, organizations have relied on measures of performance (communication activities) to justify their programs. Today, though, senior management and the public demand more. Instead of simply measuring communication activities, one should also be able to measure the effect of the communication activities. Although this type of measurement is significantly more difficult, it is a better path to improving a results-based strategic communication program.

Measures of performance. A measure of performance is a metric for assessing the accomplishment of various communication activities. It compares the quantity of communication activities to the amount of money budgeted for the activities. For example, for a specific homeland security objective, the public affairs office might count the number of brochures it produced or the number of minutes of public service announcements on the radio. Social media analytics allows one to track hundreds of measures, including hits and reach. Although these types of measures are needed, they often produce communication activities that do not focus efforts on the strategic or operational objectives of the organization.

Measures of effects. Measures of effects assess the results or impact that your communications are having. This measure shows the effect of your communication relative to the budget you have allocated to communication. Measures of effect are much more difficult to achieve. First you must determine the objective of your strategic initiative and the effect that you hope to achieve. Next you determine the impact of your communication in relationship to your desired effect. In regard to communication, effects are generally stated as attitudes, beliefs, or behaviors. For example, the Office of Emergency Preparedness (OEP) may desire to communicate with the public about earthquake preparedness. Measures of performance might tell them how many public broadcasts were delivered. Ultimately, the OEP wants to change behavior. For example, they want business owners to identify and address potential hazards, prepare disaster supply kits, and be able to protect their employees during an earthquake. By focusing on measures of effectiveness, communicators get more focused on the desired results of the communications rather than the communications themselves. In other words, the communications become the means to an end rather than the end. In this example, a measure of effects might include the number of businesses that have eliminated potential earthquake hazards or the number of businesses that have disaster supply kits on hand. More important would be to find out which communications motivated the business owners to take action.

Measures of strategic communication program effectiveness. From a macro perspective, the overarching strategic communication program and planning process must also be measured for effectiveness. This type of measure allows officials to assess the results of the overall strategic communication process. This measure can be used to assess the cost and benefits of the overarching strategic communication program. This assessment becomes the feedback mechanism for improving the strategic communication program and determining how communication budget dollars would best be spent to achieve the agency's goals.

Formative evaluation. The purpose of formative evaluations is to improve programs. Formative evaluations are conducted throughout the life cycle of a program and provide feedback for adjusting the program to meet its objectives. Formative evaluation is often accomplished through surveys, interviews, data collection, and experiments (Patton 2008).

Summative evaluation. Summative (sometimes referred to as outcome) evaluations look at the intended and *unintended* positive consequences and intended and *unintended* negative consequences of a program. Questions that might be answered as part of a summative evaluation include: "Did our strategic communication program accomplish our objectives?" or "What were the costs and benefits of the strategic communication program?"

Risk Communication

Risk communication originated in the environmental sciences in an attempt to better communicate hazards to the public and other stakeholders. The National Academy of Sciences defines risk communication as "the interactive process of exchange of information and opinion among individuals, groups, and institutions. It involves multiple messages about the nature of risk and other messages—not strictly about risk—that express concerns, opinions or reactions to risk messages or to legal and institutional arrangements for risk management" (National Research Council, Committee on Risk Perception and Communication 1989, 21).

Risk communication begins with risk assessment, which is defined as the probability of undesired effects arising from exposure to a hazard. Often it is expressed as risk = probability x consequences. Whereas scientists, engineers, and other technicians may calculate an objective notion of risk, the public's perceptions of risk vary widely. Various scholars believe that the public's perception of risk is based on the strength of fifteen different factors. These factors, which can vary in magnitude, determine the public's strength of concern, worry, anger, fear, hostility, and outrage. Understanding the source of emotions associated with risk can help professionals develop communication that is effective. These are the factors:

1. *Voluntariness.* Imposed risks are less readily accepted than those that are characterized as voluntary.
2. *Controllability.* Risks that are perceived as under the control of others are less readily accepted than those risks that are perceived to be under the control of the individual.
3. *Familiarity.* Unfamiliar risks are less acceptable than those risks that are believed to be familiar.
4. *Equity.* Inequitable or uneven risks are seen as less acceptable than those that are perceived to be equally shared.
5. *Benefits.* Risks with unclear benefits are less acceptable than those risks that appear to have clear benefits.
6. *Understanding.* Poorly understood risks are seen as less acceptable than those risks from activities that are believed to be well understood.
7. *Uncertainty.* Unknown risks or risks with uncertain dimensions are less acceptable than risks that are known to science.
8. *Dread.* Risks that induce fear, anxiety, or terror are less acceptable than risks that do not elicit fear, anxiety, or terror.
9. *Trust in institutions.* Risk associated with institutions that lack credibility or are considered untrustworthy are less acceptable than risks associated with institutions that are considered trustworthy and credible.
10. *Reversibility.* Risks with perceived irreversible effects are less acceptable than risks that are perceived to have reversible effects.

11. *Personal stake.* Risks that people believe will put them at personal risk are less acceptable than those risks that do not create a direct personal threat.

12. *Ethical or moral nature.* Unethical or morally reprehensible risks are less acceptable than risks that are considered ethical or morally acceptable.

13. *Human versus natural origin.* Human-generated risks are considered less acceptable than risks that are perceived to be caused by nature or "acts of God."

14. *Victim identity.* Risks with identifiable victims are seen as less acceptable than risks associated with victims who are simply seen as statistics.

15. *Catastrophic potential.* Risks that incur fatalities, injuries, or illness that are grouped in time and space are less acceptable than fatalities, injuries, or illnesses that are scattered and random. (Covello, von Winterfeldt, and Slovic 1986)

Crafting Risk Messages

Covello and Allen (1988) name seven cardinal rules for designing risk messages. Although these rules may seem obvious, they are frequently violated:

1. Accept and involve the public as a legitimate partner. The ultimate goal of the communication strategy is to inform the public so that they can make decisions that affect their lives and property.

2. Plan carefully and evaluate your efforts. Risk communication must be carefully planned. Establish goals, identify audiences, and evaluate your results.

3. Listen to the public's specific concerns. Do not make assumptions about people's perceptions of risk. Gather sufficient information to be able to empathize with your audience. Recognize hidden agendas, symbolic meanings, and broader economic or political considerations.

4. Be honest, frank, and open. Know that you must earn trust and credibility. It cannot be taken for granted. When you do not know answers, say so. Lean toward sharing more information than less, but be honest about what you know. Speak openly about data uncertainties, strengths, and weaknesses.

5. Coordinate and collaborate with other credible sources. Use allies to help communicate risk information. Develop collaborative relationships with allies who can jointly communicate about an issue. Collaborative

sources might include university scientists, physicians, or trusted local officials.

6. Meet the needs of the media. Media are key to disseminating information about risks. Build relationships with the media. Be accessible. Learn to communicate well with the media.

7. Speak clearly and with compassion. Use simple, nontechnical language to communicate risks. Use vivid and concrete images, examples, and anecdotes. Avoid distant, abstract language. Acknowledge and respond to the public's emotions. Tell people what you can do and what you cannot do.

Community Engagement

Community engagement's purpose is to *engage* the public in support of the DHS or subcomponent programs, activities, and issues. Engagement happens with two-way communication. Engagement can occur before, during, and after the development of federal programs and policies. Agencies can engage with the public during the problem-definition stage. By engaging the public early in the process, multiple viewpoints are considered before analyzing and framing the problem, opportunity, or issue. Involving the public early allows agencies to incorporate community ideas into the process (Bowen, Newenham-Kahindi, and Herremans 2010). This type of inclusion generally increases citizen ownership and contributes a diversity of solutions that might not otherwise be available. Examples of community engagement strategies that the DHS uses are:

Community roundtables. Roundtables bring together citizens of various backgrounds with government representatives. Other roundtables are broader and include communities with concerns relating to homeland security and civil rights and liberties.

Consultation with communities. The department learns from affected communities about their concerns and their ideas for solutions. An example of consultations includes coordinated meetings with religious leaders to hear their concerns about modesty prescriptions and airport screening, with communities of recent immigrants to discuss language-access issues, and with disability groups to discuss accessibility issues at ports of entry. Sometimes consultations result in formal products such as the recommendations that were made by a broad range of American Muslim leaders regarding appropriate terminology to be used when describing the terrorist threat (DHS 2008).

Incident Communication Coordination Team. The Incident Communication Coordination Team's goal is to provide swift federal government official communication with various community leaders in the aftermath of a terrorist act or homeland security incident.

International engagement. These initiatives aim to build a long-term network with international partners to foster integration and civic engagement.

Cultural competency and engagement training. The Office for Civil Rights and Civil Liberties trains department personnel in cultural competency and awareness.

The Central Role of the Media in Homeland Security

The media play an important role in the achievement of homeland security strategic objectives:

Role model of a free press in a democracy. In the United States we point to editorial independence as a hallmark of a free society, unlike less free societies where the government controls the media. Access to information is central to a democracy. A free press offers citizens multiple perspectives and helps citizens make responsible, informed decisions. A free press also serves to hold elected officials accountable. This responsibility often creates an inherent tension between the media and the government (Center for Democracy and Governance 1999). Thus, homeland security officials should be cognizant of their role as it relates to the role of the media. Officials should be trained to interact with the media in such a way that appreciates the role of the media in society but also effectively communicates with the public.

Dissemination of information. The nature of homeland security's work relies heavily on the mass media to disseminate information to the public. Homeland security uses mass media to prepare the public for disasters. Techniques in risk communication (described above) can help officials mitigate the risks associated with terrorism and natural disasters. Should a crisis occur, the mass media will play an important role by keeping the public informed with up-to-the-minute details of the event and providing directions. The 2007 Southern California wildfires provided a good example of how traditional media outlets are now being augmented by social media to meet the public's need for information during a disaster. Social media allowed for wide-scale interaction among the public as they collected information, disseminated information, coordinated their actions, and self-policed (Sutton, Palen, and Shklovski 2008).

With the advent of social media and other new technologies, the public is increasingly using peer-to-peer back channels to deal with disaster situations. The DHS and its subcomponent agencies can use strategic communication programs and plans not to control but to better align their efforts with the organic peer-to-peer networks.

Increasing avenues for two-way, participative communication. Web 2.0 is a means for promoting more two-way, interactive communication among homeland security's stakeholders. Social media and other technologies create opportunities for real-time sensing of the environment as well as feedback about numerous issues. The rise of social media requires homeland security to understand the impact of these technologies and begin to integrate them in meaningful ways.

Conclusion

Advancement in information and communication technology has enabled an unprecedented level of interconnectivity between the public, the media, the government, the military, and other communities and organizations in today's world. The White House's National Framework for Strategic Communication states that "across all of our efforts, effective strategic communications are essential to sustaining global legitimacy and supporting our policy aims" (2010). Thinking strategically about communication is key to meeting big-picture goals and objectives, not just for the Department of Homeland Security, but for a wide variety of agencies and organizations across the public and private sectors. Today, we recognize that communication is interpretive, and that assessing the environment, analyzing stakeholders, and choosing credible sources are important parts of a successful strategic communication plan. A two-way, participative approach that engages stakeholders is key to successful communication, both internal and external. Strategic communication must be credible, results-based, engaged, and responsive. Most important, strategic communication should always be aligned with an overall strategic intent. Establishing a strategic communication plan and process can help the Department of Homeland Security and its subcomponent agencies use communication to help reach their strategic goals.

REFERENCES

Argenti, Paul A., Robert A. Howell, and Karen A. Beck. 2005. "The Strategic Communication Imperative." *MIT Sloan Management Review* 46, no. 3: 83–89.

Arnstein, Sherry R. 1969. "A Ladder of Citizen Participation." *Journal of the American Institute of Planners* 35, no. 4: 216–224.

Axley, Stephen R. 1984. "Managerial and Organizational Communication in Terms of the Conduit Metaphor." *Academy of Management Review* 9, no. 3: 428–427.

Bowen, Frances, Alysium Newenham-Kahindi, and Irene Herremans. 2010. "When Suits Meet Roots: The Antecedents and Consequences of Community Engagement Strategy." *Journal of Business Ethics* 95: 297–318.

Bryson, John M. 2004. "What to Do When Stakeholders Matter." *Public Management Review* 6, no. 1: 21–53.

Burby, R. 2003. "Making Plans That Matter: Citizen Involvement and Government Action." *Journal of the American Planning Association* 69, no. 1: 33–50.

Center for Democracy and Governance. June 1999. "The Role of Media in Democracy: A Strategic Approach." Accessed May 9, 2011. www.usaid.gov/our_work/democracy _and_governance/publications/pdfs/pnace630.pdf.

Covello, Vincent T., and Frederick W. Allen. 1988. *Seven Cardinal Rules of Risk Communication.* Washington, DC: US Environmental Protection Agency.

Covello, Vince T., Detlof von Winterfeldt, and Paul Slovic. 1986. "Communicating Scientific Information About Health and Environmental Risks: Problems and Opportunities from a Social and Behavioral Perspective." In *Uncertainties in Risk Assessment and Management*, edited by V. Covello, L. Lave, A. Moghissi, and V. R. R. Uppuluri. New York: Plenum.

DeFleur, M. L., and E. E. Dennis. 1994. *Understanding Mass Communication.* Boston: Houghton Mifflin.

DHS. 2008. "Terminology to Define the Terrorists: Recommendations from American Muslims." http://www.dhs.gov/xlibrary/assets/dhs_crcl_terminology_08-1-08_accessible .pdf.

Dietz, Thomas, and Paul C. Stern, eds. 2008. *Public Participation in Environmental Assessment and Decision Making.* Nationa Research Council. Accessed May 15, 2011, www.nap.edu/catalog.12434.html.

Fleming, John H., Curt Coffman, and James K. Harter. 2005. "Manage Your Human Sigma." *Harvard Business Review* 83, nos. 7–8: 106–114.

Freeman, R. E. 1984. *Strategic Management: A Stakeholder Approach.* Boston: Pitman.

Kouzes, James, and Barry Posner. 2007. *The Leadership Challenge.* 4th ed. San Francisco: Jossey-Bass.

Mefalopulos, Paolo. 2003. "Theory and Practice of Participatory Communication: The Case of the FAO Project 'Communication for Development in Southern Africa.'" PhD diss., University of Texas at Austin.

National Research Council, Committee on Risk Perception and Communication. 1989. *Improving Risk Communication*. Washington, DC: National Academy Press.

Nutt, Paul. 2002. *Why Decisions Fail: Avoiding the Blunders and Traps That Lead to Debacles*. San Francisco: Berrett-Koehler.

Parmar, Bidhan L., R. Edward Freeman, Jeffrey S. Harrison, Andrew C. Wicks, Lauren Purnell, and Simone DeColle. 2010. "Stakeholder Theory: The State of the Art." *Academy of Management Annals* 4, no. 1: 403–445.

Patton, Michael Quinn. 2001. *Qualitative Research and Evaluation Methods*. 3rd ed. Thousand Oaks, CA: Sage.

————. 2008. Utilization-Focused Evaluation, 4th edition. Thousand Oaks, CA: Sage.

Sopow, Eli. 1994. *The Critical Issues Audit*. Issue Action Publications. Accessed May 9, 2011.

Sutton, Jeannette, Leysia Palen, and Irina Shklovski. 2008. "Backchannels on the Front Lines: Emergent Uses of Social Media in the 2007 Southern California Wildfires." In *Proceedings of the 5th International ISCRAM Conference*. Eds. F. Fiedrich and B. Van de Walle. Washington, DC. 624–631.

Thomas, Gail Fann. January 8, 2008. *Strategic Communication Framework*. Lecture for Strategic Communication Workshop, Center for Executive Education, Naval Postgraduate School, Monterey, CA.

US Department of Defense. 2008a. "One Team, One Mission, Securing Our Homeland: US Department of Homeland Security Strategic Plan Fiscal Years 2008–2013." Accessed May 7, 2011. www.dhs.gov/xlibrary.assets.DHS_StratPlan_FINAL_spread.pdf.

————. 2008b. *Principles of Strategic Communication*. Distributed by Robert T. Hastings, Principal Deputy Assistant Secretary of Defense for Public Affairs. Washington DC, August. www.carlisle.army.mil/DIME/documents/Principles%20of%20SC%20(22%20 Aug%2008)%20Signed%20versn.pdf.

US Joint Forces Command. 2010. *Commander's Handbook for Strategic Communication and Communication Strategy, Version 3.0*. Suffolk, VA: Doctrine and Education Group Joint Warfighting Center, US Joint Forces Command.

White House. 2010. "National Framework for Strategic Communication." http://www.fas .org/man/eprint/pubdip.pdf.

World Bank. 2008. *Development Communication Sourcebook: Broadening the Boundaries of Communication*. Washington, DC: World Bank.

Strategic Planning

SAMUEL H. CLOVIS JR.

Strategic planning is perhaps one of the most challenging, and necessary, functions of management, particularly in government organizations. Contrary to the motivations and focus that underlie planning in the for-profit private sector, government, in their component agencies, bureaus, and departments, must deal with a host of constraints, myriad stakeholders, and various uncertainties. Those uncertainties, most often resource related, are particularly compelling in today's homeland security environment. Likewise, government is complex, composed of several layers and literally thousands of entities, each of which is unique. This chapter will focus on outlining strategic planning considerations for each level of government and their respective jurisdictions. In order to inform readers about strategic planning, this chapter will similarly be focused on not so much *what to think* about planning in the homeland security environment, as *how to think* about this most important activity. The strategic thinking element will give those interested in homeland strategic planning the potential to expand the domain of solutions available to meet many of the "wicked problems" one might encounter in getting the most from the limited resources available to government enterprises, regardless of level or size. In the paragraphs that follow, we will examine the background of strategic planning and public entities. Next will be discussion of the planning methodologies that work best for government enterprises and then a review of some alternative thoughts on strategic planning for public organizations. Finally, we will explore several intellectual dimensions that will prepare homeland security practitioners to deal with planning activities and their challenges when things move from classic bureaucratic equilibrium to a transition zone of disequilibrium. This introduction of the rudimentary elements of "complexity theory" should provoke discussion and further investigation into such interdisciplinary areas of study as resilience. Though there are many "how-to" books on strategic planning with some specifically aimed at government and nonprofit management, what the student will find in this final segment of the chapter will be ideas that may break the chains of conventional thinking about strategic planning.

Background

Strategic planning is a relatively new phenomenon for public organizations. Borrowing from the business literature, public managers have for the past several decades examined ways to better demonstrate effectiveness and public value to stakeholders inside and outside of government (Bryson 2004). In fact, most governmental organizations have specific planning activities that eventually lead to some form of formal documentation such as standard operating procedures, operations manuals, or formal plans. At the federal level, these activities are directed by legislation, most prominent among these laws being the Government Performance and Results Act of 1993 (White House 1993). The original intent of the law was to provide organizing principles for the vast array of departments, agencies, and bureaus found in the executive branch of . the federal government. Congress, working with the Clinton administration, wanted to bring methods into the administrative processes of government to raise transparency and to ensure that citizens were getting the most for their investment of national treasure. All departments and separate operating agencies in the executive branch were directed to develop a strategic planning process and then periodically report *program* performance to Congress. As many of the operational programs found in government cross many agencies, such planning and reporting were intended to cut down on waste and inefficiencies inherent in such bureaucratic arrangements.

Over the years, the Office of Management and Budget (OMB), part of the executive branch, charged with program implementation, sought help from the Government Accountability Office (GAO), part of Congress, to monitor compliance among federal departments and agencies. What the GAO reported was that not all agencies were able to meet the metrics established for compliance (Kamensky 2011). To meet the needs of senior managers in government, many management "gurus" authored books outlining best practices in planning for government and nonprofit organizations. From this flood of literature, however, two volumes contained the templates that were used most often by federal agencies to establish a strategic planning process. Those volumes, authored by James Mercer and John Bryson, remain preeminent for federal government planning activities.

Overview of the Templates

Strategic planning and performance measurement have remained a challenge for most federal agencies. Buttressed by the need to cut down on waste to preserve tax dollars, the Obama administration had the intention of providing as much transparency as possible in government operations. Seeking bipartisan support, the administration was able to convince Congress to renew the Government Performance and Results Act in 2010. In January 2011, the president signed the revised legislation that provided even more guidance and structure to strategic planning at the national level. Highlights of the new legislation are:

1. Priority goals for the federal government that cut across all agencies. Rather than hundreds of priorities from all the agencies that might be in conflict or asymmetric, the executive branch will identify a few goals that all agencies will work to achieve. Also, individual agencies will limit goals to a manageable, achievable level.
2. Quarterly reviews and reports to the Office of Management and Budget to review progress on achieving national and agency goals. Lack of progress will bring increased scrutiny to the agency. If progress is not achieved at an acceptable level, the agency may lose control of the program altogether.
3. Codification of the performance framework. Over the life of the legislation, many adjuncts to the law have been initiated, including chief operating officers, performance improvement officers, and others. These adjuncts have now been formalized.
4. Realignment of planning sequence. All agencies will now align strategic plans to a four-year horizon that will take effect in the February after the inauguration of the president. (Kamensky 2011)

The new law is closely aligned with the Bryson and Mercer texts, which indicates that these two templates will continue to be relevant and useful in helping agencies complete their strategic plans.

Strategic planning at the state and local levels of government is much more challenging but is a common practice, even in the smallest of jurisdictions. Below the federal government, however, jurisdictions rather than individual departments or agencies typically develop strategic plans. Only at the state level and in the larger urban jurisdictions will one generally find individual agency and department strategic planning. Jurisdictional and agency administrative capacity in smaller jurisdictions (populations below one hundred thousand) can be problematic, as will be discussed in later paragraphs (Clovis 2008). However, strategic planning serves a multitude of functions for nearly all public enterprises and is practiced ubiquitously.

Current Environment

As was stated above, Bryson and Mercer are used most often as guideposts for developing strategic plans at the federal level. Bryson will be discussed first. Later, Mercer will be compared to the Bryson template.

Bryson (2004) outlines a ten-step process for developing strategic plans for the public and nonprofit organizations. Those steps are:

1. Initiate and agree on a strategic planning process. This, of course, means starting the process as outlined in this template.
2. Identify organizational mandates. Participants should identify the legislative and regulatory environment in which the organization operates and should determine how those mandates might influence the planning process.
3. Clarify organizational mission and values. This is perhaps the most important step in the process. Today, this is particularly challenging for many organizations with homeland security responsibilities, including the Department of Homeland Security. As missions change, morph, or migrate, bringing the focus back to accomplishing the mission can be problematic. This phenomenon has recently been identified by practitioners at all levels of government and has become the focus of new research in the field.
4. Assess the external and internal environments to identify strengths, weaknesses, opportunities, and threats (SWOT). The SWOT analysis technique is ubiquitous in both the public and private sectors.

5. Identify the strategic issues facing the organization. "Strategic issues" can be considered those events, trends, or developments deemed critical to or able to affect the organization's performance.

6. Formulate strategies to manage the issues.

7. Review and adopt the strategies or strategic plan.

8. Establish an effective organizational vision. In the private sector, this action is part of the early steps of articulating a vision, then a mission, for the organization.

9. Develop an effective implementation process. Again, this is a very challenging step in the public sector. Implementation is difficult if the strategy has not accounted for all possible consequences of actions required to execute the strategy.

10. Reassess the strategies and the strategic planning process. This is a feedback mechanism found in both the private and the public sectors.

Bryson recommends processes for entities below the department level. Large organizations, such as those found at the federal government level, have the administrative capacity to develop internal strategic plans and contribute to the strategic plans developed for the department. This, of course, is not usually the case at levels below the federal government.

Mercer (1991) offers a slightly different perspective on strategic planning for public organizations. He suggests that strategic plans contain the following six elements:

1. An environmental scan. This means some form of situational analysis, or SWOT analysis that includes both internal and external factors.

2. A mission statement that defines the fundamental purpose of the organization and its boundaries.

3. A set of strategies indicating what will be done to carry out the mission.

4. Objectives for each strategy.

5. Tactics or short-term operating plans for meeting the objectives.

6. Controls, measures, and evaluation steps to determine how well the strategic plan is progressing

Mercer also introduces a ten-step process very similar to Bryson's and offers suggestions on how to develop and then execute strategic plans. Perhaps most important, however, is the idea of developing a planning horizon, something that will be discussed later in this chapter.

Public administrators over the past two decades have done a great deal to introduce and refine strategic planning for all levels of government, especially at the state and local levels. Though many of these officials find strategic planning of little utility, the process of developing plans for organizations serves many functions that are most helpful in guiding and informing management decisions in public organizations. Now that the current environment has been addressed, how does this apply to homeland security strategic planning at all levels and in all governmental organizations?

Strategic Planning and Homeland Security

At the federal level, the Department of Homeland Security is the locus of policy development and implementation. On matters of national preparedness—those issues that affect state and local governments most—the Federal Emergency Management Agency is the principal agency. FEMA operates the Homeland Security Grant Program,[1] an element of which is the State Homeland Security Program. Since the first grants were issued in the wake of the events of 9/11, state and local governments have had to develop strategic plans that pass DHS standards to receive grant funding (Clovis 2008). Up to and including the current fiscal year grant program requirements (US Department of Homeland Security 2011), state and local governments must strive to comply with the National Preparedness Guidelines (NPG), the National Incident Management System, the National Response Framework, the National Strategy for Information Sharing, and the National Infrastructure Protection Plan.[2] These documents, along with the Homeland Security Presidential Directives and Presidential Policy Directives,[3] are considered the "national documents" and are the foundation of all national preparedness public policy for homeland security.

Federal government agencies, including the DHS, have formalized, controlled, and accountable planning processes in place. At the state and local levels, however, homeland security planning, though recognized as valuable, has had a checkered existence.

In homeland security, planning deficiencies were recognized in the immediate aftermath of the terror attacks of 9/11. In a study done by the Homeland Security Institute, researchers examined documents related to after-action and lessons-learned reports from some two thousand separate activities. In more than 50 percent of those reports, planning was identified as the single most significant deficiency in achieving operational effectiveness. Planning was identified five times more often as a deficiency than any other factor (Clovis, Dunleavy, and Bernard 2005). Thus, planning in the homeland security environment has taken on paramount importance for all individuals and jurisdictions with homeland security responsibility.

Strategic planning for homeland security at the state and local levels has proved to be challenging. Planning effectiveness, as one might imagine, may be as diverse as there are jurisdictions attempting to plan. Thus, homeland security planning is not a ubiquitous, uniform activity with a single set formula for the thirty-nine thousand jurisdictions and countless agencies and departments found in those jurisdictions. Though single approaches are often advocated, as is seen at the federal level, planning must be shaped and molded to the circumstances of the individual agency. Based on national preparedness public policy research, nearly all of the general-purpose jurisdictions in the country approach planning from a jurisdictional perspective (Clovis 2006).[4] The principal reason for this divergent approach to planning between the DHS and nearly all state and local governments is a divergence in perspective on homeland security. The DHS planning has been generally focused on antiterrorist or counterterrorism, whereas state and local governments, with few exceptions, focus on an "all-hazards" approach, of which terrorism is but one of the hazards. This divergence in perspective has created, and continues to cause, significant tensions (Clovis 2006, 2008).

The difference in outlooks at the various levels of government dictates that planning activities should also be different. Because of congressional budget mandates, the executive branch must follow specific planning activities with specific reporting requirements, as is documented above. Just as the national government has focused predominantly on terrorism, that level of government has also concentrated most of its homeland security resources on urban-center protection. One of the main grant programs offered at the DHS is the Urban Area Security Initiative program, which requires regional cooperation in large metropolitan areas.[5] Local cooperation is incentivized, with the large core cities and the respective states gaining resources with which to develop formalized mutual aid arrangement. Some of these areas might encompass as many as four hundred separate urban jurisdictions. Regardless of what level of government is involved in homeland security planning, each jurisdiction—federal, state, local, and tribal—must include some concept of risk in its strategic planning activities.

Risk assessment has turned into a cottage industry in the homeland security field, but often this activity has been separated from planning. For those with homeland security responsibilities, risk must be a part of the planning process, or both the risk assessment and the planning activity will be of little value. To either Bryson or Mercer, risk is not explicitly mentioned, but might be considered as one of the planning elements. However, logic dictates that risk calculations must be part of any planning activity related to securing a city, town, or village. In the next section, one will find a discussion of how to think about risk in homeland security planning.

Strategic Thinking for Homeland Security Planning

Generally speaking, the purpose of planning is to mitigate uncertainty related to the future of an organization by gaining and applying knowledge to reduce risk. When this notion is applied to homeland security, risk mitigation is paramount at every level of government. Based on research and operational knowledge, one can make the assertion that the more knowledge gained about the various internal and external forces that affect the organization, the more likely the organization will achieve a level of security or, in modern parlance, resilience. Learning organizations, particularly those with homeland security responsibilities, are going to enjoy greater resilience and continuity than those that remain confined by bureaucratic structures and pathologies—behaviors identified with a particular organization.

Much has been made of developing learning organizations, but that discussion is beyond the scope and intent of this chapter. However, some specific comments about learning organizations can be made as they relate to homeland security planning for jurisdictions and agencies. Birkland (2006) addresses organizational learning in the wake of disaster. He suggests that government entities engage is three types of learning (instrumental, social, political) that will affect future actions.

The first type of organizational learning is "instrumental" learning. Here officials learn what tools and techniques need to be used to mitigate risks associated with likely catastrophic events. Though instrumental learning is much like classic "lessons-learned" activities, officials actually take actions based on the instrumental learning. Such learning may be reflected in the actions of a jurisdiction in making sure that public-works personnel are trained in first aid, due to the fact that many public-works staff will be responding the same as fire and police officers to the scene of an incident.

The second form of organizational learning introduced by Birkland is "social policy" learning. Here officials must work to ensure that constituents and other stakeholders have a full appreciation of what needs to be done. Often these actions manifest themselves in actually shaping values and attitudes in the jurisdiction. An example of this might be what occurred after Hurricane Katrina, when animal-companion rescue and recovery became part of planning in jurisdictions around the country.

The third form of organizational learning is "political" learning. Here the officials of the jurisdiction learn the tactics to sell policy changes to constituents. As Machiavellian as this may sound, such learning is necessary to advance new policies within the jurisdiction. An example might be found in forming different coalitions in local school elections, so that the weight and strength of a few wealthy landowners in a community may be neutralized to enact zoning changes to alleviate future disasters by reducing risks associated with land use. Thus, if jurisdictions and agencies learn from past events, as Birkland suggests, perhaps they can use that learning to advance their planning activities, particularly when homeland security mission accomplishment is the issue.

One of the difficulties related to planning in the public sector is that often the "planning horizon" is set at some arbitrary point in the future. This type of boundary setting is not helpful, because the planning horizon should be based on the assessment of risk and uncertainty as determined by those with planning responsibilities. As planning is a necessary condition for achieving strategic outcomes, one might need to alter thinking about how one arrives at a planning horizon.

The typical approach to planning for government entities is to pick some certain time in the future and then begin the process of reverse engineering what needs to be done to achieve the established goals. Most planning approaches incorporate some form of internal analysis to measure core competencies and to determine strengths and weaknesses, opportunities and threats. Because employees are most familiar with the internal operations of an organization, this phase of planning is relatively straightforward. As important as this internal analysis might be, it is the environmental scan—identifying and understanding the nature of those influences outside (that is, external to) the organization that have the potential to impact the organization—that may be most compelling (Mercer 1991; Boyd and Reuning-Elliot 1998; Bryson 2004; Pearce and Robinson 2009). A comprehensive external analysis might well determine the success or failure of an organization.

As Pearce and Robinson (2009) point out, the external environment is composed of three components. Those components are:

1. the operational environment
2. the industrial environment
3. remote influences

The first component deals with the operational context in which the organization finds itself. This perspective is based on the operational activities of the organization (jurisdiction or agency) and how other organizations may influence those activities. This plays out in real life when agencies must compete for scarce resources. Though competition among agencies is not encouraged, the realities of bureaucratic structures today dictate that agencies must be aware of all the competing elements when laying plans for the future.

Second, the industrial environment perspective best translates for public organizations as where the agency might find itself across the rest of that level of government. The DHS might find its operational environment one in which it must determine the influence of the Department of Health and Human Services and the Department of Defense, for example. Its industrial environment might be in which the DHS fits into the rest of the executive branch, particularly when it comes to securing resources to conduct its complex mission. Where most public enterprises fall down, however, is in surveying the remote environment for influences over which the organization may or may not have control. By gathering information about the remote influences, agencies and jurisdictions may have more opportunity to identify trends and provide forecasts that will increase knowledge, thus reducing uncertainty and alleviating some elements of risk. The lower the uncertainty, the more likely an agency will meet its mission obligations. An example might be found at the state level, where corporate tax rates in bordering states are more business friendly, thus making economic development more problematic. Without the ability to attract businesses to the state, population and subsequent tax revenues will be lost. In order to overcome the competitive advantage of neighboring states, other actions must be considered in order to provide expected goods and services. In homeland security planning, one state will have fewer resources to apply to mitigation efforts, so other approaches must be found to secure citizens.

The third component is composed of the remote influences that affect jurisdictions and agencies. These influences, most likely beyond their control, may have significant effect over establishing planning horizons. These influences are:

A. economic influences
B. social influences
C. political influences
D. technological influences
E. ecological influences

The first of these influences is economic factors. Today, the country is suffering through a sluggish recovery after a dramatic economic downturn. Given these conditions, revenues at all levels of government are diminished. Uncertain economic conditions often make it impossible to adequately forecast future revenues. Therefore, government must engage in some form of mitigation planning to accommodate swings in revenue. At the state and local levels, revenue forecasting can be problematic. When the national economy is productive, state and local governments do very well in accumulating revenue. When the national economy is struggling, state and local governments may suffer even more. Thus, having an appreciation for the overall economic environment is critical for planning activities, particularly when activities, such as homeland security, are confronted by limited resources; hard decisions have to be made regarding the use of the resources (e.g., whether to keep schools open or fund Medicaid).

The second influence deals with social factors—the beliefs, values, attitudes, opinions, and lifestyles of people external to the organization. Imagine the changes in a community that has seen its largest manufacturing plants close and the jobs going overseas. The natural emigration of people away from depressed areas might well be offset by the immigration of those who are willing to work for lower wages in less structured environments. This change might also bring with it a change in language, culture, and skill sets. As high-revenue producing entities are displaced by lower-revenue generating entities, a fundamental change in the community has taken place. Also to be considered are demographic changes dealing with age and education, among other characteristics of the community.

The third influence can be found in political factors. Political, philosophical, and ideological differences might divide the nation, state, or other jurisdictions. These polar opposites bring high levels of activism and subsequently can lead to difficulties in advancing policies, regardless of level of government. Hypothetically, an administration that would encourage broader environmental regulation may operate at a high tempo until such time as the controlling party of one or both houses of Congress might change. Similarly, changes in control of state legislatures from one party to another might dramatically influence policy development and implementation. Those with strategic planning and strategy development responsibilities must be able to accommodate these changes.

The fourth influence deals with the rapidly changing technology that influences every aspect of government operation. Often, new technology emerges before jurisdictions and agencies can work their way through the often overly bureaucratic procurement systems found in the public sector. Just as a government enterprise moves to make a purchase, new technology comes out that obsolesces what is in the procurement pipeline. To illustrate what happens sometimes with technology, imagine the process of building an airplane. To design and build a new modern aircraft might take ten years from first sketch to flight test. One might not expect metallurgical changes over that ten-year period, but one would be foolish not to anticipate changes in electronics. A black box today that weighs fifty pounds might very well be a one-ounce chip in a circuit board when the aircraft is ready to roll out. Anticipating and planning on these changes are a great challenge. Over a ten-year development cycle of the aircraft, the fuel load might change, simply from saving weight and space through the changing landscape of avionics. Similarly, changes in fuel mixtures, advances in chip production, engine-compressor capacities, and any number of other advances might allow the aircraft to be "greener" than was ever originally imagined.

Climate change and rising consciousness concerning ecological issues have become points of interest for all organizations, particularly governmental entities. This fifth influence becomes important when anticipating regulatory or legislative changes that might affect resource allocations. For example, what might happen with a change in the composition and use of herbicides in agriculture? Though the material might be well tested before being used, the potential hazard to water systems and wildlife habitats might require government entities to change resource allocations to provide alternatives to ensure the safety of citizens. The influence of ecological factors is far reaching and in many cases in not fully appreciated. As more research about climate change becomes available, governments will likely have to modify strategic plans to accommodate those changes.

By introducing the discussion related to remote influences, those charged with homeland security strategic planning will gain an appreciation of how to think outside the confines of their agency or jurisdiction. To reiterate an important point, planning is essentially a task that is framed by knowledge and risk. The first step in the planning process should be to establish a realistic and threat-sensitive planning horizon—how far into the future an organization is willing to project its goals and objectives. For most public organizations, that future view into the future is fixed by mandate, directive, legislation, or some other administrative constraint. Witness the Government Performance and Results Act that requires federal agencies to modify their strategic plans every four years. This artificial constraint is unfortunate, because organizations need to conduct critical, objective analyses of their respective remote environments to adequately establish a planning horizon. The fundamental question for homeland security strategic planners is just how far into the future are they willing to look? That "time and distance" into the future must be predicated on how much risk planners are willing to accept and what objectives are to be met. The broader and deeper the knowledge of the remote environment, the further into the future the enterprise is likely to plan.

Imagine sitting in a classroom with a professor lecturing at the podium. The student has a good "knowledge" of what is likely to take place over the next few minutes in the classroom, and based on that knowledge, the risk of anything catastrophic happening is low. This inverse relationship between risk and knowledge may not always apply; for most planning activities, one might make the assumption that the further into the future one peers, the more uncertainty exists. With more uncertainty, one might assume more risk is involved with decision making. In other words, in a deliberate planning environment, when knowledge is high, risk is likewise low. Over time, however, knowledge begins to degrade, thus raising the level of risk involved in projecting the future. In Figure 11.1, one sees this relationship over time. For example, at the present time, one's knowledge about what is likely to happen in the next few seconds is high, and any risk associated with what might happen is relatively low. However, when one considers what might happen a week, a month, or a year from now, there is less certainty of the result. If one does not attempt to learn more, the current knowledge might degrade gracefully, but the risk to the organization will increase proportionately. Our planning horizon, then, should be for a time in the future when our willingness to accept degraded knowledge crosses the level of risk we are willing to accept. That time might be a year or even ten years into the future, depending on the level of risk we are willing to accept.

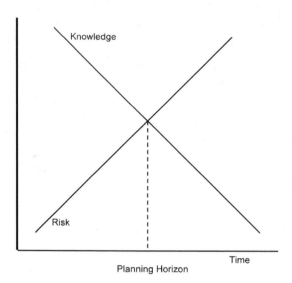

FIGURE 11.1 Establishing a planning horizon

If planners work at gaining and maintaining a higher knowledge threshold, then risk is similarly mitigated. As one examines Figure 11.2, the slope of the knowledge line changes, as does that of the risk line. The level of risk may very well be the same relative measure, but the planning horizon is now projected further into the future—a much more comfortable position for most organizations. Being able to extend the planning horizon by increasing knowledge, which might include resource allocation strategies and policy investigations, and reducing risk is perhaps one of the most important concepts related to planning that one might embrace. To look far into the future, one must do a lot of homework. Even with the best intelligence, it may not always be possible.

Planning Models

For homeland security planners, the environment is extremely complex and dynamic and requires some form of planning for all jurisdictions, regardless of the level of government or its size. Though the relationship among the federal, state, local, and tribal governments might be strained, the DHS has done a great deal to provide the tools to assist all jurisdictions in planning. Perhaps the most important tool available to all jurisdictions is the NIMS and its com-

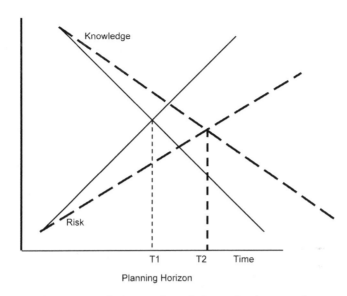

FIGURE 11.2 Increasing knowledge and reducing risk

plementary Incident Command System.[6] In the most recent NIMS document, there is a clear outline of suggested planning activities for the different communities. Further guidance can be found in the NRF and the NIPP. These documents provide guidance and suggestions on what should be considered when jurisdictions are taking on a deliberate planning activity. Within a jurisdiction, many agencies might be required to contribute to homeland security planning. This demand is especially relevant for responder disciplines like fire, police, public works, and emergency medicine. Though these FEMA documents are useful, their utility is limited. For example, although the planning procedures suggested are helpful, for most jurisdictions, much of what is offered is of little direct use. States and large urban areas might benefit from these tools and templates, but most jurisdictions with populations below one hundred thousand run out of administrative capacity very quickly (Clovis 2008). To that end, most jurisdictions must find templates that will allow them to develop plans that serve purposes other than establishing formal arrangements among agencies and between governments.

The limited resources of most jurisdictions inhibit their ability to adequately plan to respond to possible emergency situations. Based on the previous section, one might examine how risk affects various planning models. The most prevalent planning models are those based on risk calculations

TABLE 11.1   Risk-consequence matrix

RISK	High Risk II Low Consequence	High Risk I High Consequence
	Low Risk IV Low Consequence	Low Risk III High Consequence

CONSEQUENCE

(risk-based models) and those based on planning for certain scenarios (scenario-based models) (Van Der Heijden 2005). Risk models deal predominantly with assessing the risk of an event occurring and the consequences of the event, in loss of life, property damage, or, more recently, political impact. The NRF presents a risk-based perspective on preventing and responding to catastrophic events. Table 11.1 offers a rough representation of the calculus involved in risk-management models.

In quadrant I, planners might focus on events of high risk (likelihood of happening) and high consequence (probable loss of life and property damage). In the Midwest, tornadoes and flooding fall into this quadrant and are the prevalent drivers in homeland security strategic planning, especially from an all-hazards perspective. As one walks through the various quadrants, one can allocate events and consequences accordingly.

One of the great challenges strategic planners face is finding a risk-assessment template that is appropriate to the needs and demands of the jurisdiction. Most jurisdictions at the state and local levels already apply risk calculations, either implicitly or explicitly, when preparing operational budgets. Elected officials create budgets that reflect the preferences of the members of the community. Subsequently, the revenue spent on public safety, emergency management, medical first response, public health, and other competing elements in government is a reflection of some form of risk assessment. More sophisticated models can be used, but the bottom line is the application of resources to programs to ensure a predicted level of protection or mitigation of consequences based on the likelihood an event will take place.

Scenario-based models use specific events as planning instruments (Van Der Heijden 2005). At the national level, the DHS developed fifteen scenarios from which jurisdictions might develop plans to meet the specific demands of specific events (US Department of Homeland Security 2005). However, the scenarios do not accurately reflect what is most likely to occur in these jurisdictions. The scenarios are extremely useful for the federal government, states, and large urban concentrations, but not small local jurisdictions, with less administrative ability to develop their own risk models. For a town of twenty-five thousand people, dealing with the aftermath of the detonation of a nuclear device does not seem to be a worthy or likely project. However, dealing with tornadoes, floods, or active shooters is more appropriate.

Building Capacities Through Planning

There are a lot of constraints confronting most state and local governments. First is the severely limited availability of resources, and first among those resources is revenue. State and local governments are constantly looking for new revenue streams to ease pressures on taxpayers. To that end, as noted above, public budgets reflect the decisions of elected officials intent on meeting constituent preferences. However, most responder agencies and departments are often placed in precarious positions because public safety, emergency management, and homeland security activities are often the most visible to communities and the most vulnerable for budget cuts. To provide the level of prevention, protection, mitigation, response, and recovery demanded by the people, jurisdictions will have to seek mutual aid from other governmental entities. Local cooperation is problematic when more than one public good or service is involved, but there are mechanisms available to aid in building capacities outside of one community's resources (Feiock 2005).

The study of intergovernmental management is a good point of departure for examining how to build capacities in jurisdictions. To build capacities, entities will have to employ both scenario- and risk-based planning. To establish a framework for discussion, the work of Agranoff and McGuire (2001, 2003) and McGuire (2006) concerning various models of intergovernmental management is a point of reference. These scholars from Indiana University introduce four capacity-building models we can consider. The first of these models is called the top-down model (also discussed in Chapter 3). This model is typical of most current interactions among the federal, state, and local governments in the homeland security environment. Most direction comes from the DHS, with little flexibility available for implementation at the state and local levels.

The second capacity-building model is titled the donor-recipient model. This model is typified by many of the arrangements found in public health organizations or in the provision of means-tested income-security programs. The federal or state government (or both) will offer resources to support a plan, and the lower local government unit uses those resources to meet program objectives.

A third capacity-building model is called the jurisdiction model. This model is one in which the jurisdiction becomes the center of the planning universe. Particular scenarios are examined with the intent of doing "gap analysis." This type of analysis allows decision makers to determine the "gap" between current levels of capability and what might be needed to actually achieve desired outcomes if a scenario unfolds. Once the gaps are identified, then the jurisdiction attempts to locate the necessary resources; this search for resources predominantly originates with other levels of government and surrounding jurisdictions, to ensure the local government can mount an adequate response to meet the jurisdiction's needs.

The fourth model is called the network model. This approach is one where the jurisdiction, based on the "gap analysis," operationalizes its needs and then, through a series of contacts, seeks mutual support from surrounding jurisdictions or other levels of government, thus establishing an operational network. This approach is most often supported by risk-based planning, ensuring that enhanced capacities are built to the benefit of all who might be part of the network. Table 11.2 summarizes these models and their applications.

For an example of how this approach might work, imagine a city of approximately twenty-five thousand people with its own law enforcement, fire services, public works, and emergency medical response capabilities. Near the edge of town are an ethanol plant and a concentration of grain storage facilities, next to a small but busy railroad yard. In the late afternoon, an explosion is heard, and first responders move to the scene of one of the grain storage facilities. A young worker cycling dust relief ducts is injured when captured grain dust explodes. A small fire is visible, and cracks in the external wall of the grain storage silo are visible, indicating a very unstable building. Some of the debris from the explosion has fallen into the ethanol plant, where a tanker truck has caught fire. There are railcars full of coal nearby. Almost immediately, local officials determine that their ability to address the needs of this evolving scenario will be quickly overwhelmed. The police captain, the on-scene commander (first reponder), confers with his fire and public works counterparts and calls the county sheriff, who in turn alerts the state police.

TABLE 11.2   Intergovernmental models

MODELS

Top-Down	Donor-Recipient	Jurisdiction	Network
Policy development concentrated at the national level. State and local governments coerced into implementing policies with high compliance requirements and little flexibility. Funding found in categorical grants with stringent accountability.	Policies developed at the national level to treat "national" issues. State and local governments implement policies for national government but have some flexibility in implementation to suit constituent needs. Funding categorical but less stringent in compliance.	Center of policy and planning focused on the local jurisdiction. Planning is strategic in nature, placing the jurisdiction at the center of the planning process and the recipient of all potential support coming from other jurisdictions or levels of government. Funding, if available, focused on meeting constituent preferences.	Planning and policy development focused on establishing networks of cooperation and collaboration to meet common needs, particularly in times of crisis. Support based on temporary excess capacities. Network expanded to include other jurisdictions and levels of government.
Enforced Behaviors	*Mutual Dependencies*	*Centralized Planning*	*Capacity Augmentation*
Current Homeland Security Grant Program emphasizes compliance with national directives without support of accompanying legislation.	Current national, state, and local interactions related to FEMA satisfy this model.	Would allow jurisdictions to develop strategic plans that allow for deliberate, effective resource planning and management.	Would allow jurisdictions to build an expectation of augmentation to own-source capacities within the confines of own-source resources.

The state police call the state command post, and emergency management teams are mobilized to assist, but they are hours away. What is the likely outcome of this series of events?

During the deliberate planning cycle, the city had developed a plan that focused on catastrophic events near the ethanol plant (scenario planning). Though the production of ethanol is not inherently dangerous, accidents can lead to serious consequences, particularly when the plant is located near other industrial sites. Realizing there were gaps in response capabilities, the city invested in specialized firefighting and rescue equipment that would allow internal resources to contain an ethanol-plant fire until more help could arrive. The city identified that other assets were available from the state and from larger urban areas in the region to assist them. In the process of developing the plan, the city reached out to these other governmental entities to make formal arrangements for this assistance. By following the jurisdictional model, the city had in place a scenario-based plan to respond to a catastrophic event near the ethanol plant (or other similar event).

Among the dozens of phone calls made by the on-scene commander was the one made to the county sheriff. The sheriff notified all the standing and volunteer fire units from surrounding communities and all the law enforcement agencies in each of those communities as well. At a moment's notice, each jurisdiction dispatched available equipment and personnel to assist their neighboring community. Of course, all of these contacts and relationships were based on the distressed community building a network from which it might expect to see support from these other jurisdictions in the form of whatever capacity might be available. The neighboring jurisdiction might send a patrol car and officer, an engine company, or a hazardous material handling unit that is not needed in the home jurisdiction at that time. Why would all of these jurisdictions self-organize and cooperate? At some point in the future, each community might be very much in the same position. Many small-town police and fire departments will have similar arrangements on a daily basis for less serious activities. In such cases, neighboring departments will have agreements to assist during vacations and extended illness among their limited personnel.

The above scenario is not hypothetical. It loosely represents actual events that took place in a small midwestern town several years ago. Adopting intergovernmental management models and appropriate planning activities saved the city, the grain elevator, the ethanol plant, and the young man's life. The more formal scenario-based planning helped the community identify capacity and capability gaps that would need to be filled if such a scenario developed.

Obviously, no scenario-based plan can adequately capture every possible contingency, but nevertheless, thorough and mindful planning will help inform decision makers about potential problems and will allow for a more effective allocation of resources. Using risk-based strategic planning, built upon a much less formal approach, helped the community build a network of potential supporters based on a shared understanding of risk. Not all communities are the same, but most communities share risk quotients based on local circumstances. Helping a neighbor is made easier if one knows that assistance is also available.

This scenario highlights the need to introduce some other concepts into the discussion. The first of those concepts is recognizing the differences associated with planning requirements for what are referred to as "point events" and "regional events." Point events are those that occur at a particular point and are generally contained in one jurisdiction. Tornadoes can be one example. When a tornado touches the ground, it is on the ground for a short period of time, though the destruction can be overwhelming. The damage, though intense, is usually, but not always, isolated to a relatively small geographic area. In contrast, a regional event is one that covers multiple jurisdictions, such as a flood or a blizzard. Given the nature of large-scale regional events, jurisdictions would be hard-pressed to share resources with immediate neighbors due to the fact that each jurisdiction and agency are likely overwhelmed. If help is to come to the region, it must come from outside the region. Such an event in recent history would be captured in the response to Hurricanes Katrina and Rita.

The other concept is that of *excess capacity*. Most of the national documents outlined above are predicated on the assumption that there is an ideal state of preparedness for each jurisdiction and for the nation. This is simply not reality. Preparedness is fluid and changes with each day and location. On any given day, a city may have responders out sick, equipment in for maintenance, and events that require concentration of effort or any number of other factors that might affect the ability of a jurisdiction to respond to an event. At any given time, however, a community might be able to dispatch an ambulance, a cruiser with a couple of officers, or some maintenance equipment to a community that might need some temporary help. This *excess capacity* is available only until such time as it is needed back in its home jurisdiction. For jurisdictions to take advantage of the excess capacity that exists inside their networks, they must also be willing to deliver excess capacity if called upon to do so (Clovis 2008).

There are some downsides to basing planning on reciprocation. Some jurisdictions purposely underdevelop capacities based on the notion that perhaps larger and more affluent jurisdictions will provide help in times of crisis (Cohen, Gerber, and Stewart 2004). Other factors might influence this underdevelopment of own-source capacities, as well. Jurisdictions may not have a culture of learning and might be bureaucratically "hind bound" (Meyer 2006). Others simply project present circumstances into the future without taking advantage of available lessons learned (Birkland 2006). This behavior, of course, raises the risk quotients of these governmental entities.

Planning seems straightforward, whether using a scenario- or risk-based model. If one works to increase knowledge to mitigate uncertainty, planning activities are likely to be successful and will likely lead to appropriate and adequate responses in times of crisis. This begs the question, however, about what happens when things do not go as expected.

Planning for the Unexpected

The classic characterization of a public organization is one of a bureaucratic entity possessing all the features found within. Bureaucracies, whether intended or not, function "best" in a stable environment. These organizations tend toward a perpetual state of equilibrium and resist any movement away from that innate stability. However, emerging literature might cast this paradigm in a different light. What if public organizations were more closely aligned with complex adaptive systems?[7] How might that change one's consideration of planning activities? Perhaps one should explore such a proposition.

Public organizations today are much more fragile than in the past. As was discussed above, organizational uncertainty is increased because knowledge about the future is less certain and because the number of stakeholders has increased dramatically. Along with this change in numbers (revenues and stakeholders), one is also confronted by bounded rationality—knowing only so much—and, subsequently, the number of variables in play becomes problematic (Anderson 1999). The dynamics associated with changing political, economic, and sociological forces are enough to push otherwise stable organizations closer to instability. The instability might manifest itself in an organization or jurisdiction as an inadequate response to a disaster, much as what was seen in the response to Hurricane Katrina. Mitigating this situation by preventing the jurisdiction from moving into a chaotic state can best be accomplished through effective homeland security strategic planning. Further examination of "chaos" and its effect on organizational performance should be examined, however.

To understand "chaos," one must acknowledge that organizations are, rather than stable enterprises, "nonlinear dynamic systems" subject to the forces of stability and instability that interact to push the organization toward chaos (Thietaut and Forgues 1995). Rather than imagining that an organization might return to stability naturally, one must accept the idea that once an organization passes into a chaotic state, any newly established equilibrium will be for a changed organization. How, then, does one plan for such eventualities? Planning functions are altered dramatically to accommodate this new state of being for the enterprise. One should focus on building organizations that are adaptive so that organizations can retain resiliency during and after catastrophic events.

Uncertainty based on a constantly changing environment might lead individuals who do not recognize the circumstances to blindly follow structured paradigms that will eventually lead to underperforming organizations that have planned for the wrong events, marshaled the wrong resources, and taken the wrong actions when events occurred. To avoid these pitfalls, planners must assist decision makers in building organizations that can adapt.

The first step in preparing an organization to be adaptive is to assess the complexity of the environment. This step harks back to the suggestion of an environmental scan presented above. An individual agency inside a jurisdiction or a small jurisdiction will have a different perspective on complexity than might a state or large urban jurisdiction. Because complexity is directly related to the number of variables one encounters in the assessment, the more complex the environment, the less knowable the environment becomes and, hence, the greater the need for homeland security strategic planning. Further, the more complex the environment, the more ambiguous organizational operations become (Anderson 1999). If an organization is in a complex environment, small changes in conditions can have long-term and very large consequences.

These complex systems (i.e., complexity theory) are held in place by energy being infused by all the entities involved. However, this energy will dissipate over time, and unless the energy level is maintained, the system (network) will begin to decay. If entities are removed and the associated energy is taken away, the system might very well reach its "tipping point"—that point at which the system disintegrates. Homeland security strategic planners need to be aware of complexity theory and how this theory helps to describe the homeland security environment in which they might find themselves. Noting that understanding and predicting the future will be problematic, planners need to account for the uncertainty that may be more prevalent than is the ability to gain knowledge to mitigate risk. Perhaps the best approach is for planners to build resilient organizations that service resilient communities.

Resilience is an emerging concept that many experienced and cynical practitioners see as nothing more than the most current buzzword or emergency management fad. This author is more sanguine about the future of this concept, based mostly on continuing research in the area. Planners will play a significant role in building resilient communities, because the skills required to inform decision making are the ones planners use to mitigate uncertainty and risk. Resilience, as defined for this chapter, is the ability of a community to return to a perceived state of normalcy after a catastrophic event. The city of Parkersburg, Iowa, demonstrated resilience after a devastating tornado literally destroyed the city. The city of New Orleans could not be characterized as a resilient city, as any semblance of normalcy is still a long way down the road. To measure, and support by planning, resilience, one must be familiar with four disciplines: geography, economics, sociology, and demographics. Geography deals with land use and topography. The economics component deals with the income levels of the average resident, the tax base, and the other components that contribute to the economic health of a community. The sociology element requires examination of the culture, history, and dynamics of the people who populate the community. By studying demographics, planners will be able to see connections between educational attainment, poverty rates, ethnic and racial diversity, and a host of other factors that might influence the government and governance of the jurisdiction.

One can easily see that the planning principles and situations presented earlier in this chapter would be wholly appropriate for helping build resilient communities. With more resilience, planning will be an easier task, and preparing for that slip into chaos may not be as urgent as if nothing were done.

Conclusion

Strategic planning and thinking for homeland security are often scripted and based on long-established, conventional approaches advocated by the DHS and other federal agencies. Except for a few states and localities that possess the administrative capacity to comply with federal guidelines, most jurisdictions in the country must find planning models that will work for them. Although a one-size-fits-all approach offered by federal agencies is hardly adaptable to most communities, the main components and much of the logic in the federal plans can serve as useful points of departure for most strategic planners.

Perhaps most important, strategic planning for homeland security must be driven by the need to understand and manage uncertainty, risk, and the pursuit of intelligence and knowledge that reduce uncertainty. By better understanding the nature, structures, events, and challenges that confront their organization, planners will reduce risk and the associated uncertainty that inhibits good decision making.

Ultimately, there tend to be several models one might follow when strategic planning for homeland security. By examining useful intergovernmental management models and using both risk-based and scenario-based planning models, communities can reduce risk and build capacities beyond their own-source limitations.

As the complexity of the environment changes, so do the dynamics of the public organization. As organizations struggle to survive in less stable environments, homeland security planners must assist decision makers by building adaptive organizations that can maintain effectiveness even during times of extreme uncertainty. By concentrating on building resilience in community structures and organizations, the task of maintaining stability and protecting the people is made decidedly more efficient.

NOTES

1. FEMA, "FY 2011 Homeland Security Grant Program," August 23, 2011, http://www.fema.gov/government/grant/hsgp/.

2. FEMA, "Resource Record Details: National Preparedness Guidelines," 2007, http://www.fema.gov/library/viewRecord.do?id=3773; FEMA, NIMS Resource Center, accessed July 8, 2011, http://www.fema.gov/emergency/nims/; FEMA, *National Response Framework*, 2008, http://www.fema.gov/pdf/emergency/nrf/nrf-core.pdf; National Strategy for Information Sharing, 2007, http://www.fas.org/sgp/library/infoshare.pdf; DHS, National Infrastructure Protection Plan, 2009, http://www.dhs.gov/xlibrary/assets/NIPP_Plan.pdf.

3. See also PDD-8, National Preparedness, 2011, http://www.dhs.gov/xabout/laws/gc_1215444247124.shtm.

4. A general-purpose jurisdiction is defined as one in which two or more services are provided, such as fire and police services, supported by taxes and fees and administered by a board of elected or appointed officials. According to the US Census Bureau, there are eighty-seven thousand separate government entities in America including one national government, six territorial governments, fifty state governments, and more than three thousand county governments. The rest are composed of single-function districts, such as

are found in our public school system. Including county governments, there are 39,000 general-purpose jurisdictions in the country.

5. See FEMA, "FY 2011 Urban Area Security Initiative (UASI) Nonprofit Security Grant Program (NSGP)," 2011, http://www.fema.gov/government/grant/nsgp/.

6. FEMA, "Incident Command System (ICS)," accessed July 4, 2011, http://www.fema.gov/emergency/nims/IncidentCommandSystem.shtm.

7. Complex adaptive systems are an area of study related to the interaction of entities inside a "system." The actions of one entity might influence another. For the most part, complex adaptive systems operate in a state of equilibrium. In government, bureaucratic pathologies dictate, and demand, equilibrium. If that equilibrium is disrupted by a catastrophic event, the system may move into a region of disequilibrium where an action that is normally predictable with a predictable outcome might very well lead to even more disruptive outcomes. This "chaos" is what happens when disequilibrium occurs in these systems. The old saw about a butterfly flapping its wings in the Amazon causing a hurricane in the Gulf of Mexico is illustrative.

REFERENCES

Agranoff, R., and M. McGuire. 2001. "American Federalism and the Search for Models of Management." *Public Administration Review* 61, no. 6: 671–681.

———. 2003. "Inside the Matrix: Integrating the Paradigms of Intergovernmental Management and Network Management." *International Journal of Public Administration* 26, no. 12: 1401–1422.

Anderson, P. 1999. "Complexity Theory and Organization Science." *Organizational Science* 10, no. 3: 216–232.

Birkland, T. 2006. *Lessons from Disasters: Policy Change After Catastrophic Events*. Washington, DC: Georgetown University Press.

Boyd, B., and E. Reuning-Elliot. 1998. "A Measurement Model of Strategic Planning." *Strategic Management Journal* 19, no. 2: 181–192.

Bryson, J. 2004. *Strategic Planning for Public and Non-profit Organizations*. 3rd ed. San Francisco: Jossey-Boss.

Clovis, S. 2006. "Federalism, Homeland Security, and National Preparedness: A Case Study in the Development of Public Policy." *Homeland Security Affairs Journal* 2, no. 3: 1–24.

———. 2008. "Promises Unfulfilled: The Suboptimization of Homeland Security National Preparedness." *Homeland Security Affairs Journal* 4, no. 3: 1–21.

Clovis, S., B. Dunleavy, and S. Bernard. 2005. *Lessons Learned Analysis*. Publication RP05-013-01. Arlington, VA: Homeland Security Institute.

Cohen, D., B. Gerber, and K. Stewart. 2004. "State and Local Actions on Homeland Security: Explaining Variations in Preparedness Efforts." Paper presented at the annual meeting of the Midwestern Political Science Association, April 15–18, Chicago.

Feiock, R. 2005. "Institutional Collective Action and Local Governance." Paper prepared for Creating Collaborative Communities: Management Networks, Services Cooperation, and Metropolitan Governance Symposium, Wayne State University, October 31, 2005, Detroit.

Kamensky, J. 2011. "Congress Overhauls Results Act, Wants Results." *PA Times* 34, no. 2: 8.

McGuire, M. 2002. "Managing Networks: Propositions on What Managers Do and Why They Do It." *Public Administration Review* 62, no. 5: 599–609.

———. 2006. "Intergovernmental Management: A View from the Bottom." *Public Administration Review* 66: 677–679.

Mercer, J. 1991. *Strategic Planning for Public Managers.* Westport, CT: Quorum Books.

Meyer, R. 2006. "Why We Under-prepare for Hazards." In *On Risk and Disaster: Lessons from Hurricane Katrina*, edited by R. Daniels, D. Kettl, and H. Kunreuther, 153–173. Philadelphia: University of Pennsylvania Press.

Pearce, J., and R. Robinson. 2009. *Competitive Strategy.* 11th ed. Boston: McGraw-Hill.

Thietaut, R., and B. Forgues. 1995. "Chaos Theory and Organizations." *Organizational Science* 6, no. 1: 19–31.

US Department of Homeland Security. 2005. *National Planning Scenarios.* Washington, DC: US Department of Homeland Security.

———. 2007. *National Preparedness Guidelines.* Washington, DC: US Department of Homeland Security.

———. 2008a. *National Incident Management System.* Washington, DC: US Department of Homeland Security.

———. 2008b. *National Response Framework.* Washington, DC: US Department of Homeland Security.

———. 2009. *National Infrastructure Protection Plan.* Washington, DC: US Department of Homeland Security.

———. 2011. *Fiscal Year 2011 Homeland Security Grant Program.* Washington, DC: US Department of Homeland Security.

Van Der Heijden, K. 2005. *Scenarios: The Art of Strategic Conversation.* Chichester, UK: John Wiley and Sons.

White House. 1993. *The Government Performance and Results Act of 1993.* Washington, DC: White House.

———. 2011. *The Government Performance and Results Modernization Act of 2010.* Washington, DC: White House.

Terrorism and Counterterrorism

GEORGE MICHAEL

The events of September 11, 2001, catapulted terrorism to the top of the US national security agenda. These attacks provoked a ferocious response from the American government that set in motion a chain of events leading to two protracted wars. But even prior to the 9/11 attacks, terrorism bedeviled the United States. During the 1990s, the primary focus of counterterrorism efforts was on domestic right-wing extremists. The 1995 bombing of the Alfred P. Murrah Federal Building in Oklahoma raised the specter of loosely organized "lone-wolf" domestic terrorists who could carry out lethal attacks without the support of a formal organization. Occasionally, international terrorists made headlines as well. On February 26, 1993, a small circle of radical Muslims based in Brooklyn and led by a shadowy figure from Baluchistan, Ramzi Yousef, attempted to topple one of the World Trade Center towers into the other with a truck bomb parked in an underground garage beneath the edifice.

This chapter examines the nature of contemporary terrorism and its challenges to America. First, there is a review of some of the various definitions of terrorism that have been advanced to explain the concept. Next, the nature of the "new" versus the "old" terrorism is compared and contrasted. Following is a discussion on domestic terrorism in America. The main terrorist theaters outside of the United States are covered as well. After that, there is a brief discussion on the potential threat of weapons of mass destruction. This is followed by a brief review of America's efforts to confront terrorism both at home and abroad. Finally, the conclusion speculates on the future of terrorism that appears to be moving in the direction of "leaderless resistance," or lone-wolf operations, in which individuals, or very small cohesive groups, engage in terrorism independent of any official movement, leader, or network of support.[1]

Terrorism Defined

Scholars have long struggled to define terrorism. There are many variants of political violence that are sometimes designated under the rubric of terrorism, including guerrilla warfare, sabotage, assassination, and, according to some observers, even hate crimes. To most observers, the phenomenon of terrorism seems obvious; nevertheless, the study of terrorism is not without its normative squabbles, as the cliché "One man's terrorist is another man's freedom fighter" demonstrates. Depending on their perspectives, observers often classify and interpret political violence through their own nationality or ideological predilection. For example, during their guerrilla struggle against the Soviets during the 1980s, the Afghan mujahideen were heralded as valiant freedom fighters in the West. Today, however, that image has reversed, as the Taliban and the Afghan insurgency are conflated with the al-Qaeda terrorist network and its deceased leader, Osama bin Laden. Previously, some "progressive" scholars sympathized with left-wing terrorists, characterizing them as desperate idealists who were driven to violence by conditions such as poverty, discrimination, and oppression. The rise of right-wing violence in the 1980s and 1990s, however, removed much of the idealistic veneer of terrorism in the academic community.[2]

Terrorism remains difficult to define for several reasons. First, it is generally a pejorative term used to delegitimize those who practice it. As a consequence, routine crimes assume greater importance when they are designated as terrorism.[3] Labeling a particular incident as an act of terrorism can influence the response to the incident. Political movements can be undermined when their followers are designated as terrorists. For instance, Hamas—a Palestinian group that rejects accommodation with Israel—at one time operated an office in Springfield, Virginia. In the mid-1990s, however, the US State Department designated Hamas as a foreign terrorist organization. As a result, Hamas was forced to close its office in Virginia. More recently, Mujahedeen-e-Khalq—an opposition group in Iraq that opposes the Iranian government—was also designated a foreign terrorist organization by the US State Department. As a consequence, the Iraqi government announced that Mujahedeen-e-Khalq must leave the country. Inasmuch as Shiites (members of a denomination in Islam) now control the Iraqi government, there are efforts to improve relations with Iran, which also has a majority Shiite population.

Another reason terrorism can be difficult to define is because the terms *terror* and *terrorism* become intertwined. Some actors can provoke terror but are not really terrorists, at least not in the traditional sense of the term. Over the past two decades, for instance, street gangs have been responsible for far more fatalities in the United States than terrorists. In fact, the total number of deaths attributed to intergang violence in Los Angeles for just one year alone (1991) was greater than the estimated number of all terrorist fatalities in the United States from 1955 through 1998.[4] Be that as it may, street gangs are generally considered more of a criminal and law enforcement problem than a counterterrorism issue.

Inasmuch as terrorism is a socially defined phenomenon, it often eludes concise and clear definitions on which all people can agree. Moreover, the term changes within social and historical contexts as definitions of terrorism vary depending on who defines the concept. According to Martha Crenshaw, terrorism must be studied in context. There are several contextual issues that can give us a better understanding of terrorism, including history, political power, motivation, and the media. As she sees it, terrorism cannot be defined unless the act, target, and possibility of success are analyzed. According to Brent Smith, the main factor separating the average criminal from the average terrorist is motivation.[5] Terrorists are motivated by some ideology, religion, or belief system.

Some observers emphasize the nonstate quality of terrorists and the innocence (i.e., civilian status) of their victims. According to historian Walter Laqueur, terrorism constitutes the illegitimate use of force to achieve a political objective by targeting innocent people. In a similar vein, Alex Schmid sees terrorism as a method of combat in which the victims serve as symbolic targets. Similarly, Brian Jenkins once called terrorism the use or threatened use of force designed to bring about a political change. Cindy Combs defines terrorism as a synthesis of war and theater. In that sense, terrorism is played out before an audience in the hope of creating an atmosphere of fear for political purposes. Her components of terrorism include the use of violence against innocent victims (i.e., civilians not connected to the government) that is communicated to an audience often through media coverage intended to induce fear in a segment of the population. In her schema, terrorists are connected to some political, ideological, religious, or social goal.[6]

The Federal Bureau of Investigation—the chief government agency responsible for investigating and preventing terrorism in the United States—offers one of the most succinct and practical definitions of terrorism: "The unlawful use of force or violence against persons or property to intimidate or coerce a government, the civilian population, or any segment thereof, in furtherance of political or social objectives."[7]

Still, problems remain in our effort to conceptualize terrorism. For instance, the FBI is often inconsistent in its own designation of acts of terrorism. Prior to 9/11, most acts of terrorism in the United States were usually treated as criminal activity and not a special category known as terrorism. However, with the enactment of the USA PATRIOT Act, a more aggressive approach to combating terrorism was launched.

Extracting from the FBI, the US Code, the US State Department, and the Department of Defense, the following commonalities exist across all definitions:

- the acts are deliberate
- the acts are all violent, and the violence is focused upon innocent people
- the acts are designed with the psychology of producing fear
- the acts are dynamic and intended to be sensationalistic
- the acts are designed toward achieving some sort of goal, such as political, social, or religious change

Although no firm consensus on the definition of terrorism has been formulated, many observers believe that there are important qualitative differences between terrorism today and terrorism in the past.

The New Terrorism

Terrorism has been around for time immemorial. For example, the Sicari—a Jewish terrorist sect that was active in the first century AD—sought to expel the Romans from the Holy Land. Another example, the Assassins, was an Islamic cult that was active from about the eleventh to the thirteenth centuries in the Middle East, which murdered prominent rival leaders. In India the Thugs, a Hindi terrorist cult that was active from about the sixteenth to the nineteenth centuries, preyed upon hapless travelers, whom they sacrificed to placate their goddess, Kali.

During much of the 1970s and 1980s, terrorists were seen as rational actors. Although they committed some horrible attacks, it was generally believed that they were reluctant to inflict mass casualties. If they were to do so, they would offend too many people and lose sympathy from the international community. As Brian Jenkins once stated, terrorists wanted "a lot of people watching, not a lot of people dead."[8] Terrorists wanted just enough drama to get their message across; they did not, however, want the violence to be so horrific that it would alienate supporters and sympathizers. Left-wing terrorists and Palestinian rejectionists tended to follow this dictum during the 1970s and 1980s. Furthermore, the terrorists risked serious reprisals from the country or the community that they targeted. Largely secular in orientation, these terrorists tended to be pragmatic in their demands. Rather than seeking to destroy their enemies, which was unrealistic, they hoped to gain a seat at the negotiating table, or so the argument went.

By contrast the so-called new terrorists are thought to be less constrained in their operations and have less compunction about inflicting mass casualties. One of the reasons suggested for this development is that contemporary terrorists—both domestic and international—are more likely to be inspired by religion than their predecessors. At first blush, this may sound paradoxical. After all, one would assume that a religious person would be more reluctant to inflict casualties, especially on innocent people. Presumably, there should be ethical constraints that would inhibit the terrorist from engaging in indiscriminate killing. According to the theory, however, religiously inspired terrorists believe that God is on their side and, as a result, are more self-assured in their mission, thus loosening their inhibitions to inflict mass casualties.[9] What is more, the enemy is vilified to a much greater degree than in the past, as the struggle is often framed in absolutist terms by contemporary terrorist groups. Once the enemy is so demonized, terrorists believe that nearly all measures are justified to bring about its defeat; some would say that the term *religious terrorism* is just another oxymoron.

One of the principal concerns of the so-called new terrorism is this combination of religious fanaticism and technology. Earlier terrorists could not avail themselves of the level of technology that we have today. Over the past twenty-five years, there has been a technological revolution, or, more to the point, an information revolution. Terrorists now have information more readily available to them because of new technological developments, such as the

Internet. Information flows more freely than it did in the past. What is more, some of these contemporary terrorists groups have demonstrated that they are willing to use methods that were not used in the past; for example, members of the Japanese cult Aum Shinrikyo released sarin gas in the Tokyo subway, killing twelve persons, injuring thousands. To some observers, this attack presaged even more lethal terrorism in the future because of the potential it had for greater casualties.

Finally, the organizational structure of terrorist groups has changed. Previously, terrorist groups, at least the more successful and enduring groups, exhibited hierarchical organizational structures. This top-down leadership structure included leaders at the top, followed by some middle managers, and finally the rank-and-file members at the bottom. By contrast, terrorist groups today are more likely to have loose, amorphous organizational structures. Al-Qaeda exemplifies this trend. Although there is somewhat of a hierarchical structure for the core of the network, the periphery is much more amorphous, which has enabled the organization to persist despite efforts to destroy it. More recently, so-called lone-wolf terrorists, such as Timothy McVeigh, Ted Kaczynski, and Eric Rudolph, have demonstrated that they can cause havoc without any direct affiliation to a formal organization. In fact, this type of terrorist has become the most frequent type in the United States, which has a long tradition of political violence.

Domestic Terrorism in the United States

In essence, "domestic terrorism" is any terrorist activity occurring within one country, by a group or individual operating within that country, without foreign direction, to create fear and produce change within that same country. The effect of this terrorist activity is most significant when these violent acts are forced upon the civilian, noncombatant population. Domestic terrorists, often called "homegrown terrorists," are responsible for most of the terrorist activity within the United States. Domestic terrorists can exhibit radical philosophies from either end of the political spectrum or be cause based, as in the case of environmentalism, animal rights, or abortion.

Terror from the Extreme Right

For the most part, there was a lull in political violence following World War I until a new era of domestic terrorism commenced in the 1960s. The civil rights movement was the catalyst for a renascent Ku Klux Klan in the South.

In the aftermath of the Supreme Court's *Brown v. Board of Education* decision (1954) on segregation in schooling, the extreme Right and assorted segregationists became increasingly visible in American politics. Though unable to defeat integration, the movement has remained actively opposed to African American demands for integration. Although the Klan has demonstrated a proclivity for violence in the past, traditionally, the movement was not revolutionary in orientation. For much of its history it has been the defender of a racial status quo and has not sought to really overthrow or radically change the government.[10] However, there has been an internecine debate in Klan circles, with one faction calling for revolutionary violence and the other arguing for nonviolence.[11] Violent Klan groups have been active, but usually not for long, due to vigilant prosecution on the part of federal authorities.[12] Over time the extreme Right has evolved from a movement characterized by ultrapatriotism to one increasingly characterized by racial revolution.

Global events influenced the orientation of the extreme Right as well, most notably the demise of the Soviet Union and the declining appeal of international communism. For many years, some in the movement saw communism as a diversion, a distraction from the "real" enemy. With the removal of communism as a major force in geopolitics, the extreme Right could now focus more attention on the Jews and their putative vehicle, the US government, as the prime source of evil.[13] Although anti-Semitism had loomed large in the extremist subculture for many years, Jews had shared this animus with others as well, including liberals, "insiders" (a term John Birch Society members would use to refer to the shadowy plutocrats who allegedly ruled America), the Illuminati, the Trilateral Commission, the Council on Foreign Relations et al. What accelerated in the 1980s was the identification of Jews as the primary enemy—the puppet master of all of the enemies, in the extreme Right's worldview. Indeed, Jews have become an idée fixe, as evidenced by the popularity of the ZOG (Zionist Occupation Government) discourse. In the minds of those on the extreme Right, ZOG is viewed as a global Leviathan with tentacles reaching into the innermost recesses of government and society, a Pax Judaica, if you will.

The Order,[14] led by Robert Jay Matthews, conducted a campaign of terror in the Pacific Northwest that included several armored-car heists, bank robberies, bombings, and homicides. Since the demise of the Order, there has not really been any organized threat of terrorism and violence from the extreme Right. Nevertheless, inasmuch as the revolutionary racialist Right has virtually no hope of achieving power through the electoral process, terrorism remains an attractive alternative in that members generally consider the broad white masses as too indifferent to listen to their message. Consequently, terrorism could serve as a form of "shock therapy" to destabilize the state and society and, in doing so, gain the attention of the masses.[15] Toward this end, some extreme-Right activists have endeavored to create a network in which they could operate surreptitiously, without the scrutiny of authorities. In this vein, Louis Beam advocated the strategy of "leaderless resistance" as a method by which to thwart government infiltration of dissident groups. In recent years, virtually all right-wing violence has been perpetrated by individuals, or "lone wolves," who act on their own initiative without any directive from the extremist groups with which they are sometimes affiliated. The most notable example occurred on April 19, 1995, two years to the day of the culmination of the Waco tragedy, when the Alfred P. Murrah Federal Building in Oklahoma City was bombed, leaving at least 168 dead and many others wounded. Until 9/11 this attack was the most lethal act of domestic terrorism ever carried out on American soil. The subsequent investigation would identify Timothy McVeigh as the chief culprit for the attack. He also had some accomplices, including Terry Nichols and Michael Fortier.[16] McVeigh and Nichols are reported to have attended meetings of the Michigan Militia, but the group did not welcome them. Although McVeigh may not have had any formal affiliation with extremist groups, there is evidence to suggest that he was a denizen of the subterranean world of the Far Right.

The presidential candidacy of Barack Obama alarmed segments of the white nationalist movement. In October 2008, two young men, Daniel Cowart of Bells, Tennessee, and Paul Schlesselman of West Helena, Arkansas, were arrested for an alleged plot to rob a gun store, target students at a largely black high school, and then attempt to assassinate Obama.[17] In October 2010, a *Time* cover story attributed a resurgence of the radical Right to "the tectonic shifts in American politics that allowed a black man with a foreign-sounding name and a Muslim-born father to reach the White House."[18] The Obama presidency and the persistent economic recession have emboldened the Far Right. For instance, in the spring of 2010, an organization calling itself the Guardian of the Republic issued letters to all fifty state governors, urging them to resign within three days or face removal. Around the same time, the FBI arrested nine members of the Hutaree militia group after they allegedly conspired to kill police officers in a plot to trigger a civil war and bring about the collapse of the federal government.[19] The militia movement, which had been in retreat since the Oklahoma City bombing in 1995, has experienced a resurgence. The Southern Poverty Law Center reported a sharp increase—almost a tripling—in the number of extremist groups (519) in the months after Obama's election.[20] A Department of Homeland Security report released in April 2009 speculated that the prolonged economic downturn could create a fertile recruiting ground for extremist groups. The most serious threat, the report mused, came from lone wolves who embrace the tactics of leaderless resistance and carry out acts of violence.[21] In America consternation over immigration has fueled the rise of self-styled vigilante groups such as the Minuteman Project, which Chris Simcox and James Gilchrist created in 2004 to patrol the US-Mexican border. According to the Southern Poverty Law Center, a considerable number of white nationalists have volunteered for the Minutemen.[22]

Since the early 1980s, the American extreme Right has evolved from a movement characterized by ultrapatriotism to one increasingly characterized by a revolutionary outlook. This can be explained in large part by the fact that various social trends over the past several decades have significantly changed the texture of the United States. For those on the extreme Right, America is not the same country they once knew, and only radical solutions, they believe, can save the nation and race. However, recent developments such as the economic downturn, consternation over immigration and outsourcing, and the election of Barack Obama seem to have energized the broader conservative movement. Ironically, many of the same issues seem to be able to revitalize the radical Left as well.

Terror from the Radical Left

The Vietnam War was the catalyst for the campaign of terrorism initiated by the radical Left in the late 1960s. One small group, the Weather Underground—a violent offshoot of the Students for a Democratic Society—turned to terrorism in 1969. Their attacks peaked in 1971 and then declined erratically. With the end of the Vietnam War, left-wing terrorism went into a steep decline, but, in 1981, various members of the long-dormant Weather Underground, Black Liberation Army, and the Black Panthers coalesced to form the May 19th Communist Organization. The new group began a terrorist campaign that included the robbery of a Brinks armored car. Moreover, the May 19th Communist Organization established links with and provided assistance to the Armed Forces of National Liberation, a Puerto Rican separatist terrorist group.

Initially after the Cold War, Far Left groups lost a credible ideology, as even the broader political Left became more concerned about social and identity issues rather than socialism and economic redistributive policies. The collapse of the Soviet Union ushered in a new era of global integration that eschewed grand ideological schemes. Francis Fukuyama's 1989 article "The End of History?" presaged the coming zeitgeist. As he observed of the events of that year, governments around the world were converging on a model consisting of democracy and free markets. According to his analysis, all other ideologies had been effectively exhausted and discredited; thus, no credible alternatives remained. Supposedly, all that was left was mere fine-tuning.[23]

Nevertheless, elements of the Far Left developed a critique of the ongoing historical process of globalization that resonates with sections of disaffected youth around the world. Self-styled anarchists endeavor to create an alternative globalization based on leftist precepts, including opposition to corporations, antiwar activism, and minority rights. Although the movement is stridently critical of capitalism, it has not really offered an alternative to be taken seriously. Not unlike its forebears in the early twentieth century, contemporary anarchists endeavor to create a nonhierarchical society based on left-wing precepts. Contemporary anarchists employ "black bloc" tactics[24] as ways of both confronting a system seen as oppressive and creating an alternative space of freedom, justice, and dignity. The neoanarchists, who eschew government and other institutions, seek to replace the neoliberal (free-market) "Washington Consensus" capitalist economy with one that is more inclusive and egalitarian.

As a consequence of the dissolution of the Soviet Union in the early 1990s, and the general decline in the fortunes of Marxism, many young people turned to environmentalism, which they sought to combine with a left-wing ideology.[25]

The Radical Environmental and Animal Liberation Movements

So-called ecoterrorists have been responsible for a considerable amount of property damage, though not many fatalities. There are indications, however, that some representatives of the movement have adopted a more apocalyptic and misanthropic worldview and could be more inclined to wage lethal attacks in the future. Similarly, some of the more radical activists in the animal liberation movement have targeted personnel affiliated with animal testing laboratories and could escalate their campaign of harassment to include deadly attacks. Although the radical environmental movement has caused substantial property damage, it has failed to alter public opinion in any meaningful way. It has, however, managed to make previously labeled "radical environmental" organizations, such as Greenpeace and the Sierra Club, appear more moderate to the public. Although the radical environmental and animal liberation movements are essentially single-issue movements, they nevertheless have traditionally leaned toward the political Left. As the number of such groups' attacks mounted, the US government took notice. Since the late 1990s, on numerous occasions, the FBI has identified violent eco-extremists and radical animal liberation activists, such as the Earth Liberation Front and the Animal Liberation Front, as the most serious domestic terrorism threat in the country. Despite a lack of demonstrable achievement, the radical environmentalist movement persists.

The Radical Antiabortion Movement

Still another example of single-issue terrorism comes from the radical antiabortion movement. The movement includes violent, militant antiabortion direct-action organizations such as Operation Rescue and Lambs of Christ and organizations that advocate or perpetuate violence against abortion providers and patients, such as the Army of God and American Coalition of Life Activists, as well as lone-wolf terrorists, such as James Kopp and Eric Rudolph. Usually, representatives of the mainstream antiabortion movement have sought to distance themselves from the violent activists. Nevertheless, there is some overlap between the two camps. On the one hand, pro-life sentiments have been expressed by pillars of the establishment, including Presidents Ronald Reagan and George W. Bush. Reagan's FBI director, William Webster, actually downplayed the significance of antiabortion violence and, for a while, even refused to classify clinic bombings and arson as terrorism. Even pro-choice candidates are loath to come out unequivocally for abortion, instead choosing to couch their support in the guarded language of individual choice and reproductive rights as inherently personal decisions. And legislation, such as the Hyde Amendment, bars federal funds that would pay for abortions. On the other hand, violent antiabortion activists have been condemned not only by leading public figures and the media, but also by their more mainstream colleagues. Legislation designed to protect reproductive rights, such as the Freedom of Clinic Entrances Act of 1994, imposed restrictions on abortion clinic protests. Even the murder of Dr. George Tiller merely occasioned condemnation throughout America. Just prior to his murder, Dr. Tiller was put on trial for failing to obtain a second independent opinion that a late-term abortion he performed was necessary, as required by Kansas law. His acquittal may have been a motive in the attack. The assailant, Scott Roeder, was reputed to have had ties to the antigovernment "Sovereign" movement. The abortion issue continues to polarize public opinion in America. However, in recent years, despite sporadic violence, the radical antiabortion movement appears to be in retreat. More potent, however, appears to be the allure of radical Islam to disaffected Muslim youth.

Radical Islam in America

Prior to 9/11, terrorism by Islamic radicals in the United States was infrequent. Neither foreign residents nor native Muslim Americans were particularly active, although the first attempt to destroy the World Trade Center Towers in 1993 indicated that attacks could occur. Although various radical Islamic groups have frequently attacked US interests overseas, they have generally refrained from striking domestic US targets. Historically, Islamist activity in the United States centered more on fund-raising and recruiting than on terrorism.[26] However, with the country's liberal immigration and student visa policies and porous borders, foreign extremists have been able to penetrate the United States under the radar screen of intelligence agencies, thus allowing Islamist groups to establish a presence in the United States that culminated in the 9/11 terrorist attacks in New York and Washington, DC. In the aftermath of 9/11, there was a great fear that Islamic extremists in numerous sleeper cells would spring into action. Although fears of al-Qaeda sleeper cells in America appear to be overblown, there have been plots by both foreign and domestic groups that have been uncovered. Some of the more deadly attacks to date, however, have come from solitary individuals, so-called lone wolves, who have self-identified with the global jihad. Over the years, radical Islam has gained traction in the United States.

The increasing role of Adam Gadahn, as terrorism analyst Peter Bergen observes, is indicative of the Americanization of the leadership of al-Qaeda.[27] Gadahn, a.k.a. "Azzam the American," has emerged as one of al-Qaeda's leading spokesmen. Amazingly, the young native of California and convert to Islam was able to ingratiate himself into the highest echelons of al-Qaeda. A seemingly alienated youth, he underwent a radicalization process and made his way to Pakistan, where he was recruited and served as a translator for the terrorist organization. He has emerged as somewhat of an Internet celebrity on websites such as YouTube.[28] Another important figure is Anwar al-Awlaki, a recently killed Yemini cleric who grew up in New Mexico. Al-Awlaki had played an important operational role for al-Qaeda in the Arabian Peninsula and was known to reach out to several American jihadists. For example, he exerted a strong influence on Major Nidal Malik Hasan, with whom he exchanged e-mails several times before the attack at Fort Hood on November 5, 2010. Al-Awlaki also met with Umar Farouk Abdulmutallab (a.k.a. the "Underwear Bomber"), who was arrested for his ill-fated attempt to blow up a Detroit-bound flight on Christmas Day in 2009. Al-Awlaki's sermons also inspired Faisal Shahzad, who unsuccessfully attempted to set off a car bomb in New York's Times Square in May 2010, and Zachary Chesser, a Fairfax, Virginia, man who was arrested in July 2010 on charges of trying to join the Somali Islamic terrorist group al-Shabaab. Once characterized as the "Bin Laden of the Internet," al-Awlaki's pronouncements have been broadcast on sites such as YouTube.[29]

In the United States, Islam is one of the fastest-growing religions, due not only to immigration but also to conversions, most notably in the African American community. Some observers now suspect that trends in the West, such as identity politics, are actually furthering the development of militant Islam. Such was the case of the nineteen hijackers responsible for 9/11 who were radicalized not in the Middle East, but rather in the West. The noted French scholar of Islam Oliver Roy observes that, cut off from families and acquaintances while in the West, young Muslims experience a sense of anomie and alienation and thus find solace in attaching themselves to a "virtual *umma*," or community, enabled by Internet technology.[30] Despite the growth of the Muslim population of America, demographically, radical Islam can have only limited influence on a nationwide basis. Nevertheless, there are indications that US authorities are increasingly concerned about radical Islam in America. In March 2011, the US Congress held hearings called by Representative Peter T. King (R-NY) on the topic that occasioned controversy.[31] Another worrisome prospect is that Islamic terrorists might strike Jewish targets in the United States. Inasmuch as the Jewish Diaspora supports Israel, Muslim terrorists justify their attacks on Jewish targets outside of Israel. In turn, it is possible that such violence could embolden Jewish extremists in America.

Jewish Extremism in America

Militant Judaism, or Jewish extremism, is based on an interpretation of the Bible and other Jewish holy texts that God has promised Jews the land of Israel. The principal organization in this regard, the Jewish Defense League (JDL), was actually created in response to a conflict in New York City involving public schools in which many of the teachers were Jewish and many of the pupils were African Americans. At the time, there were some tensions between the two communities. The JDL first provided protection to Jewish neighborhoods against outside threats. More important, though, to the rise of Jewish extremism in the United States have been events overseas. The JDL frequently targeted the Soviet Union for its failure to allow Jewish citizens to emigrate. In addition, the JDL launched attacks against the Soviet Union and other countries for anti-Israeli votes in the United Nations. After years of FBI surveillance and prosecutions, the JDL went into retreat. Rabbi Meir Kahane went on to found a right-wing extremist political party in Israel called the Kach movement, which was eventually dissolved by Israeli authorities because of the party's extremist platform. On November 5, 1990, El Sayyed Nosair, a Muslim, assassinated Kahane as the latter was addressing a conference of the Zionist Emergency Evacuation Rescue Operation in a hotel in downtown Manhattan.

Offshoots of the JDL continued to engage in terrorist violence, but they have been less active and often have not lasted as long. Most notable was the Jewish Defense Organization, which was founded by Mordechai Levi. The group attained notoriety in 2001, when its national chairman, Irv Rubin, and another member, Earl Krugel, were charged with conspiracy in an alleged plot to bomb the King Fahd Mosque in Culver City, California, and the office of an Arab American member of the US House of Representatives, Darrell Issa (R-CA). In November 2002, Rubin committed suicide as he awaited trial in prison.

Although domestic terrorists do not constitute an existential threat in the United States since they have not engendered much public support, transnational terrorists have demonstrated that they can coordinate lethal strikes against America, as evidenced by the attack on September 11, 2001. An examination of the transnational terrorist threat is in order.

Transnational Terrorism

Origins

In essence, transnational terrorism involves citizens or the territory of more than one country. The principal transnational terrorist challenge facing the United States comes from radical Islam. The global Islamic resistance movement has endured despite a multinational effort to eradicate it after 9/11. To some observers, militant Islam, or Islamism, is a retrograde phenomenon, a rearguard action against the inexorable march of modernity and globaliza-tion.[32] To its supporters, however, it represents an effort to return man to the righteous guidance of Allah as expressed in the Koran. Islamists seek to revi-talize the universalistic fervor of early Islam and repackage it as a viable polit-ical ideology. According to Daniel Pipes, Islamism is essentially an effort to transform the religion of Islam into a contemporary political ideology, usually with a radical bent, not unlike fascism and communism. Islamism offers a vanguard philosophy with a complete program to improve man and remake society. In short, it is an Islamic attempt to come to terms with the challenge of modernization.

The most enduring institution of Islamism, the Muslim Brotherhood (al-Ikhwan al-Muslimun), was founded by Hassan al-Banna in Egypt in 1928. Rapidly, the movement spread throughout the Islamic world.[33] Eventually, al-Banna ran afoul of the Egyptian regime, and he was assassinated in 1949, on the orders of King Farouk. However, Farouk's days as the Egyptian leader were also numbered. Arab nationalism would prove to be a dynamic force that the monarch could not squelch. Initially, relations between the Muslim Brother-hood and Gamel Abdel Nasser were amicable. The Muslim Brotherhood even supported Nasser and his Free Officers in their 1952 coup over King Farouk. By 1954 Nasser had taken over full control of the state, but not long into his tenure, some Islamic fundamentalists began to criticize his regime. Relations broke down irrevocably between the government and the Muslim Brother-hood in 1954 when a member, Mahmud 'Abd al-Latif', attempted to assassi-nate Nasser while he gave a speech in Alexandria. Soon thereafter, the regime fiercely repressed the Brotherhood, as many members were sent to prison and the movement was driven underground. This failed to silence the opposition, and indeed it became more emboldened. Chief among the critics of the regime was Sayid Qutb.

Sayid Qutb and Milestones

The ideological roots of al-Qaeda can be traced to Egypt's prisons of the 1960s and 1970s, when some of the most prominent Islamist thinkers were de-tained.[34] The chief ideologist of Islamism, Sayid Qutb (1906–1966), inspired some of the most prominent Muslim leaders, including Osama bin Laden. In Qutb's analysis, the societies of the contemporary Muslim world were not au-thentically Islamic. Rather, they still existed in a state of *jahiliyya*—a Koranic term designating a pre-Islamic state of barbarism and ignorance. According to Qutb, it was the duty of Muslims to implement the sharia, or Islamic law, so that the sovereignty of God would rule alone.[35] For Qutb, the only places on earth that could genuinely be called *Dar-al-Islam* (the abodes of Islam) were those countries and territories in which an Islamic state had been established, where the sharia was recognized as the law, and where Muslims administered the affairs of the state with mutual consultation (*shura*). The rest of the world was *Dar-al-Harb* (home of hostility). Based on this reasoning, Qutb argued that Muslims could have only two possible relations with *Dar-al-Harb*: peace with a contractual agreement or war.[36] Presciently, Qutb predicted that one day Islam would be engaged in a global war with the United States.[37]

Perhaps Qutb's most significant contribution to Islamism was his exegesis on jihad, *Milestones*. Qutb searched for a way to legitimize his revolt against secular authorities. To do so, he invoked the concept of jihad to justify revolt against Arab regimes that were, he claimed, Muslim in name but *jahiliyya* in practice.[38] He exhorted Muslims to assume their individual duties to "execute the will of Allah" as they saw fit, regardless of whether they had the capability of coordinating their actions through a single organization.[39] Thus, in order to create a genuine Islamic society, good Muslims must wage jihad against their local governments.[40]

Qutb's authorship of *Milestones* was not without great cost, as it would eventually be used against him in a trial that concluded with a death sentence. Until the end of his life, he would serve as the supreme guide of the Muslim Brotherhood, yet the group was sharply divided over how to achieve power.[41] One faction favored a legal approach, while the other faction favored revolutionary violence.

Osama bin Laden and al-Qaeda

The origins of al-Qaeda came out of the jihad against the Soviet Red Army in Afghanistan.[42] The 1979 Soviet invasion of Afghanistan sounded the clarion call for jihad throughout the Islamic world. The Afghan war stimulated Islamic terrorism in three ways. First, it provided terrorist-related skills to non-Afghan volunteers (the so-called Afghan Arabs) who came to fight in the Afghan jihad. Second, the war provided the opportunity for Muslims from many different nationalities to create a truly global network. Veterans of the war traveled back to their countries to wage jihad against apostate regimes.[43] Estimates of the total number of Afghan Arab fighters who eventually participated in war range from fourteen to twenty-two thousand.[44] Finally, Afghanistan has tremendous symbolic and emotive importance for the jihadist movement insofar as it was the country in which the mujahideen defeated the Red Army. Although it is widely believed in the Arab and Islamic world that the mujahideen defeated the USSR unilaterally, the United States played a significant role in arming, training, and bankrolling the mujahideen.

The event that ultimately drove Osama bin Laden to the point of no return from the Saudi government was the first Gulf War. To many Muslims, the Saudi government is viewed as the custodian of the two most sacred places in Islam, that is, Mecca and Medina. Not long after Saddam Hussein's August 1990 invasion of Kuwait, tens of thousands of US troops began deploying in Saudi Arabia as part of a troop buildup for what would ultimately become Operation Desert Storm. The Saudi government's decision to allow US troops on the holiest soil of Islam was too galling for him. Fresh from victory in Afghanistan, he approached the royal family and offered to raise an army of five thousand veteran mujahideen volunteers to thwart any aggression by Iraq.[45] Not wanting to risk the same fate that had befallen Kuwait, the Saudi royal family declined his offer and instead decided to accept American military assistance.

By the early 1990s, the security services in the Middle East were beginning to demonstrate that they were able to contain the radical Islamist movements in their countries.[46] Frustrated by their lack of progress in their own countries in the Middle East, jihadists began to consider alternative strategies to effect their goals. Into this void, Osama bin Laden reached. The marginalization of jihadist groups in various Arab nations made available a large number of recruits for al-Qaeda.[47] With the connections and moral authority he established during his exploits in Afghanistan, Bin Laden found sanctuary in Sudan, where he was welcomed by Hassan al-Turabi, a charismatic cleric who led the National Islamic Front, which ruled the country at that time.[48] Bin Laden's stay in Sudan overlapped with that of many other terrorists, which enabled al-Qaeda to forge more links and turn itself into a global umbrella organization.[49] From this secure base, he intensified his operations, expanded his terrorist network, and planned attacks against America. On November 13, 1995, a car bomb exploded in the courtyard of a Saudi Arabia National Guard building in Riyadh, killing two Indian nationals and five American servicemen. This attack put Bin Laden on the CIA's radar screen. In January 1996, the CIA Counter-terrorist Center in Langley, Virginia, created a special Bin Laden task force.[50] In August 1996, Osama bin Laden formally announced himself as an enemy of the United States with a formal declaration of war.[51] The September 11, 2001, attacks on the World Trade

Center and Pentagon were the culmination of al-Qaeda's terrorist campaign against the United States.

Al-Qaeda 2.0

Initially, Islamists were adversely affected by the 9/11 attacks in that they provoked a massive response from the United States and its allies. Moreover, the ensuing backlash provided the political elite in the Middle East the opportunity to suppress the Islamists and other oppositional voices in the name of fighting terrorism.[52] According to some estimates, by early 2003, roughly two-thirds of the leadership has been killed or captured since 9/11, including many of the top leaders.[53] With the commencement of Operation Enduring Freedom in October 2001, al-Qaeda initially lost its sanctuary in Afghanistan. Consequently, the organization was deprived of vital resources, and much of its financial assets were confiscated.[54] Although al-Qaeda had skillfully employed terrorism in the past, some observers believe that the leadership gravely miscalculated by provoking a ferocious response for which the organization was unprepared.[55]

Nevertheless, al-Qaeda quickly reformulated from a centralized organization into a series of autonomous organizations driven by local concerns, which allowed the network to endure. Since Operation Enduring Freedom commenced in October 2001, al-Qaeda began a process of transformation into a more diffuse terrorist network that can still strike at US targets abroad.[56] Al-Qaeda 2.0, as defined by Peter Bergen, suggests a decentralized alliance of terrorists spread throughout the world.[57] The flexibility enables al-Qaeda to effectively prosecute asymmetric warfare.[58] In some ways al-Qaeda has become an "imagined jihadist community" or a "state of mind" organization. Although there is somewhat of a hierarchical structure at the core of the network, the periphery is much more amorphous. There is evidence to suggest that disparate individuals and groups that are inspired by the al-Qaeda ideology are coordinating and conducting attacks on their own initiative—a genuine form of leaderless resistance in practice. Significantly, nearly all Islamist terrorist attacks since 2002 have been conducted by either a franchise or an unaffiliated group.[59] In short, jihadists are exhorted to think globally, but act locally.

Al-Qaeda remains the vanguard organization providing crucial knowledge and methodology to mobilize both foreign and domestic jihadist groups. Although the central organization's numbers are quite small—in June 2010, CIA director Leon Panetta estimated the figure to be between fifty and one hundred—al-Qaeda still exerts a substantial influence over the global jihadist movement, as the group's ideology and tactics have spread throughout the Islamic world.[60] Ensconced in the Federally Administered Tribal Areas in Pakistan, the leadership of al-Qaeda has survived and still manages to plan key operations and terrorist attacks, not only in Pakistan and Afghanistan, but also through affiliated groups and migrant populations in the West.[61] Following the loss of al-Qaeda's central base in Afghanistan, Europe has become even more important to the organization.[62] In fact, virtually every major attack carried out by al-Qaeda throughout the world has had some link to Europe.

Social networks are also vital to terrorism. The Internet is an important aspect of al-Qaeda's campaign, as Dr. Ayman al-Zawahiri once opined: "We are in a battle, and more than half of this battle is taking place in the battlefield of the media. We are in a media battle for the hearts and minds of our *umma* [community of Muslims]."[63] To that end, al-Qaeda has a media committee led by a jihadist with the nom de guerre "Abu Reuter." Presently, the leadership operates more as a communications company, producing occasional videotapes rather than actual terrorism.[64] In essence, al-Qaeda has become the strategic communicator for the larger global Salafist movement.[65] Over the years, al-Qaeda has stepped up its media operations.[66] The most susceptible to the propaganda are Muslims living in conflict zones and in their immediate neighborhoods, as well as Muslims living in the migrant and diasporic communities.[67]

The Internet is an important contributing factor that makes jihadist terrorism more global in scope, insofar as it reduces the need for physical contact and makes possible the formation of a decentralized structure of autonomous groups that share the same ideology. Furthermore, the anonymity of the Internet allows extremists to interact more freely with fewer constraints than in a real-world setting in which monitoring is almost ubiquitous.[68] Such trends make leaderless jihad possible.

Leaderless Jihad

Since the war in Afghanistan commenced in October 2001, al-Qaeda has been moving toward a more decentralized approach to terrorism in which loosely affiliated groups that have only slight connections to the central organization commit acts of terrorism of their own volition. Such groups tap into Bin Laden's "franchise" and adopt al-Qaeda's brand name.[69] Leaderless resistance has now caught on in the jihadist movement. Ironically, the American extreme Right movement has done the most theorizing on the concept. In 1992

Louis Beam, a long-standing activist, released the seminal essay "Leaderless Resistance" in which he argued that the traditional hierarchical organizational structure was untenable under current conditions.[70] This essay was disseminated through computer networks that Beam was a pioneer in exploiting in the 1980s.

A Syrian member of al-Qaeda, Abu Musab al-Suri, advanced an operational strategy of decentralization to fit contemporary conditions. His sixteen-hundred-page online tome, *A Global Islamic Resistance*, seeks to provoke a global Islamic uprising led by autonomous cells and individual jihadists. In it he argues that it was folly for the movement to fight from fixed locations because their units could be trapped where Western forces could eventually invade and destroy them. Furthermore, he saw the traditional hierarchical model of a terrorist group as outdated because if authorities could capture one member, then it could put the whole organization at risk. Taking into account these factors, al-Suri proposed a "jihad of individual terrorism" in which self-contained cells implement their own terrorist template to start their own jihad. What is critical is a shared ideology that serves to create a feeling of common cause and unity of purpose. There would be no formal organizational links between the cells. This model fosters adaptability and creativity in the realm of terrorism. He advises Islamists to focus on jihad in their own countries of residence.[71]

The power of the Internet is integral to al-Suri's strategy of individual terrorism in that it serves as a mobilization tool. To make leaderless resistance orderly, al-Suri recognized that it was necessary to direct such actions through strategic guidance from al-Qaeda's leaders so that they would work with a unity of purpose. In that regard, al-Qaeda's leaders have taken his advice, as demonstrated by the cases in which locally recruited cells carry out attacks under the guidance of the parent organization, such as in the cases of the Madrid and London attacks.[72]

A few examples are illustrative of this tactical approach. On August 1, 2007, an al-Qaeda website promised that a big surprise would soon occur. Although the message did not specify the precise nature of the surprise, the accompanying visual displayed a montage of President Bush with then visiting Afghan president Hamid Karzai and Pakistani president Pervez Musharraf against a backdrop of the White House in flames, thus suggesting that they should be targeted. This was followed on August 5 by a video in which Gadahn warned that US embassies would be attacked. Such threats have of course become commonplace in al-Qaeda discourse; as terrorism analyst

Brian Jenkins observes, they are part of the organization's communications strategy. Gadahn's videotape threatened no specific action; rather, it identified targets that ought to be attacked and left it up to jihadists to act on their own initiative.[73] Not long thereafter, he appeared in another video in which he seemingly commanded sleeper agents to attack nuclear power plants inside the United States.[74] By instilling a sense of nuclear anxiety through Bin Laden's pronouncements on the suitability of acquiring nuclear weapons, al-Qaeda has managed to induce nuclear terror in the United States.[75] More threats would follow. In March 2010, al-Qaeda's media army, as-Sahab, released a videotape in which Gadahn commended Major Hasan, the Fort Hood shooter, calling him an "ideal role model" whose lone-wolf terrorism should be a model of emulation for other jihadists in America and the West.[76] Such threats, often conveyed through the news media, are an integral part of al-Qaeda's grand strategy.

In essence, al-Qaeda is mounting a global version of fourth-generation warfare against the United States and its allies. As Thomas X. Hammes explains, fourth-generation warfare is an evolved form of insurgency that endeavors to use all available networks, political, social, and military, to convince the enemy's decision makers that their strategic goals are unattainable or not worth the cost.[77] Based on this reasoning, Bin Laden's strategic approach has viability. He was greatly influenced by his experiences in the Soviet-Afghan war of the 1980s and even went so far as to take credit for the downfall of the Soviet Union. That war set in motion various trends and developments that ultimately contributed to the dissolution of the Soviet Union. It is one of the foundational beliefs of al-Qaeda that a major setback in the Middle East could usher in a similar scenario for the United States. Al-Qaeda's grand strategy appears to be aimed at bleeding America to exhaustion and bankruptcy and, in doing so, forcing the United States to withdraw from the Muslim world so that its regional allies will collapse, while simultaneously inciting a mass uprising within the Islamic world.[78]

Despite setbacks, al-Qaeda has proved to be highly adaptable, as it has devolved to regional affiliates much of the responsibility for waging global jihad with little centralized planning from the parent organization.[79] Still, the influence al-Qaeda has in those countries in which its most important local affiliates reside—Saudi Arabia, Yemen, Jordan, Pakistan, and elsewhere—is rapidly shrinking, due to the efforts of the security services and substantial assistance from the United States.[80] Nevertheless, al-Qaeda has regrouped and remains a formidable force.[81] The movement simultaneously inspires, motivates, and animates radicalized Muslims around the world to join their global jihad. Moreover, al-Qaeda central still exercises command-and-control capabilities by directing the implementation of terrorist attacks.[82] It is now possible for very small cells, and even individuals, to cause considerable damage due to the greater availability of weapons of mass destruction.

Weapons of Mass Destruction

Historically, technological advances enhanced the disruptive potential of terrorism. In fact, one reason for the rise of modern terrorism was the increasing availability of firepower to groups wishing to overthrow the government. For example, the introduction of dynamite was a catalyst for the anarchist movement that launched bombing campaigns in Europe and America. More recently, the attacks on 9/11 changed the seriousness of the perception of terrorism in the United States because it brought together two threats that were much more serious in combination than they were isolation—that is, radical Islam and the availability of weapons of mass destruction.[83] The major variants of WMD are chemical, biological, radiological, and nuclear.

Today, there is much consternation over the increasing availability of WMDs. The most worrisome aspect of modern terrorism is the prospect of a radical group obtaining a nuclear weapon. In fact, on the eve of the Nuclear Security Summit in April 2010, President Barack Obama announced that the prospect of nuclear terrorism was "the single biggest threat to U.S. security, both short-term, medium-term and long-term."[84] During the Cold War, the nuclear balance of terror—mutually assured destruction—was thought to follow a certain logic, in that the United States and the Soviet Union pursued their foreign policy goals in a rational fashion. Some observers fear, however, that nuclear-armed extremist groups would not follow such logic because of their radical worldviews.[85]

What is all the more troubling is that some terrorist organizations with the most violent histories, such as al-Qaeda and Aum Shinrikyo, were at one time believed to have the requisite financial ability to purchase WMDs.[86] For his part, Osama bin Laden explicitly stated his ambition to acquire a WMD on more than one occasion.[87] The potential damage stemming from nuclear terrorism could be catastrophic. A study conducted by the RAND Corporation of a hypothetical attack on the port of Long Beach in California estimated that a nuclear device would kill 60,000 persons instantly or soon thereafter, while exposing another 150,000 persons to harmful radioactive water and sediment. The total economic cost of such an attack would exceed $1 trillion.[88]

Although the probability of nuclear terrorism is still quite low, it is so consequential as to merit consideration. Nevertheless, despite the alarming prospect of nuclear terrorism, the obstacles to obtaining such capabilities are formidable. First, neither nuclear weapons nor nuclear technology has proliferated to the degree that was once feared. What is more, even if a terrorist group purloined a nuclear warhead or procured one on the black market, sophisticated security measures would be difficult to surmount. Acquiring fissile material with which to build a bomb would also be challenging in that states would be reluctant to convey such material to underground groups. Uranium enrichment is a very complex process, far beyond the capacity of terrorist groups operating in a clandestine environment. The single most difficult obstacle to producing a nuclear weapon is acquiring weapons-grade highly enriched uranium, the production of which would require large facilities, sophisticated equipment, and highly skilled expertise that in total would be beyond the capabilities of a nonstate entity. Obtaining highly enriched uranium material on the black market would be one way to short-circuit this process; however, there would still be tough obstacles in constructing the actual nuclear bomb. If states that aspire to obtain nuclear capability face such difficulties, it would follow that it would be even more challenging for terrorist groups with far fewer resources and without a secure geographic area in which to undertake such a project. States would be reluctant to convey nuclear weapons to underground groups, for to be implicated in doing so they would run the risk of serious retaliation from the targeted country as well as the international community. Alternatively, terrorists could attempt to purloin a weapon from a nuclear stockpile; however, absconding with a nuclear weapon would be problematic for a terrorist group because of tight security measures at installations. A sympathetic insider would be one way to short-circuit some of the hurdles facing the group. Conceivably, rogue elements in a regime might be willing to assist a terrorist group in obtaining a nuclear weapon. A terrorist group might also be able to acquire a nuclear weapon in the event of political turmoil when security is compromised. If a regime collapsed, state control over nuclear weapons could evaporate, thus allowing a terrorist or criminal group to obtain weapons from the nuclear arsenal. Still another scenario could involve a collapsing regime that would transfer a nuclear weapon to a terrorist group in order to exact revenge against an adversary.[89]

With the technological hurdles to obtaining nuclear weapons so high, terrorists could settle for less sophisticated alternatives, such as nuclear sabotage or radiological dispersion devices. Nuclear power facilities are "hardened," but, nevertheless, they remain "fixed targets" and are thus vulnerable to sabotage.[90] Many research nuclear reactors are located on urban university campuses that terrorists might be able to access. As the accident at Chernobyl in 1986 illustrated, the effects of an attack or sabotage could be potentially devastating without an explosion ever taking place. Likewise, the damage inflicted on the earthquake-stricken reactors in March 2011 in Japan demonstrated the potential vulnerability of nuclear power plants. Conceivably, this disaster could have a demonstration effect on terrorists who might opt for nuclear sabotage as a more viable option in lieu of the more challenging proposition of constructing an improvised nuclear device.

For small groups, or lone wolves intent on inflicting nuclear terrorism, employing a dirty bomb would be the most feasible option. In essence, a dirty bomb consists of radioactive material conjoined with conventional explosives, which when detonated disperses harmful radiation, thus possibly rendering an area uninhabitable for a considerable length of time. Radioactive materials are used in a variety of commercial applications in industrial economies and are thus widely accessible. Many sites containing high-risk radioactive materials remain vulnerable to theft. Although not as deadly as a device capable of a nuclear detonation, a dirty bomb's primary threat would be economic and societal disruption. Cleaning up the radiation after an attack would entail laborious cleansing of surfaces and potentially removing some materials that could not be decontaminated.

Unlike nuclear devices, chemical weapons would be well within the reach of individuals and small groups. If disseminated effectively, chemical weapons could produce mass casualties. Despite this potential lethality, the effective dispersal of chemical weapons is a difficult task. As the case of Aum Shinrikyo illustrates, chemical weapons suitable for mass-casualty attacks could conceivably be acquired by nonstate actors with moderate technical skills. On March 20, 1995, members of Aum Shinrikyo released sarin gas in the Tokyo subway attack, which killed 12 persons and caused an estimated 6,000 people to seek medical attention.[91] If Aum Shinrikyo had acquired high-grade sarin and dispensed it as an aerosol, then the Tokyo attack might have resulted in thousands of casualties.[92] Striking an industrial chemical facility would be one method of amplifying the effect of a conventional attack. Conventional explosives could disperse dangerous chemicals, thus contaminating adjacent people and property.

Biological weapons could potentially be even more lethal than nuclear bombs, as diseases killed scores of people in the last century. The prospect of smallpox being used as a bioweapon still exists, as vaccinations for the disease have long since ceased.[93] The October 2001 anthrax-laced letters demonstrated the possibility that weapons could be diverted by an insider. Adding to these fears is the fact that biological weapons are difficult to detect. Nevertheless, from the perspective of terrorists, biological weapons pose a number of logistical problems. First, a pathogenic or toxin-producing organism must be acquired. Second, the microorganism or toxin must be produced in bulk. And finally, the most significant technical hurdle would be weaponizing a biological agent that is capable of being dispersed at an infectious or toxic concentration as a respirable aerosol.

According to Fred Schreier, the main reason terrorists have so seldom resorted to WMDs in the past is because they are difficult to obtain and employ. As the case of Aum Shinrikyo illustrates, the effective use of WMD is still challenging. The group pursued sophisticated weaponry, including nuclear, biological, and chemical weapons. Furthermore, the group's formidable resources (according to some estimates, its coffers reached an estimated $1 billion) enabled the group to carry out serious plans for the procurement and development of such weapons. Nevertheless, given the expenditures that were used for these ventures, it is conceivable that far more destruction and casualties could have been inflicted using conventional explosives.

Counterterrorism and the US Government Response

The September 11th attacks on the World Trade Center and Pentagon brought home the issue of terrorism as no other previous attack in America's history had. The government was strongly criticized in many quarters for its failure to anticipate and prepare for such a horrific eventuality. Despite this perception, the Clinton administration had actually given high priority to the issue of domestic terrorism on its policy agenda. In fact, throughout President Bill Clinton's tenure, a flurry of new antiterrorist laws and measures were enacted, including the Anti-Terrorism and Effective Death Penalty Act of 1996.[94] Funding for counterterrorism was substantially increased during this period as well.[95] Much of the impetus for these efforts actually came from the perceived threat of domestic right-wing extremists and self-styled citizen militias. The April 19, 1995, bombing of the Alfred P. Murrah Federal Building in Oklahoma City was ominously seen as a harbinger of further domestic terrorism. Various government officials, policy analysts, and blue-ribbon panels argued that the country must do more to protect against terrorism. For instance, the Gilmore Commission recommended the creation of a National Homeland Security Agency that would have responsibility for planning and coordinating US government activities involved in homeland security. Likewise, the United States Commission on National Security/21st Century, more popularly known as the Hart-Rudman Commission, called for the consolidation of agencies involved in homeland security into one cabinet-level department.[96] Although President Clinton placed counterterrorism high on his policy agenda, it was mostly behind the scenes, and he did not attempt any sustained public education on the issue. In consequence, when George W. Bush took office, there was not much public or congressional pressure to respond to the threat posed by Osama bin Laden and al-Qaeda.[97]

USA PATRIOT Act

As would be expected, in the aftermath of 9/11, the federal government, with support from the American public and US Congress, called for more vigilant measures to root out potential terrorists at home and abroad.[98] To meet the exigencies of the new terrorist threat, Congress passed the USA PATRIOT Act, which was signed into law by President Bush on October 26, 2001. The thrust of the new law was to give authorities more options for surveillance with less judicial supervision.[99] It contains several features that grant authorities new measures to combat terrorism. First, it authorizes the use of so-called roving wiretaps to tap any phones that a suspected terrorist may be using. Second, it permits surveillance of a suspect's Internet activity and gives the FBI greater latitude in conducting secret searches of a suspect's home. Third, it allows for greater sharing of information among grand juries, prosecutors, and intelligence agencies. Fourth, it expands the powers of agencies such as US Immigration and Customs Enforcement and US Customs and Border Protection to detain immigrants suspected of terrorist activities. Fifth, it gives the government greater power to penetrate banks suspected of being involved in the financing of terrorist groups and activities. And finally, the new law statutorily creates new crimes, enhances penalties, and increases the length of statutes of limitation for certain crimes.[100]

Arguably the most ambitious governmental effort in the wake of 9/11 was the creation of the Department of Homeland Security. Toward this end, on October 8, 2001, President Bush issued Executive Order 13228, which established the Office of Homeland Security. The new office guided a comprehensive effort to safeguard the nation's population, property, government, and critical infrastructure by preparing for, protecting against, and managing the consequences of terrorist attacks and related crises.[101] This initiative constituted the most ambitious governmental reorganization since the creation of the Department of Defense and the Central Intelligence Agency in 1947.

Reforming the Intelligence Sector

The extremely well-coordinated attacks of September 11th underscored the gaping hole in the area of human intelligence. The *9/11 Commission Report* found that the US government was structured to fight the Cold War, with an emphasis on symmetric confrontations rather than combating terrorism and other asymmetrical threats. As a consequence, the Department of Defense and the defense support of civilian authorities were not as well structured to deal with counterterrorism. To meet the challenges of the new security environment, the report called for the creation of the position of national intelligence director to coordinate intelligence among all government agencies. Previously, a so-called firewall between the CIA and the FBI hindered intelligence sharing, as there was a history of entrenched bureaucratic resentment and distrust between the two agencies.[102] Actually, an interagency effort to combine US government information and analysis was established in the late 1980s, when the CIA created the Counterterrorist Center, which coordinates the intelligence collection and evaluation of many government agencies involved in counterterrorism issues.[103] Now called the National Counterterrorism Center, the program has been expanded since 9/11.[104]

Military Response

The terrorist attacks on 9/11 provoked a ferocious response from the US government. Initially, there was broad-based sympathy for America, as many countries offered assistance, even if only nominal and symbolic, which nevertheless provided tremendous legitimacy to US efforts to eradicate the Taliban and al-Qaeda in Afghanistan. For the first time in its history, NATO invoked Article 5 of its charter, which mandates alliance members to come to the defense of a member when it is attacked. Although Operation Enduring Freedom was mainly a unilateral US military effort, NATO countries did play a leading role in the stabilization and reconstruction phases of the mission.

Concerning the broader international community, the United States invoked Article 51 of the UN Charter, which states that member nations have the right to self-defense in response to an armed attack. In its interpretation of Article 51, the US government also theorized that an armed attack could be launched by nonstate actors. As a consequence, a principle of state responsibility implies that a country has an obligation to prevent terrorists from operating on their soil; otherwise, it could become a target. In order to bolster this claim, the Bush administration first demanded that the Taliban hand over Osama bin Laden and other parties responsible for the attacks on 9/11 or else the United States would be free to commence military operations. For the war effort, the United States entered into a number of bilateral agreements with individual countries, most critically Pakistan, whose cooperation was essential. Despite regional rivalries, Russia supported the US intervention by allowing the United States to use bases in the former Soviet republics in central Asia over which it still exerted a strong influence. Middle Eastern governments helped out as well.[105] Amazingly, during the conventional phase of the conflict, an estimated 100 CIA officers, 350 special forces soldiers, and 15,000 Afghanis defeated a Taliban army of approximately 50,000 to 60,000 as well as several thousand al-Qaeda fighters.[106]

Fresh from quick victory in Afghanistan, by April 2002, President Bush began to publicly call for a policy of regime change in Iraq. By June 2002, he announced that he would launch preemptive strikes against those countries believed to pose a serious threat to the United States. Furthermore, he added that the United States would be willing to take unilateral and preemptive action if support from the UN and traditional allies was not forthcoming. This approach would later be dubbed "the Bush Doctrine." Ultimately, President Bush became convinced that a strategy of preemption was necessary. Two factors featured prominently in his decision. First was the prospect of another massive surprise attack similar to 9/11. Second, the proliferation of weapons of mass destruction added to the potential lethality of future terrorism. If these two factors converged in the hands of terrorists, or a rogue state, then the United States could suffer terrorism of an unprecedented magnitude.[107]

Conclusion

Over the past several years, the face of terrorism has undergone substantial change. Although the US government is understandably concerned about well-established and enduring terrorist organizations, there is a discernible trend indicating the increasing prevalence of so-called lone-wolf attacks by individuals and small cells with little or no connections to larger groups. Increasingly, individuals and small groups are responsible for some of the most lethal acts of terrorism. To be sure, well-established organizations, such as Hezbollah, Hamas, FARC, the Tamil Tigers, and al-Qaeda, continue to mount operations; however, individuals and much smaller cells, sometimes inspired by the ideologies that inform the more established groups, are able to autonomously mount operations without central direction.

Additionally, the emergence of new technology also has the potential to serve as a force multiplier for terrorists. For example, the Internet allows like-minded activists to operate on their own initiative without the direction of a formal organization—hence, the emergence of leaderless resistance as a new operational strategy and the miniaturization of terrorist and insurgent movements around the world today. These developments mark a major departure from previous paradigms of warfare, although there is an ongoing debate in the field of terrorism studies on the significance of leaderless resistance and the degree to which al-Qaeda central exercises direct control over its affiliates.[108] Furthermore, leaderless resistance is not confined to radical jihadists. As mentioned earlier, the American extreme Right has been in the forefront in theorizing on the concept. Arguably, the most adept at its actual implementation are the radical environmentalists and animal liberation activists.[109] Some US officials warned that the death of Osama bin Laden in early May 2011 could speed up the trend over the past few years that has seen al-Qaeda become more decentralized and therefore more difficult to stop.[110]

In an era of US-dominated globalization, states presumably would have more to gain by accommodation with the West rather than confrontation. This development militates against the viability of the larger terrorist organizations in that they are more vulnerable to state repression and disruption because governments coordinate their counterterrorist efforts with the United States. US-led efforts to counter terrorism both at home and abroad include intelligence sharing, enhanced homeland security, military action, and interstate cooperation. Increasingly, the United States is promoting an international agenda that seeks to create a less congenial world for terrorism. This effort, however, has had great costs. As of June 2011, 6,058 US soldiers and DOD civilians have died in the various theaters in the Global War on Terror.[111] According to some estimates, the financial cost of fighting Bin Laden's network has reached $3 trillion.[112]

NOTES

1. As described in Jeffrey Kaplan, "Leaderless Resistance," *Terrorism and Political Violence* 9, no. 3 (1997): 80.

2. Walter Laqueur explains this change in thinking in *The New Terrorism: Fanaticism and the Arms of Mass Destruction* (New York: Oxford University Press, 1999), 9.

3. Jonathan R. White, *Terrorism and Homeland Security*, 6th ed. (Belmont, CA: Thompson/Wadsworth, 2009), 4.

4. Combining Christopher Hewitt's figure of 501 domestic terrorist fatalities for the period 1955–1998 with the fatalities resulting from the Oklahoma City bombing adds up to a figure of 669. Hewitt, "Patterns of American Terrorism, 1955–1998: An Historical Perspective on Terrorism-Related Fatalities, 1955–98," *Terrorism and Political Violence* 12, no. 1 (2000): 5. The number of gang-related deaths in Los Angeles County for 1991 exceeded 700. Jesse Katz, "Gang Killings in LA County Top a Record of 700," *Los Angeles Times*, December 8, 1991, A1, 24, 26.

5. Martha Crenshaw, ed., *Terrorism in Context* (University Park: Pennsylvania State University Press, 2001); Brent L. Smith, *Terrorism in America: Pipe Bombs and Pipe Dreams* (Albany: State University of New York Press, 1994).

6. Jonathan R. White, *Terrorism and Homeland Security*, 5th ed. (Belmont, CA: Thompson/Wadsworth, 2006), 4–5; Cindy C. Combs, *Terrorism in the Twenty-First Century* (Upper Saddle River, NJ: Prentice-Hall, 1997).

7. FBI, *Terrorism in the United States, 1998* (Washington, DC: FBI, 1999), i.

8. Brian Michael Jenkins, *Will Terrorists Go Nuclear?* (Amherst, NY: Prometheus Books, 2008), 101.

9. Bruce Hoffman, *Inside Terrorism* (New York: Columbia University Press, 2006).

10. As David M. Chalmers, a noted historian of the Klan, opines, "Throughout its history the Klan has been a conservative, not a revolutionary, organization. . . . The Klan has basically been a *revitalization movement*." Chalmers, *Hooded Americanism: The History of the Ku Klux Klan*, 3rd ed. (Durham, NC: Duke University Press, 1981), 425 (emphasis in the original).

11. Louis Beam and Dennis Mahon exemplified the revolutionary faction. Thom Robb is the leading proponent for the nonviolent approach. Beam and Mahon have since parted from their respective Klan organizations. For more on this debate, see Jeffrey Kaplan, *The Encyclopedia of White Power: A Sourcebook on the Radical Racist Right* (New York: Alta Mira Press, 2000), 163–166.

12. One terrorist expert, David Rapoport, estimates that the life expectancy of at least 90 percent of terrorist organizations is less than one year. Rapoport, "Terrorism," in *Routledge Encyclopedia of Government and Politics*, edited by Mary Hawkesworth and Maurice Kogan (London: Routledge, 1992), 2:1067. I do not know if Rapoport included the violence-prone Klan organizations in his analysis, but I suspect that his findings would hold up for them as well. However, in earlier eras, violent Klan organizations did have some staying power.

13. Mattias Gardell, "Black and White Unite in Fight?," in *The Cultic Milieu: Oppositional Subcultures in an Age of Globalization*, edited by Jeffrey Kaplan and Heléne Lööw (New York: Alta Mira Press, 2002), 168.

14. The organization used several names, including "the Silent Brotherhood" and a German version of that same title, the Brüder Schweigen.

15. Walter Laqueur, *No End to War: Terrorism in the Twenty-First Century* (New York: Continuum, 2003), 195.

16. In February 2007, Nichols claimed in a nineteen-page signed declaration that McVeigh told him that he was taking instructions from a former FBI official named Larry Potts. Supposedly, McVeigh had been recruited back in 1992 while he was still in the army to carry out undercover missions. According to Nichols, McVeigh acquired the knowledge on how to make bombs while traveling the gun-show circuit. Nichols claimed that he knew McVeigh was building a bomb back in November 1994 and thus left for the Philippines to avoid being implicated in the plot. Geoffrey Fattah, "Nichols Says Bombing Was FBI Op," *Deseret Morning News*, February 21, 2007.

17. "Assessing White Supremacists Groups in the U.S." National Public Radio, October 30, 2008, http://www.npr.org/templates/story/story.php?storyId=96329575&ps=rs.

18. Barton Gellman, "Locked and Loaded," *Time*, October 11, 2010, 24–33.

19. Nicholas Köhler, "America Is Angry," *Maclean's*, April 19, 2010, 30.

20. Mark Potok, "Rage on the Right," *Intelligence Report*, no. 137 (Spring 2010), http://www.splcenter.org/get-informed/intelligence-report/browse-all-issues/2010/spring/rage-on-the-right.

21. US Department of Homeland Security, *Rightwing Extremism: Current Economic and Political Climate Fueling Resurgence in Radicalization and Recruitment*, April 2009, http://www.fas.org/irp/eprint/rightwing.pdf.

22. Stuart Wright, "Strategic Framing of Racial-Nationalism in North America and Europe: An Analysis of a Burgeoning Transnational Network," *Terrorism and Political Violence* 21 (2009): 199.

23. This article was developed in more detail in Francis Fukuyama, *The End of History and the Last Man* (New York: Free Press, 2006).

24. "Black blocs" refer to those activists who are often clad in black attire and wearing masks that use so-called direct-action tactics to physically confront "the establishment" and its icons and protective forces. José Pedro Zúquete, "'Hell Yes, We're Fighting!': Revolutionary Anarchism's Call for Destruction and Creation," in *Extremism in the United States: An Overview*, edited by George Michael (Gainesville: University Press of Florida, forthcoming).

25. Laqueur, *New Terrorism*, 204.

26. In the United States, radical Islamists have sometimes received support from the more respectable Islamic organizations. Their oft-expressed enmity for America notwithstanding, Islamists are ironically drawn to the country for a number of reasons. In their home countries they often face repression by the police and security agencies. Thus, they find it attractive to flee to the United States, a country with the rule of law, separation of church and state, wealth, and excellent communication and transportation. Furthermore, by and large Muslims, as a demographic group, seem to fare very well in the United States. The average income for Muslims appears to be higher than the average income in the United States; a 1996 survey found that their median household income was forty thousand dollars, versus thirty-two thousand dollars for the country as a whole. Daniel Pipes, *Militant Islam Reaches America* (New York: W. W. Norton, 2002), 157.

27. Peter Bergen, "Why Bin Laden Still Matters," *Newsweek*, September 4, 2010, http://www.fas.org/programs/ssp/nukes/nuclearweapons/nukestatus.html.

28. For more on Gadahn, see George Michael, "Adam Gadahn and al Qaeda's Internet Strategy," *Middle East Policy* 16, no. 3 (2009): 135–152.

29. Aamer Madhani, "Cleric al-Awlaki Dubbed 'Bin Laden of the Internet,'" *USA Today*, August 25, 2010.

30. Olivier Roy, *Globalized Islam: The Search for a New Ummah* (New York: Columbia University Press, 2004).

31. David A. Fahrenthold and Michelle Boorstein, "Rep. Peter King's Muslim Hearings: A Key Moment in an Angry Conversation," *Washington Post*, March 9, 2011, http://www.washingtonpost.com/wp-dyn/content/article/2011/03/09/AR2011030902061.html.

32. See, for example, Thomas P. M. Barnett, *Great Powers: America and the World After Bush* (New York: Putnam, 2009).

33. Amir Taheri, *Holy Terror: Inside the World of Islamic Terrorism* (Bethesda, MD: Adler and Adler, 1987), 48.

34. Thomas Rid and Marc Hecker, *War 2.0: Irregular Warfare in the Information Age* (Westport, CT: Praeger Security International, 2009), 185.

35. Sayid Qutb, *Milestones* (Cedar Rapids, IA: Mother Mosque Foundation, n.d.), 9.

36. Ibid., 118.

37. One of his contemporary admirers, Sheikh Abdel-Fatah al-Khalidi, portrayed Qutb as a great prognosticator and quasi-Nostradamus figure who predicted the so-called clash of civilizations between the United States and Islam. In 1985 al-Khalidi compiled Qutb's unpublished writings into a book titled *Amreeka Kamaa Ra'aytu*. LCDR Youssef Aboul-Enein, "Sheik Abdel-Fatah al-Khalidi Revitalizes Sayid Qutb," Combating Terrorism Center guest commentary, accessed September 7, 2011, http://ctc.usma.edu/publications/pdf/Khalidi-Qutb.pdf.

38. Qutb had drawn upon the previous writings of an Indian Muslim, Mawlana abu al-Ala Mawdudi, to formulate his theory of jihad. Mawdudi had used the term *jahiliyya* in an abstract way to describe the system of beliefs and ideas in India during the early twentieth century. However, Qutb took Mawdudi's ideas out of context and applied them to his own theories of jihad and *jahiliyya*. See Marc Sageman, *Understanding Terror Networks* (Philadelphia: University of Pennsylvania Press, 2004), 6–9.

39. Taheri, *Holy Terror*, 57.

40. Qutb, *Milestones*, 70.

41. Taheri, *Holy Terror*, 264.

42. Rid and Hecker, *War 2.0*, 185.

43. Paul L. Williams, *Al Qaeda: Brotherhood of Terror* ([Parsippany, NJ?]: Alpha, 2002), 99–101.

44. Simon Reeve put the estimate at fourteen to seventeen thousand. Reeve, *The New Jackals: Ramzi Yousef, Osama bin Laden, and the Future of Terrorism* (Boston: Northeastern University Press, 1999), 3. Adam Robinson put the figure at fifteen to twenty-two thousand. Robinson, *Bin Laden: Behind the Mask of the Terrorist* (New York: Arcade, 2001), 114.

45. Rohan Gunaratna, *Inside al Qaeda: Global Network of Terror* (New York: Columbia University Press, 2002), 27–28.

46. Paul R. Rich, introduction to *Small Wars and Insurgencies* 14, no. 1 (2003): 10.

47. Paul R. Rich, "Al Qaeda and the Radical Islamic Challenge to Western Strategy," *Small Wars and Insurgencies* 14, no. 1 (2003): 43.

48. Roland Jacquard, *In the Name of Osama Bin Laden: Global Terrorism and the Bin Laden International* (Durham, NC: Duke University Press, 2002), 31.

49. Steven Emerson, *American Jihad: The Terrorists Living Among Us* (New York: Free Press, 2002), 145.

50. Reeve, *New Jackals*, 184–185.

51. Bin Laden, "Declaration of War (August 1996)," in *Anti-American Terrorism and the Middle East: A Documentary Reader*, edited by Barry Rubin and Judith Colp Rubin (Oxford: Oxford University Press, 2002), 137.

52. Montasser al-Zayyat, *The Road to al-Qaeda: The Story of Bin Laden's Right-Hand Man* (London and Sterling, VA: Pluto Press, 2004), 4–5.

53. "Al-Qaeda 'Extinct Within a Year,'" October 9, 2003, http://www.news.com.au /common/story _page/o,4057,7431422%5E1702,00.html.

54. Sageman, *Understanding Terror Networks*, 52.

55. Thomas X. Hammes, *The Sling and the Stone: On War in the 21st Century* (St. Paul, MN: Zenith Press, 2004), 130–152.

56. Numerous "number-three" al-Qaeda leaders have been killed or captured since 9/11: Mohamed Atef, Abu Zubaydah, Khalid Sheikh Mohammed, and Saif al-Adel. Faye Bowers, "Al Qaeda's Profile: Slimmer but Menacing," *Christian Science Monitor*, September 9, 2003.

57. Peter Bergen, *The Osama bin Laden I Know: An Oral History of al Qaeda's Leader* (New York: Free Press, 2006).

58. Rich, "Al Qaeda and the Radical Islamic Challenge to Western Strategy," 47.

59. Barry R. Schneider, "Al Qaeda's Modus Operandi: Anticipating Their Target Selection," in *The World's Most Threatening Terrorist Networks and Criminal Gangs*, edited by Michael T. Kindt, Jerrold Post, and Barry R. Schnieder (New York: Palgrave Macmillan, 2009), 34.

60. Bergen, "Why Bin Laden Still Matters."

61. Rohan Gunaratna, "Al-Qaedastan: The Sanctuary of the Afghan-Pakistan Border," Intel File, 12, http://events.fcw.com/events/2008/GLR/downloads/GLR08_T1_GUNARATNA _THE%20TERRORIST%20SANCTUARY%20OF%20THE%20AFGHAN -PAKISTAN%20BORDER.pdf.

62. Lorenzo Vidino, *Al Qaeda in Europe: The New Battleground of International Jihad* (Amherst, NY: Prometheus Books, 2006), 17.

63. Hanna Rogan, "Abu Reuter and the E-Jihad: Virtual Battlefronts from Iraq to the Horn of Africa," *Georgetown Journal of International Affairs* (Summer–Fall 2007): 89.

64. Fareed Zakaria, *The Post-American World* (New York: W. W. Norton, 2008), 13.

65. *Salaf* is Arabic for "ancient one." The Salafist movement refers to Muslim fundamentalists who believe that modern Muslims have lost their way and are not living lives true to the core principles of Mohammed or Islam. Salafists are ideologically nonviolent and instead call not for a revolt against whomever holds power, but for Muslims to reintegrate with fundamental Islam on a personal and daily basis. The fact that al-Qaeda is

working more closely with the larger Salafist movement indicates a potential shift in how fundamentalist Islam views its role in the world.

66. As Rohan Gunaratna found, "In the twelve-month period ending December 2007, al Qaeda produced a cassette, sermon, or video every three days." Gunaratna, "Al-Qaedastan." In the six years following 9/11, Osama bin Laden appeared in more than twenty videos and audiotapes. His chief lieutenant, Dr. Ayman al-Zawahiri, communicated more frequently, as he appeared in more that forty productions during that period. Jenkins, *Will Terrorists Go Nuclear?*, 247.

67. Interview with Rohan Gunaratna, May 28, 2008. According to a study of al-Qaeda's media outreach efforts, important themes in the media pronouncements of Bin Laden and al-Zawahiri, in descending order of frequency, include the call to jihad, the clash of civilizations, "apostate" Muslim leaders that betray Islam, the US-Israel connection, the call for Muslim unity, the "weakening" of the United States, and the "theft" of Muslim oil. Carl J. Ciovacco, "The Contours of al Qaeda's Media Strategy," *Studies in Conflict and Terrorism* 32 (2009): 858.

68. Lia Brynjar, "Al-Qaeda Online: Understanding Jihadist Internet Infrastructure," *Jane's Intelligence Review*, January 1, 2006.

69. Adam Elkus, "Future War: The War on Terror After Iraq," *Athena Intelligence Journal* 2, no. 1 (2007): 20.

70. See Louis Beam, "Leaderless Resistance," *Seditionist*, no. 12 (February 1992); "Understanding the Struggle; or, Why We Have to Kill the Bastards," in *Essays of a Klansman* (Hayden Lake, ID: AKIA Publications, 1983), 45–51; and "Understanding the Struggle, Part II," in *Essays of a Klansman*, 52–72. For more on the extreme Right's theorizing on the leaderless-resistance concept, see George Michael, *Confronting Right-Wing Extremism and Terrorism in the USA* (New York and London: Routledge, 2003), 113–123.

71. Paul Cruickshank and Mohannad Hage Ali, "Abu Musab al Suri: Architect of the New Al Qaeda," *Studies in Conflict and Terrorism* 30, no. 1 (2007): 1–14.

72. Brynjar Lia, *Architect of Global Jihad: The Life of al-Qaida Strategist Abu Mus'ad al-Suri* (New York: Columbia University Press, 2008).

73. Jenkins, *Will Terrorists Go Nuclear?*, 127–129.

74. "Al-Qaida American Was Poster Boy for USC Muslim Student Association," *WorldNetDaily*, July 14, 2006, http://www.worldnetdaily.com/news/article.asp?ARTICLE_ID =51050.

75. Jenkins, *Will Terrorists Go Nuclear?*

76. "Al-Qaeda on Alleged Fort Hood Killer: 'Ideal Role Model,'" *USA Today*, March 7, 2010.

77. Hammes, *Sling and Stone*.

78. Noted authority on counterinsurgency David Kilcullen uses the metaphor of an infection to explain the process of how al-Qaeda is able to take advantage of hot spots in the Islamic world and establish a local presence from which to attack US and Western interests. In the infection state, al-Qaeda inserts itself into remote areas and creates alliances with local communities. Once ensconced, a contagion phase begins in which the group's influence spreads. By exporting violence, al-Qaeda prompts a Western response, thus leading to the third stage, intervention. The organization then exploits this backlash against the

intervention to generate support for its Islamist agenda, which finally results in the emergence of local insurgents, or "accidental guerillas," who fight to evict the foreign occupiers, not so much out of some radical Islamist ideology, but rather out of a more elemental desire to resist a foreign body, akin to antibodies fighting an infection. Kilcullen, *The Accidental Guerilla: Fighting Small Wars in the Midst of a Big One* (New York: Oxford University Press, 2009).

79. F. A. Gerges, *The Far Enemy* (New York: Cambridge University Press, 2005), 247.

80. Ibid., 249.

81. Gerges conceptualizes four dimensions of the al-Qaeda movement. The first category—al-Qaeda central—comprises the core leadership and remains centered on or around the Afghanistan and Pakistan border region. The second category—affiliates—includes groups such as al-Qaeda in Mesopotamia and the Islamic Movement of Uzbekistan. The third category—locals—is dispersed cells of al-Qaeda adherents who have had some connection with al-Qaeda, no matter how tenuous or evanescent. Examples include Ahmed Ressam, who was a planner of the Millennium Plot, and the four British Muslims who were responsible for the July 7, 2005, bombings of mass-transit targets in London. Finally, the fourth category—the al-Qaeda network—consists of homegrown Islamic radicals as well as converts who have no direct connection to the parent organization, but nevertheless gravitate toward each other to plan and mount terrorist attacks in solidarity with al-Qaeda's global agenda. Bruce Hoffman, "From the War on Terror to Global Counterinsurgency," in *Annual Editions*, edited by Thomas J. Badey, 11th ed. (New York: McGraw-Hill, 2009), 210.

82. Ibid., 208.

83. Francis Fukuyama, *America at the Crossroads: Democracy, Power, and the Neoconservative Legacy* (New Haven: Yale University Press, 2006), 66–94.

84. David E. Sanger and William J. Broad, "Leaders Gather for Nuclear Talks as New Threat Is Seen," *New York Times*, April 11, 2010, http://www.nytimes.com/2010/04/12 /world/12nuke.html.

85. Benjamin Netanyahu, *Fighting Terrorism: How Democracies Can Defeat the International Terrorist Network* (New York: Farrar, Straus, Giroux, 2001), 126.

86. Terrorism analyst Jessica Stern identifies several indicators of a terrorist group's ability to overcome technical hurdles to the development of WMD: previous use of high-tech weapons; state sponsorship; access to significant financial resources; a relatively large, well-educated membership; and links and ties with corrupt government officials, scientists, or organized crime. Jessica Stern, *The Ultimate Terrorists* (Cambridge, MA: Harvard University Press, 1999), p. 77.

87. As Bin Laden said in one interview, "Acquiring weapons for the defense of Muslims is a religious duty. If I have indeed acquired these weapons [WMD], I am carrying out a duty. It would be a sin for Muslims not to try to possess the weapons that would prevent the infidels from inflicting harm on Muslims." Quoted in Gunaratna, *Inside al Qaeda*, 48. Not long thereafter, he remarked, "At a time when Israel stocks hundreds of nuclear warheads and when the Western crusaders control a large percentage of this [type of] weapon, we do not consider this an accusation but a right, and we reject anyone who accuses us of this. We congratulated the Pakistani people when they achieved this nuclear weapon, and

we consider it the right of all Muslims to do so." "Interview with Usama bin Ladin (December 1998)," in *Anti-American Terrorism and the Middle East*, edited by Rubin and Rubin, 154–155.

88. Kenneth R. Timmerman, "Fear of a Nuclear D-Day," *Newsmax*, May 2010, 59–60.

89. Charles D. Ferguson and William C. Potter, *The Four Faces of Nuclear Terrorism* (New York and London: Routledge, 2005).

90. Although power plants are designed to withstand earthquakes, tornadoes, and other natural disasters, according to the Nuclear Regulatory Commission, the vast majority of the 106 operating nuclear reactors in the United States were not designed to withstand the impact of a large jet airliner. What is all the more worrisome is that twenty-one of these reactors are located within five miles of an airport. Although experts do not agree as to whether a nuclear power plant could withstand a direct hit by a commercial jet without releasing dangerous radioactive material, the prospect is serious enough to warrant trepidation. The specter of nuclear sabotage arose in November 1972 when three Americans hijacked Southern Airways Flight 49 and ordered the pilot to begin a steep descent on the nuclear facility in Oak Ridge, Tennessee, in order to press their ransom demands. Graham Allison, *Nuclear Terrorism: The Ultimate Preventable Catastrophe* (New York: Times Books, 2004), 7, 55.

91. Holly Fletcher, Council on Foreign Relations, "Aum Shinrikyo," May 28, 2008, http://www.cfr.org/japan/aum-shinrikyo/p9238.

92. Jonathan B. Tucker, introduction to *Toxic Terror: Assessing Terrorist Use of Chemical and Biological Weapons* (Cambridge, MA: Monterey Institute of International Studies, 2001), 6.

93. Although the deadly disease was effectively eradicated through a global inoculation effort, most people in the world are no longer vaccinated against it. Vaccinations ceased in the 1970s. The poxvirus still exists in laboratories. It would take considerable effort to reintroduce the vaccine in the wake of another global outbreak. In the previous century, wiping out the disease involved the labor of 150,000 people working over an eleven-year period. Michael T. Osterholm and John Schwartz, *Living Terrors: What America Needs to Know to Survive the Coming Bioterrorist Catastrophe* (New York: Random House, 2000), 108.

94. For example, President Clinton issued Presidential Decision Directive 39 in 1995, which was the first directive to make terrorism a national top priority and also concluded that the United States was threatened from within. This policy further articulated and defined the roles of members of the US counterterrorism community. The FBI was designated as the chief government agency responsible for investigating and preventing domestic terrorism. Robert M. Blitzer, "FBI's Role in the Federal Response to the Use of Weapons of Mass Destruction: Statement of Robert M. Blitzer, Chief Domestic Terrorism/Counter-terrorism Planning Section FBI, Before the U.S. House of Representatives Committee on National Security," November 4, 1997. White House, Office of the Press Secretary, "Fact Sheet: Combating Terrorism: Presidential Decision Directive 62," May 22, 1998, http://www.au.af.mil/au/awc/awcgate/ciao/62factsheet.htm.

95. The various new laws and initiatives nearly doubled the amount of money spent on counterterrorism to $11 billion a year. Jim Redden, *Snitch Culture* (Venice, CA: Feral

House, 2000), 71. Much of the money went to the FBI, whose antiterrorism budget jumped from $78 million to $609 million a year. Furthermore, between fiscal years 1993 and 2000, the number of FBI special agents assigned to counterterrorism programs increased from 550 to 1,669—approximately a 224 percent increase. Statement for the Record of Dale L. Watson, Executive Assistant Director of Counterterrorism and Counterintelligence, Federal Bureau of Investigation, on the Terrorist Threat Confronting the United States, Before the Senate Select Committee on Intelligence, February 6, 2002, http://www.fbi.gov/news/testimony/the-terrorist-threat-confronting-the-united-states; R. Pillar, *Terrorism and U.S. Foreign Policy* (Washington, DC: Brookings Institution Press, 2003), 80.

96. George Michael, "Homeland Defense Initiative and U.S. Counterterrorism Policy," in *Encyclopedia of World Terrorism, 1996–2002* (Armonk, NY: M. E. Sharpe, 2003), 57.

97. Timothy Naftali, *Blind Spot: The Secret History of American Counterterrorism* (New York: Basic Books, 2005), 285.

98. For example, in the Senate by a vote of 98–0, and in the House of Representatives by a vote of 420–1, Congress passed a joint resolution authorizing President Bush to use "all necessary and appropriate force" for those responsible for the September 11th terrorist attack.

99. Susan Herman, "The USA PATRIOT Act and the U.S. Department of Justice: Losing Our Balances?," *Jurist,* http://law.pitt.edu/forum/formnew40htm.

100. Michael, "Homeland Defense Initiative and U.S. Counterterrorism Policy," 59.

101. Eric V. Larson and John E. Peters, *Preparing the U.S. Army for Homeland Security: Concepts, Issues, and Options* (Santa Monica, CA: RAND), 2001, xv–xvi.

102. "September 10, 2001: The Way We Were," in *To Prevail: An American Strategy for the Campaign Against Terrorism,* edited by Kurt M. Campbell and Michele A. Flournoy (Washington, DC: CSIS Press, 2001), 15.

103. Amos A. Jordan, William J. Taylor, and Michael J. Mazarr, *American National Security,* 5th ed. (Baltimore: Johns Hopkins University Press, 1999), 167.

104. In August 2004, President Bush renamed it the National Counterterrorism Center by an executive order. Naftali, *Blind Spot,* 318–319. The NCTC is located in an unmarked office complex in northern Virginia and has become the centerpiece of reform efforts to integrate the various intelligence agencies in the United States. Most of the work focuses on analysis. Analysts from the CIA, FBI, and National Security Agency in the NCTC monitor unfolding plots and investigations and produce continually updated reports called "Threat Threads" on the most dangerous cases. Kevin Whitelaw, "The Eye of the Storm," in *Annual Editions,* edited by Badey, 192–195.

105. B. Mendelsohn, *Combating Jihadism: American Hegemony and Interstate Cooperation in the War on Terrorism* (Chicago: University of Chicago Press, 2009), 188–189.

106. S. G. Jones, *In the Graveyard of Empires: America's War in Afghanistan* (New York: W. W. Norton, 2009).

107. Bob Woodward, *Bush at War* (New York: Simon and Schuster, 2002), 330, 349.

108. See Bruce Hoffman, "The Myth of Grass-Roots Terrorism: Why Osama bin Laden Still Matters," *Foreign Affairs* (May–June 2008); and Elaine Sciolino and Eric Schmitt, "A Not Very Private Feud over Terrorism," *New York Times,* June 8, 2008.

109. Paul Josse, "Leaderless Resistance and Ideological Inclusion: The Case of the Earth Liberation Front," *Terrorism and Political Violence* 19, no. 3 (2007): 351–367; Donald R. Liddick, *Eco-Terrorism: Radical Environmental and Animal Liberation Movements* (Westport, CT: Praeger, 2006).

110. Tucker Reals, "What's Next for al Qaeda?," CBS News, May 2, 2011, http://www.cbsnews.com/8301-503543_162-20058796-503543.html.

111. "U.S. Military Casualties," US Department of Defense, accessed June 7, 2011, http://www.defense.gov/news/casualty.pdf.

112. Tim Fernholz and Jim Tankersley, "The Cost of Bin Laden: $3 Trillion over 15 Years," *National Journal*, May 6, 2011, http://www.nationaljournal.com/magazine/the-cost-of-bin-laden-3-trillion-over-15-years-20110505?mrefid=site_search&page=1.

CHAPTER 13

America and Terrorism in the Twenty-First Century

MICHAEL L. HUMMEL

Terrorism is not a "modern phenomenon," and although terrorism has been around for centuries, the tactics, targets, weapons, technology, and rationale behind the actions have changed over time.[1] The modern-day terrorists are tactical, sound, well trained, well resourced, and well educated, and they have a psychological will that drives them to sacrifice anything, including their own lives and the lives of their immediate families, in order to accomplish their goal. Most have absolutely no consideration for human life or suffering as accepted in the West and will employ any tactic necessary to destroy the United States of America.

Transnational terrorism has been described as a military tactic, a political strategy, a crime, and as jihad, or religious duty/struggle. It is basically accepted that for terrorists, any conflict, regardless of the political motives or the nature of the unconventional tactics, cannot be engaged without violence and death. To the civilized world, a terrorist's tactics and techniques lack legitimacy because they violate the generally accepted standards of decency regarding helpless and innocent people who are not part of the fight but who are precisely the target. Nevertheless, terrorists often and purposely use

351

violence aimed at innocent parties in order to influence politics or some other part of society.[2]

The Nature of the Threat and Tactics

The more significant concerns about terrorism are ingrained not merely within the definitions of *violence, murder, intimidation, coercion, fear*, and *exploitation*, but also in the mind-set of the extremists who will commit these crimes against humanity. In the past decade extremist groups have been increasingly interested in widening the level of destruction and fear.[3] Further, terrorists are seemingly considering a broader range of soft targets and using a broader range of tactics that are very difficult to locate, preempt, or contain. Complicating matters are two distinct variants: copycat terrorists who attempt to emulate more well-known terrorist activities and homegrown terrorists operating domestically.

The Use of Citizen Groups in Counterterrorism Strategy

In any counterterrorism strategy, it is important to use all of the tools at one's disposal. Even then, we may not have enough of the right kind of tools. Perhaps this is what former DHS secretary Michael Chertoff meant when he suggested in his book *Homeland Security* that sometimes new tools will need to be invented. Our homeland security strategy must be developed considering a holistic approach. For example, we know that terrorists work hard to understand our culture, laws, technology, and economic and financial systems. They understand physics, chemistry, psychology, sociology, unconventional military tactics, and the use of intelligence, and they can bring these disciplines together in their quest to destroy our society. Terrorists are patient and will slowly bleed our economy and financial systems, influence our government to focus on security instead of good domestic and international policy, weaken our public confidence in our government's ability to protect us, and attempt to force our citizens to live without the full spectrum of freedom. They will focus their main effort on destroying the very fabric of our democratic society.

A holistic approach to counterterrorism strategy should include partnerships among civilian, community, and federal entities. Building, resourcing, and training these partnerships will allow us to use all our resources in the most economical and practical manner possible. The use of community policing is already well established in both practice and the criminal justice and law enforcement literatures. Citizen groups and organizations can work hand in hand with local and federal law enforcement officials as well as private and public safety officers to identify terrorist tactics and techniques. To enhance the impact community groups can have, they must have training in risk analysis and a thorough understanding of what makes some targets attractive, such as schools, cyberspace, sporting events, and entertainment venues, and what the vulnerabilities are in the structures and processes that are critical to our economy.

Red Teams as a Function of Counterterrorism Tactics

Sun Tzu posits, "The general who wins a battle makes many calculations in his temple before the battle is fought. Without such diligence, the battle will surely be lost."[4] Complacency can result in serious consequences when dealing with an enemy that is bent on destroying the very fabric of a society. As such, it is prudent to be as proactive as possible in both counterterrorism strategy and counterterrorism tactics. You must know the enemy and, thus, better understand your own capabilities and countermeasures.[5] "As a time-proven concept used in U.S. government and commercial enterprises, 'red teaming' deepens the understanding of options that are available to counter adaptive adversaries."[6]

The *red team* concept requires us to adopt the mind-set and be able to emulate the thoughts and aspirations of potential terrorists. Red teaming will force public safety officials and communities to think and prepare before the threat materializes into harm. We analyze their tactics, techniques, case studies, and culture. We analyze our target environment. We identify the key threats, weigh their probability and criticality, and then develop viable countermeasures and contingency plans. The success of this effort develops confidence within the public, because we are developing countermeasures before an attack occurs, thus increasing the probability of preventing, deterring, and mitigating an attack.[7]

Red teams can be assembled at any level of government or community. They can include highly financed professional teams, local volunteers, police officers, military units, fire departments, professors and teachers, informed citizens, and public officials. To enhance creativity, red team members are encouraged to think *outside the box*. The rule is: nothing is too *out of the ordinary*. The Christmas Day bomber is a good example of how terrorists think unconventionally. Umar Farouk Abdulmutallab attempted to detonate a unique blend of explosives sewn into his underwear. A top al-Qaeda explosives expert in Yemen, where Abdulmutallab received the explosive materials and detonation instructions, constructed the underwear bomb (but chose not to wear it himself). Abdulmutallab boarded Northwest Airlines Flight 253 to Detroit with eighty grams of PETN sewn into his underwear. PETN is an ingredient of another highly explosive chemical, Semtex, which is undetectable by airport scanners and metal detectors. The inexperience of the bomber resulted in a failed attempt to properly inject the trigger fluid into the PETN powder. The package containing the PETN ignited, burned Umar's legs, and resulted in a fire on the aircraft. The courage and quick reaction of passengers and crew quickly contained the situation.[8]

Risk Analysis as a Function of Counterterrorism Tactics

The same local group of volunteers consolidated for the red team's work could serve as the team that develops one of the most important activities to countering terrorist attacks, that is, *risk analysis*. Risk analysis is the foundation for any good counterterrorism plan. Risk analysis is a management method for identifying and evaluating the potential risks to the safety and security of people, property, or the environment.[9] A risk analysis is accomplished using a variety of subjective and objective measures.[10] It should be completed in any environment where safety and security are concerns: schools, public buildings, malls, theaters, rail yards, police stations, military installations, bus stations, and any other potential targets. As Secretary Chertoff pointed out, "Responding to disasters after they occur is not risk management; it is compensating for the adverse consequences of risk mismanagement."[11] Risk analysis necessarily includes the following steps: threat assessment, risk assessment, determination and implementation of threat-specific countermeasures, and contingency plans. Each of these steps is described below.

Step 1. Threat Assessment

The first step in the risk-analysis process is threat assessment, which involves determining (identifying) and characterizing the various hazards—natural, technological, or man-made—that can inflict harm on the asset needing protection, such as the public, infrastructure, or property. Threat assessment results in an inventory of threats and hazards considered willing or able to cause harm.[12] A preliminary inventory of threats or hazards can be developed based on the analysis by a red team or a local security committee consisting of well-informed and experienced volunteers or paid security consultants. Intelligence reports, historical facts, case studies of attacks, demographics, criminal records, budgets, and the local political culture can all have an impact on the threat list. These potential threats should be further elucidated using intense research, analysis, and dialogue among the team.

Step 2. Risk Assessment

Risk assessment consists of two separate categories: (1) the probability that the threat will take place and (2) the criticality or the extent of the impact in terms of physical or emotional damages, monetary value, human cost, or social marginal cost. Once an inventory of credible threats or hazards is completed, a quasi-scientific selection process is used to rank them on the pretense of the all-hazards approach. This ranking includes the assignment of two separate weighted values (such as 1 to 10) applied to each threat based on the presumed likelihood of occurrence and the criticality of the damage created were the threat to come to fruition. *Damage* can mean loss of market share, economic loss, loss of life, property or environmental damage, loss of function, and more. For example, a higher-value weight indicates a greater predictive likelihood of the threat occurring or a higher criticality. The product of the likelihood and criticality is calculated for each threat, and a rank-ordered list is made, with the highest value indicating the "worst" threat facing the organization. The risk-analysis team determines the weighted values for the threats, and they transform their subjective assessment into a numerical value.[13] For example, to determine both likelihood and criticality weights, the team can use historical case studies (such as the Oklahoma City bombing), insurance records, and criminal records on terrorist incidents, plots, and alleged plots.[14] Impact can be assessed in dollars lost, estimates to infrastructure damage, social marginal cost, psychological damage, and cost in human life.[15] Once the risk analysis and rank order have been determined, then the third step in the process, developing countermeasures, can begin.

Step 3. Determination and Implementation of Countermeasures

A countermeasure is an action or practice implemented to prevent a threat from occurring or reduce the probability of the threat unfolding.[16] It is defensive in nature and is a form of antiterrorism. Its primary purpose is to prevent the threat from reaching its climax. For example, a sound community-policing program could result in the community residents sharing information about the location of a garage that is being used to construct improvised explosive devices. This countermeasure could also result in the prevention of planting the explosive and result in an arrest and more useful intelligence.

Countermeasures can take many forms and fall under several categories. Basic security has three categories or facets that "must be considered."[17] The first facet includes physical security. Physical security focuses on hardening the target of opportunity, such as a school, chemical plant, or federal building. Countermeasures could include cameras, barricades, armed guards, or fencing. The second facet is operational security. Operational security focuses on preventing terrorists from obtaining information on the regular activities of people or operations in the target area. The third facet is personnel security, which places the responsibility of security on the employees and management. This requires extensive training in various techniques, such as identifying intelligence-gathering techniques, computer security, understanding operations security, denial of information, vigilance, and reporting procedures.[18] Any sound countermeasure plan within a risk analysis, at a minimum, must consider these facets of security.

Step 4. Contingency Plans

Contingency plans typically go into action when your countermeasures fail. If a terrorist had been successful in setting off the vehicle bomb at the tree-lighting ceremony in Portland, Oregon, what would the reaction plan have been? Although a contingency plan seems to be reactive in nature, a good plan could serve as a deterrent to a terrorist's attacks. Terrorists typically like to hit soft, unprepared targets. This creates more fear and chaos. In the homeland security arena, everybody's vigilance and role are important. Contingency planning should become a part of our daily lives; therefore, we should also consider risk analysis and contingency planning "on a smaller scale."[19] For example, the US Coast Guard develops its own comprehensive area contingency plan (ACP). The ACP defines the roles, responsibilities, resources, and procedures necessary to respond to a variety of terrorist attacks.[20] The basic substance of a contingency plan should involve key players such as police, firefighters, emergency medical personnel, community leadership, public health officials, medical and air medical evacuation, air support for supplies, CBRNE support, engineers, search-and-rescue experts, federal agencies, state agencies, military units, public affairs officials, the US Coast Guard, and public works officials. The key players will depend on the nature and location of the incident. Developing a contingency for a specific threat can be a very detailed process and can require a highly coordinated planning committee, professional consultants, or local public officials and citizens. Regardless of the size of the team and the detail of the plan, it must include intense training, rehearsals, and evaluated exercises.

Community-Oriented Policing as a Counterterrorism Tactic

DHS secretary Janet Napolitano stated that the most effective strategy to counter terrorism is through community-oriented policing and empowering individual citizens.[21] Former secretary Michael Chertoff stated, "We must use every tool in the security toolbox, and in the coming years we will have to invent a few tools that do not yet exist."[22] Defending our homeland requires the efforts and involvement of all citizens and public safety organizations. Working as coordinated security teams, our public safety professionals along with the communities they serve can produce the synergistic effect that is critical for safeguarding our communities. "Community policing is both a philosophy and a culture based on shared police and community values." Partnerships are developed with the common goal of problem solving and safety. It is critical for police and communities to collaborate to identify problems and develop courses of action to prevent these problems from escalating. Community policing empowers communities to take responsibility for their own backyards in conjunction with police resources.[23]

Intelligence-Oriented Policing as a Counterterrorism Tactic

Incorporated within the concept of community-oriented policing should be intelligence-oriented policing. This is the "application of preventative measures" that includes working with the communities to prevent criminal or terrorist activity.[24] "The gathering, processing, reporting, analyzing, and sharing of suspicious activity is critical to preventing crimes, including those associated with domestic and international terrorism." Intelligence-oriented policing includes the use of intelligence on both covert and overt terrorist activity.[25] "Effective intelligence operations can be applied equally well to terrorist threats and crimes in the community; homeland security and local crime prevention are not mutually exclusive. Officers on the beat are an excellent resource for gathering information on all kinds of potential threats and vulnerabilities."[26] The citizens who live and work in the area communities are also an excellent resource for gathering information. In fact, the citizenry is sometimes in a better position to observe, collect, and report information than law enforcement agencies. Citizens are more intimately in tune with local customs, rhythms, and the dynamics of daily business and basic behavior within their businesses, communities, and social functions. Citizens are inherently "undercover" and may even find themselves interacting with the terrorists, whereas terrorists will avoid the uniformed police at all costs. Given the large number of citizens relative to law enforcement, citizens have a much higher probability of being in the right place at the right time to observe an opportunity and to collect information that could be turned into intelligence. The following are examples of observations that could be useful intelligence:

- Terrorists conduct extensive reconnaissance operations. They conduct dry runs or reduced-force rehearsals.[27]
- Terrorists will attempt to make unusual purchases, such as large amounts of market materials, pool chemicals, peroxide, fuel, fertilizer, firing circuit devices such as toggle switches, batteries, gunpowder, PVC pipe, and fifty-five-gallon drums; rent trucks and vans; or attempt to acquire work uniforms of trades or professions without a purpose or documentation. They will attempt to acquire *official-appearing vehicles*, such as emergency or government vehicles.
- Terrorists will solicit information through friendly conversations. Questions could focus on operational security information, plant hours of operation, shift changes, times school buses drop off students, number of security personnel, and so on.
- Terrorists will leave packages, suitcases, backpacks, bags, or a boxes in a high-traffic area such as an airport or subway and then briskly or casually walk away.
- Terrorists will leave a vehicle in a secured or restricted location or a highly trafficked area such as a government building, concert, school, airport, or sporting event.
- Terrorists will attempt to stockpile large amounts of cash or make unusual monetary transactions at the bank.

There are various forms of information that could be transformed into useful intelligence. For example, *criminal intelligence* is information collected and analyzed for the purpose of preventing more general terrorist activity. In contrast, *tactical intelligence* is information pertaining to a specific terrorist event and can be used immediately by operators to plan for tactical operations.[28]

Educating and Special Training for the Public as a Counterterrorism Tactic

One of the most powerful tools in our toolbox is the individual person who lives and works in the community. This includes business owners, store managers, public works employees, clergy, teachers, senior citizens, students, and workers in professional organizations; anyone who is a legitimate member of the community is important. As former chairman of the 9/11 Commission Thomas Kean points out, "Community vigilance is critical. Terrorists come from all walks of life, even from within our communities. Terrorist leadership is becoming Americanized or simply home-grown: American born, heading overseas for training and coming back to the states to kill us. It is the citizens, their neighbors, who will ultimately have the best chance of discovering the preparation phase or the execution phase of the attack, and we must depend on them to tell police."[29]

However, information gathering and reporting are two pieces of a larger and more comprehensive plan that must be in place to adequately provide security and response to any terrorist attack. It is likely that the first persons on the scene of an attack would be members of the community, such as meter readers, public works crews, or mail carriers. Since they would be the actual *first responders*, they are in a position to take appropriate action to assist officials once they arrive. However, citizens need to understand "scene awareness and scene control" and be prepared to assist the professional first-responder personnel with information- and performance-oriented tasks, such as applying first aid, carrying wounded, making phone calls to 911, or guiding emergency vehicles and traffic. As Hillyard points out, "A knowledgeable, trained citizenry will be much more capable of controlling emotions and actively becoming part of the solution instead of passively being part of the problem—a response instrument instead of a helpless target."[30]

Before any viable community-policing program for homeland security can be developed and integrated into the community, several milestones must be reached. First, there must be support from the community leadership. The leadership within the local government must be involved—mayor; council;

business leaders; legal counsel; school leadership; public safety leaders such as the sheriff, police chief, fire chief, and emergency management chief; academics from colleges; public works leaders; and citizens with special qualifications. Second, there must be support from the community—citizens at large. Everyone must know about the policing program, how it works, and what their role in it entails. Citizens must also be rehearsed and tested in the program. This could be very time-consuming and labor-intensive, but is absolutely critical to the success of the program. The best-intended program in the world is useless if it is not implemented and executed well.

Several forms of rehearsals or practice are possible. For example, practice might include "table top exercises"[31] involving the primary management team, that is, reduced-force rehearsals or exercises involving certain primary elements such as law enforcement and the crisis negotiating team, emergency management services, and fire and rescue, with well-planned and realistic scenarios with role players. Consider the annual training event known as the Mock Disaster, held in Moundsville, West Virginia.[32] This event welcomes agencies from all over the world to participate. It is a medium-scale, well-planned, and well-resourced event and can serve as an excellent training opportunity and model for any local community program. Implementing these types of exercises and, when possible, involving all players in these events build the trust, team confidence, experience, self-confidence, self-esteem, camaraderie, competency, and morale needed for a good security program to survive and be effective.

Education and Special Training for Public Safety Officers

Public safety officers are often on the front lines of protecting the community from threats. These frontline officers must have regular special tactical training and equipment, just as special operations, military police, or SWAT officers receive, with "consideration given to the [front]line officer's education, training, skills, capabilities, and equipment."[33] Every patrol shift should be a quick-reaction force capable of effectively engaging, containing, and eliminating organized hostile attacks as soon as possible. For example, when an attack is initiated, the closest patrol vehicle in the sector can respond almost immediately. These officers will have the education, training, and equipment to successfully engage the perpetrator, including body armor, a Kevlar helmet, personal protection equipment, and weapons stored in the patrol vehicle.

Conclusion

Renowned terrorism expert Bruce Hoffman wrote, "Al-Qaeda's newfound vitality is the product of a fresh strategy that plays to its networking strength and compensates for its numerical weakness. In contrast to its plan on Sept. 11, which was to deliver a knock-out blow to the United States, al-Qaeda's leadership has now adopted a 'death by a thousand cuts' strategy."[34] This new al-Qaeda strategy is to empower and motivate individuals to commit acts of violence entirely outside any terrorist chain of command. Hatred and ideology, a psychological tie to al-Qaeda, and extremism influence American jihadists and extremists without their being an official part of a group. "The emergence of these self-generated violent Islamist extremists who are radicalized online presents a challenge," the report concluded, "because lone wolves are less likely to come to the attention of law enforcement." That is, "At least until they start shooting."[35]

Our homeland security strategy must be developed considering a holistic approach. Terrorists understand how to "level the playing field." They understand our culture, our laws, our technology, our economic and financial systems, physics, chemistry, psychology, sociology, unconventional military tactics, and the use of intelligence, and they can bring these disciplines together in their quest to destroy our societal values and institutions. Terrorists bring a new form of warfare that has advanced to the point of being nearly impossible to prevent. Using a holistic counterterrorism strategy that includes a well-educated and -trained and engaged citizenry, we will be better able to prevent violence and tragedies before they occur.

NOTES

1. Cindy C. Combs, *Terrorism in the Twenty-First Century*, 6th ed. (New York: Longman, 2011), 18.

2. Ibid., 12.

3. Mark A. Sauter and James Jay Carafano, *Homeland Security* (New York: McGraw-Hill, 2005), 80.

4. Caleb Bartley, "The Art of Terrorism: What Sun Tzu Can Teach Us About International Terrorism" *Comparative Strategy* 24, no. 3 (2005): 237–251.

5. Gerald Michaelson, *Sun Tzu for Success: How to Use the Art of War to Master Challenges and Accomplish the Important Goals in Your Life* (Avon, MA: Adams Media, 2003), 50–51.

6. Department of Defense, Defense Science Board, *Defense Science Board Task Force on the Role and Status of DOD Red Teaming Activities* (Washington, DC: Office of the Under

Secretary of Defense for Acquisition, Technology, and Logistics, September 2003), 1, 15, 16, appx. 1.

7. US Army Training and Doctrine Command, Deputy Chief of Staff for Intelligence, Assistant Deputy Chief of Staff for Intelligence—Threats, *Terror Operations: Case Studies in Terrorism*, DCSINT Handbook No. 1.0115 (Fort Leavenworth, KS: US Army Training and Doctrine Command, Deputy Chief of Staff for Intelligence, August 2005). See http://www.dtic.mil/cgi-bin/GetTRDoc?Location=U2&doc=GetTRDoc.pdf&AD=AD A456281.

8. "Indictment in *U.S. v. Abdulmutallab*," CBS News, January 6, 2010.

9. P. J. Ortmeier, *Introductions to Security Operations and Management*, 3rd ed. (Upper Saddle River, NJ: Prentice-Hall, 2009), 180.

10. Ibid., 95.

11. Michael Chertoff, *Homeland Security: Assessing the First Five Years* (Philadelphia: University of Pennsylvania Press, 2009), 125.

12. Mary Clifford, *Identifying and Exploring Security Essentials* (Upper Saddle River, NJ: Prentice-Hall, 2004), 75.

13. Robert J. Fischer and Gion Green, *Introduction to Security*, 7th ed. (New York: Elsevier, 2004), 139.

14. Ernest Sternberg, "The Urban Region as Locus of Security Problems," *Journal of Applied Security Research* 3, no. 1 (2007): 18–19.

15. Karen M. Hess and Henry M. Wrobleski, *Introduction to Private Security*, 4th ed. (St. Paul, MN: West Publishing, 1996), 429.

16. Clifford, *Identifying and Exploring Security Essentials*, 81.

17. Combs, *Terrorism in the Twenty-First Century*, 203.

18. Ibid., 205–206.

19. "Mind Tool, Contingency Planning, Developing a Good Plan B," accessed December 9, 2010, http://www.mindtools.com/pages/article/newLDR_51.htm.

20. US Department of Homeland Security and US Coast Guard, *Area Contingency Plan*, 2009, 14, https://homeport.uscg.mil/mycg/portal/ep/contentView.do?channelId= -18361&contentId=141921&programId=88121&programPage=%2Fep%2Fprogram%2 Feditorial.jsp&pageTypeId=13489&contentType=EDITORIAL&BV_SessionID=@@@ @0228286867.1316912378@@@@&BV_EngineID=cccdadfejkfejhecfjgcfgfdffhdghj.0.

21. Janet Napolitano, Department of Justice Assistance Conference, CSPAN-2, December 11, 2010.

22. Chertoff, *Homeland Security*, 54.

23. Edwin Meese III and P. J. Ortmeier, *Leadership* (Upper Saddle River, NJ: Prentice-Hall, 2009), 233–234.

24. Jerry H. Ratcliff, "No. 248, Intelligence Led Policing," *Australian Institute of Criminology* (April 2003): 2.

25. Bureau of Justice Assistance, US Department of Justice; Major Cities Chiefs Association; DOJ's Global Justice Information Sharing Initiative; Findings and Recommendations of the Suspicious Activity Report Support and Implementation Project, June 2008, 13, http://nsi.ncirc.gov/documents/SAR_Report_January_2009.pdf.

26. US Department of Justice, https://www.ncjrs.gov/pdffiles1/bja/210681.pdf.

27. "Arrested Chesapeake Bay Bridge Videographer on Terror Watch List," Free Republic, August 24, 2004, http://www.freerepublic.com/focus/f-news/1198393/posts.

28. Marilyn Peterson, *Intelligence Led Policing* (Washington, DC: U.S. Department of Justice, Office of Justice Programs, September 2005), 39, 40.

29. Governor Thomas Kean, "Terrorism and Future of US Foreign Policy," CSPAN-2, October 11, 2010.

30. Michael J. Hillyard, *Homeland Security and the Need for Change: Organizing Principles, Governing Institutions, and American Culture* (Chula Vista, CA: Aventine Press, 2003), 126–127.

31. Sauter and Carafano, *Homeland*, 343.

32. US Department of Justice, National Institute of Justice, National Law Enforcement, Corrections Training and Technology Center, "Mock Disaster," accessed December 23, 2010, http://www.ncjrs.gov/App/Publications/abstract.aspx?ID=233410.

33. Willard M. Oliver, *Homeland Security for Policing* (Upper Saddle River, NJ: Prentice-Hall, 2007), 170.

34. Hoffman, "Al-Qaeda Has a New Strategy. Obama Needs One, Too."

35. http://www.time.com/time/magazine/article/0,9171,1938698,00.html.

CHAPTER 14

Foundations of Homeland
Security Education

JOHN M. PERSYN and CHERYL J. POLSON

Most American adults vividly remember where they were on September 11, 2001, when they first learned of the attacks on the World Trade Center and the Pentagon. That event is imprinted in our memories, just as the assassination of President Kennedy and the attack on Pearl Harbor were for previous generations. Certainly, the terrorist attacks of 9/11 transformed our perspectives and shattered our paradigms about what it means to be secure in our homeland. For millions of Americans, other events have had a similar impact. In 1995 residents of Oklahoma City were shaken by the bombing of the Alfred P. Murrah Federal Building. Until September 2001, the Oklahoma City bombing had been the most destructive terrorist attack on US soil (A&E Television Networks n.d.). For Gulf Coast residents, memories of Hurricanes Katrina and Rita in 2005 may very well overshadow their 9/11 memories. In 2007 natural disasters across the country indelibly marked the memories of other Americans. In Greensburg, Kansas, a 1.7-mile-wide EF-5 tornado cut a swath of annihilation through the landscape of Kansas and the lives of its residents. In California wildfires displaced more than 300,000 persons, destroying nearly 1,700 homes and causing more than $120 million in property damage. Across Alabama, Arkansas, Kentucky, Mississippi, and Tennessee, devastating storms spawned more than 100 tornadoes in a single day, killing more than 50 innocent victims (US Congress 2008). In April 2011, the widespread devastating storm scenario was eerily replayed as the single-day total again reached more than 100 tornadoes and shattered the previous record of 267 tornadoes in a single month with a new record, nearly 300. In this latest demonstration of nature's fury, more than 350 people in seven states were killed by tornadoes and flash floods caused by severe thunderstorms that spanned the country from Texas to New York (Reuters 2011). On the heels of these devastating thunderstorms came widespread flooding all along the 5,000-mile length of the Mississippi River, surpassing record levels set in 1927. Thousands of citizens were displaced from their homes, as levees were deliberately breached to protect the lives of millions more in population centers (Neuman 2011).

Combined, the events described above have directly and personally impacted millions of victims, emergency responders, community managers, and support personnel from the local areas and surrounding regions. Yet these are merely recent examples of the potentially life-destroying events that threaten Americans. Older adults will also remember the Loma Prieta Earthquake that rocked San Francisco in 1989, or Hurricane Andrew overwhelming Florida in 1992, or the Northridge Earthquake that struck Los Angeles in 1994. Earlier generations faced their own devastating disasters. In terms of lives lost, the 1900 Galveston Hurricane and the 1928 Okeechobee Hurricane both far exceeded the death toll of Hurricane Katrina, with an estimated 8,000 and 2,000 deaths, respectively (National Hurricane Center n.d.); in 1925 the single Tri-State Tornado caused nearly 700 deaths (National Weather Service n.d.), twice the total for the hundreds of tornadoes in the devastating storms of 2007 and 2011 combined. During the Great Flood of 1927, more 130,000 homes were lost and 700,000 people were displaced, far more than in 2011, despite the higher river levels and vastly greater populations in 2011. Sadly, it seems that virtually all Americans have been, or eventually will be, directly touched by a catastrophic event at some point in their lives. Homeland security and emergency management are relevant to us all on a very personal level. But, as these examples also show, effective planning, preparation, and response have helped to mitigate the loss of life in the more recent situations, despite their similarities in magnitude and scope with earlier examples. Effective homeland security and emergency management by skilled, educated, and well-trained professionals save lives and money.

This observation raises some questions: What constitutes homeland security education? What specific skills and capabilities do you need? What education is required to develop these fundamental skills? In short, what do you need to know as a future homeland security professional, or, if you are already in the field, what knowledge exists that can enhance your preparedness? For the past decade, these questions have guided efforts to improve the quality and value of homeland security education programs. Indeed, such has been the focus of this textbook. This chapter provides an overview of the fundamental knowledge areas and skills that every homeland security professional should possess and that previous chapters covered in greater detail.

A Brief History of Homeland Security Education

The Homeland Security Educational Landscape in September 2001

In 2002 David McIntyre critiqued the homeland security education landscape that existed in the early days following the attacks of 9/11: "There is no nationally recognized program of higher education at all. In fact, there is no generally accepted curriculum for homeland security, because there is no generally accepted body of knowledge upon which to base an academic discipline" (3). McIntyre describes a homeland security educational process that was still very much in its infancy in 2002, born out of the sudden national awareness of its importance. But the conception of what was required to improve homeland security education had actually already begun. Even before the 9/11 attacks, the Office for Domestic Preparedness was examining whether existing training programs were meeting the needs of the various jurisdictions within the US Department of Justice. In August 2001, during the course of developing the ODP Training Strategy, a collaborative team of subject-matter experts, trainers, educators, and strategic planners identified key gaps in existing training programs (Center for Homeland Defense and Security 2009a). The team recommended that those gaps be filled by adopting an educational approach in some areas—specifically, those involving the more complex upper-level leadership challenges requiring critical thinking and problem-solving approaches. The 9/11 attacks just a month later provided momentum to the ODP recommendations, and in April 2002, with the support of Congress, the US Department of Justice and the US Department of Defense signed an interagency agreement to establish the Center for Homeland Defense and

Security (CHDS) at the Naval Postgraduate School in Monterey, California. The center immediately began development of the first post-9/11 homeland security higher-education program—a graduate program designed around policy, practice, and program needs identified through empirical research (Center for Homeland Defense and Security 2009a).

Despite the success of the CHDS graduate program, as a federally provided program, it is available only to government officials at the federal, state, or local level and is not open to attendees representing the private sector. Because some private-sector industries represent an important component of critical infrastructure, their vulnerability to deliberate attacks or unintentional accidents could pose a serious threat to our security. But with limited numbers of accessible academic programs, the educational needs were largely unmet for homeland security professionals working in key private-sector industries, including civilian nuclear power, chemicals and hazardous materials (including oil and natural gas), electricity service, and food and agriculture (Congressional Budget Office 2004). These educational gaps would need to be filled by other institutions. In response, colleges and universities around the country have rallied to fill this void, albeit without much guidance or any consensus as to what their curricula should contain.

Nearly a decade after those first wobbly steps, homeland security higher education has matured significantly. National emphasis on homeland security has soared, resulting in the creation of hundreds of homeland security higher-education programs at the community-college and four-year undergraduate levels, as well as graduate certificate and degree programs for homeland security professionals. In 2007 the Homeland Security Education Survey Project reported that there were 215 homeland security–related degree and certificate programs (Rollins and Rowan 2007a, 2007b). By January 2011 that number had grown significantly, as evidenced by the 334 graduate and undergraduate programs listed on the website of the CHDS partner institutions (Center for Homeland Defense and Security n.d.). Without the benefit of governance structures such as specialized accreditation, several scholarly studies attempted to articulate what should and should not be in an HS curriculum. Examples include the Kansas State study (Polson, Persyn, and Cupp 2010), the Embry-Riddle Aeronautical University Study (Ramsay, Cutrer, and Raffel 2010), the Winegar study (Winegar 2008), and the Workshop on National Needs study (Texas A&M University, Integrative Center for Homeland Security 2007).

Relationship with Emergency Management, Public Administration, and Other Related Areas

As recent experiences in all types of disasters have highlighted, catastrophic events require the collective and integrated efforts of all members of the homeland security team, including public officials at every level, emergency managers and responders, and law enforcement. Effective integration of these diverse and often disparate elements demands that they have common and synchronized communications systems and procedures and that they have a shared understanding of the roles and responsibilities of the numerous participants in the response and recovery from such disasters. McCreight highlights the challenge of meeting the expectations of both homeland security and emergency management camps:

> Probably the first of several issues deserving attention, and one of the most intriguing aspects of the educational challenge to be addressed, entails the reconciliation of homeland security and emergency management itself. One topic focuses heavily on terrorism preparedness and prevention, while the other aims to build skills in addressing the "all-hazards" spectrum of emergencies. In an educational program finding ways to bridge these differences is not easy. The initial task, therefore, is to build a curriculum that does its best to accomplish this without sacrificing the integrity of either approach. Splitting attention between these two different policy and managerial challenges in a coherent curriculum with appropriate course design and content is not easy. There is also a genuine risk the curriculum itself will tilt towards the emergency management set of issues and downplay terrorism preparedness subjects, acknowledging a belief that local emergency managers can get whatever supplementary training on these issues they desire from periodic online programs. (2009)

The Growing Emphasis on Education as a Means to Mitigate Future Threats

Through the years, various authors and organizations have sought to define the desired focus of educational programs relating to homeland security. From the content areas proposed by McIntyre to the 2009 CHDS Model Curriculum Conference (discussed below), authors and organizations have sought to definitively answer this question: *What do students in homeland security education programs need to know in order to be prepared to plan or prepare for and to respond effectively to homeland security incidents when necessary?*

McCreight notes the difficulty of finding common ground among the diverse disciplines that are homeland security:

> The question of meeting student needs and fulfilling career-relevant demands merits paramount attention. However, building a boundary-spanning interdisciplinary educational strategy remains an alien concept, and it arguably has become the victim of benign neglect. As an example, most of our graduate schools offering MBAs still offer a periodic course on "Business Continuity" as an elective, and you will find few, if any, schools of public health dealing with the subject of pandemics and mass casualty management. Even many schools of public policy still regard emergency management or homeland security courses as distantly relevant, unsure of where such programs that emphasize contingency thinking and strategic analysis ought to fit. (2009)

In part, the difficulty in defining a universal set of common standards stems from the lack of a shared understanding about what homeland security is and from parochial views about what is most important within the broadly defined field. Viewpoints are as wide as the field itself. Yet, despite the difficulty, McCreight (2009) asserts that practitioners, scholars, and related professionals should work together to define the fundamental topic areas that should be part of undergraduate and graduate programs. Such defining events as the 9/11 attacks, Hurricane Katrina, and other significant national challenges have also served to unify the diverse homeland security disciplines as they strive toward a common and noble goal of protecting the homeland. With that shared vision, the collective homeland security community has made significant progress toward defining a universal set of common standards.

CHDS Model Curriculum Conference, 2009

The preceding review has described diverse viewpoints and varied influences that have shaped efforts to define what students in homeland security education programs need to know and what common academic areas are required to provide that knowledge. Certainly, the diverse interests and needs within the homeland security field present a challenge to establish a "one-size-fits-all" set of standards that all programs might include. Nevertheless, common themes have emerged that provide a good starting point as the core academic foundation for homeland security–related programs. Recently, these common and recurrent themes have been consolidated by a group seeking to define a model curriculum for undergraduate homeland security programs.

In June 2009, selected members of the CHDS University and Agency Partnership Initiative met to seek consensus regarding the essential elements that should be included in homeland security undergraduate certificate and degree programs (Center for Homeland Defense and Security 2009b). At this CHDS Model Curriculum Conference, a concentrated effort was made to examine undergraduate curricula and to establish a baseline for what all programs should include if new and current homeland security practitioners were going to be prepared for the often complex and overlapping components of the homeland security profession. What follows are the areas that the homeland security community has decided might constitute a comprehensive homeland security curriculum.

The Eleven Areas of Focus

The conference members collaborated to produce the main academic focus areas as recommendations for institutions considering development of homeland security undergraduate degree programs—but fell short of actually developing consensus on student learning outcomes or learning levels for each outcome (Center for Homeland Defense and Security 2009b). The following are the eleven main focus areas determined in the Model Curriculum Conference as well as the subtopics that were recommended to be covered in an HS program:

1. Administering Homeland Security
   - leadership and management: definitions, differences, and application (case studies)
   - homeland security financial aspects: budgets, planning, and grants
   - homeland security logistics
   - human resources and personnel management
   - organizational behavior
   - public administration in homeland security
   - current homeland security policy mechanisms

2. Intelligence
   - Intelligence Community history and evolution
   - Intelligence Community current structure and capabilities
   - state and local intelligence capabilities
   - the intelligence cycle
   - counterintelligence
   - covert or clandestine activities
   - policing and actionable intelligence

3. Public- and Private-Sector Partnerships
   - private-sector role in homeland security
   - public-private partnerships
   - private-sector motivations
   - business continuity and resilience
   - public relations and public education
   - private-sector role in planning
   - public- versus private-sector organizational functions

4. Research and Analysis
   - information literacy, collection, and management
   - theory awareness and application
   - inductive and deductive reasoning
   - applied statistics
   - spatial analysis and geographic information systems
   - evaluation research
   - quantitative and qualitative analyses

5. Emergency Management
   - all-hazards approach: natural and unintentional human caused
   - definitions of important terms: *emergency, catastrophe, disaster, hazards, threats, prevention, mitigation, preparedness, response, recovery, continuity of operations and government, delegation, accountability,* and *communications*
   - types and history of hazards (natural and human caused)
   - land-use planning and resilient community design
   - developing preparedness and instilling resilience
   - risk and its components: hazards, threats, vulnerabilities, consequences, and probability

  - conduct risk assessments using a variety of methods
  - apply risk-management perspectives in the context of federal, state, local, and private-sector applications
- special and vulnerable population needs (homeless, disabled, pets, and others)
- exercise and evaluation programs
- employing technology (e.g., geographic information systems, communications, remote sensing, other)
- budgeting, grants, and management

6. Critical Infrastructure (and Its Protection)
   - critical infrastructure (CI) and key resources (KR) and interdependencies
   - strategies, policies, programs, and agencies involved in CI/KR
   - critical components in CI/KR within a context (local, state, federal, national, or business sector)
   - global security threats and hazards impacting CI components
   - required performance or level of protection of CI/KR in prevention, mitigation, response, and recovery to security threats and natural or human-caused hazards
   - organizational, engineering, procedural, security, and response methods to achieve levels of protection
   - scalable assessment methodologies for micro- and macrolevel risk at all levels
   - financial and operational relationships between critical infrastructure protection and business

7. Strategic Planning
   - integrated planning systems
   - disaster planning models for local, state, federal, international, and private sectors
     - risk-based and scenario-based planning
     - deliberate and crisis-action planning
   - interagency and interorganizational coordination and planning
   - ties to the grant process (leveraging resources)
   - National Incident Management System, Incident Command System, National Infrastructure Protection Plan, and National Response Framework

8. Strategic Communications
   - risk communication
   - cultural awareness and audience identification
   - communication planning and synchronization of messages
   - interoperability of messaging and strategies
   - role of the media
   - agencies and organizations (local, tribal, state, federal, and international)
   - public affairs, education, emergency communication
   - means and technology issues and challenges
   - community outreach

9. Law and Policy
   - society and civics
   - constitutional law, principles, and federalism
   - current government agencies, private agencies, and organizational structures
   - major statutes, executive directives, and orders
   - national strategies
   - regional, state, and local policies and strategies
   - international treaties, obligations, and cooperative efforts
   - sector-specific laws and authorities
   - civil-military relations
   - policy-making process and analysis
   - administrative law and regulatory processes

10. Technology and Systems
    - role of technology in homeland security
    - types of technology used in homeland security
    - approaches to framing technology
    - ethical and privacy considerations
    - technology development cycle
    - network and cyber infrastructure protection
    - consequences (unintended and intended)
    - limitations and interoperability

11. Terrorism: Causes and Consequences
    - definitions and distinctions

- history, root causes, motivations, grievances
- theories of who joins or supports terror groups (radicalization and extremism)
- how terror groups operate (tactics, organization, support)
- role of the media and Internet
- effects of terrorism
- counterterrorism (resources, application, policies), including military roles in counterterrorism

Supporting Areas and Themes

In addition to the focus areas considered to be critical to undergraduate homeland security programs, the CHDS Model Curriculum Conference attendees identified supporting themes that should be part of a program, whether or not they are discrete topics to be taught. These areas include such underlying concepts as ethics; the defense support of civil authorities; critical thinking; oral and written communications; a "whole of society" (Chertoff 2010) approach to policies, resources, and operations; and planning. The fact that these skills have been repeatedly cited as important for homeland security professionals suggests that these skills are particularly significant in the complex, ambiguous, and hazardous world of homeland security, where the consequences of ineffective communication can be disastrous or catastrophic.

Conclusion

Homeland security education has matured substantially in the past decade. This growth has been the result of thoughtful and deliberate efforts throughout the homeland security profession and educational community to ensure that educational programs are designed to help students learn what they need to be successful. As a result, homeland security professionals educated through the wide range of undergraduate programs currently available will be better prepared for the often complex and uncertain demands they will face in the future. Collectively, the programs, and the graduates they produce, have dramatically improved the nation's ability to prevent recurrences of 9/11-type events and to respond more effectively to catastrophic events—both natural and man-made, like those presented in the beginning of this chapter. Over the past six years, hundreds of graduate and undergraduate programs across the country have been constructed to provide the necessary educational foundation for homeland security professionals. Many of these have been built on the institutions' strengths and expertise in specific areas: public health, emergency management, law enforcement, and other areas. Thus, a wide variance of courses can be found within curricula. However, the past decade has also shown that, despite these variances across the spectrum of homeland security education programs, some common themes have also emerged that define a core undergraduate program. Sound academic programs integrate the identified core competencies discussed throughout this chapter and book while building upon their unique institutional strengths.

REFERENCES

A&E Television Networks. n.d. "Oklahoma City Bombing." http://www.history.com/topics/oklahoma-city-bombing.

Bellavita, Christopher, and Ellen M. Gordon. 2006. "Changing Homeland Security: Teaching the Core." *Homeland Security Affairs* 2, no. 1: article 1, 1–28.

Center for Homeland Defense and Security. 2009a. *Education: The Key to Homeland Security Leadership*. Monterey, CA: US Naval Postgraduate School, Center for Homeland Defense and Security.

———. 2009b. "Undergraduate Curriculum: Recommended Areas of Focus [PowerPoint Slides]." Paper presented at the University and Agency Partnership Initiative, Naval Postgraduate School, Monterey, CA, June 11–12.

———. n.d. "HSDEC Graduate Course Recommendations." University and Agency Partnership Initiative. https://www.chds.us/courses/course/view.php?id=322.

Chertoff, Michael. 2010. "Remarks." Delivered at the fourth annual Homeland Defense and Security Education Summit, George Washington University, Washington, DC.

Congressional Budget Office. 2004. "Homeland Security and the Private Sector." http://www.cbo.gov/ftpdocs/60xx/doc6042/12-20-HomelandSecurity.pdf.

Fugate, Craig. 2011. "Remarks." Delivered at the fifth annual Homeland Defense and Security Education Summit, University of Maryland University College, Adelphi.

Homeland Security Council. 2007. *National Strategy for Homeland Security*. Washington, DC: White House.

McCreight, Robert. 2009. "Educational Challenges in Homeland Security and Emergency Management." *Journal of Homeland Security and Emergency Management* 6, no. 1: article 34.

McIntyre, David H. 2002. "Education for Homeland Security: The Critical Need." *ETS News* (Winter).

National Commission on Terrorist Attacks upon the United States, Thomas H. Kean, and Lee Hamilton. 2004. *The 9/11 Commission Report: Final Report of the National Commission on Terrorist Attacks upon the United States*. New York: W. W. Norton.

National Hurricane Center. n.d. "Hurricane History." National Oceanic and Atmospheric Administration. http://www.nhc.noaa.gov/HAW2/english/history.shtml.

National Weather Service. n.d. "NOAA/NWS 1925 Tri-State Tornado Web Site." National Oceanic and Atmospheric Administration. http://www.crh.noaa.gov/pah/?n =1925_tor_ss.

Neuman, Scott. 2011. "High Water Doesn't Mark an End for Flood Victims." NPR, May 19. http://www.npr.org/2011/05/19/136464035/high-water-doesnt-mark-an-end-for -flood-victims?ps=cprs.

Oklahoma Department of Civil Emergency Management. 1995. *Alfred P. Murrah Federal Building Bombing, 19 April 1995 in Oklahoma City, Oklahoma*. Oklahoma City: Oklahoma Department of Civil Emergency Management.

Polson, Cheryl Jean, John Michael Persyn, and O. Shawn Cupp. 2010. "Partnership in Progress: A Model for Development of a Collaborative Homeland Protection Graduate Degree Program." *Homeland Security Affairs* 6, no. 2. https://www.hsaj.org/?article =6.2.3.

Ramsay, Jim, Daniel Cutrer, and Robert Raffel. 2010. "Development of an Outcomes-Based Undergraduate Curriculum in Homeland Security." *Homeland Security Affairs* 6, no. 2.

Reuters. 2011. "April Tornado Insured Losses $3.7–5.5 Billion: AIR." May 9. http://www .reuters.com/article/2011/05/09/us-usa-weather-losses-idUSTRE7484OU20110509.

Rollins, John, and Joseph Rowan. 2007a. *The Homeland Security Academic Environment: A Review of Current Activities and Issues for Consideration*. Fairfax, VA: Homeland Security and Defense Education Consortium.

———. 2007b. "Homeland Security Education Survey Project. [PowerPoint Slides]." Paper presented at the spring 2007 symposium "NPS/HSDEC/DHS Education Summit," Fairfax, VA, February 27–28.

Texas A&M University, Integrative Center for Homeland Security. 2007. *Workshop on National Needs: What Employers Want from Graduate Education in Homeland Security*. After-Action Report, Homeland Security and Defense Education Consortium and Texas A&M University, College Station.

US Congress, Senate, Ad Hoc Subcommittee on Disaster Recovery of the Committee on Homeland Security and Governmental Affairs. 2008. "Major Disaster Recovery: Assessing FEMA's Performance Since Katrina." 110th Cong., 2nd sess., July 17.

US Northern Command. n.d. "About USNORTHCOM." US Northern Command. http://www.northcom.mil/about/history_education/history.html.

Winegar, Scott. 2008. "Developing the Bench: Building an Effective Homeland Security Undergraduate Program." Master's thesis, Naval Postgraduate School.

Epilogue

JAMES D. RAMSAY

Since the terror attacks on September 11, 2001, and the subsequent formation of the US Department of Homeland Security in 2003, the field of homeland security has continued to evolve in a fascinating mix of politics, policy, strategy, and tactics. As a social and economic function of the federal government, homeland security is a complex, dynamic, and often value-laden enterprise that requires the joint tasking of dozens—if not hundreds—of players, including federal, state, local, and tribal governmental agencies; nongovernmental organizations; private industry; members of the local, state, and federal law enforcement community; and community-based organizations. In addition, there have been dozens of laws and regulations brought to bear on how homeland security activities are to be organized and carried out. Together, such laws and regulations and all the agencies and organizations strive to work together in order to achieve a common set of missions; that is, they all strive to maintain law and order, to protect civil liberties, to assist the nation in preparation and recovery from natural disasters, and to safeguard the effective and efficient functioning of the infrastructures critical to our economy. This milieu of agencies, partnerships, organizations, and missions is collectively referred to as the "homeland security enterprise."

From the perspective of a student in homeland security, it is clear that the *enterprise* provides careers that embody the best aspects of a democracy, including the protection of life, liberty, property, and the preservation of the environment. Careers in homeland security also enable and support liberty and the pursuit of economic opportunity. However, as the threats facing our nation and the world continue to evolve, so must the nature and composition of the homeland security enterprise evolve. Accordingly, over the past ten years, we have witnessed changing national security strategies, shifts in the structure of the DHS, modified laws, the growth of hundreds of academic- and research-based programs, and, more recently, an emergent set of public-private partnerships that work at the local, state, and national levels. Altogether, these changes represent our collective national effort to secure the homeland from a wide variety of technological threats (aging power grids, roads, bridges, telecommunications networks, and the like), threats due to natural disasters (hurricanes, floods, tornadoes, earthquakes, tsunamis, wildfires, and so on), and threats due to terrorist states (e.g., Iran, North Korea, Syria),[1] foreign terrorist organizations (e.g., al-Qaeda, al-Shabaab, Basque Fatherland and Liberty [ETA], Abu Sayyaf Group, Hezbollah),[2] domestic terrorist groups (e.g., Animal Liberation Front, Christian Identity Movement, Aryan Nations, Ku Klux Klan, Weather Underground),[3] insurgent groups (e.g., the Taliban, Hamas, Irish Republican Army, Shining Path),[4] and individuals (e.g., Ayman al-Zahwahiri, Daniel San Diego, Saif al-Adel, Jamal Ahmed Mohammed Ali al-Badawi).[5]

From the mix of all that has transpired since September, 11, 2001, there are at least three main themes that have evolved in the practice of homeland security. First, the complexity of the threat environment begets constant change, which in turn requires policy makers and practitioners to work jointly across organizational and national lines and be nimble and adaptive. The second theme concerns the ascendancy of academic homeland security programs and their emerging role in the profession. The third theme is the relationship of homeland security to the health of the economy. Each theme is briefly introduced below.

Constant Change: The scope and breadth of this text have, we hope, demonstrated that homeland security is an exciting, complex, and dynamic enterprise where change is constant. Its practice requires constant vigilance, the need for agencies, organizations, and governments to be adaptive and to work seamlessly together, whether the objective is to track and contain domestic or transnational terrorists or to stabilize communities or nations struck by large-scale natural disasters. From the 2008–2013 *DHS Strategic Plan*, we learn the mission of the US Department of Homeland Security: "We will lead the unified national effort to secure America. We will prevent and deter terrorist attacks and protect against and respond to threats and hazards to the Nation. We will secure our national borders while welcoming lawful immigrants, visitors, and trade."[6]

Though this mission is logical and sensible, it is more complex in practice than one may initially think. For example, in the years following its formation, the US Department of Homeland Security experienced changes in its leadership, its organizational structure, and the mission set of organizations under the DHS, such as the Transportation Security Administration. These transformations have been the direct result of changing political philosophy about where the professional boundaries of HS begin and end and about what the HS enterprise should, and what it possibly should not, emphasize. For example, early on in its life cycle, the DHS under both Secretary Tom Ridge and Secretary Michael Chertoff emphasized counterterrorism. This was logical, given the events of 9/11. Later on, however, and as evidenced in the remarks made about the US critical infrastructure at the Brookings Institution,[7] Secretary Chertoff relayed that the United States simply cannot afford to protect all its assets all the time from all threats and that HS must be more centered on risk-management principles and be as interested in emergency preparedness as it is in counterterrorism—the so-called all-hazards approach. The damage of Hurricane Katrina showed quite plainly how failure to prepare for and confusion in responding to natural disasters can cause long-term damage to communities, states, and even the nation.

Clearly, how best to protect and secure America and its interests remains a complex question. Nowhere has this aspect of HS been more clearly seen than in the Global War on Terror generally and the pursuit of Osama bin Laden specifically. As a foreign terrorist organization, al-Qaeda operates as a loose affiliation of transnational, substate actors. This means that they have no national boundaries; they do not represent a government; cells of al-Qaeda tend to operate independently, making the traditional notion of negotiation almost impossible; and there is really no one to surrender in the classical sense. As the mastermind of the September 11, 2001, attacks (as well as several others), Bin Laden was considered public enemy number one over the past ten years. In the years since 9/11, counterterrorism experts agree that the al-Qaeda network has evolved significantly and has learned to function more independently from the direct influence of Bin Laden. So upon the death of Bin Laden, the policy question becomes how the United States and its allies should continue to prosecute the Global War on Terror in a world without him. So far, the answer seems to be "just as vigilantly as before." In other words, the presence or absence of Bin Laden does not change the fact that there are still many terrorist organizations both within the United States and outside the United States with a transnational capability, and there are still state sponsors of terrorism. For example, vocal offshoots of the original al-Qaeda network such as al-Qaeda in the Arabian Peninsula are striving to establish a global reputation, and the Taliban's influence in Afghanistan causes great turmoil in that nation's efforts to modernize and develop.

In some ways, the world of counterterrorism seems as complicated and deadly as ever. As incredibly symbolic to the West as the death of Bin Laden is, it remains quite clear that the struggle for peace, liberty, and human dignity continues in a world with a seemingly endless supply of evil organizations and groups. Consequently, not only do policy and strategy need to continue to evolve to match the changing threat environment, but so do the education and skill sets of homeland security professionals.

Academic Homeland Security Programs: Though still in its infancy, one might accurately describe the academic study of homeland security as a metadiscipline. For example, the study of homeland security combines the wisdom and talents of a variety of academic fields and professional expertise, including (at a minimum) emergency management, risk management, intelligence studies, law and policy studies, transportation and industrial security management, international relations, languages, political science, sociology, strategic studies, and public health and safety. In addition, academic homeland security embraces new and vivacious fields that are evolving in order to answer difficult questions about how best to keep America secure and how best to protect its economy, fields including environmental security studies, critical infrastructure protection, public and private partnerships, and the ever-evolving challenges for the defense support of civil authorities.

Although it is clear that there are differences across university programs in homeland security,[8] it is also clear that most programs aspire to support the profession by producing students who are capable and critical thinkers and collaborative workers who possess an interdisciplinary mind-set and are well versed in the various disciplines that constitute the *academic HS enterprise*. In this sense, academic homeland security is a broad field, applied social science that is characterized by numerous professional opportunities to defend and support our democracy. The field is new, undeveloped, and maturing. For example, how best to educate students and exactly which student learning outcomes should be taught continue to be debated at national conferences and in peer-reviewed journals. Indeed, not only are the need to establish governance structures over the curriculum (such as program-level accreditation), a consensus professional definition of homeland security, and theoretical foundations for academic homeland security that can be subjected to empirical testing and revision key components to the maturation of homeland security as a bona fide discipline, but their development is also the obligation of academics working closely with policy makers and practitioners. As such, and by comparison to other more established academic and professional disciplines such as engineering, law, and medicine, academic HS should be considered an *emergent discipline* in higher education. However, despite the indeterminate nature of academic HS, programs all over the United States and the world have continued to be popular choices among students, and higher education has witnessed literally hundreds of new programs in the past five years.[9]

In addition, students should keep in mind the ever-changing nature of the practice that will motivate tomorrow's generation to define, resource, and even practice homeland security in ways that may significantly differ from today's generation. As a result, and as the practice of homeland security evolves, academic programs will need to evolve with it. This is not a bad thing, and indeed such change characterizes all established professional disciplines, including medical education, legal education, and engineering education, to name a few. This challenge will be nothing new, as America has a long and rich history of adapting its politics, educational and legal systems, and governmental structures and laws in order to better manage changes in social and political conditions and advancements in science and technology.

Homeland Security and the Health of the Economy: Still, as dynamic as the administrative structures have been, and as complex as the mission set is, what has been more stable are the foci of the overall HS enterprise: fighting terrorism and guarding communities and infrastructure against the ravages of natural disasters. Obviously, the ongoing security of the American people and the country's infrastructures seems to be more art than science at this point, and investments in safeguarding and revitalizing existing critical infrastructure have not been a core political objective to date. The irony of such is not lost. For example, we have made the point that homeland security does indeed have a central role to play in protecting the health of the US economy. This can be seen quite interestingly as the department's mission from the 2011 fiscal-year budget report: "The Department of Homeland Security will lead the unified national effort to secure America. We will prevent and deter terrorist attacks and protect against and respond to threats and hazards to the nation. We will ensure safe and secure borders, welcome lawful immigrants and visitors and promote the free-flow of commerce."[10]

Although still evolving, how best to fight terrorism, shore up our emergency preparation and response capabilities, and safeguard systems and structures critical to our economy has proved to be a complicated and dynamic challenge to both practitioners and policy makers alike. As such, these are challenges for academic programs as well.

As mentioned above, directly following the events of September 11, 2001, US national security policy and strategy were logically highly focused on counterterrorism. This included broad national efforts at learning more about terrorist groups and counterterrorism strategies; developing better counterterrorism policy and strategy and better counterinsurgency tools; improving intelligence-gathering, -sharing, and -analysis techniques; gaining better fusion of law enforcement and intelligence; and working to enhance communication, operations, and partnerships between civilian and military entities. Meanwhile, as the importance of our critical infrastructures to the health of the US economy was becoming clearer each time natural disasters struck, in comparison, there was relatively little done to improve preparedness techniques, plans, or procedures or to improve the resilience of our infrastructures. Then, in August 2005 Hurricane Katrina showed us how expensive Mother Nature can be. The economic impact of Katrina has been estimated to be more than $100 billion in response and recovery costs to the US government, with more than $40–$60 billion in insured losses,[11] and one might argue that to some degree, some areas of the Gulf Coast have yet to fully recover economically or emotionally. Outside the United States, one only needs to recall two tragedies from the first six months of 2011, the Australian floods and the Japanese earthquake, tsunami, and nuclear power–plant meltdown, to see the enormous economic impact that natural disasters can have. For instance, the Japanese tsunami is estimated to cost almost four times what Katrina did.[12] Ultimately, these events demonstrate the tremendous impact Mother Nature can have on any nation's economy, and therefore the impact on any nation's security, without involving a single "bad guy."

These incidents, and many others, serve to remind us that homeland security is as much about natural disasters, infrastructure resilience, and economic sustainability as it is counterterrorism. As a US department, one major challenge facing the DHS is how best to find a way to equally appreciate and emphasize counterterrorism as well as how best to integrate resilience into US infrastructures that will mitigate the impacts of both natural disasters as well as failures in technologies on which we all depend (such as the Internet, water and energy support and delivery systems, agriculture, health care systems, transportation systems, and so forth). When one considers that the vast majority (precise numbers are not known, but estimates are up to 80 percent) of critical infrastructure is owned and operated by the private sector, it becomes clear just how important interdisciplinary partnerships are to critical infrastructure protection and how important and central the role homeland security plays in society.

This text is meant to provide a thoughtful and thorough overview of the practice of homeland security as it exists today, and by virtue of its content, an overview of curricula in homeland security in higher education. Students are encouraged to consider the plethora of careers that such an overview presents. Careers abound in such fields as critical infrastructure protection, law enforcement, intelligence analysis, environmental protection, law and policy studies, strategic studies, the military, international relations, public health, and even academia as scientists and educators. Homeland security is a vital and valued function of the US government, and as such places students at the center of many exciting and rewarding possibilities.

NOTES

1. US State Department, accessed August 15, 2011, http://www.state.gov/s/ct/c14151.htm.

2. Ibid.

3. Council on Foreign Relations, accessed August 15, 2011, http://www.cfr.org/terrorist-organizations/militant-extremists-united-states/p9236.

4. USAF Air University, accessed August 15, 2011, http://www.au.af.mil/au/aul/bibs/tergps/tg98tc.htm.

5. FBI, accessed August 15, 2011, http://www.fbi.gov/wanted/wanted_terrorists/@@wanted-group-listing.

6. *US DHS Strategic Plan, 2008–2013*, 3, accessed June 25, 2011, http://www.dhs.gov/xlibrary/assets/DHS_StratPlan_FINAL_spread.pdf.

7. Michael Chertoff, Secretary of the US Department of Homeland Security, remarks at Brookings Institution on September 5, 2008, http://www.dhs.gov/xnews/speeches/sp_1220876790967.shtm.

8. Scott Winegar, "Developing the Bench: Building an Effective Homeland Security Undergraduate Program" (master's thesis, Naval Postgraduate School, 2008), 4.

9. The Center for Homeland Defense and Security maintains a database of academic homeland security programs, numbered at 316 at the time of this writing: http://www .chds.us/?partners/institutions (accessed July 2, 2011).

10. 2011 fiscal year DHS budget, 1, accessed May 2, 2011, http://www.dhs.gov/xlibrary /assets/budget_bib_fy2011.pdf.

11. US CRS Report, "Hurricane Katrina: Insurance Losses and National Capacities for Financing Disaster Risk," September 15, 2005, http://www.au.af.mil/au/awc/awcgate/crs /rl33086.pdf.

12. US Congressional Research Service, *Japan's 2011 Earthquake and Tsunami: Economic Effects and Implications for the United States*, 7-5700 (Washington, DC: US Congressional Research Service, March 25, 2011).

Acknowledgments

We would like to thank our families, most especially our spouses, for their support and understanding while we worked on the writing and editing of this book. A special thank-you to Nicole Beauregard, a recent graduate of Kutztown University, who provided assistance in researching and reviewing material for this book.

We appreciate the time and effort that each of the authors took from their busy schedules, and their families, to contribute to writing this book. Our appreciation also extends to Stan Supinski, Naval Postgraduate School (NPS), and Steve Recca, NPS, who encouraged us to write this book, and the other members of NPS's Center for Homeland Defense and Security University and Agency Partnership Initiative with whom we worked to develop a core undergraduate homeland security curriculum proposal that provided key areas of focus for this book.

Those additional members are:

- John Barbrey, Longwood University
- Emily Bentley, Savannah State University
- Marion Cane, Emergency Management Institute, FEMA
- Mike Chumer, New Jersey Institute of Technology
- Keith Clement, California State University–Fresno
- Mike Collier, Eastern Kentucky University
- Steve Hart, United States Military Academy
- Vincent Henry, Long Island University
- Linda Kiltz, Texas A&M–Corpus Christi
- Jeff Maxfield, Utah Valley University
- Greg Moore, Notre Dame College
- Sam Morgan, Central Pennsylvania College

- Greg Moser, University of Denver
- Tim Murphy, University of Findlay
- Shawn Peppers, Utah Valley University
- Phil Schertzing, Michigan State University
- Lydia Staiano, Long Island University
- George Tanner, Department of Homeland Security
- Dan Turner, California Polytechnic University
- Bert Tussing, Army War College
- James Walsh, University of North Carolina–Charlotte
- Scott Winegar, National Guard Bureau

Keith Gregory Logan,
Kutztown University

James D. Ramsay,
Embry-Riddle Aeronautical University

About the Editors and Authors

EDITORS

Keith Gregory Logan, JD, is an Associate Professor in the Department of Criminal Justice at Kutztown University; he teaches such courses as Homeland Security, Defense and Intelligence, Criminal Law and Procedure, and Contemporary Legal Issues. He holds an undergraduate degree in political science, a master's degree in criminal justice, and a law degree. He is a member of the District of Columbia Bar and the Virginia State Bar. A former federal law enforcement officer and security officer, he also served as a special assistant US attorney in the District of Columbia and the Eastern District of Virginia (EDVA) and represented the United States Attorney's Office, EDVA, before the Fourth Circuit Court of Appeals. His federal service includes a short tour as a congressional staff assistant for a New York congressman, and he later served with the following agencies during his career: Drug Enforcement Administration, Agency for International Development, General Services Administration, Department of the Interior, Department of Education, Environmental Protection Agency, and Nuclear Regulatory Commission. He received numerous awards during his federal service. For several years he worked on government contracts and was a consultant to the nuclear industry regarding whistle-blower–retaliation investigations. In 2007 he was a guest lecturer at the Russian Federation Diplomatic Academy in Moscow. While a member of the US Army Reserves, he achieved the rank of major, Military Police Corps, and was an NBC/CBR defense instructor.

He is the editor and contributing author of *Homeland Security and Intelligence* (2010). He presented "Motor Vehicle Search Incident to Arrest: Will the Court Move in a New Direction?" at the 2008 annual conference of the American Society of Criminology and "Fiction as a Didactic Tool in Teaching Criminal Justice/Homeland Security" at the 2007 conference. Several of his recent publications include "Domestic Terrorism" and "Transnational Terrorism," in *Transnational Crime and Justice*; "Border Patrol," "*Sheppard v. Maxwell*," and "Lindberg Law," in *Social History of Crime and Justice*; "Son of Sam Laws" in *Victimology and Crime Prevention*; "*United States v. Booker* and *United States v. Fanfan*," in *Race and Crime*; "*People v. Lee*," in *Forensic*

Science; the "Foreign Intelligence Surveillance Act," in *Battleground: Criminal Justice*; and "DEA Intelligence" and "EPIC," in *Encyclopedia of U.S. Intelligence*.

James D. Ramsay, PhD, is currently a Certified Safety Professional, Professor, and Coordinator of the Homeland Security Program at Embry-Riddle Aeronautical University in Daytona Beach, Florida. Dr. Ramsay developed the Homeland Security Program at Riddle in 2006. He was recently appointed by the US secretary of health and human services to serve on the Board of Scientific Counselors to the director of the National Institute of Occupational Safety and Health in the Centers for Disease Control (CDC). Dr. Ramsay also serves on the board of directors for ABET, Inc. In addition, he serves on the education standards committees for both the International Association for Intelligence Education and the American Society of Safety Engineers (ASSE), where he also chairs the committee.

He is a charter member of the ASSE Academics Practice Specialty and has served on the ASSE Foundation Research and Technology Committees. He was the 2008 recipient of the ASSE Tarrants Award as the Outstanding Safety Educator in the nation, won the ASSE Outstanding Service Award for the Council on Practices and Standards in 2005, and won the Academics Practice Specialty Safety Professional of the Year Award in 2003. He was a codeveloper of the peer-reviewed *Journal of Homeland Security Education*, where he also serves as a reviewer. Dr. Ramsay developed the peer-reviewed *Journal of Safety, Health, and Environmental Research*, where he also served as editor in chief from 2002 to 2009. Dr. Ramsay serves as a reviewer for the *Journal of Homeland Security and Emergency Management* and the *Homeland Security Affairs Journal*. He has served as an ABET accreditation program evaluator and past commissioner on the Applied Sciences Commission. He has served numerous times as a scientific reviewer to the CDC, as both chair and reviewer to the NIOSH National Occupational Research Agenda, and on several special working groups for the CDC/NIOSH.

AUTHORS

Emily Bentley, JD, is an Assistant Professor and Coordinator of the Homeland Security and Emergency Management Program at Savannah State University. Bentley previously served as executive director of the Emergency Management Accreditation Program, a national standards and assessment program for state and local government emergency management. A former journalist and lawyer, Bentley has a broad background in public policy, particularly in comprehensive emergency operations and continuity planning, process improvement, and interstate cooperation, to address issues of national interest. She received her bachelor's degree from Auburn University and juris doctorate from the Jones School of Law at Faulkner University.

Michael Chumer, PhD, is a Research Professor within the Department of Information Systems at the New Jersey Institute of Technology (NJIT), specializing in homeland security and emergency management. He is also a faculty member in the State of

New Jersey's Preparedness College, advisory board director of the Business Emergency Operations Center Alliance, and director of the NJIT MS Emergency Management and Business Continuity program. As a homeland security private-sector advocate and subject-matter expert, he is called upon to provide guidance on collaborative communication models that engage the private sector with the public sector during all dimensions of homeland security emergency management. He is a participant in the Highlands Forum, a Department of Defense think tank that advises the assistant secretary of defense on networks and information integration. His research focuses on command and control as used in the military and its application to emergency response during multiagency collaboration such as experienced in Katrina and the recent tsunami disasters. He has written about command and control and is incorporating that knowledge into command-center operations that benefit the public and private sectors during homeland security–enabled emergency management. He is coeditor of *Managing Knowledge: Critical Investigations of Work and Learning,* a book that investigates issues surrounding the present formulation of IT-based knowledge management. Chumer is the principal investigator in a research grant from the Department of Defense in the area of homeland security and homeland defense. He is a 1964 graduate of the US Naval Academy and a 1970 graduate of Georgia Tech in information science. He earned his PhD from Rutgers University in communication and information science.

Samuel H. Clovis Jr., PhD, Chairperson of the Department of Business Administration and Economics, Morningside College, has more than thirty years of managerial and executive experience in the public, private, and nonprofit sectors. He holds the rank of full professor and leads the largest academic department on campus. After twenty-five years of highly successful service in the federal government, he entered the private sector, subsequently managing the Strategic Solutions Division for Logicon, providing support to clients in human factors engineering, in scenario-based decision support, and software engineering. He left the private sector to take a teaching position at William Penn University, eventually taking the position of founding dean of the College of Business and Management Science. He later accepted positions in business development and consulting with Northrop Grumman and Booz Allen Hamilton. At the Homeland Security Institute, he served as a principal analyst and acting fellow, providing security-issue policy analysis. Clovis has a BS in political science from the USAF Academy, an MBA in management from Golden Gate University, and a doctorate in public administration from the University of Alabama.

Randy R. Griffith is an Associate Professor of Aerospace Electronics at Embry-Riddle Aeronautical University in Daytona Beach, Florida. He received a BS in aviation technology and a master's in business administration in aviation from Embry-Riddle. He has been active in the areas of aviation communication, navigation, and identification equipment for more than thirty-five years and holds both a Federal Aviation Administration Airframe and Powerplant Certificate and a Federal Communications

Commission General Radiotelephone Operator License. He is the author of an article on the use of computer software in electronic circuit analysis for the Association for Avionics Education and several laboratory manuals used in electronics courses at Embry-Riddle.

Steven D. Hart, PhD, is a Lieutenant Colonel in the US Army Corps of Engineers with more than twenty-two years of service in both command and staff positions in Iraq, Kuwait, Panama, Germany, Korea, and the United States. He is currently assigned as an Assistant Professor in the Department of Civil and Mechanical Engineering at West Point, where he is teaching courses on Infrastructure Engineering and Critical Infrastructure Protection. His other teaching experience includes Design of Steel Structures, Design of Concrete Structures, Advanced Structural Analysis, Soil Mechanics, and the Civil Engineering Capstone Course. His active areas of research include infrastructure protection and resiliency and engineering education. He is active in the American Society of Engineering Education; the American Society of Civil Engineers, including service on the Committee on Critical Infrastructure; and the Infrastructure Security Partnership.

Michael L. Hummel, PhD, received his doctorate degree from Columbia University, New York, and is currently an Associate Professor of Leadership and Security Studies in the Department of Justice, Law, and Society and Director of the Serene Leadership Institute at California University of Pennsylvania. He is an Adjunct Professor at the University of Pittsburgh, Graduate School of Public and International Affairs, and teaches courses on terrorism and homeland security. He is a retired military officer with twenty-three years of experience in security, law enforcement, and special operations–related areas. He served as an Assistant Professor in the Department of Social Sciences, US Military Academy, West Point. He served as the director of the Performance Assurance, Safety, and Security Division at the Savanna River Site for the Department of Energy and is the president and owner of Shield Investigations and Security.

William J. Lahneman, PhD, is an Assistant Professor of Political Science at Towson University in Towson, Maryland, and a Senior Research Scholar at the Center for International and Security Studies at the University of Maryland's School of Public Policy. He holds a PhD in international relations from Johns Hopkins University's School of Advanced International Studies, an MA in national security affairs from the Naval Postgraduate School, and a BS from the US Naval Academy. He has held academic positions as Associate Director for programs at CISSM, where he conducted several research projects for different parts of the US Intelligence Community, and as Associate Chair of the Political Science Department at the US Naval Academy. A former career naval officer, Commander Lahneman, US Navy (retired), was a surface warfare officer with specializations in strategic planning, international negotiations, and nuclear propulsion. He is the author of *Keeping U.S. Intelligence Effective: The Need for a Revolution in Intelligence Affairs* (2011).

George Michael received his PhD from George Mason University's School of Public Policy. He is a Professor of Nuclear Counterproliferation and Deterrence Theory at the Air War College in Montgomery, Alabama. Previously, he was an Associate Professor of Political Science at the University of Virginia's College at Wise. He is the author of five books: *Confronting Right-Wing Extremism and Terrorism in the USA* (2003), *The Enemy of My Enemy: The Alarming Convergence of Militant Islam and the Extreme Right* (2006), *Willis Carto and the American Far Right* (2008), *Theology of Hate: A History of the World Church of the Creator* (2009), and *The New Insurgents: The Rise of Leaderless Resistance and Lone Wolf Terror* (2012). In addition, his articles have been published in the *Chronicle of Higher Education, Skeptic, Journal of International Security Affairs, Terrorism and Political Violence, Small Wars and Insurgencies, Defence Studies, Middle East Quarterly, Middle East Policy, Studies in Conflict and Terrorism, Totalitarian Movements and Political Religions, Journal of Church and State, Patterns of Prejudice, Population and Environment*, and the *Fort Worth Star-Telegram*.

Terrence M. O'Sullivan, PhD, is Associate Director of the Center for Emergency Management and Homeland Security Policy Research, Assistant Professor in the Department of Political Science, and Adjunct Professor of the Consortium of Eastern Ohio Master of Public Health Program at the University of Akron. Previously, he was a researcher at the University of Southern California's Center for Risk and Economic Analysis of Terrorism Events, a Department of Homeland Security Academic Center of Excellence. His research dealt with terrorism, weapons of mass destruction (biological, chemical, and unconventional weapons' risks to aviation and transportation critical infrastructure in particular), homeland security disaster management, and global public health security policy. Current projects include an analysis of the recent White House homeland security restructuring. He is the author of several articles and is writing a book on the global defense, public health, intelligence, and institutional governance challenges from converging biological and nanotechnologies in the private and public sectors.

John M. Persyn, PhD, is an Assistant Professor at the US Army Command and General Staff College. He currently teaches faculty development and curriculum development courses for the Faculty and Staff Development Division. He has previously taught national strategy, joint operations, and homeland security courses in the college's Directorate of Joint, Interagency, and Multinational Operations. He earned a master's and a doctorate in adult education from Kansas State University and a master's in national security and strategic studies from the Naval War College.

Cheryl J. Polson, PhD, is an Associate Dean of the Graduate School at Kansas State University and the Director of Kansas State at Fort Leavenworth. She oversees all university graduate degree programs offered at Fort Leavenworth and is responsible for new degree program initiatives at this off-campus site. Dr. Polson is leading Kansas State's homeland security curriculum development efforts and served as a member of the Homeland Security Defense and Education Consortium Association's accreditation committee. Her recent publications focus on homeland security curriculum development. She earned her doctorate at Kansas State University in higher-education administration and completed postdoctoral course work in adult education at the University of Missouri–Kansas City.

Scott Robinson, PhD, is an Associate Professor in the Department of Public Service and Administration, Bush School of Government and Public Service, Texas A&M University. After earning a doctorate in political science from Texas A&M in 2001, he taught at both Rice University and the University of Texas at Dallas. His research focuses on the management and politics of public agencies and the dynamics of public policy, with special attention paid to education management and emergency management. His work has been published in the *Policy Studies Journal, Review of Policy Research, American Review of Public Administration, Political Research Quarterly, Public Manager*, and *American Journal of Political Science*. He currently serves on the editorial board of the *Policy Studies Journal*.

Gail Fann Thomas, EdD, is an Associate Professor in the Graduate School of Business and Public Policy at the Naval Postgraduate School. She conducts research on strategic communication and interagency collaboration and serves as program manager for strategic communication in the Center of Executive Education at NPS. In 2004 she was awarded the Distinguished Member Award by the Association for Business Communication (ABC). In 2005 she received ABC's Outstanding Research Award and NPS's Richard W. Hamming Award for Excellence in Graduate Teaching. She has published in several academic journals and recently coauthored a booklet on conflict and teams. This booklet builds on the Thomas-Kilmann Conflict Mode Instrument, which allows team members to identify their predominant modes for dealing with conflict and then use that information to maximize team effectiveness.

Bert Tussing is the Director of the Homeland Defense and Security Issues Group at the US Army War College's Center for Strategic Leadership and holds the Elihu Root Chair of Military Studies. He joined the Center in October 1999 following nearly twenty-five years in the US Marine Corps. He is a Distinguished Graduate of both the Marine Corps Command and Staff College and the Naval War College, and he holds master's degrees in National Security Strategy and Military Strategic Studies. He has served on three Defense Science Boards; the Center for Strategic and International Studies' *Beyond Goldwater-Nichols Study*; and on the Senior Advisory Group for DoD's *Strategy for Homeland Defense and Civil Support*. He is a senior fellow on George Washington University's *Homeland Security Policy Institute* and Long Island University's *Homeland Security Management Institute*; a member of the Board of Experts for the University of California–Irvine's *Center for Unconventional Security Affairs*; a member of the Pennsylvania State University's Homeland Defense and Security Council; and on the Homeland Security Board of Advisors for Kansas State University and the US Army Command and General Staff College. In 2009 he served on Department of Homeland Security's *Homeland Security Advisory Council*, assisting in the development of the Department's first *Quadrennial Homeland Security Review*.

Index